JOHN CONSTANTINE, HELLBLAZER: STATIONS OF THE CROSS

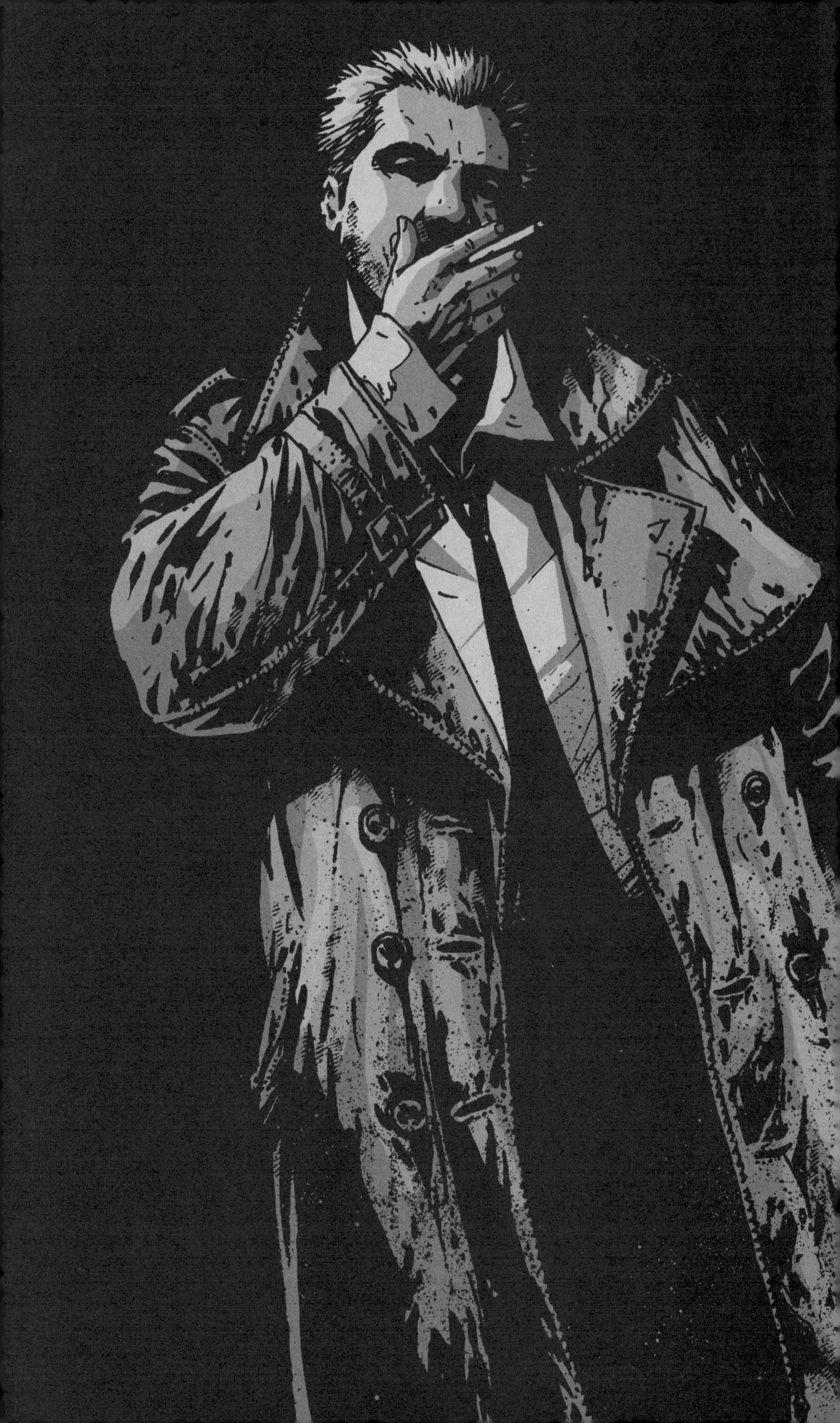

JOHN CONSTANTINE, HELLBLAZER:

STATIONS OF THE CROSS

Mike Carey
Writer

Leonardo Manco
Chris Brunner
Marcelo Frusin
Steve Dillon
Artists

Lee Loughridge
Colorist

Clem Robins
Letterer

Tim Bradstreet
Original Series Covers

JOHN CONSTANTINE, HELLBLAZER: STATIONS OF THE CROSS

Published by DC Comics. Cover and compilation copyright ©
2006 DC Comics. All Rights Reserved.

DC Comics, 1700 Broadway, New York, NY 10019
A Warner Bros. Entertainment Company
Printed in Canada. First Printing.

ISBN: 1-4012-1002-3
ISBN 13: 978-1-4012-1002-1

Cover illustration by Tim Bradstreet.
Logo design by Nessim Higson.

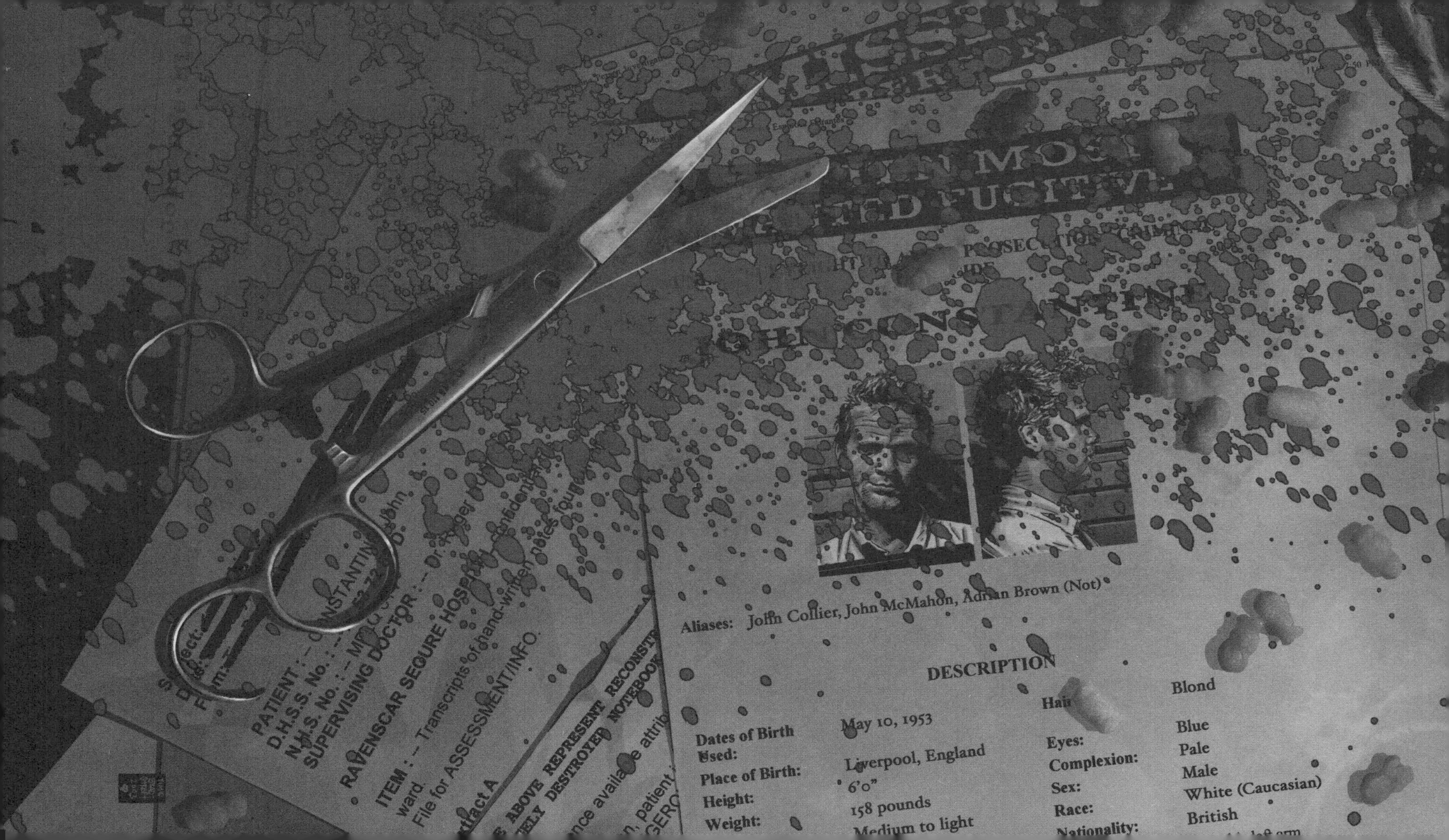
Aliases: John Collier, John McMahon, Adrian Brown (Not)
DESCRIPTION
Dates of Birth Used: May 10, 1953
Place of Birth: Liverpool, England
Height: 6'0"
Weight: 158 pounds
Medium to light
Hair Blond
Eyes: Blue
Complexion: Pale
Sex: Male
Race: White (Caucasian)
Nationality: British
PATIENT
D.H.S.S. No.
N.H.S. No.
SUPERVISING DOCTOR
RAVENSCAR SECURE HOSPITAL
ITEM : -- Transcripts of hand-written notes found
ward.
File for ASSESSMENT/INFO.
ABOVE REPRESENT RECONSTR
DESTROYED NOTEBOOK

IF YOU MOVE--IF YOU SO MUCH AS BREATHE--
--YOU'RE DEAD. YOU HEAR ME?
HANDS EHIND YOUR ACK. NOW.
COME ON COME ON COME ON! FUCKING DO IT!
LOVELY! NOW THE LEGS.
BIT LATE TO RUN AWAY AT THIS POINT ANYWAY, RIGHT?
RIGHT. THANK CHRIST. I CAN PUT THIS THING AWAY NOW.
I HATE GUNS. KILLING SOMEONE WITH A GUN--
--THAT'S LIKE SHAGGING WITH A RUBBER ON.

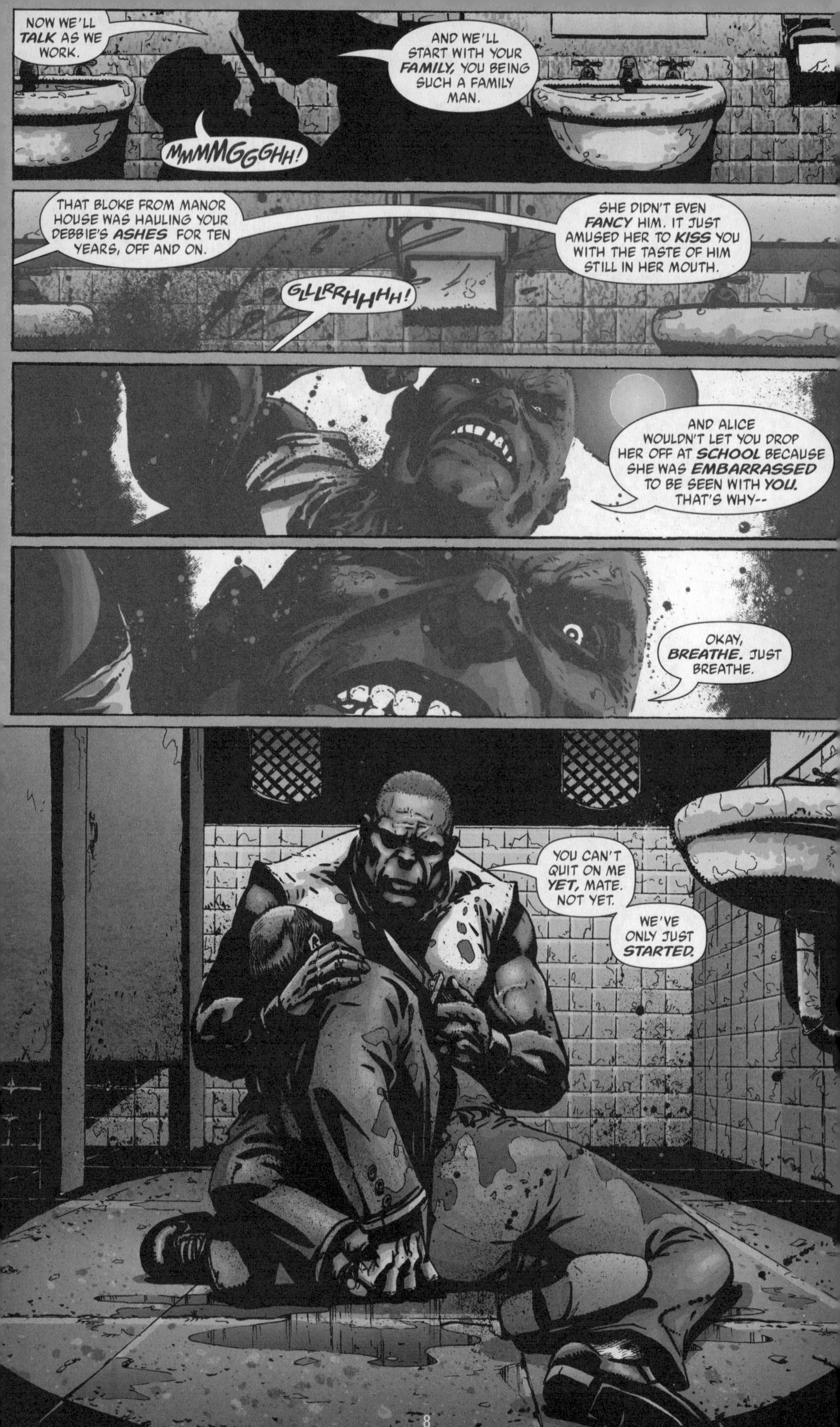
NOW WE'LL TALK AS WE WORK.
AND WE'LL START WITH YOUR FAMILY, YOU BEING SUCH A FAMILY MAN.
MMMMGGGHH!
THAT BLOKE FROM MANOR HOUSE WAS HAULING YOUR DEBBIE'S ASHES FOR TEN YEARS, OFF AND ON.
SHE DIDN'T EVEN FANCY HIM. IT JUST AMUSED HER TO KISS YOU WITH THE TASTE OF HIM STILL IN HER MOUTH.
GLLLRRHHHH!
AND ALICE WOULDN'T LET YOU DROP HER OFF AT SCHOOL BECAUSE SHE WAS EMBARRASSED TO BE SEEN WITH YOU. THAT'S WHY--
OKAY, BREATHE. JUST BREATHE.
YOU CAN'T QUIT ON ME YET, MATE. NOT YET.
WE'VE ONLY JUST STARTED.

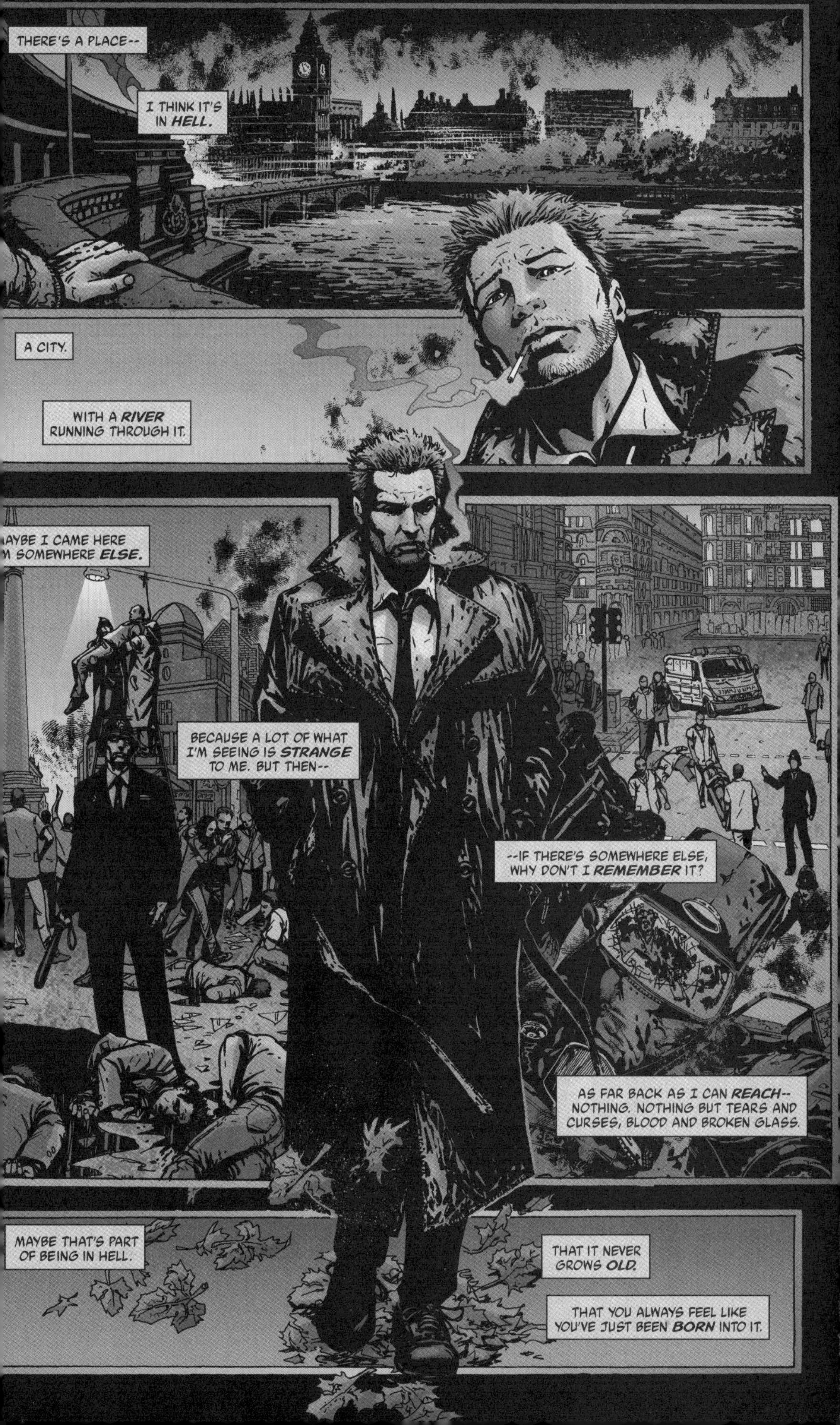

THERE'S A PLACE--
I THINK IT'S IN HELL.
A CITY.
WITH A RIVER RUNNING THROUGH IT.
AYBE I CAME HERE
M SOMEWHERE ELSE.
BECAUSE A LOT OF WHAT I'M SEEING IS STRANGE TO ME. BUT THEN--
--IF THERE'S SOMEWHERE ELSE, WHY DON'T I REMEMBER IT?
AS FAR BACK AS I CAN REACH-- NOTHING. NOTHING BUT TEARS AND CURSES, BLOOD AND BROKEN GLASS.
MAYBE THAT'S PART OF BEING IN HELL.
THAT IT NEVER GROWS OLD.
THAT YOU ALWAYS FEEL LIKE YOU'VE JUST BEEN BORN INTO IT.

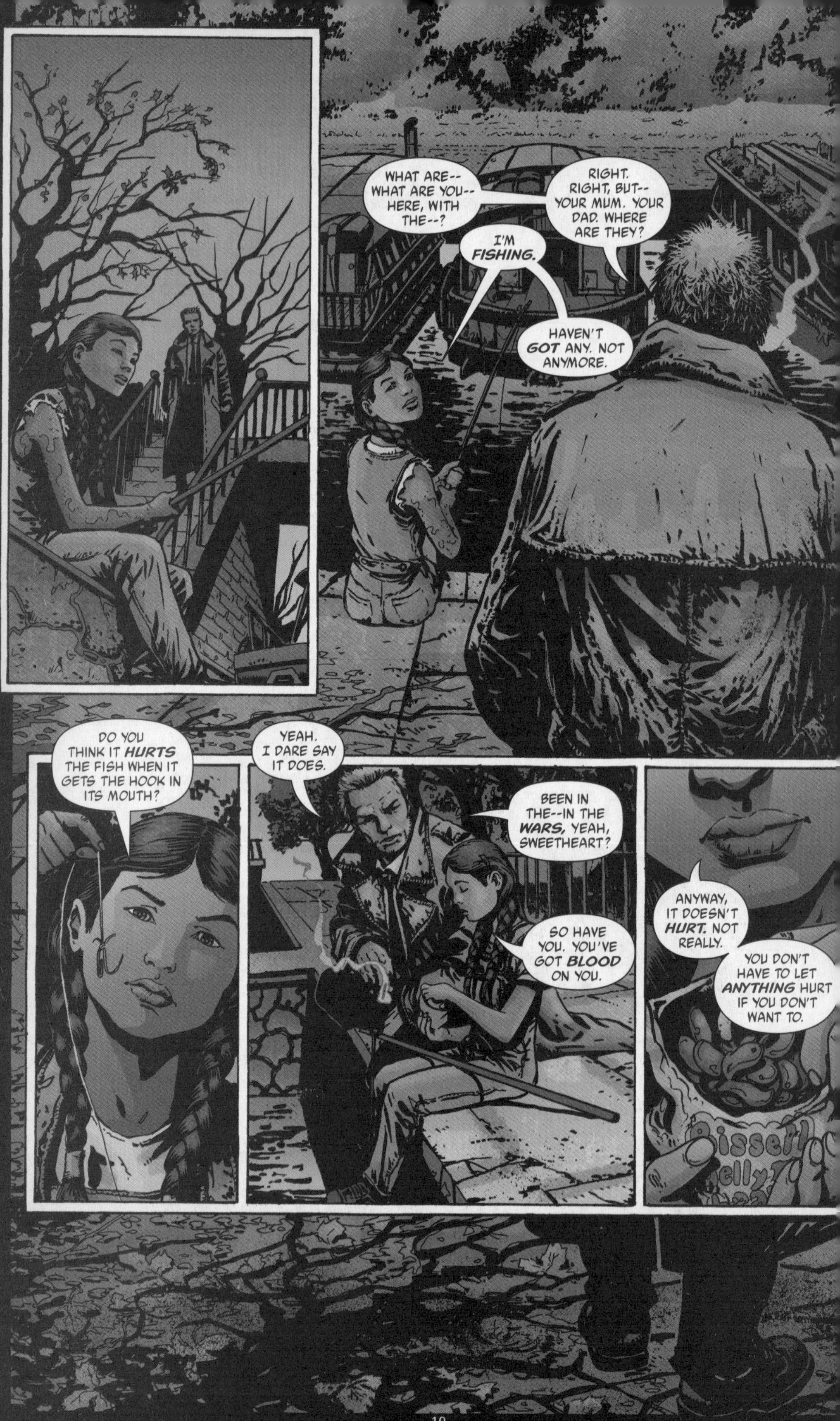
WHAT ARE--
WHAT ARE YOU--
HERE, WITH
THE--?
RIGHT.
RIGHT, BUT--
YOUR MUM. YOUR
DAD. WHERE
ARE THEY?
I'M
FISHING.
HAVEN'T
GOT ANY. NOT
ANYMORE.
DO YOU
THINK IT HURTS
THE FISH WHEN IT
GETS THE HOOK IN
ITS MOUTH?
YEAH.
I DARE SAY
IT DOES.
BEEN IN
THE--IN THE
WARS, YEAH,
SWEETHEART?
SO HAVE
YOU. YOU'VE
GOT BLOOD
ON YOU.
ANYWAY,
IT DOESN'T
HURT. NOT
REALLY.
YOU DON'T
HAVE TO LET
ANYTHING HURT
IF YOU DON'T
WANT TO.

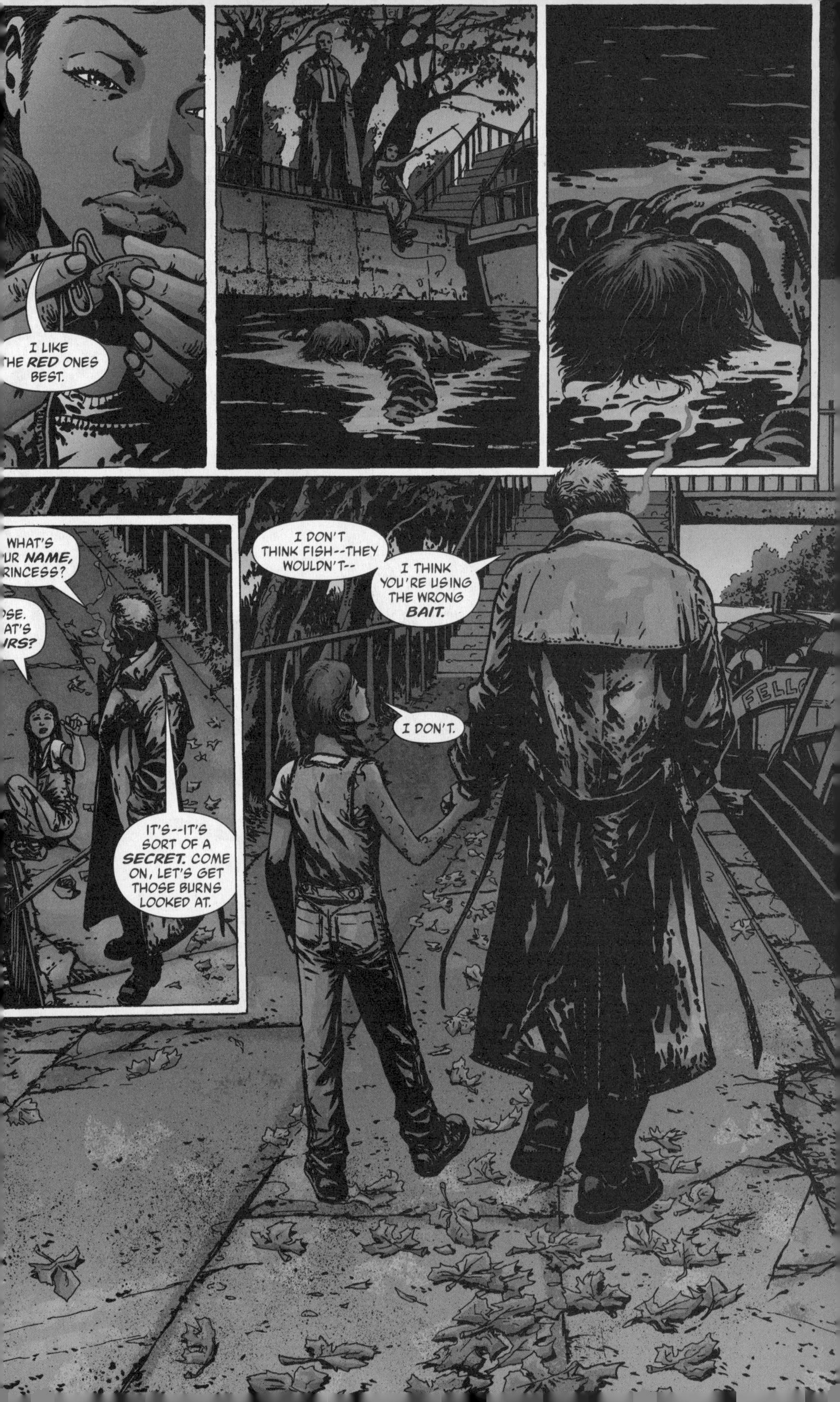
I LIKE THE RED ONES BEST.
I DON'T THINK FISH--THEY WOULDN'T--
I THINK YOU'RE USING THE WRONG BAIT.
I DON'T.
WHAT'S UR NAME, RINCESS?
OSE. AT'S IRS?
IT'S--IT'S SORT OF A SECRET. COME ON, LET'S GET THOSE BURNS LOOKED AT.

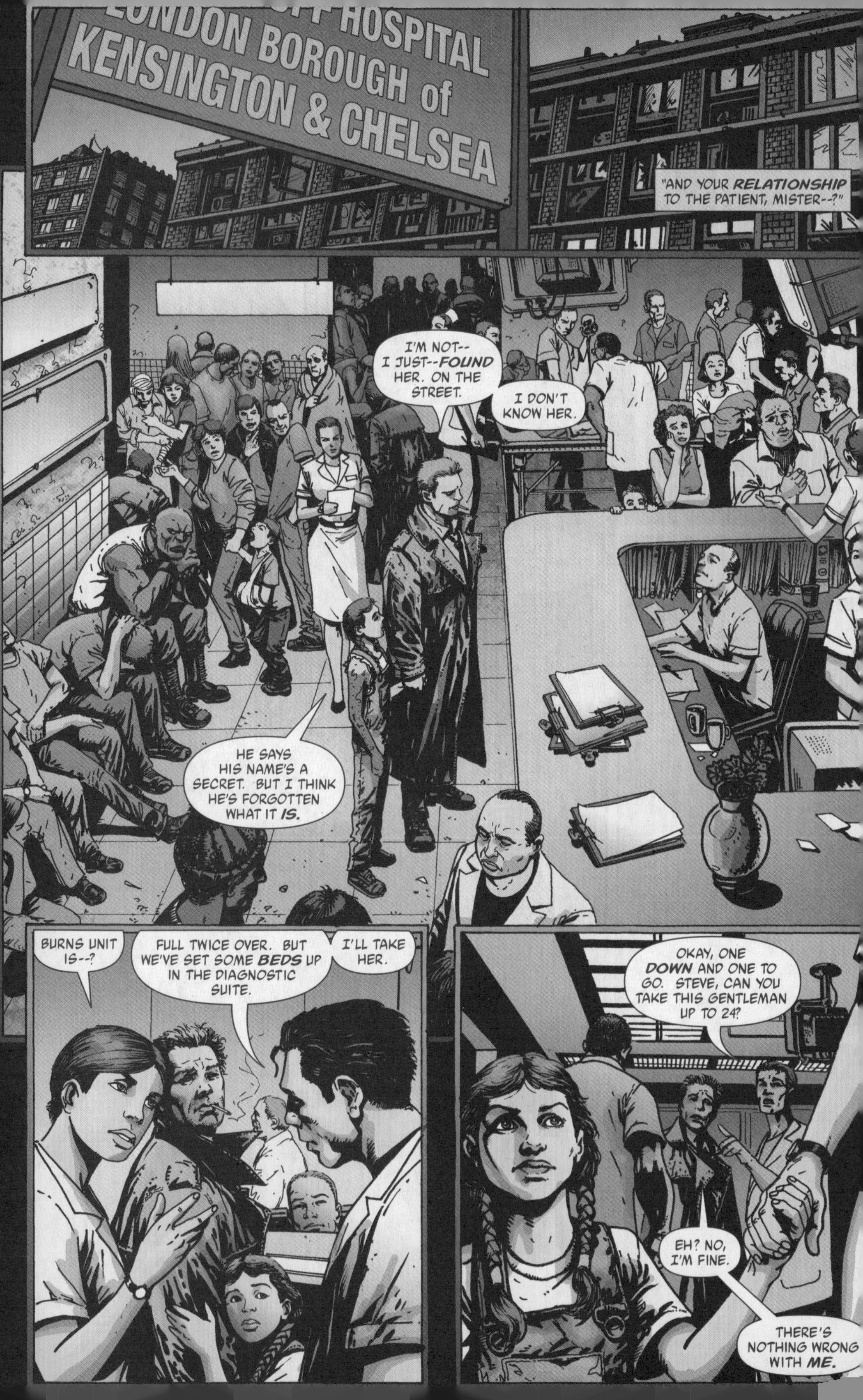
LONDON BOROUGH of
KENSINGTON & CHELSEA
HOSPITAL
"AND YOUR RELATIONSHIP TO THE PATIENT, MISTER--?"
I'M NOT-- I JUST--FOUND HER. ON THE STREET.
I DON'T KNOW HER.
HE SAYS HIS NAME'S A SECRET. BUT I THINK HE'S FORGOTTEN WHAT IT IS.
BURNS UNIT IS--?
FULL TWICE OVER. BUT WE'VE SET SOME BEDS UP IN THE DIAGNOSTIC SUITE.
I'LL TAKE HER.
OKAY, ONE DOWN AND ONE TO GO. STEVE, CAN YOU TAKE THIS GENTLEMAN UP TO 24?
EH? NO, I'M FINE.
THERE'S NOTHING WRONG WITH ME.

I HAVEN'T FORGOTTEN-- I WAS--I WAS *JOKING* WITH HER.

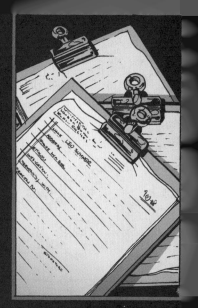

YOU'VE TAKEN SOME KIND OF *WOUND* TO THE THROAT. YOU'RE PROBABLY IN *SHOCK.*

FORGETTING YOUR *NAME* ISN'T A GOOD SIGN.

MY NAME'S-- *SUMNER.*

MY NAME'S LEO SUMNER.

WELL I DON'T THINK YOU'RE READY TO GO BACK OUT ON THE *STREET,* LEO.

I THINK YOU SHOULD LET A *DOCTOR* TAKE A LOOK AT YOU.

COME ON, MR. SUMNER.

WELL, NO. I'VE GOT TO--

BELIEVE ME, YOU'LL *THANK* US FOR THIS IN THE MORNING.

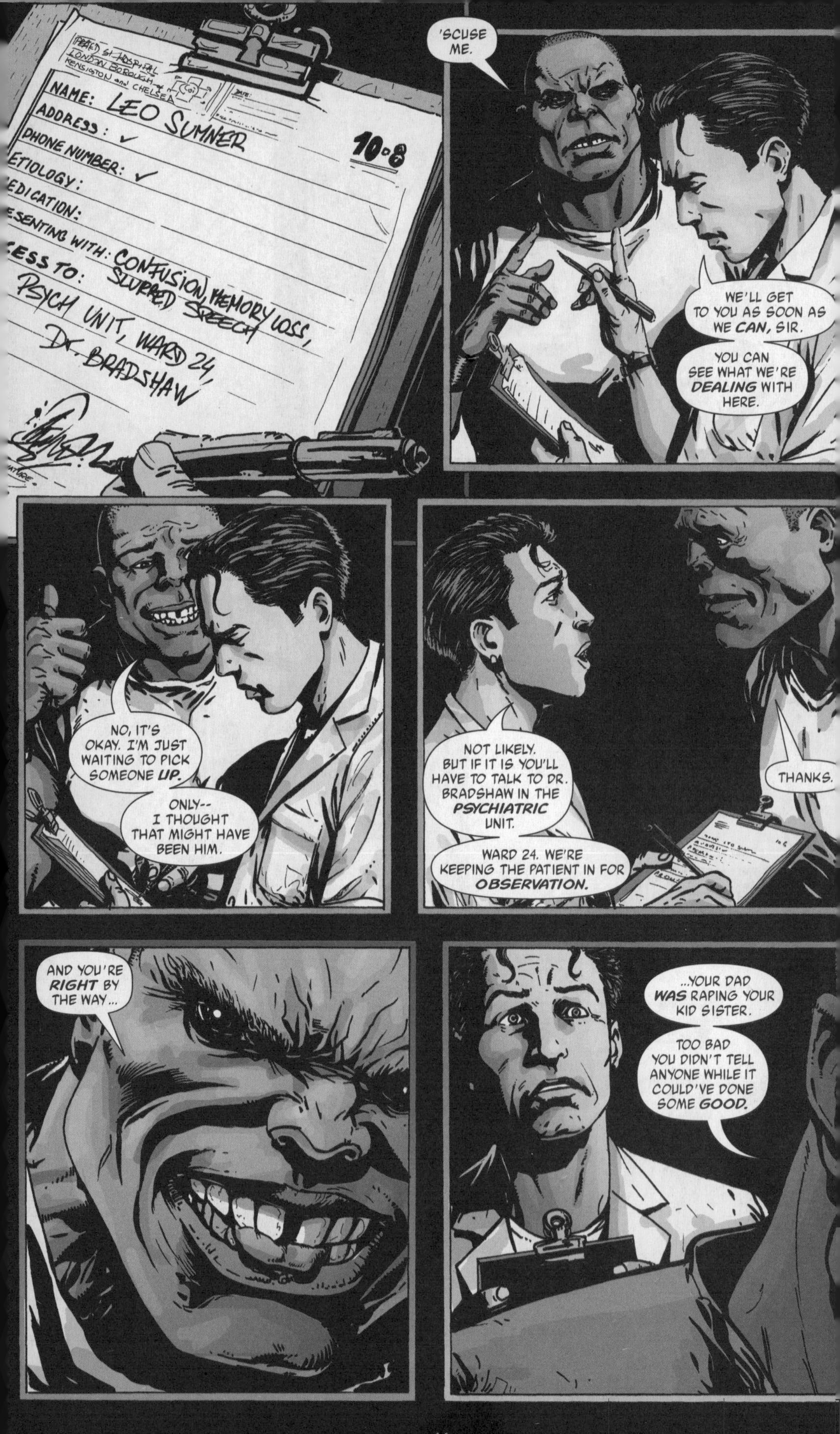
LONDON BOROUGH
KENSINGTON and CHELSEA
NAME: LEO SUMNER
ADDRESS: ✓
PHONE NUMBER: ✓
ETIOLOGY:
EDICATION:
ESENTING WITH: CONFUSION, MEMORY LOSS, SLURRED SPEECH
CESS TO: PSYCH UNIT, WARD 24, DR. BRADSHAW
10-8
'SCUSE ME.
WE'LL GET TO YOU AS SOON AS WE **CAN**, SIR.
YOU CAN SEE WHAT WE'RE **DEALING** WITH HERE.
NO, IT'S OKAY. I'M JUST WAITING TO PICK SOMEONE **UP**.
ONLY-- I THOUGHT THAT MIGHT HAVE BEEN HIM.
NOT LIKELY. BUT IF IT IS YOU'LL HAVE TO TALK TO DR. BRADSHAW IN THE **PSYCHIATRIC** UNIT.
WARD 24. WE'RE KEEPING THE PATIENT IN FOR **OBSERVATION.**
THANKS.
AND YOU'RE **RIGHT** BY THE WAY...
...YOUR DAD **WAS** RAPING YOUR KID SISTER.
TOO BAD YOU DIDN'T TELL ANYONE WHILE IT COULD'VE DONE SOME **GOOD.**

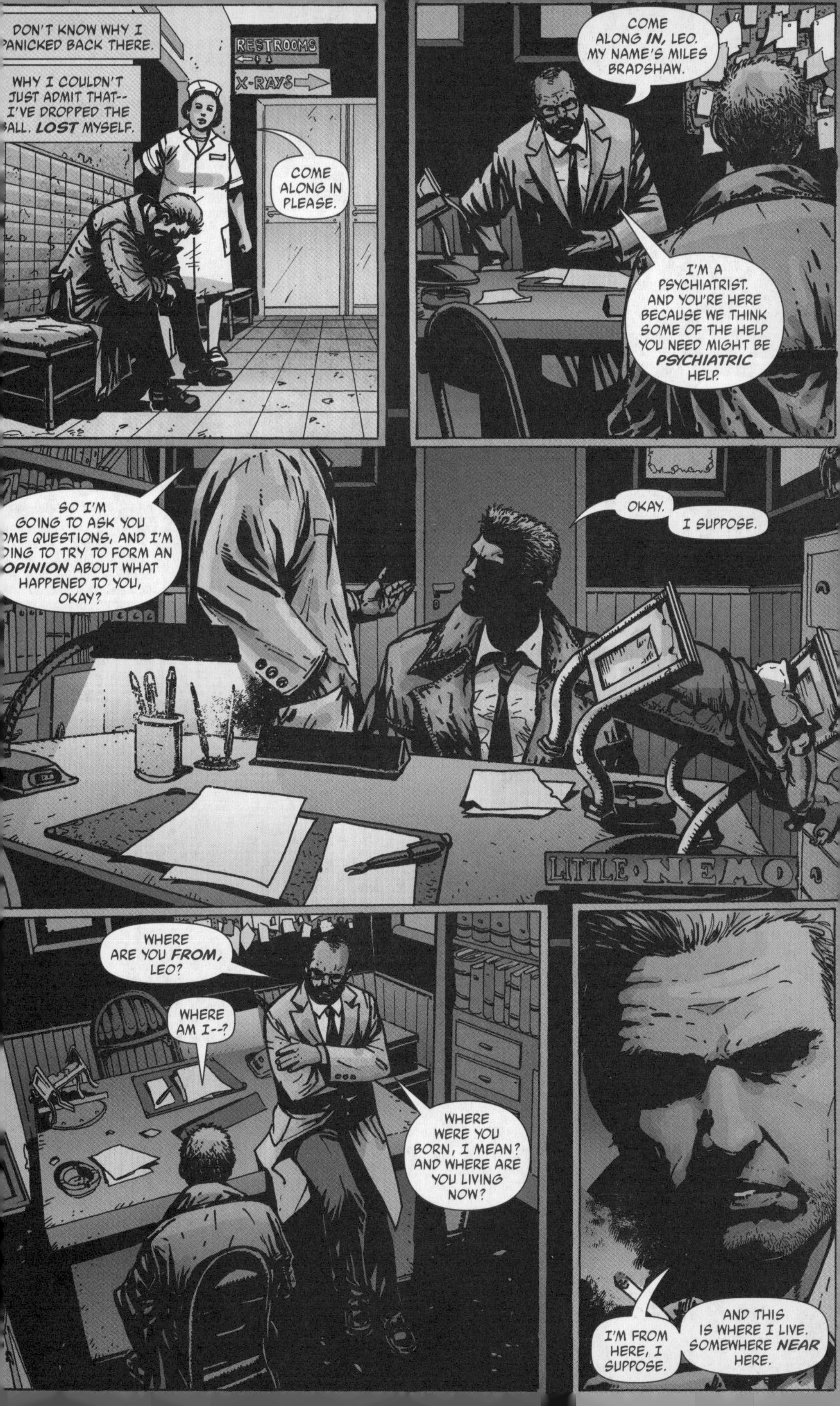
DON'T KNOW WHY I PANICKED BACK THERE.
WHY I COULDN'T JUST ADMIT THAT-- I'VE DROPPED THE BALL. LOST MYSELF.
RESTROOMS
X-RAYS
COME ALONG IN PLEASE.
COME ALONG IN, LEO. MY NAME'S MILES BRADSHAW.
I'M A PSYCHIATRIST. AND YOU'RE HERE BECAUSE WE THINK SOME OF THE HELP YOU NEED MIGHT BE PSYCHIATRIC HELP.
SO I'M GOING TO ASK YOU SOME QUESTIONS, AND I'M GOING TO TRY TO FORM AN OPINION ABOUT WHAT HAPPENED TO YOU, OKAY?
OKAY.
I SUPPOSE.
LITTLE NEMO
WHERE ARE YOU FROM, LEO?
WHERE AM I--?
WHERE WERE YOU BORN, I MEAN? AND WHERE ARE YOU LIVING NOW?
I'M FROM HERE, I SUPPOSE.
AND THIS IS WHERE I LIVE. SOMEWHERE NEAR HERE.

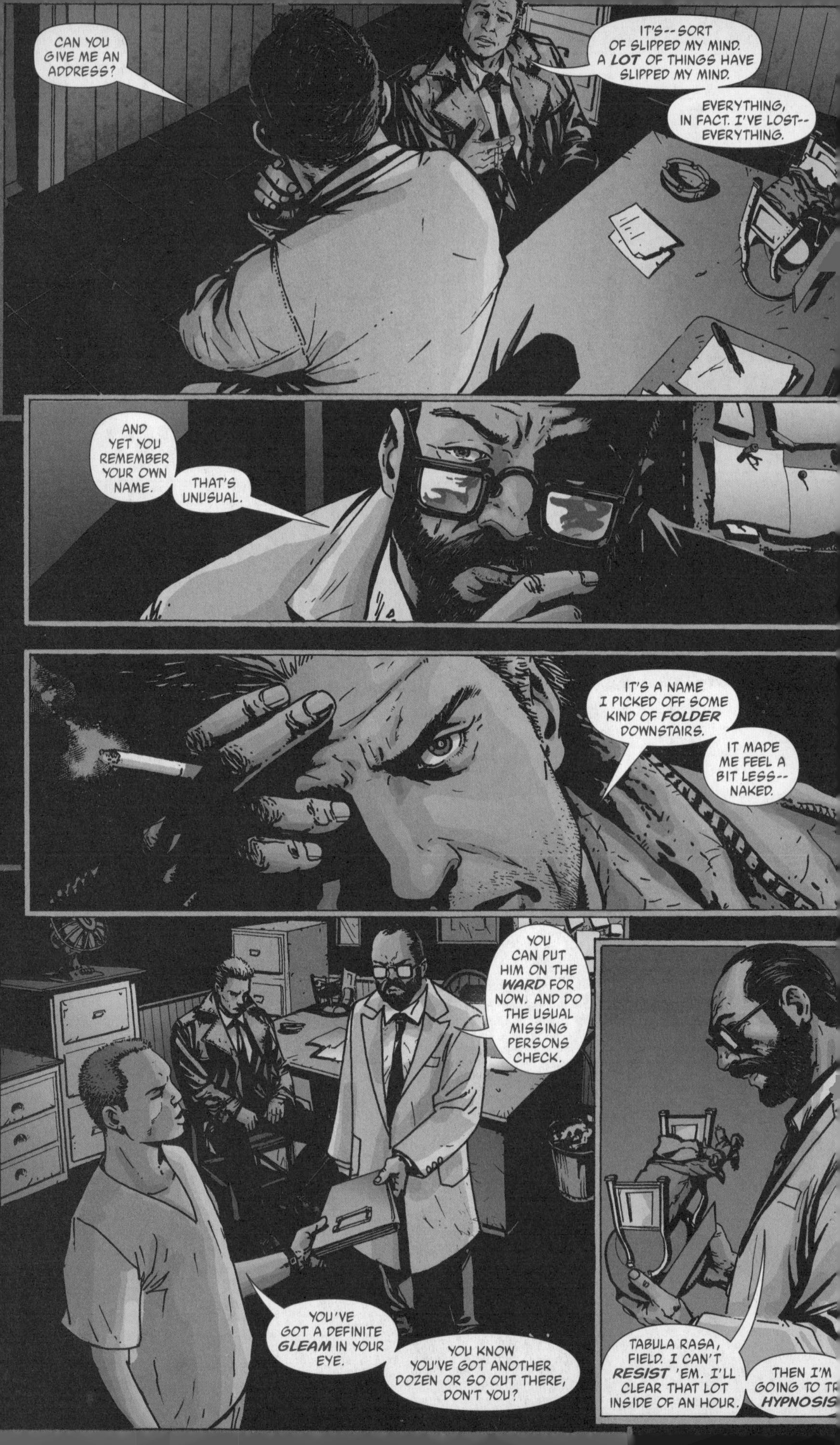
CAN YOU GIVE ME AN ADDRESS?
IT'S--SORT OF SLIPPED MY MIND. A LOT OF THINGS HAVE SLIPPED MY MIND.
EVERYTHING, IN FACT. I'VE LOST--EVERYTHING.
AND YET YOU REMEMBER YOUR OWN NAME.
THAT'S UNUSUAL.
IT'S A NAME I PICKED OFF SOME KIND OF FOLDER DOWNSTAIRS.
IT MADE ME FEEL A BIT LESS--NAKED.
YOU CAN PUT HIM ON THE WARD FOR NOW. AND DO THE USUAL MISSING PERSONS CHECK.
YOU'VE GOT A DEFINITE GLEAM IN YOUR EYE.
YOU KNOW YOU'VE GOT ANOTHER DOZEN OR SO OUT THERE, DON'T YOU?
TABULA RASA, FIELD. I CAN'T RESIST 'EM. I'LL CLEAR THAT LOT INSIDE OF AN HOUR.
THEN I'M GOING TO TR
HYPNOSIS

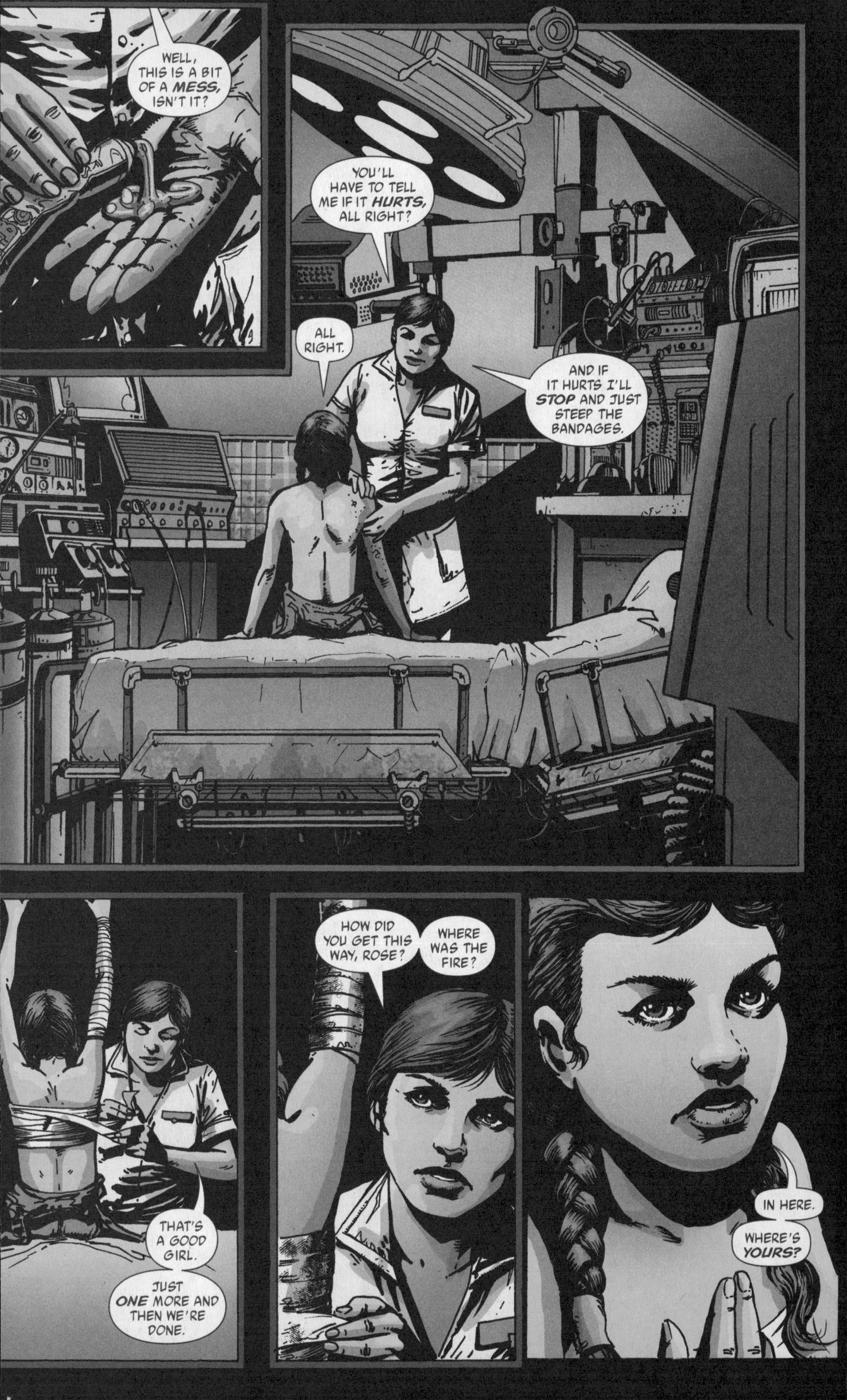
WELL, THIS IS A BIT OF A **MESS,** ISN'T IT?
YOU'LL HAVE TO TELL ME IF IT **HURTS,** ALL RIGHT?
ALL RIGHT.
AND IF IT HURTS I'LL **STOP** AND JUST STEEP THE BANDAGES.
THAT'S A GOOD GIRL.
JUST **ONE** MORE AND THEN WE'RE DONE.
HOW DID YOU GET THIS WAY, ROSE?
WHERE WAS THE FIRE?
IN HERE.
WHERE'S **YOURS?**

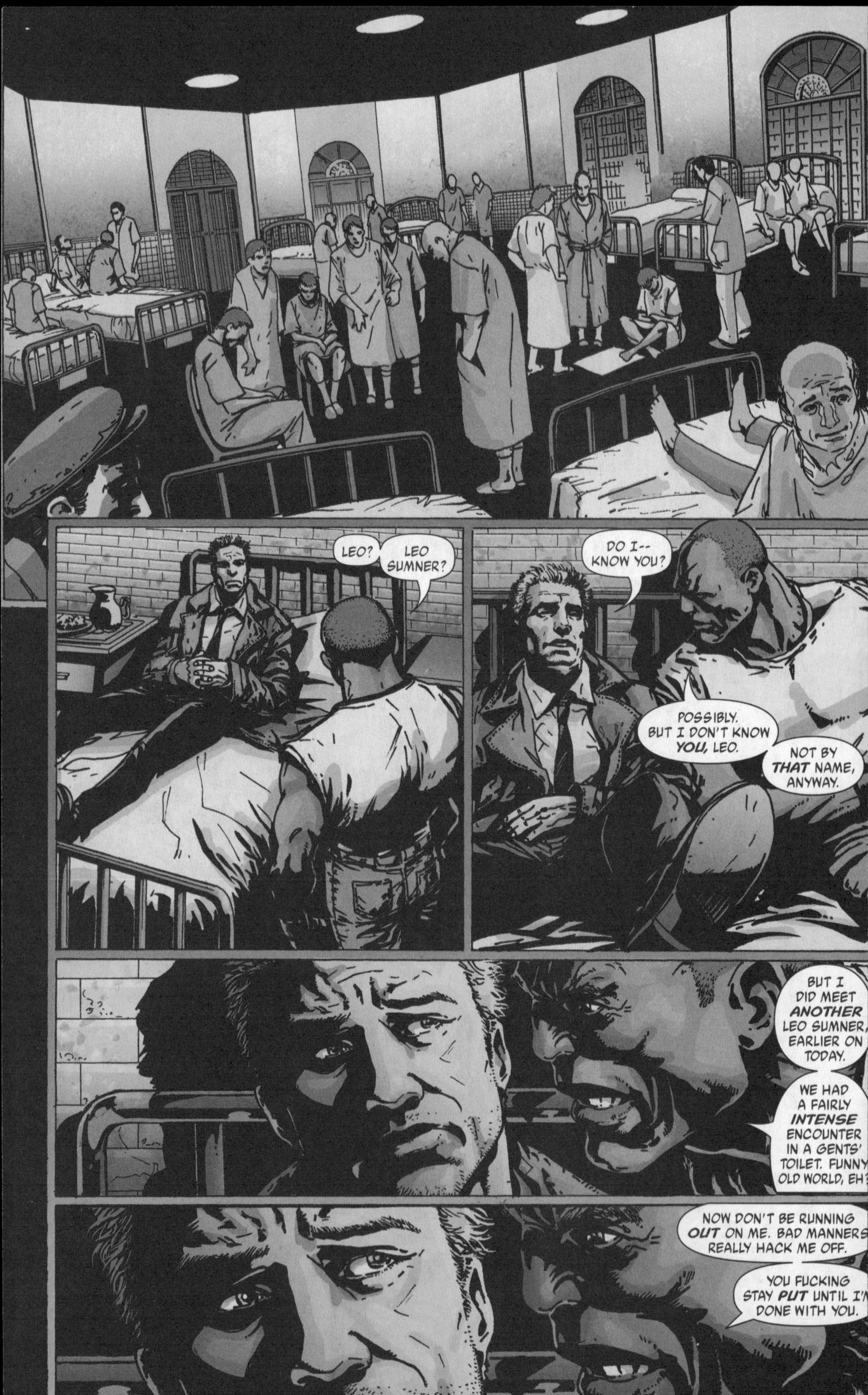
LEO? LEO SUMNER?
DO I-- KNOW YOU?
POSSIBLY. BUT I DON'T KNOW YOU, LEO.
NOT BY THAT NAME, ANYWAY.
BUT I DID MEET ANOTHER LEO SUMNER, EARLIER ON TODAY.
WE HAD A FAIRLY INTENSE ENCOUNTER IN A GENTS' TOILET. FUNNY OLD WORLD, EH?
NOW DON'T BE RUNNING OUT ON ME. BAD MANNERS REALLY HACK ME OFF.
YOU FUCKING STAY PUT UNTIL I'M DONE WITH YOU.

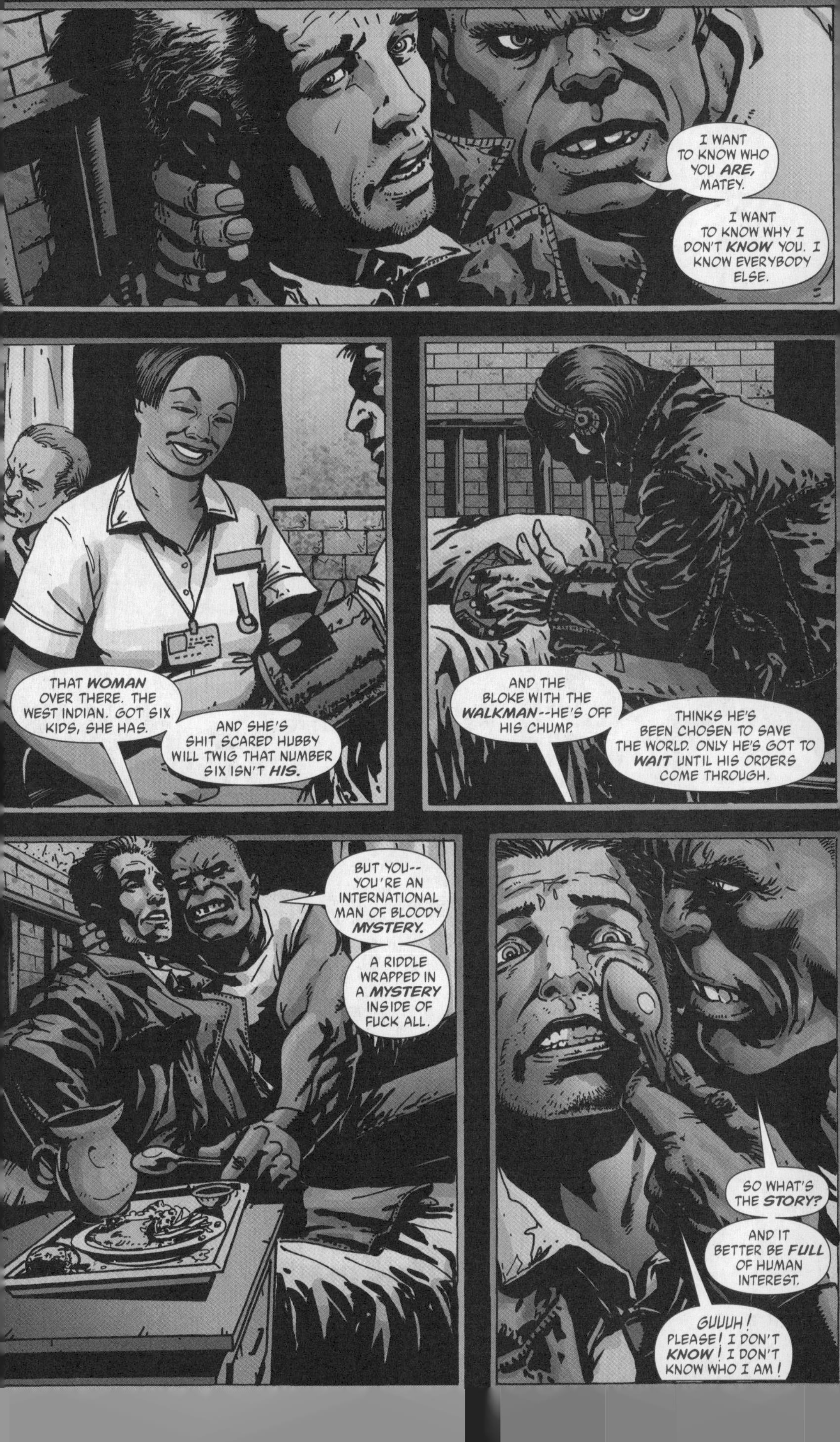
I WANT TO KNOW WHO YOU *ARE,* MATEY.
I WANT TO KNOW WHY I DON'T *KNOW* YOU. I KNOW EVERYBODY ELSE.
THAT *WOMAN* OVER THERE. THE WEST INDIAN. GOT SIX KIDS, SHE HAS.
AND SHE'S SHIT SCARED HUBBY WILL TWIG THAT NUMBER SIX ISN'T *HIS.*
AND THE BLOKE WITH THE *WALKMAN*--HE'S OFF HIS CHUMP.
THINKS HE'S BEEN CHOSEN TO SAVE THE WORLD. ONLY HE'S GOT TO *WAIT* UNTIL HIS ORDERS COME THROUGH.
BUT YOU-- YOU'RE AN INTERNATIONAL MAN OF BLOODY *MYSTERY.*
A RIDDLE WRAPPED IN A *MYSTERY* INSIDE OF FUCK ALL.
SO WHAT'S THE *STORY?*
AND IT BETTER BE *FULL* OF HUMAN INTEREST.
GUUUH! PLEASE! I DON'T *KNOW!* I DON'T KNOW WHO I AM!

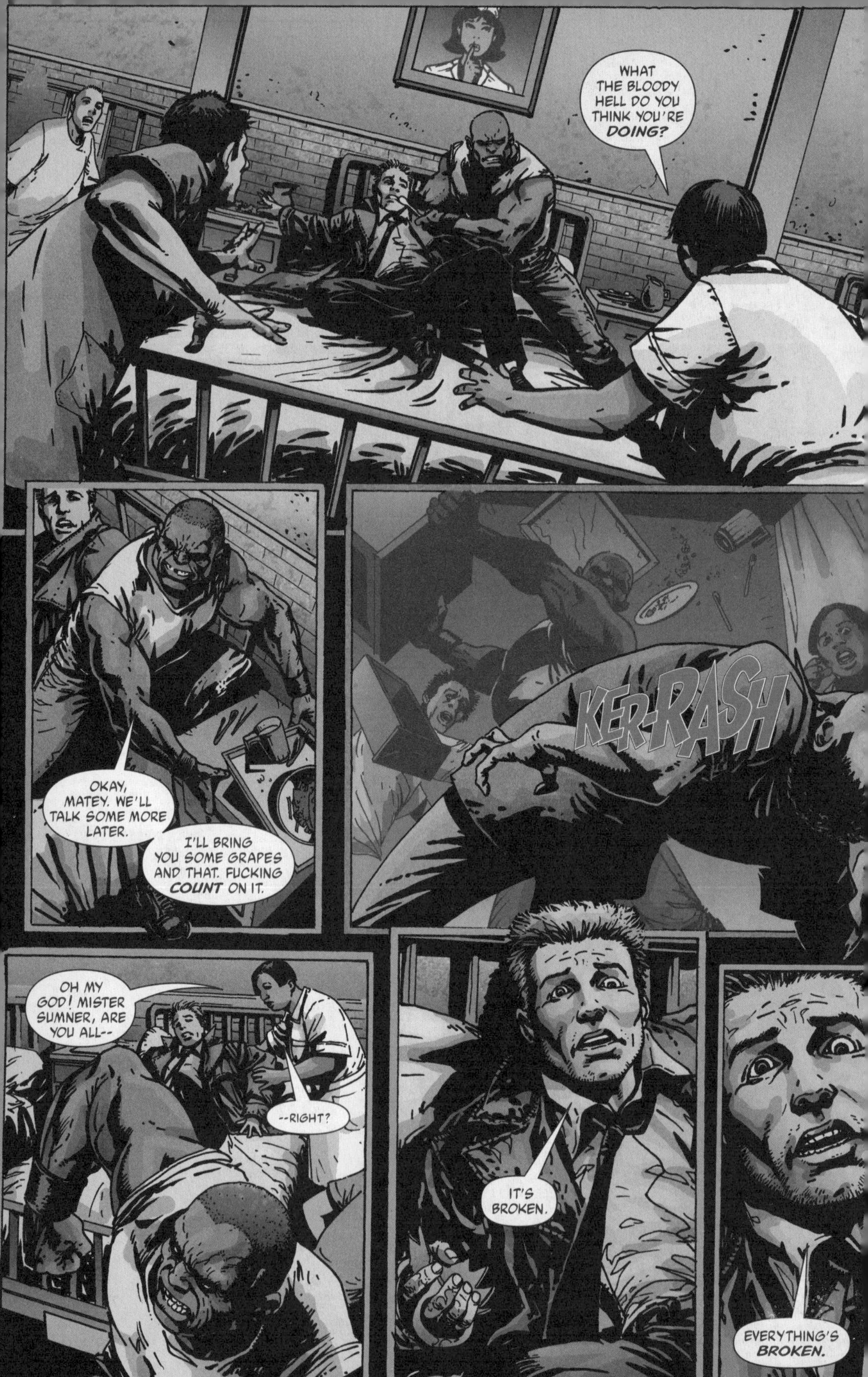
WHAT THE BLOODY HELL DO YOU THINK YOU'RE *DOING?*
OKAY, MATEY. WE'LL TALK SOME MORE LATER.
I'LL BRING YOU SOME GRAPES AND THAT. FUCKING *COUNT* ON IT.
KER-RASH
OH MY GOD! MISTER SUMNER, ARE YOU ALL--
--RIGHT?
IT'S BROKEN.
EVERYTHING'S *BROKEN.*

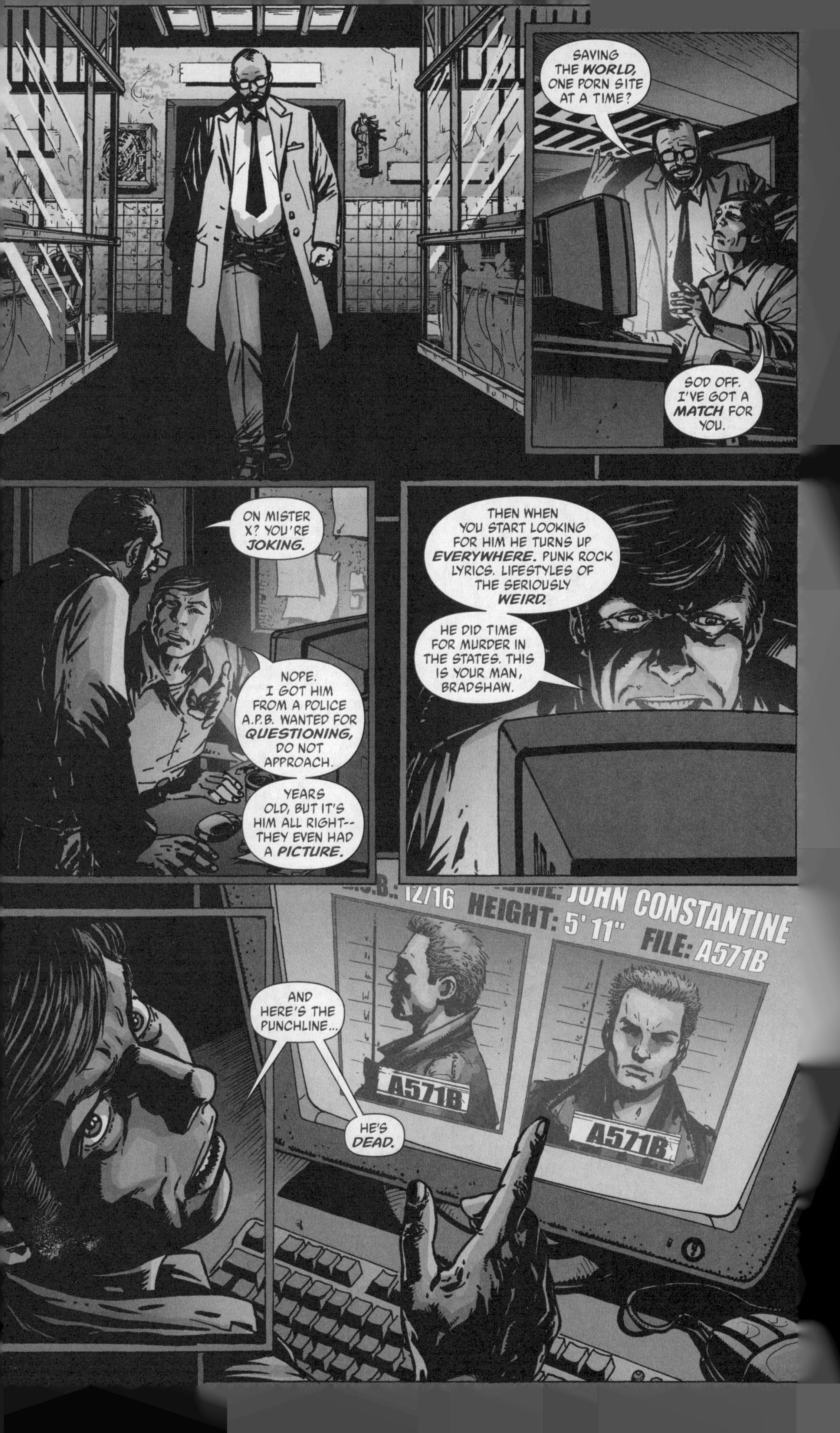
SAVING THE WORLD, ONE PORN SITE AT A TIME?
SOD OFF. I'VE GOT A MATCH FOR YOU.
ON MISTER X? YOU'RE JOKING.
NOPE. I GOT HIM FROM A POLICE A.P.B. WANTED FOR QUESTIONING, DO NOT APPROACH.
YEARS OLD, BUT IT'S HIM ALL RIGHT-- THEY EVEN HAD A PICTURE.
THEN WHEN YOU START LOOKING FOR HIM HE TURNS UP EVERYWHERE. PUNK ROCK LYRICS. LIFESTYLES OF THE SERIOUSLY WEIRD.
HE DID TIME FOR MURDER IN THE STATES. THIS IS YOUR MAN, BRADSHAW.
12/16
JOHN CONSTANTINE
HEIGHT: 5' 11"
FILE: A571B
AND HERE'S THE PUNCHLINE...
A571B
A571B
HE'S DEAD.

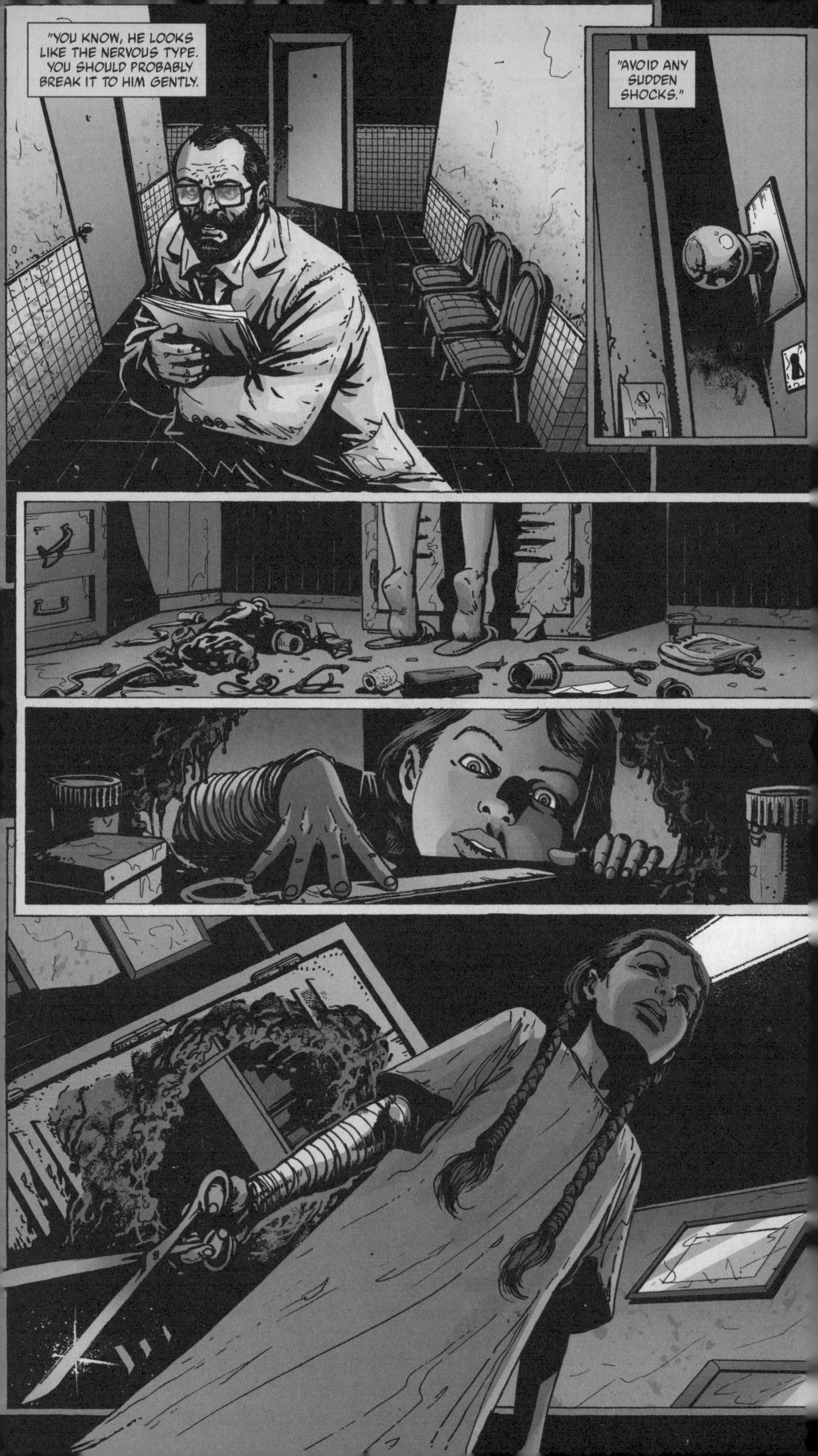
"YOU KNOW, HE LOOKS LIKE THE NERVOUS TYPE. YOU SHOULD PROBABLY BREAK IT TO HIM GENTLY.
"AVOID ANY SUDDEN SHOCKS."

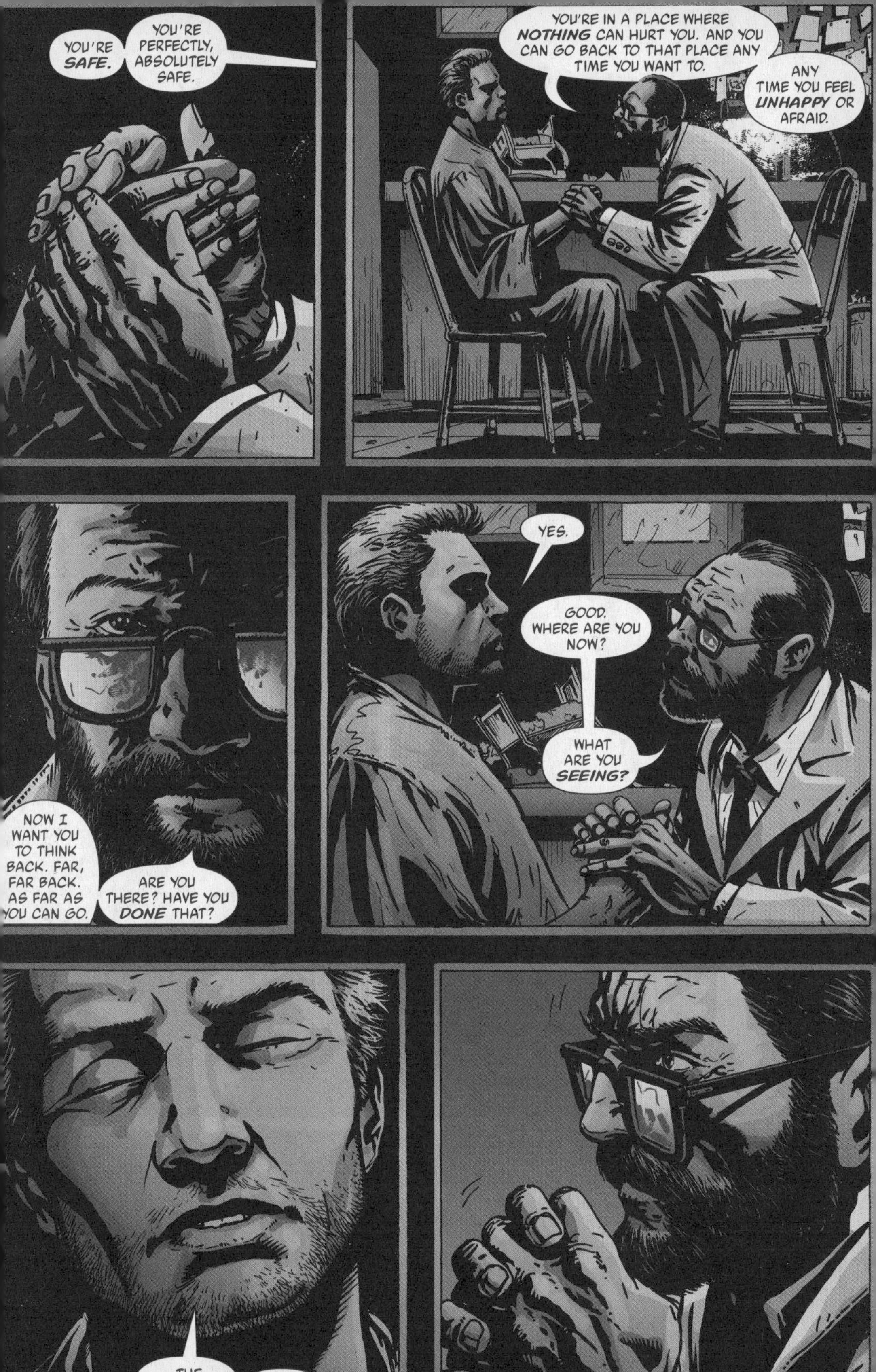
YOU'RE SAFE.
YOU'RE PERFECTLY, ABSOLUTELY SAFE.
YOU'RE IN A PLACE WHERE NOTHING CAN HURT YOU. AND YOU CAN GO BACK TO THAT PLACE ANY TIME YOU WANT TO.
ANY TIME YOU FEEL UNHAPPY OR AFRAID.
NOW I WANT YOU TO THINK BACK. FAR, FAR BACK. AS FAR AS YOU CAN GO.
ARE YOU THERE? HAVE YOU DONE THAT?
YES.
GOOD. WHERE ARE YOU NOW?
WHAT ARE YOU SEEING?
THE MIST ON THE RIVER.
THIS MORNING.

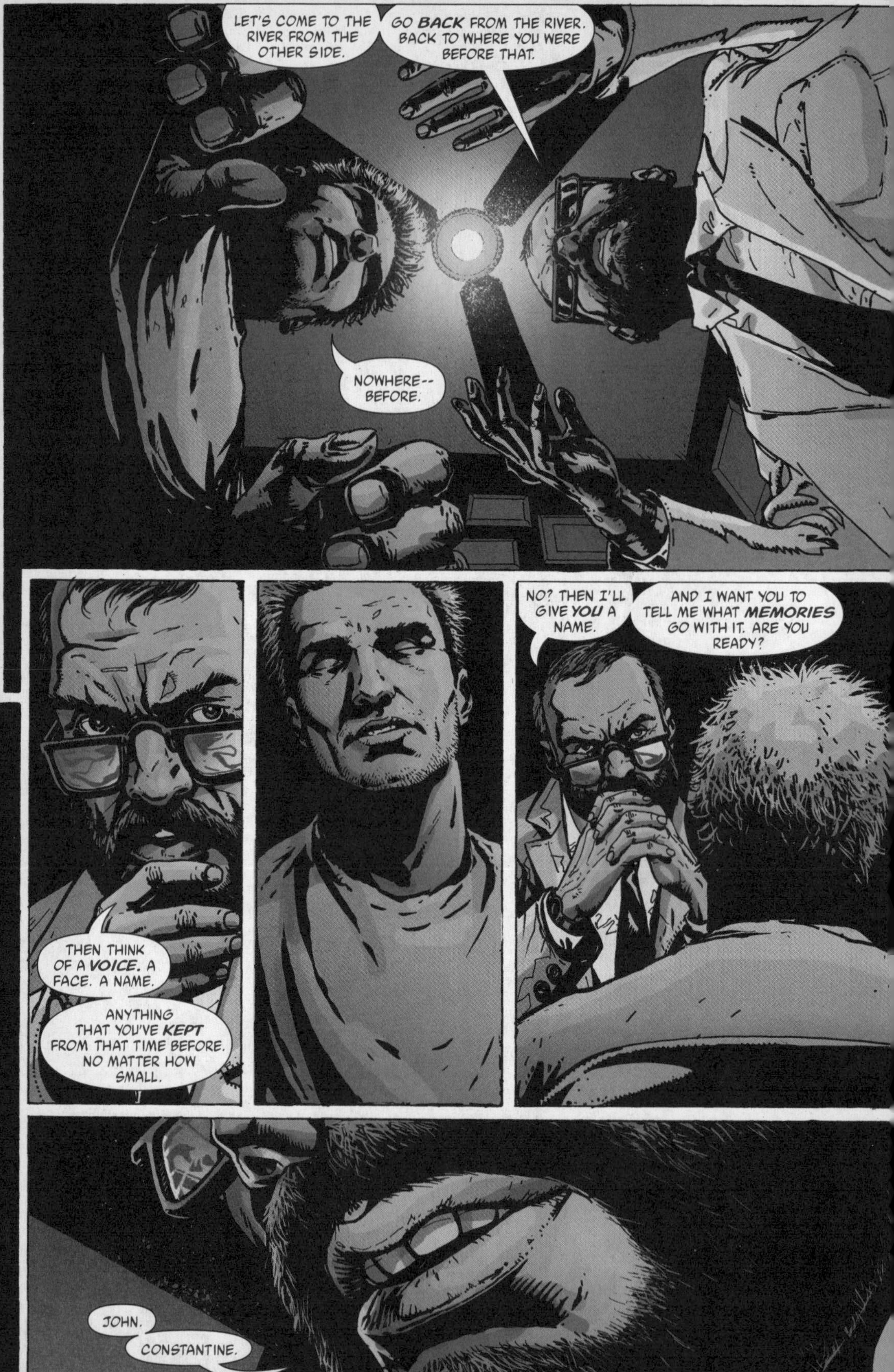
LET'S COME TO THE RIVER FROM THE OTHER SIDE.
GO BACK FROM THE RIVER. BACK TO WHERE YOU WERE BEFORE THAT.
NOWHERE-- BEFORE.
THEN THINK OF A VOICE. A FACE. A NAME.
ANYTHING THAT YOU'VE KEPT FROM THAT TIME BEFORE. NO MATTER HOW SMALL.
NO? THEN I'LL GIVE YOU A NAME.
AND I WANT YOU TO TELL ME WHAT MEMORIES GO WITH IT. ARE YOU READY?
JOHN.
CONSTANTINE.

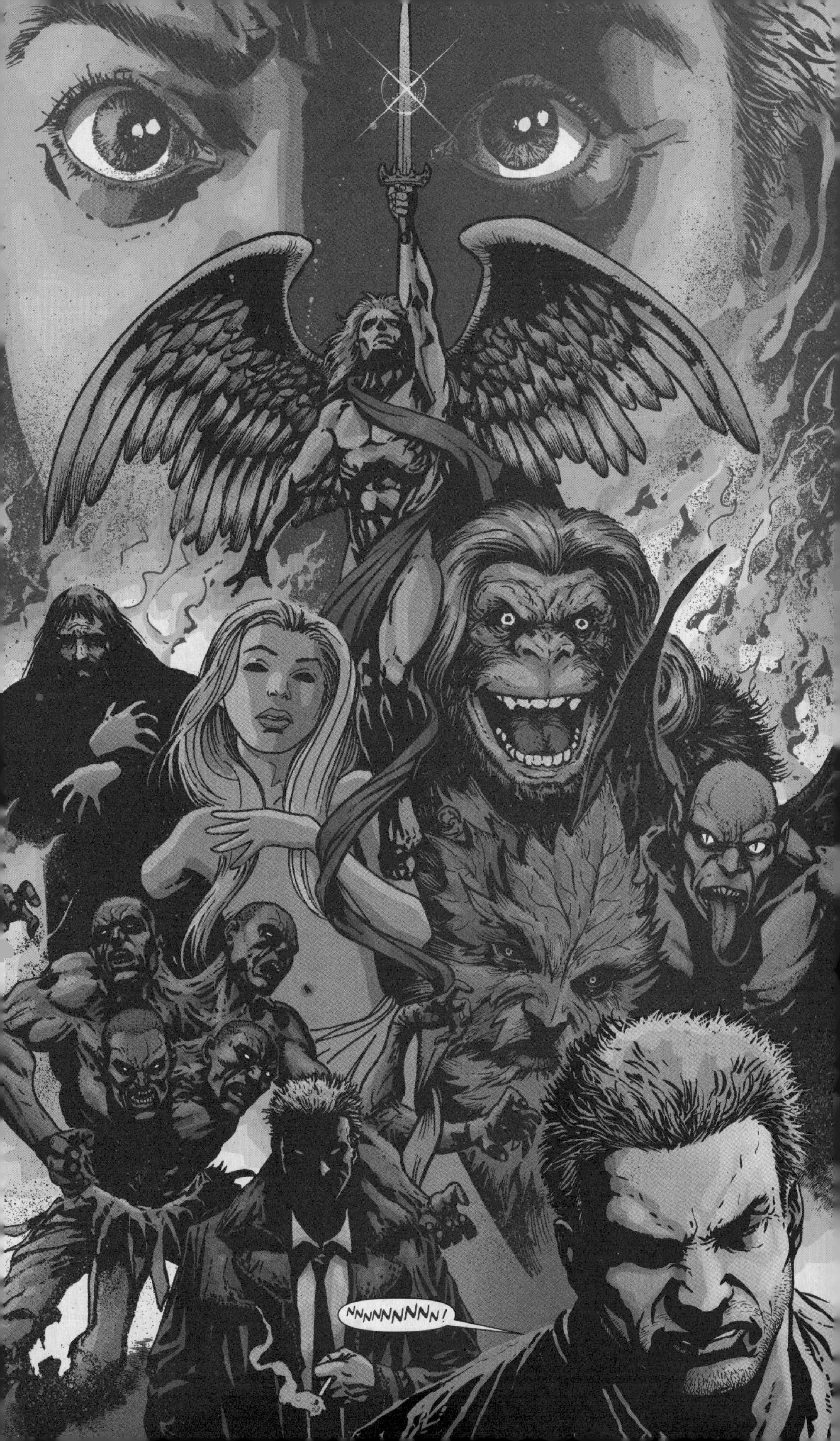
NNNNNNNNN!

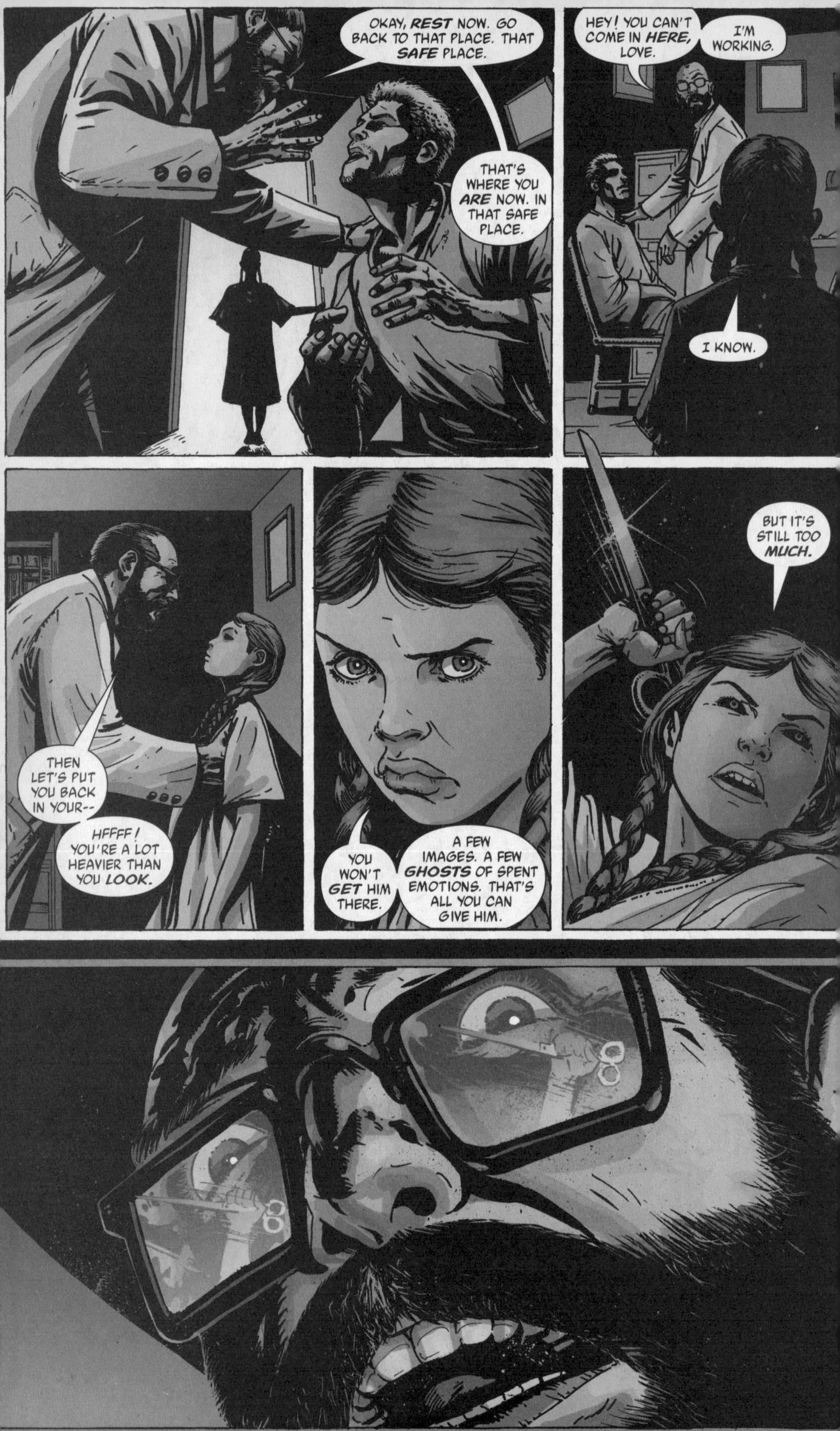

OKAY, REST NOW. GO BACK TO THAT PLACE. THAT SAFE PLACE.
THAT'S WHERE YOU ARE NOW. IN THAT SAFE PLACE.
HEY! YOU CAN'T COME IN HERE, LOVE.
I'M WORKING.
I KNOW.
THEN LET'S PUT YOU BACK IN YOUR--
HFFFF! YOU'RE A LOT HEAVIER THAN YOU LOOK.
YOU WON'T GET HIM THERE.
A FEW IMAGES. A FEW GHOSTS OF SPENT EMOTIONS. THAT'S ALL YOU CAN GIVE HIM.
BUT IT'S STILL TOO MUCH.

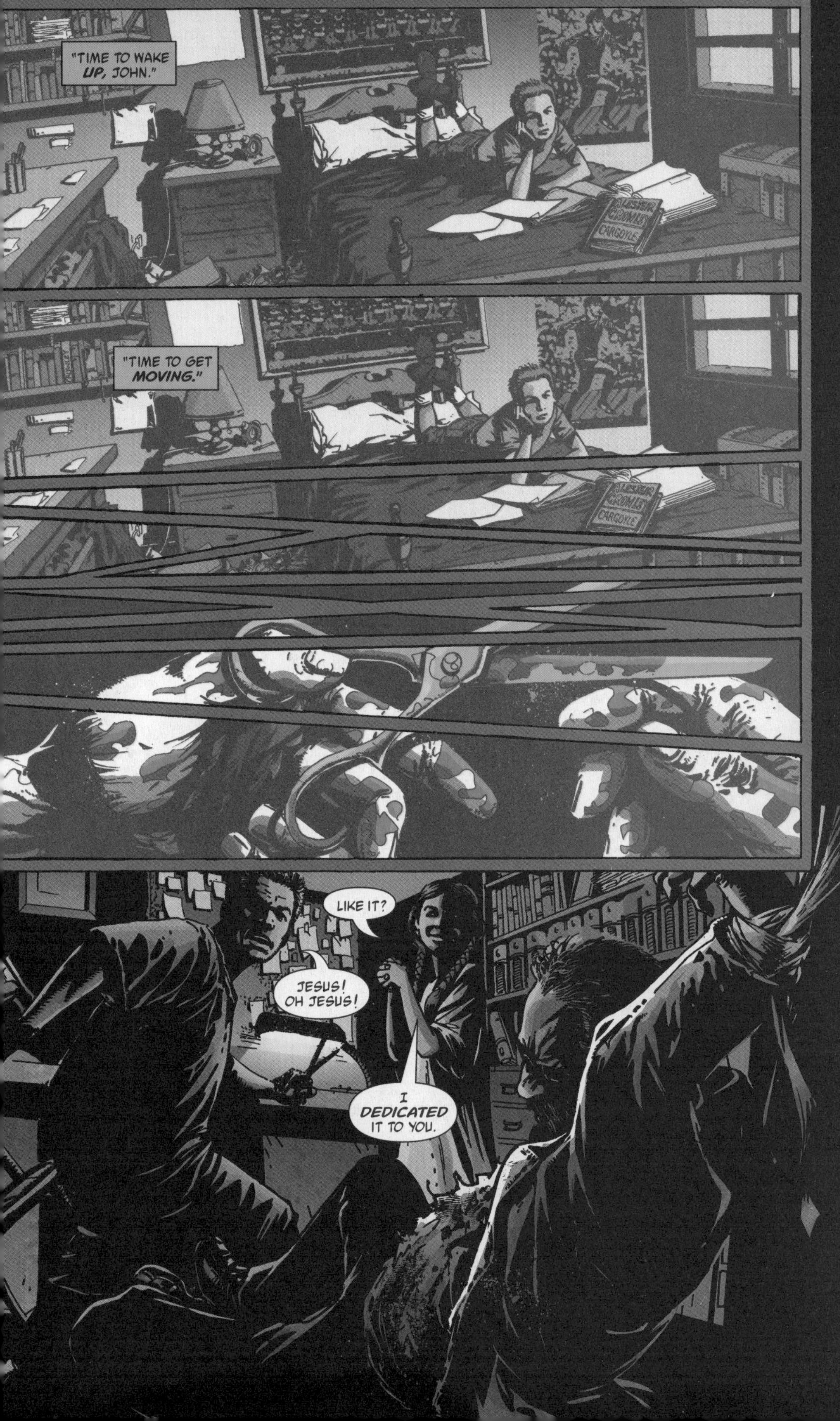
"TIME TO WAKE UP, JOHN."
ALEISTER CROWLEY
GARGOYLE
"TIME TO GET MOVING."
ALEISTER CROWLEY
GARGOYLE
LIKE IT?
JESUS! OH JESUS!
I DEDICATED IT TO YOU.

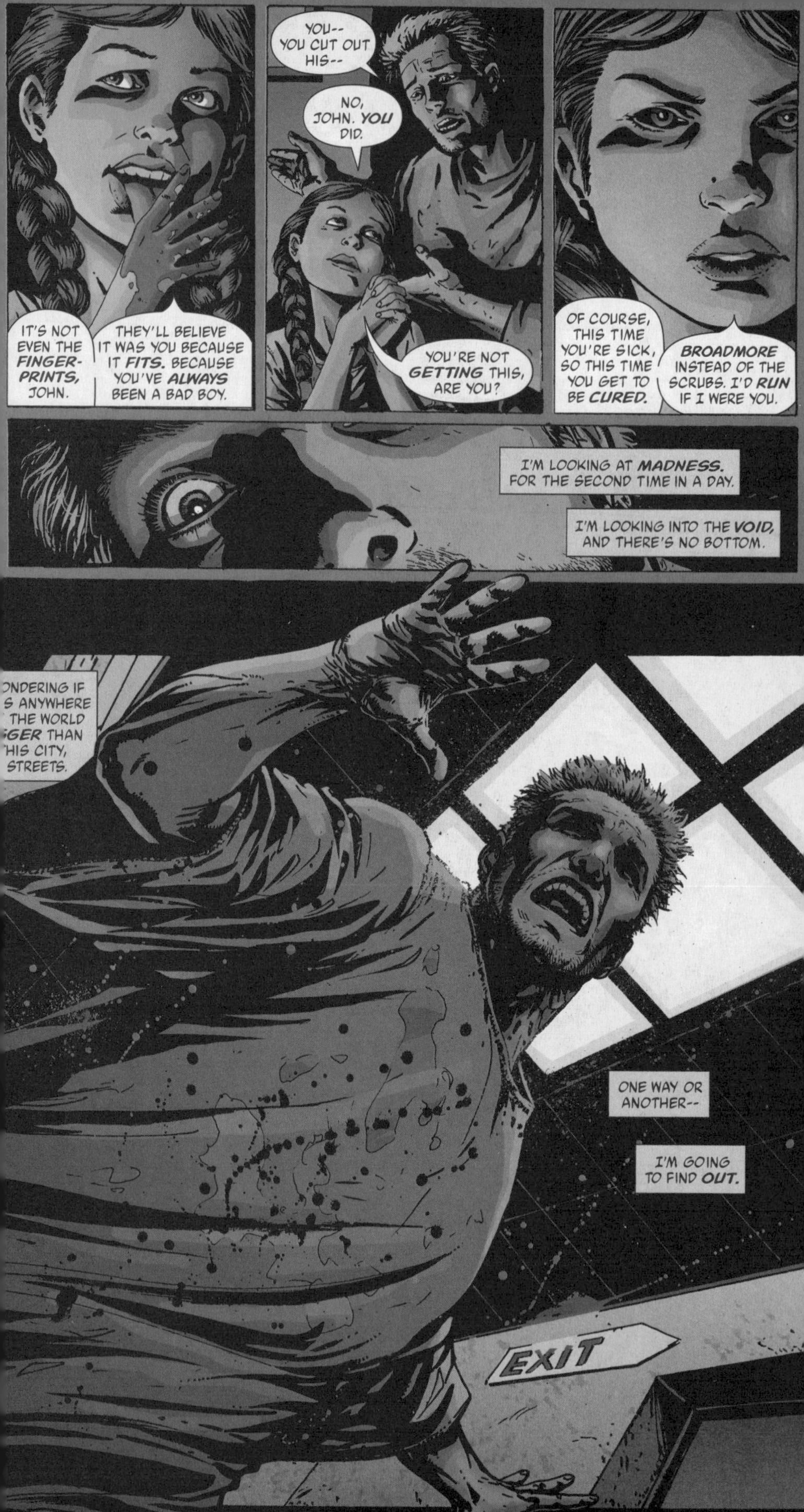
IT'S NOT EVEN THE FINGER-PRINTS, JOHN.
THEY'LL BELIEVE IT WAS YOU BECAUSE IT FITS. BECAUSE YOU'VE ALWAYS BEEN A BAD BOY.
YOU-- YOU CUT OUT HIS--
NO, JOHN. YOU DID.
YOU'RE NOT GETTING THIS, ARE YOU?
OF COURSE, THIS TIME YOU'RE SICK, SO THIS TIME YOU GET TO BE CURED.
BROADMORE INSTEAD OF THE SCRUBS. I'D RUN IF I WERE YOU.
I'M LOOKING AT MADNESS. FOR THE SECOND TIME IN A DAY.
I'M LOOKING INTO THE VOID, AND THERE'S NO BOTTOM.
ONDERING IF S ANYWHERE THE WORLD GER THAN THIS CITY, STREETS.
ONE WAY OR ANOTHER--
I'M GOING TO FIND OUT.
EXIT

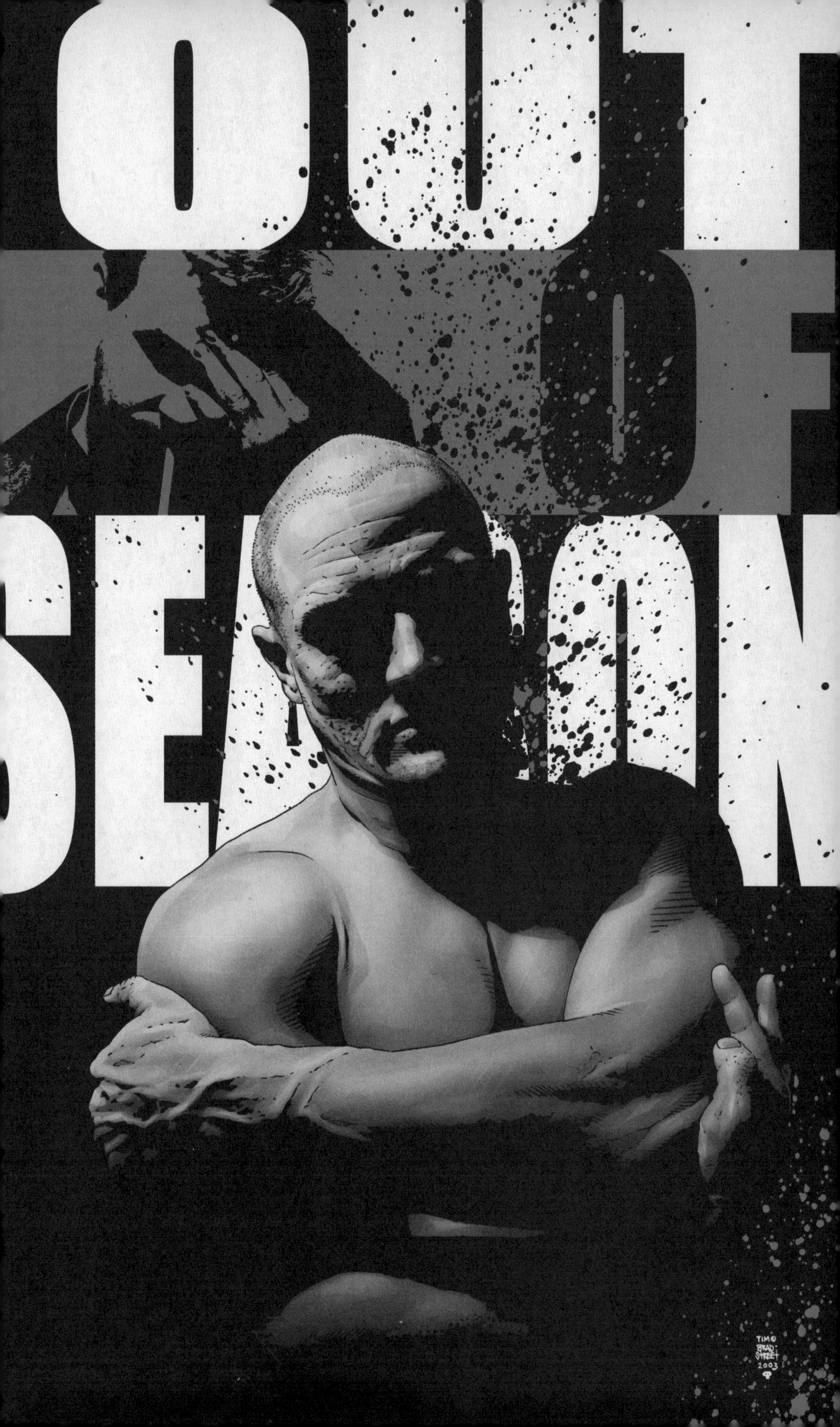
OUT
OF
SEASON

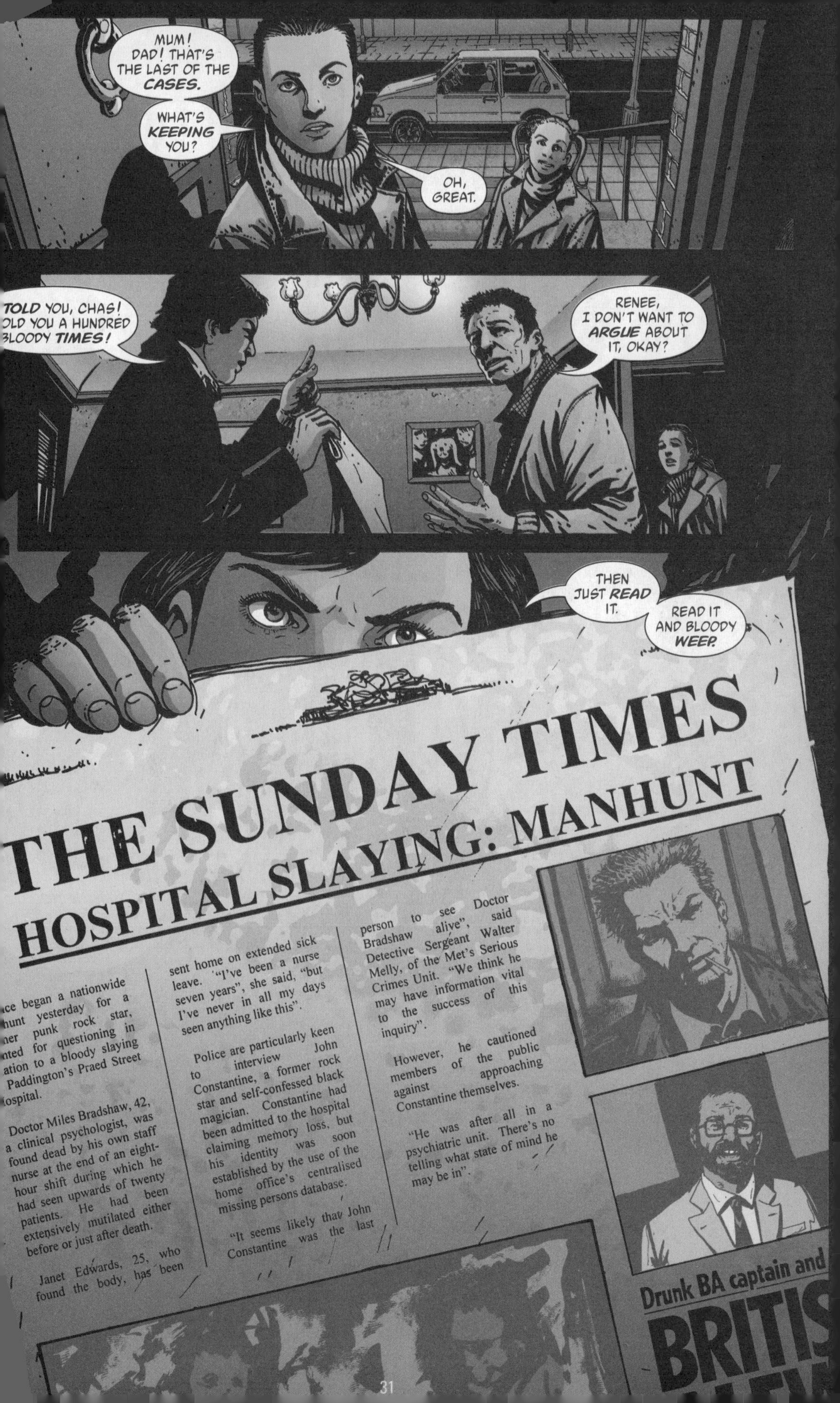

MUM! DAD! THAT'S THE LAST OF THE CASES.
WHAT'S KEEPING YOU?
OH, GREAT.
TOLD YOU, CHAS! OLD YOU A HUNDRED BLOODY TIMES!
RENEE, I DON'T WANT TO ARGUE ABOUT IT, OKAY?
THEN JUST READ IT.
READ IT AND BLOODY WEEP.
THE SUNDAY TIMES
HOSPITAL SLAYING: MANHUNT
ce began a nationwide hunt yesterday for a ner punk rock star, nted for questioning in ation to a bloody slaying Paddington's Praed Street ospital.
Doctor Miles Bradshaw, 42, a clinical psychologist, was found dead by his own staff nurse at the end of an eight-hour shift during which he had seen upwards of twenty patients. He had been extensively mutilated either before or just after death.
Janet Edwards, 25, who found the body, has been sent home on extended sick leave. "I've been a nurse seven years", she said, "but I've never in all my days seen anything like this".
Police are particularly keen to interview John Constantine, a former rock star and self-confessed black magician. Constantine had been admitted to the hospital claiming memory loss, but his identity was soon established by the use of the home office's centralised missing persons database.
"It seems likely that John Constantine was the last person to see Doctor Bradshaw alive", said Detective Sergeant Walter Melly, of the Met's Serious Crimes Unit. "We think he may have information vital to the success of this inquiry".
However, he cautioned members of the public against approaching Constantine themselves.
"He was after all in a psychiatric unit. There's no telling what state of mind he may be in".
Drunk BA captain and
BRITIS

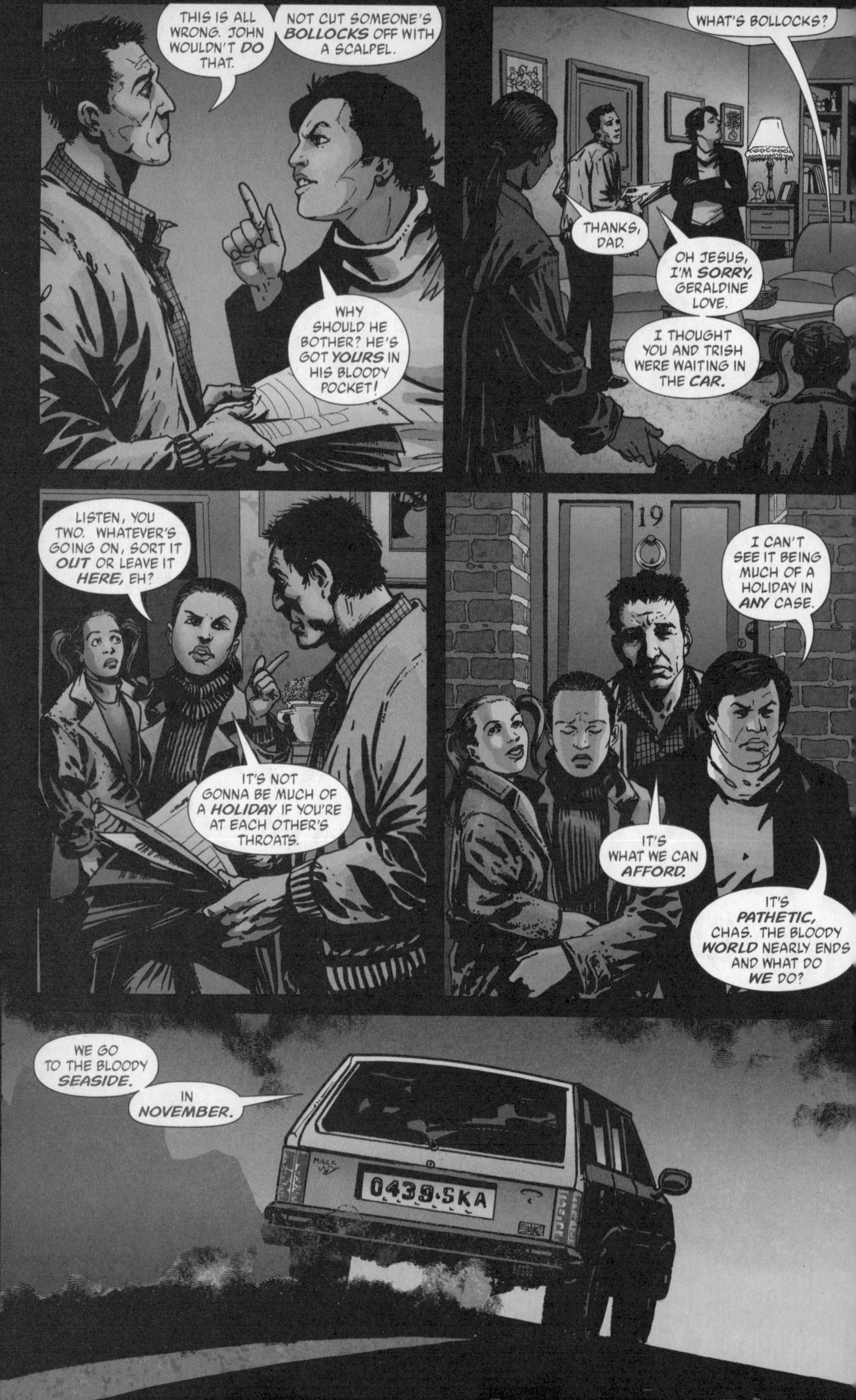
THIS IS ALL WRONG. JOHN WOULDN'T DO THAT.
NOT CUT SOMEONE'S BOLLOCKS OFF WITH A SCALPEL.
WHY SHOULD HE BOTHER? HE'S GOT YOURS IN HIS BLOODY POCKET!
WHAT'S BOLLOCKS?
THANKS, DAD.
OH JESUS, I'M SORRY, GERALDINE LOVE.
I THOUGHT YOU AND TRISH WERE WAITING IN THE CAR.
LISTEN, YOU TWO. WHATEVER'S GOING ON, SORT IT OUT OR LEAVE IT HERE, EH?
IT'S NOT GONNA BE MUCH OF A HOLIDAY IF YOU'RE AT EACH OTHER'S THROATS.
19
I CAN'T SEE IT BEING MUCH OF A HOLIDAY IN ANY CASE.
IT'S WHAT WE CAN AFFORD.
IT'S PATHETIC, CHAS. THE BLOODY WORLD NEARLY ENDS AND WHAT DO WE DO?
WE GO TO THE BLOODY SEASIDE.
IN NOVEMBER.
0439·SKA

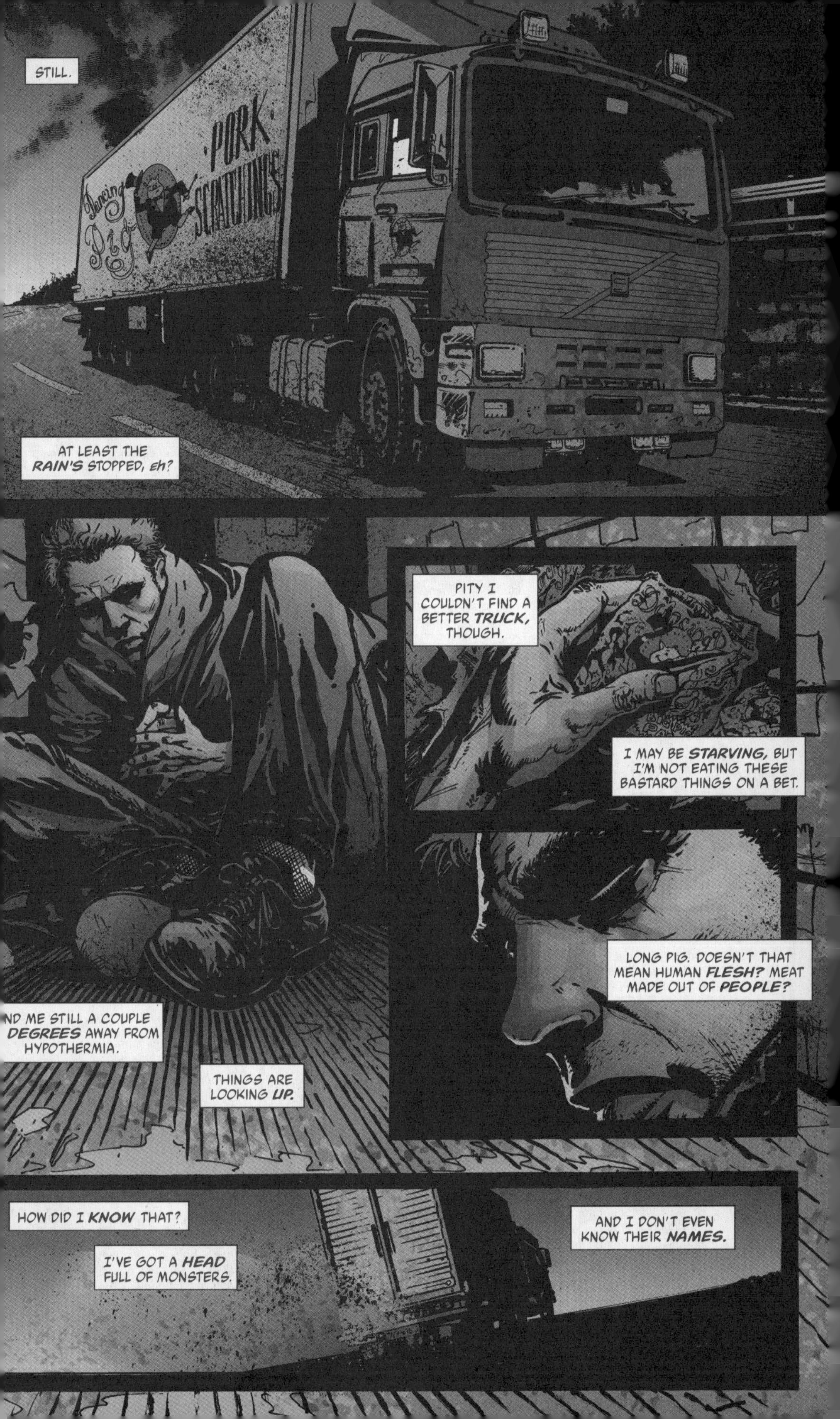
STILL.
AT LEAST THE RAIN'S STOPPED, eh?
Dancing Pig
PORK SCRATCHINGS
ND ME STILL A COUPLE DEGREES AWAY FROM HYPOTHERMIA.
THINGS ARE LOOKING UP.
PITY I COULDN'T FIND A BETTER TRUCK, THOUGH.
I MAY BE STARVING, BUT I'M NOT EATING THESE BASTARD THINGS ON A BET.
LONG PIG. DOESN'T THAT MEAN HUMAN FLESH? MEAT MADE OUT OF PEOPLE?
HOW DID I KNOW THAT?
I'VE GOT A HEAD FULL OF MONSTERS.
AND I DON'T EVEN KNOW THEIR NAMES.

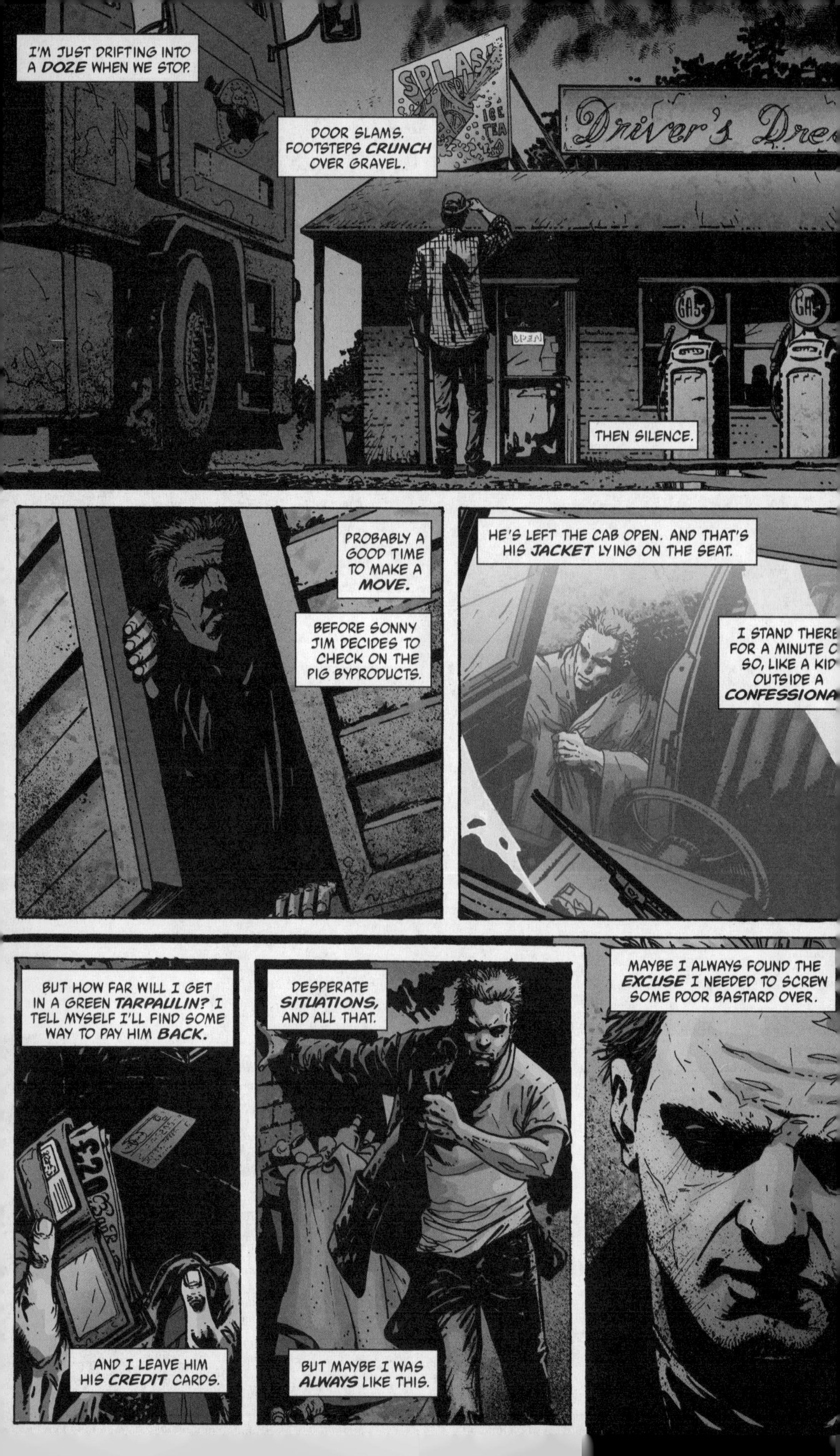

I'M JUST DRIFTING INTO A DOZE WHEN WE STOP.
SPLASH
ICE TEA
Driver's Dre
DOOR SLAMS. FOOTSTEPS CRUNCH OVER GRAVEL.
GAS
OPEN
THEN SILENCE.
PROBABLY A GOOD TIME TO MAKE A MOVE.
BEFORE SONNY JIM DECIDES TO CHECK ON THE PIG BYPRODUCTS.
HE'S LEFT THE CAB OPEN. AND THAT'S HIS JACKET LYING ON THE SEAT.
I STAND THERE FOR A MINUTE SO, LIKE A KID OUTSIDE A CONFESSIONA
BUT HOW FAR WILL I GET IN A GREEN TARPAULIN? I TELL MYSELF I'LL FIND SOME WAY TO PAY HIM BACK.
AND I LEAVE HIM HIS CREDIT CARDS.
DESPERATE SITUATIONS, AND ALL THAT.
BUT MAYBE I WAS ALWAYS LIKE THIS.
MAYBE I ALWAYS FOUND THE EXCUSE I NEEDED TO SCREW SOME POOR BASTARD OVER.

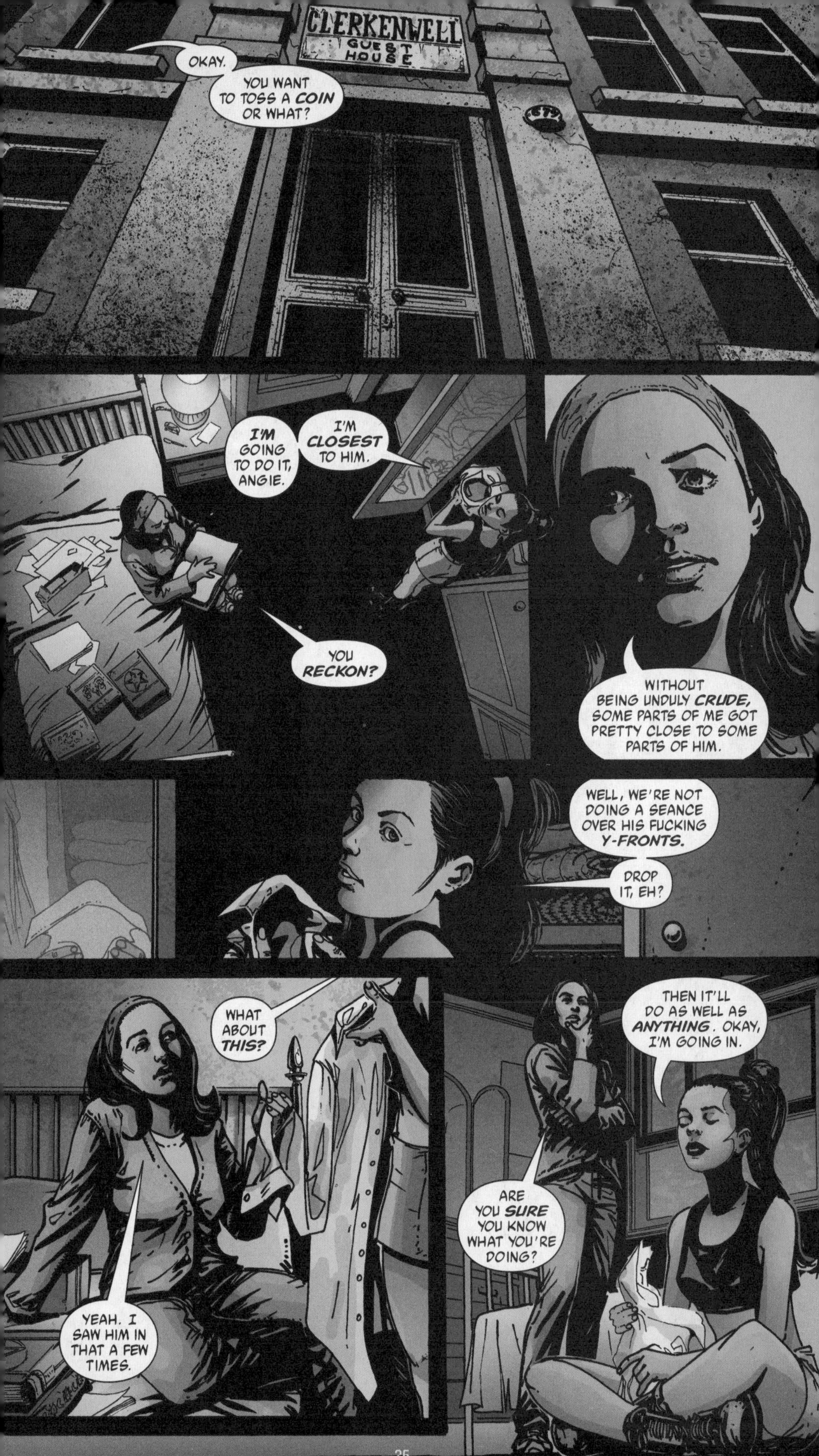
CLERKENWELL GUEST HOUSE
OKAY.
YOU WANT TO TOSS A COIN OR WHAT?
I'M GOING TO DO IT, ANGIE.
I'M CLOSEST TO HIM.
YOU RECKON?
WITHOUT BEING UNDULY CRUDE, SOME PARTS OF ME GOT PRETTY CLOSE TO SOME PARTS OF HIM.
WELL, WE'RE NOT DOING A SEANCE OVER HIS FUCKING Y-FRONTS.
DROP IT, EH?
WHAT ABOUT THIS?
YEAH. I SAW HIM IN THAT A FEW TIMES.
THEN IT'LL DO AS WELL AS ANYTHING. OKAY, I'M GOING IN.
ARE YOU SURE YOU KNOW WHAT YOU'RE DOING?

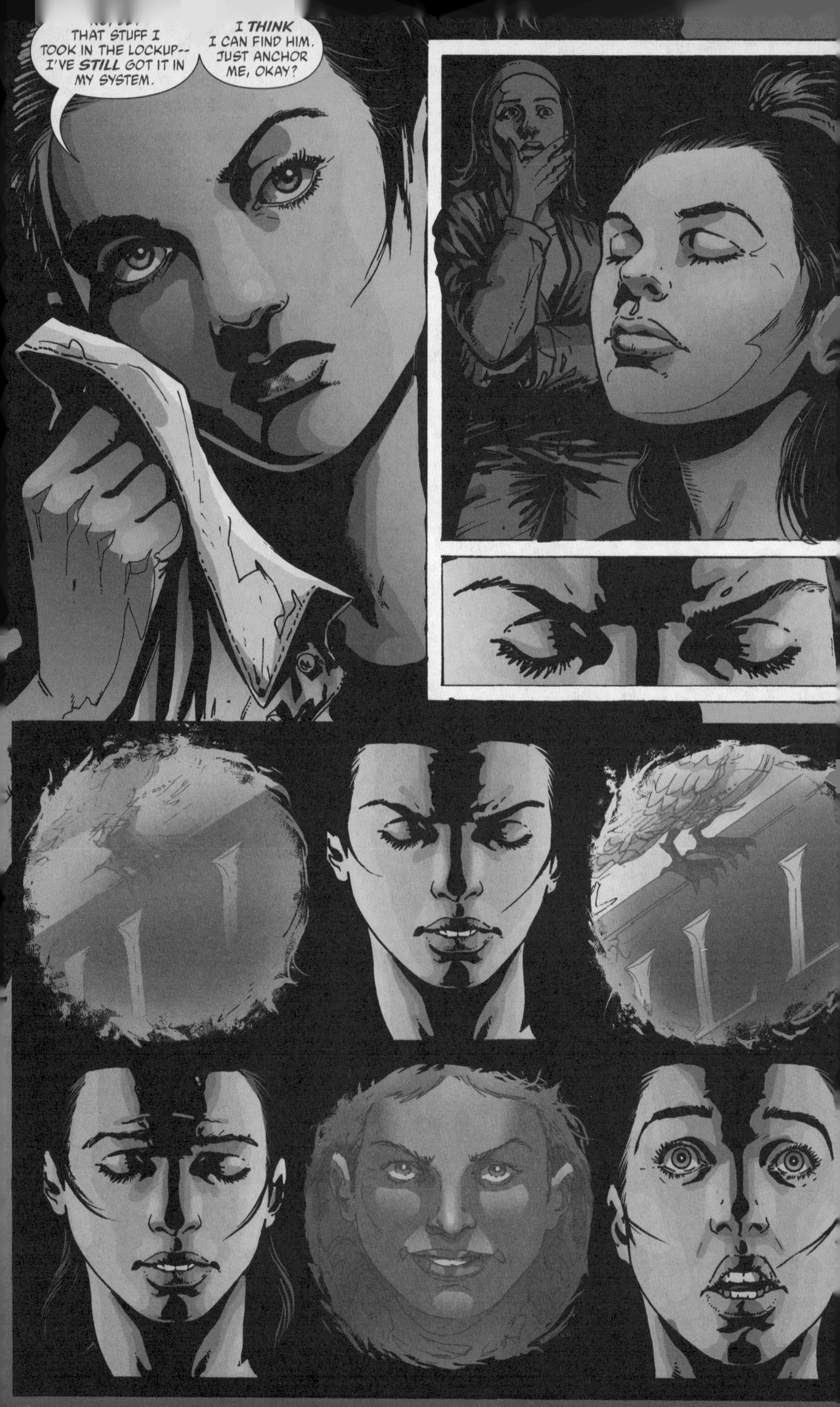
THAT STUFF I TOOK IN THE LOCKUP-- I'VE **STILL** GOT IT IN MY SYSTEM.
I **THINK** I CAN FIND HIM. JUST ANCHOR ME, OKAY?

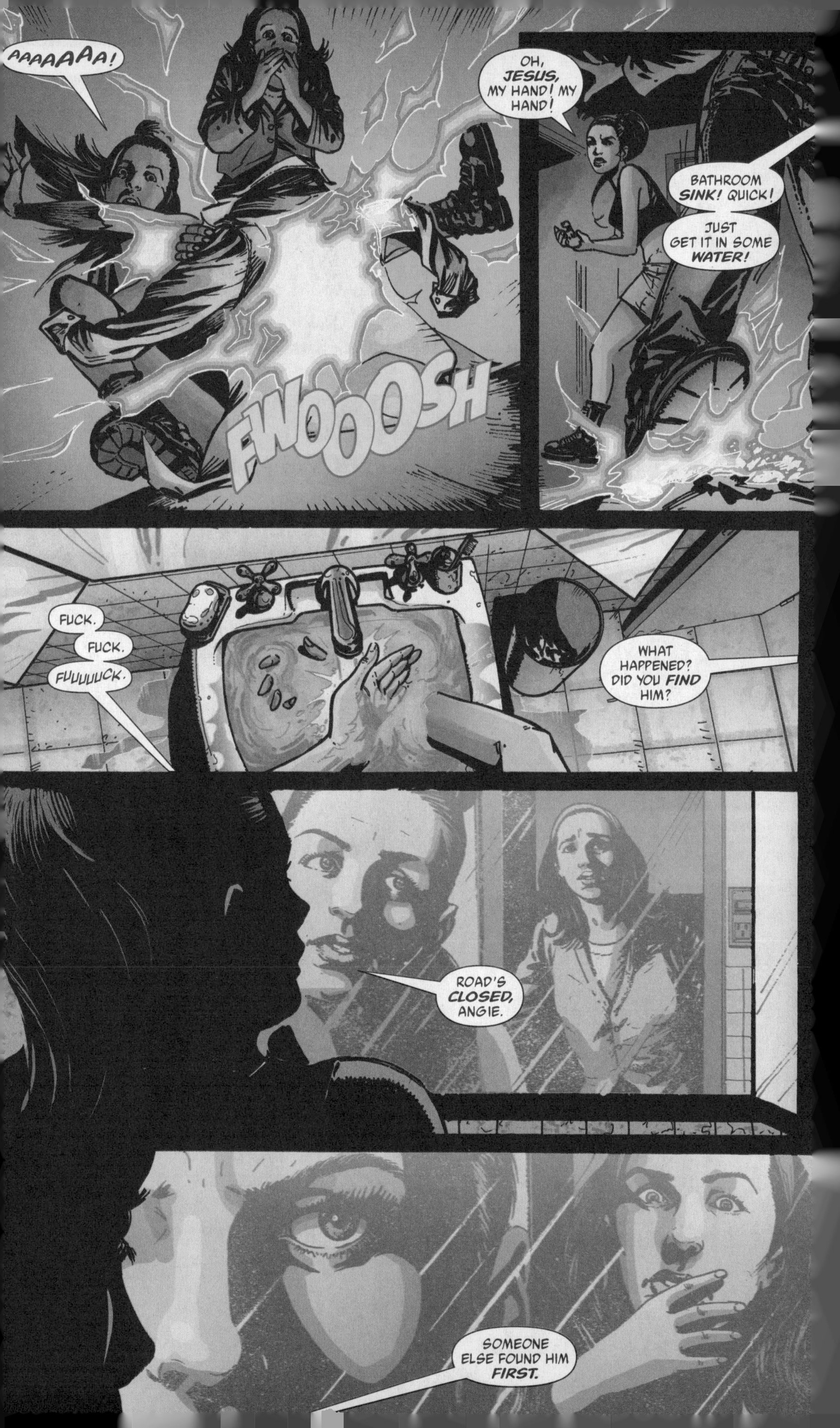
AAAAAAA!
FWOOOSH
OH, JESUS, MY HAND! MY HAND!
BATHROOM SINK! QUICK!
JUST GET IT IN SOME WATER!
FUCK.
FUCK.
FUUUUUCK.
WHAT HAPPENED? DID YOU FIND HIM?
ROAD'S CLOSED, ANGIE.
SOMEONE ELSE FOUND HIM FIRST.

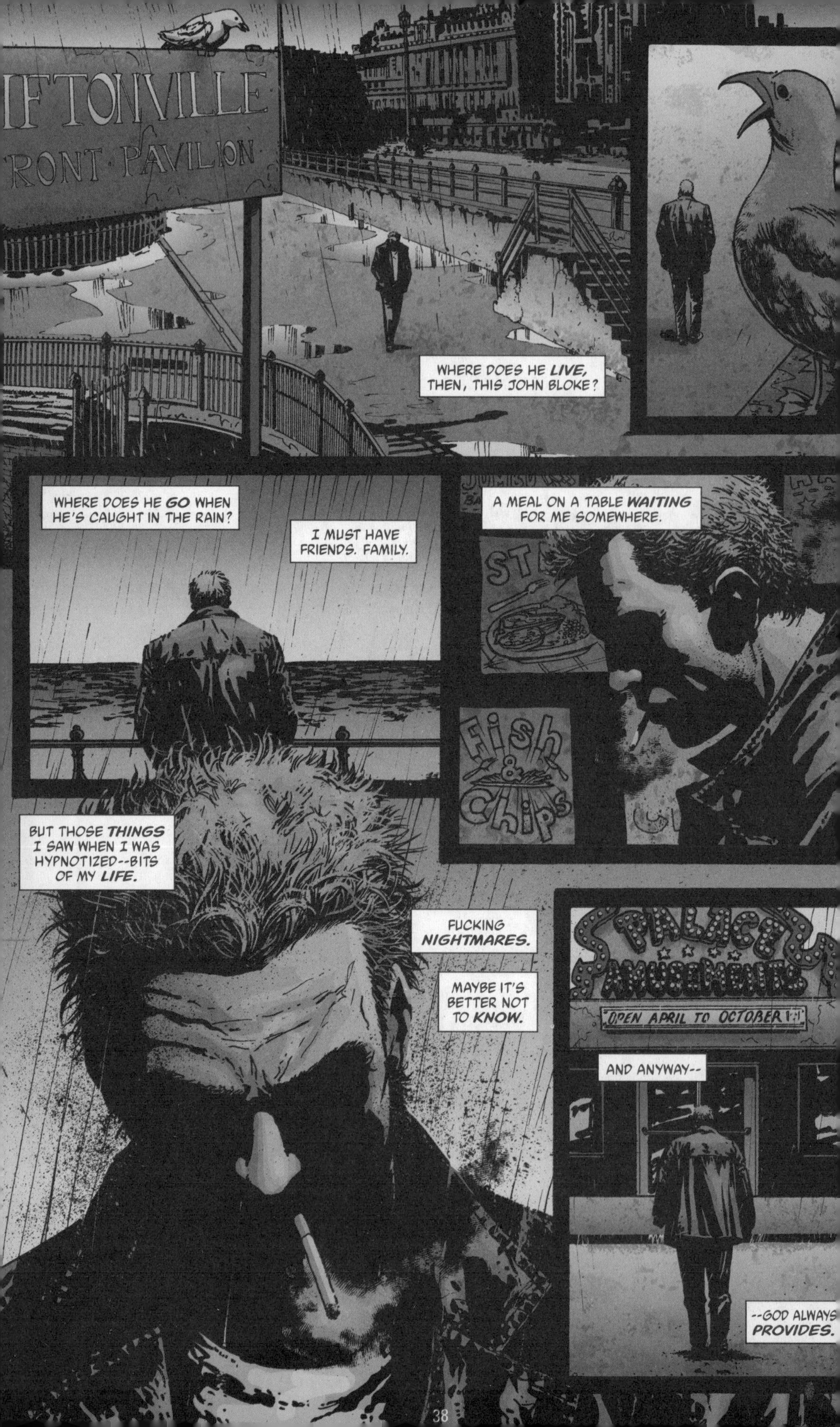
IFTONVILLE
RONT PAVILION
WHERE DOES HE LIVE, THEN, THIS JOHN BLOKE?
WHERE DOES HE GO WHEN HE'S CAUGHT IN THE RAIN?
I MUST HAVE FRIENDS. FAMILY.
A MEAL ON A TABLE WAITING FOR ME SOMEWHERE.
Fish & Chips
BUT THOSE THINGS I SAW WHEN I WAS HYPNOTIZED--BITS OF MY LIFE.
FUCKING NIGHTMARES.
MAYBE IT'S BETTER NOT TO KNOW.
PALACE AMUSEMENTS
OPEN APRIL TO OCTOBER
AND ANYWAY--
--GOD ALWAYS PROVIDES.

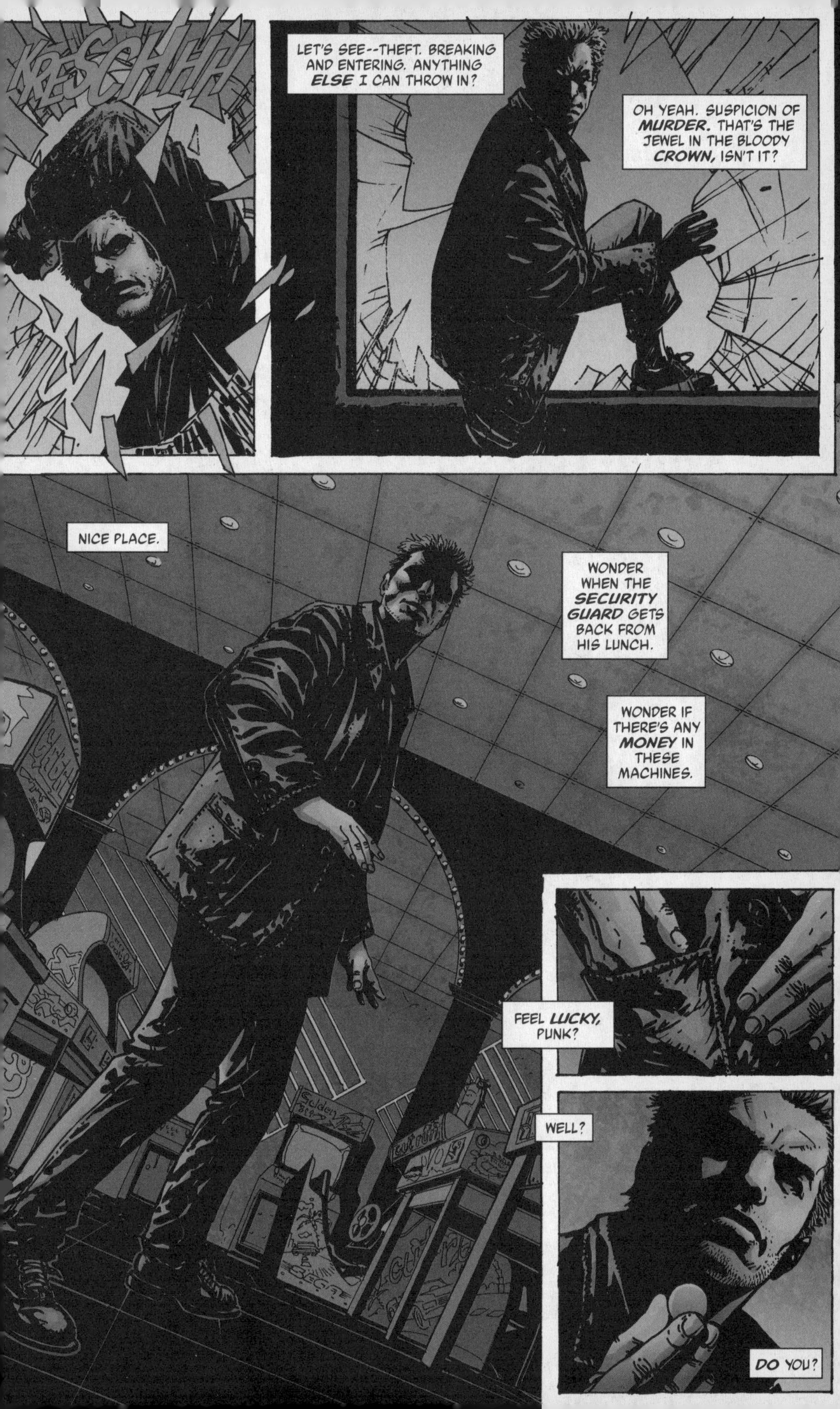

KRESCHHH
LET'S SEE--THEFT. BREAKING AND ENTERING. ANYTHING ELSE I CAN THROW IN?
OH YEAH. SUSPICION OF MURDER. THAT'S THE JEWEL IN THE BLOODY CROWN, ISN'T IT?
NICE PLACE.
WONDER WHEN THE SECURITY GUARD GETS BACK FROM HIS LUNCH.
WONDER IF THERE'S ANY MONEY IN THESE MACHINES.
FEEL LUCKY, PUNK?
WELL?
DO YOU?

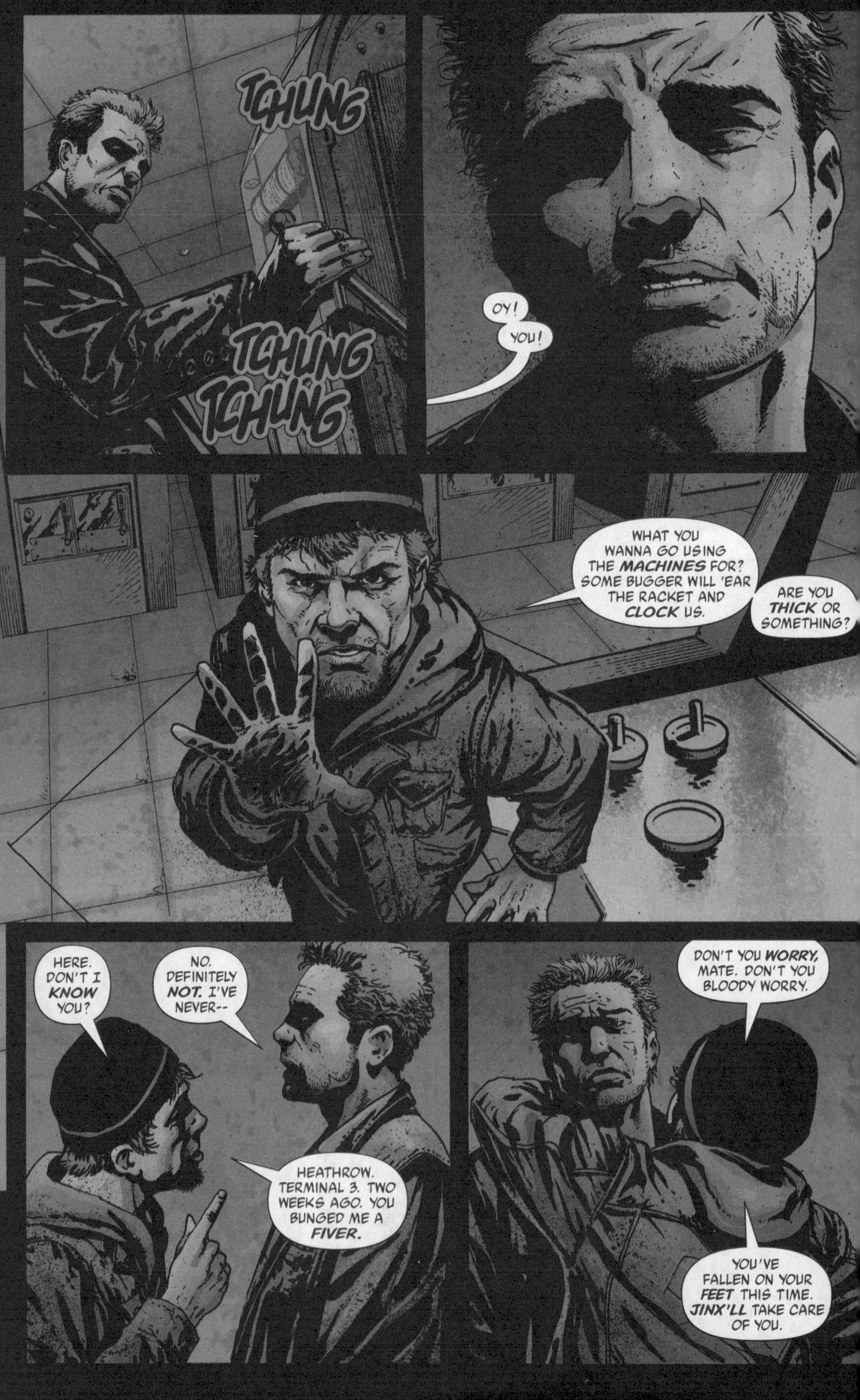
TCHUNG
TCHUNG
TCHUNG
OY!
YOU!
WHAT YOU WANNA GO USING THE MACHINES FOR? SOME BUGGER WILL 'EAR THE RACKET AND CLOCK US.
ARE YOU THICK OR SOMETHING?
HERE. DON'T I KNOW YOU?
NO. DEFINITELY NOT. I'VE NEVER--
HEATHROW. TERMINAL 3. TWO WEEKS AGO. YOU BUNGED ME A FIVER.
DON'T YOU WORRY, MATE. DON'T YOU BLOODY WORRY.
YOU'VE FALLEN ON YOUR FEET THIS TIME. JINX'LL TAKE CARE OF YOU.

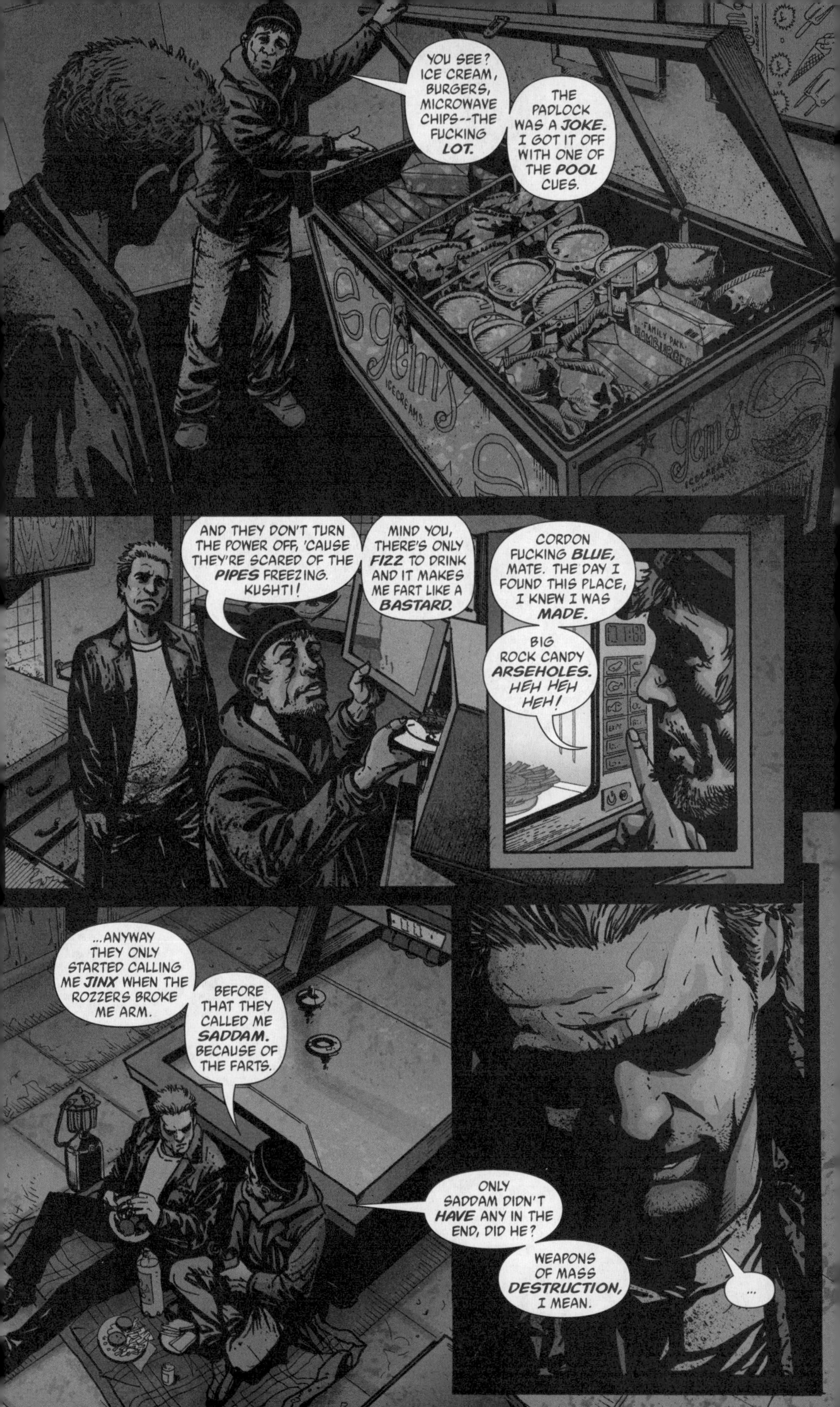

YOU SEE? ICE CREAM, BURGERS, MICROWAVE CHIPS--THE FUCKING LOT.
THE PADLOCK WAS A JOKE. I GOT IT OFF WITH ONE OF THE POOL CUES.
AND THEY DON'T TURN THE POWER OFF, 'CAUSE THEY'RE SCARED OF THE PIPES FREEZING. KUSHTI!
MIND YOU, THERE'S ONLY FIZZ TO DRINK AND IT MAKES ME FART LIKE A BASTARD.
CORDON FUCKING BLUE, MATE. THE DAY I FOUND THIS PLACE, I KNEW I WAS MADE.
BIG ROCK CANDY ARSEHOLES. HEH HEH HEH!
...ANYWAY THEY ONLY STARTED CALLING ME JINX WHEN THE ROZZERS BROKE ME ARM.
BEFORE THAT THEY CALLED ME SADDAM. BECAUSE OF THE FARTS.
ONLY SADDAM DIDN'T HAVE ANY IN THE END, DID HE?
WEAPONS OF MASS DESTRUCTION, I MEAN.
...

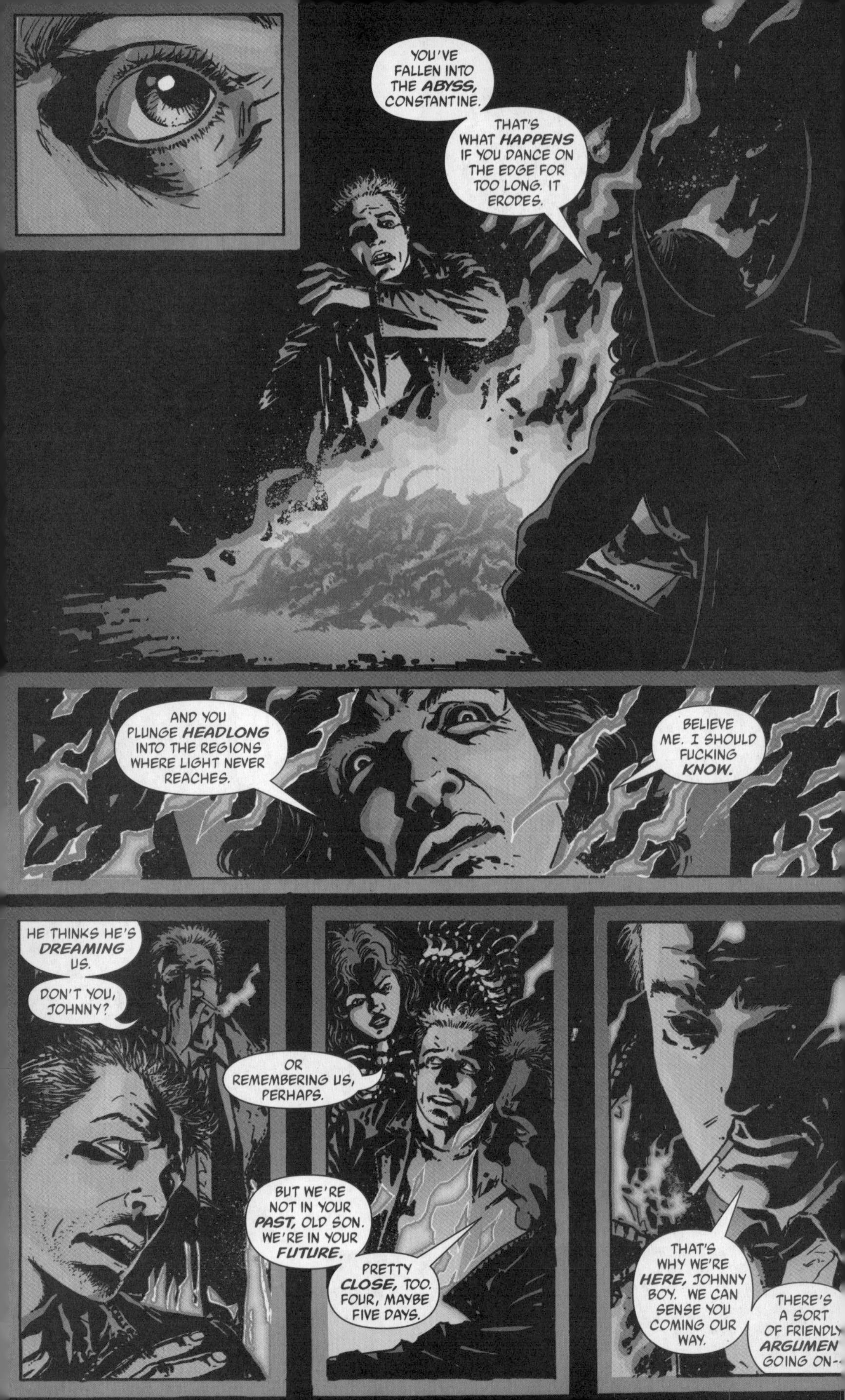
YOU'VE FALLEN INTO THE ABYSS, CONSTANTINE.
THAT'S WHAT HAPPENS IF YOU DANCE ON THE EDGE FOR TOO LONG. IT ERODES.
AND YOU PLUNGE HEADLONG INTO THE REGIONS WHERE LIGHT NEVER REACHES.
BELIEVE ME. I SHOULD FUCKING KNOW.
HE THINKS HE'S DREAMING US.
DON'T YOU, JOHNNY?
OR REMEMBERING US, PERHAPS.
BUT WE'RE NOT IN YOUR PAST, OLD SON. WE'RE IN YOUR FUTURE.
PRETTY CLOSE, TOO. FOUR, MAYBE FIVE DAYS.
THAT'S WHY WE'RE HERE, JOHNNY BOY. WE CAN SENSE YOU COMING OUR WAY.
THERE'S A SORT OF FRIENDLY ARGUMEN GOING ON--

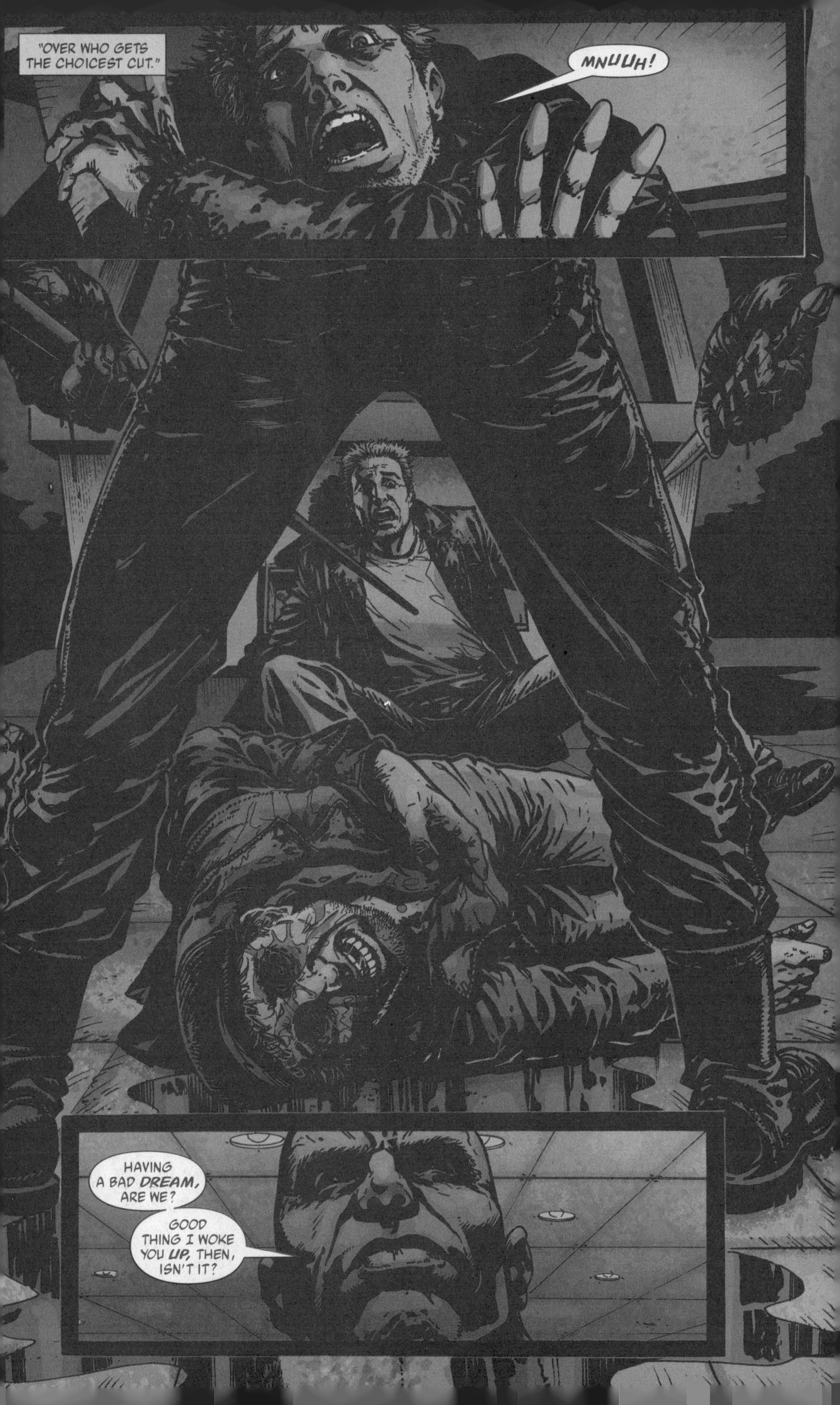
"OVER WHO GETS THE CHOICEST CUT."
MNUUH!
HAVING A BAD DREAM, ARE WE?
GOOD THING I WOKE YOU UP, THEN, ISN'T IT?

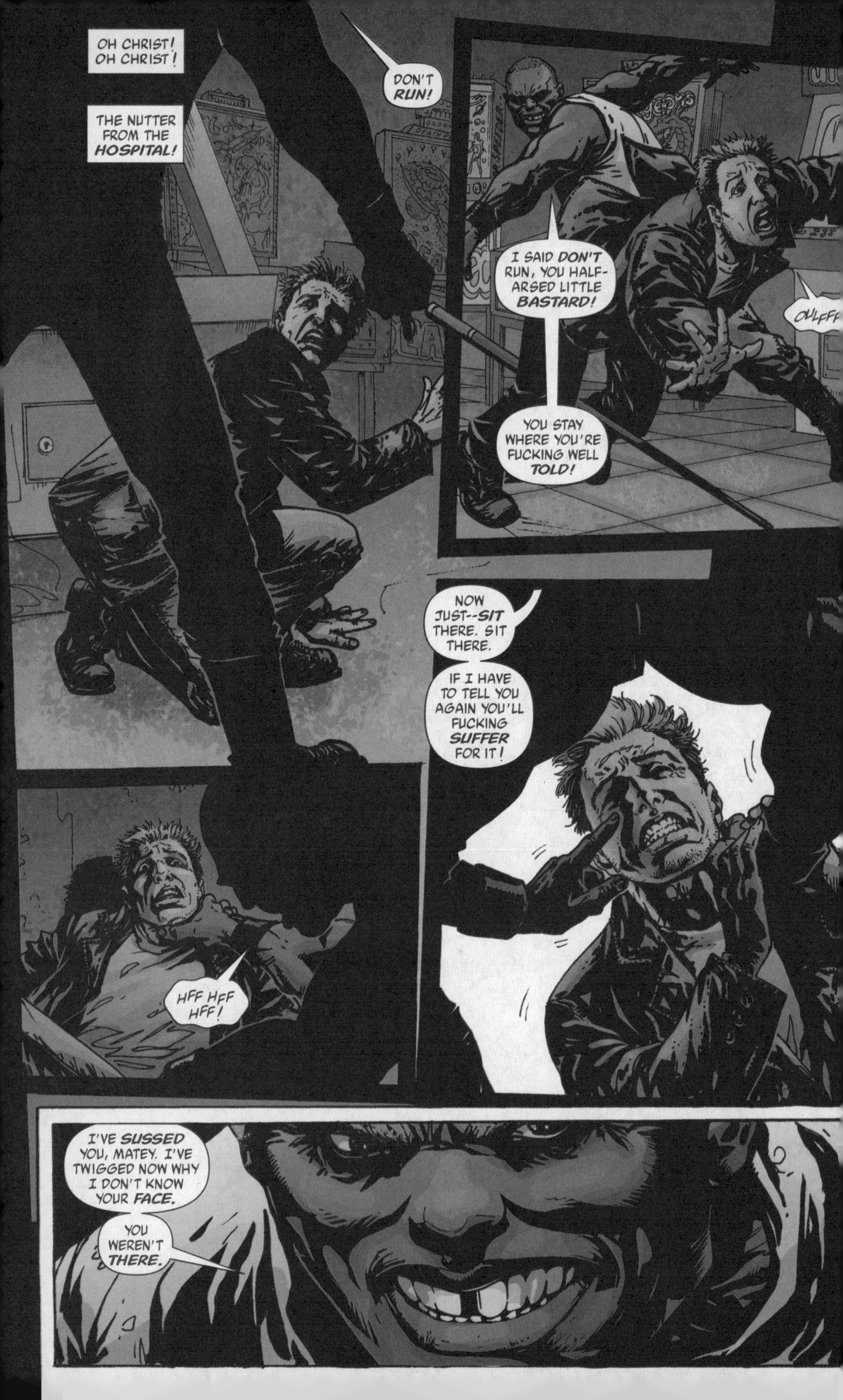
OH CHRIST! OH CHRIST!
THE NUTTER FROM THE HOSPITAL!
DON'T RUN!
I SAID DON'T RUN, YOU HALF-ARSED LITTLE BASTARD!
YOU STAY WHERE YOU'RE FUCKING WELL TOLD!
OULFFF
HFF HFF HFF!
NOW JUST--SIT THERE. SIT THERE.
IF I HAVE TO TELL YOU AGAIN YOU'LL FUCKING SUFFER FOR IT!
I'VE SUSSED YOU, MATEY. I'VE TWIGGED NOW WHY I DON'T KNOW YOUR FACE.
YOU WEREN'T THERE.

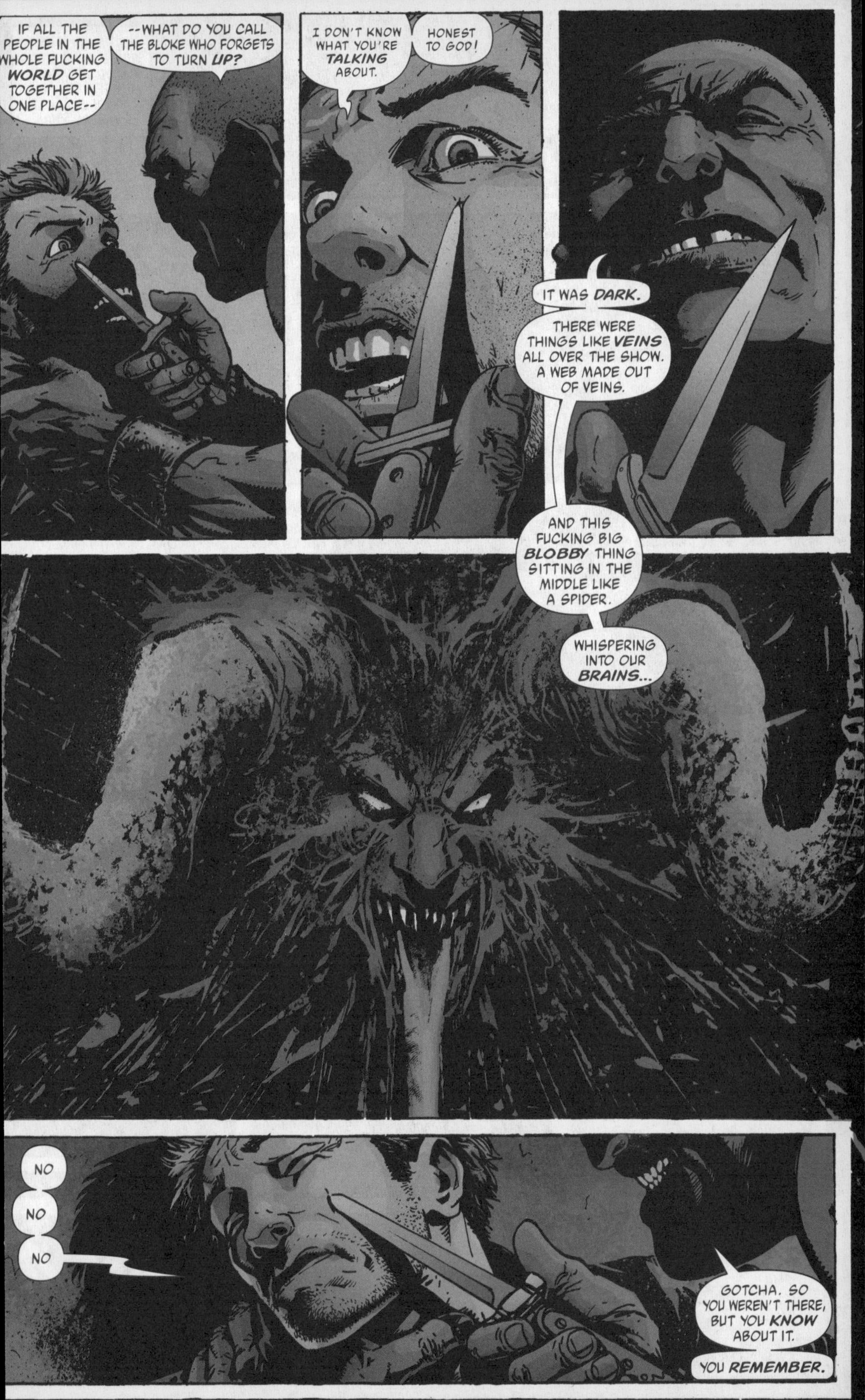
IF ALL THE PEOPLE IN THE WHOLE FUCKING WORLD GET TOGETHER IN ONE PLACE--
--WHAT DO YOU CALL THE BLOKE WHO FORGETS TO TURN UP?
I DON'T KNOW WHAT YOU'RE TALKING ABOUT.
HONEST TO GOD!
IT WAS DARK.
THERE WERE THINGS LIKE VEINS ALL OVER THE SHOW. A WEB MADE OUT OF VEINS.
AND THIS FUCKING BIG BLOBBY THING SITTING IN THE MIDDLE LIKE A SPIDER.
WHISPERING INTO OUR BRAINS...
NO
NO
NO
GOTCHA. SO YOU WEREN'T THERE, BUT YOU KNOW ABOUT IT.
YOU REMEMBER.

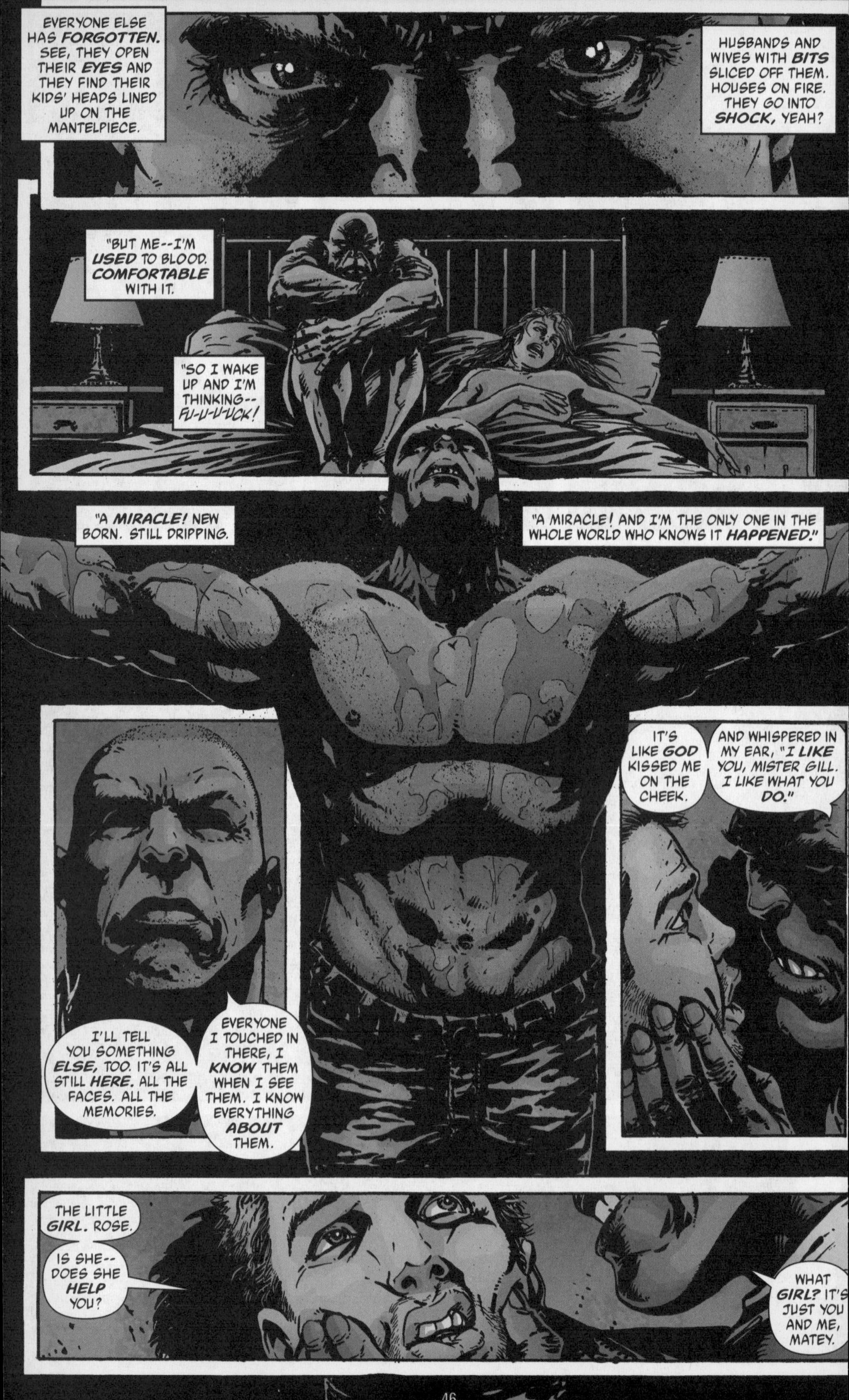
EVERYONE ELSE HAS FORGOTTEN. SEE, THEY OPEN THEIR EYES AND THEY FIND THEIR KIDS' HEADS LINED UP ON THE MANTELPIECE.
HUSBANDS AND WIVES WITH BITS SLICED OFF THEM. HOUSES ON FIRE. THEY GO INTO SHOCK, YEAH?
"BUT ME--I'M USED TO BLOOD. COMFORTABLE WITH IT.
"SO I WAKE UP AND I'M THINKING-- FU-U-U-UCK!
"A MIRACLE! NEW BORN. STILL DRIPPING.
"A MIRACLE! AND I'M THE ONLY ONE IN THE WHOLE WORLD WHO KNOWS IT HAPPENED."
IT'S LIKE GOD KISSED ME ON THE CHEEK.
AND WHISPERED IN MY EAR, "I LIKE YOU, MISTER GILL. I LIKE WHAT YOU DO."
I'LL TELL YOU SOMETHING ELSE, TOO. IT'S ALL STILL HERE. ALL THE FACES. ALL THE MEMORIES.
EVERYONE I TOUCHED IN THERE, I KNOW THEM WHEN I SEE THEM. I KNOW EVERYTHING ABOUT THEM.
THE LITTLE GIRL. ROSE.
IS SHE-- DOES SHE HELP YOU?
WHAT GIRL? IT'S JUST YOU AND ME, MATEY.

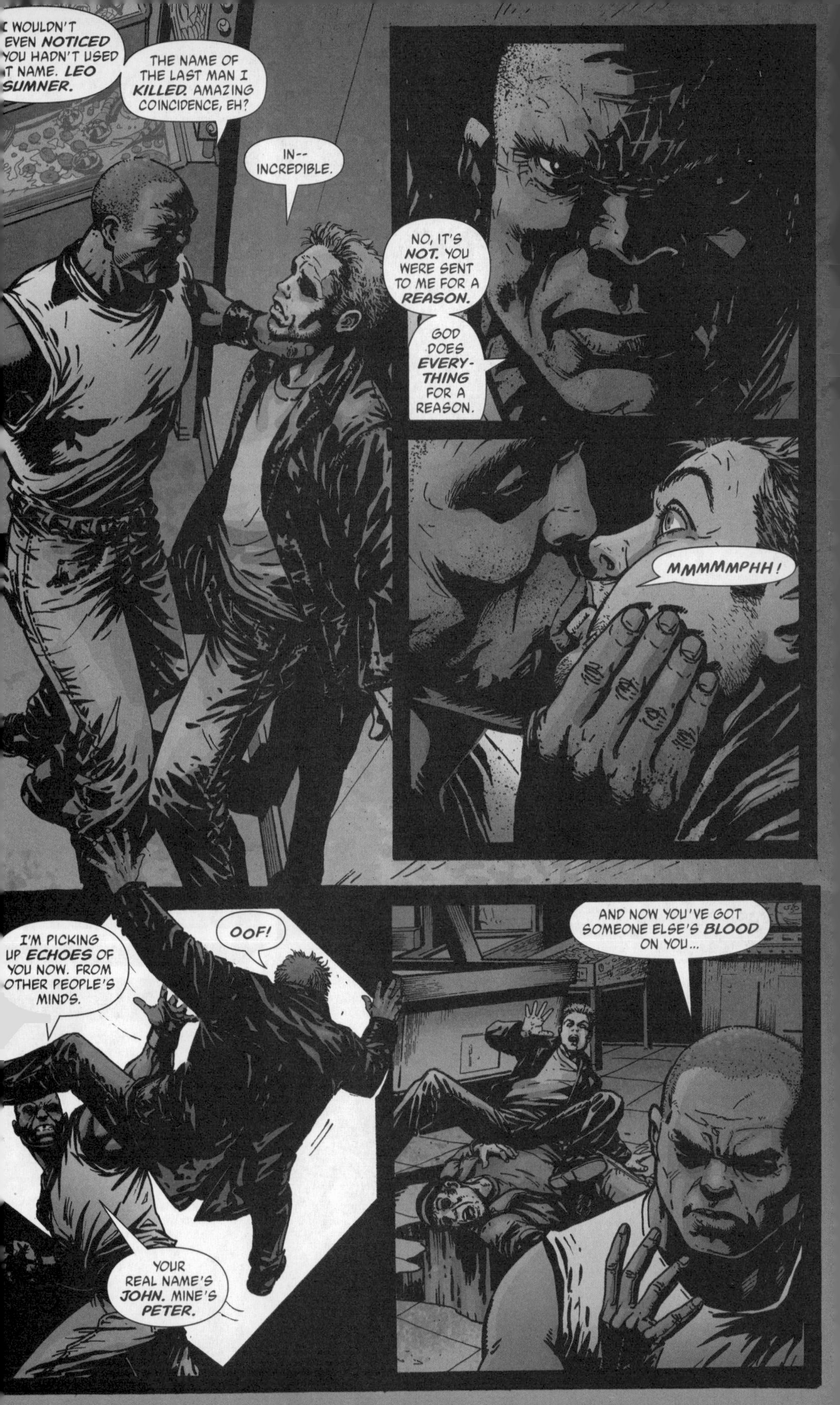

I WOULDN'T EVEN NOTICED YOU HADN'T USED IT NAME. LEO SUMNER.
THE NAME OF THE LAST MAN I KILLED. AMAZING COINCIDENCE, EH?
IN-- INCREDIBLE.
NO, IT'S NOT. YOU WERE SENT TO ME FOR A REASON.
GOD DOES EVERY-THING FOR A REASON.
MMMMMPHH!
I'M PICKING UP ECHOES OF YOU NOW. FROM OTHER PEOPLE'S MINDS.
OOF!
YOUR REAL NAME'S JOHN. MINE'S PETER.
AND NOW YOU'VE GOT SOMEONE ELSE'S BLOOD ON YOU...

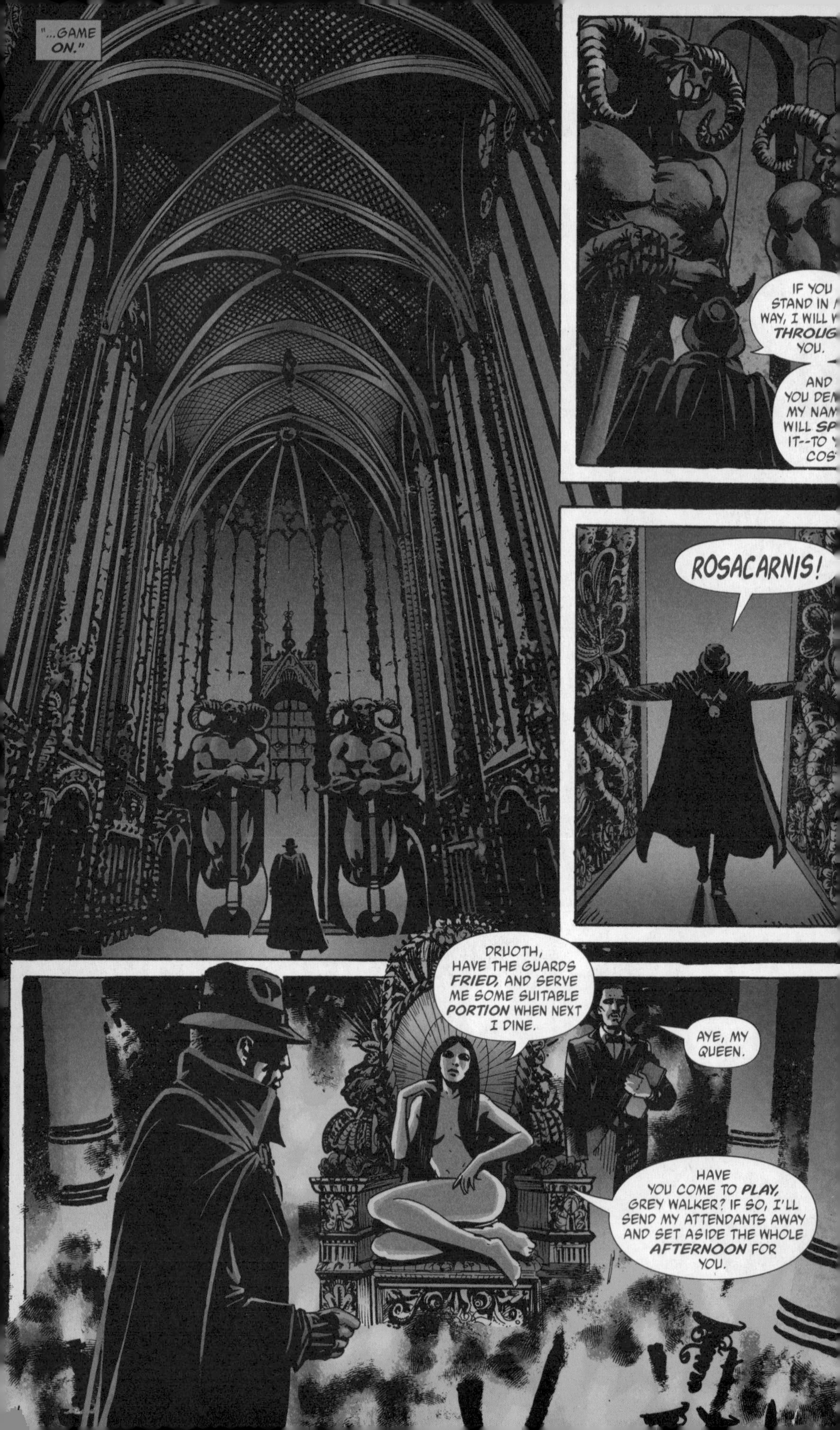
"...GAME ON."
IF YOU STAND IN WAY, I WILL YOU.
AND MY WILL
ROSACARNIS!
DRUOTH, HAVE THE GUARDS FRIED, AND SERVE ME SOME SUITABLE PORTION WHEN NEXT I DINE.
AYE, MY QUEEN.
HAVE YOU COME TO PLAY, GREY WALKER? IF SO, I'LL SEND MY ATTENDANTS AWAY AND SET ASIDE THE WHOLE AFTERNOON FOR YOU.

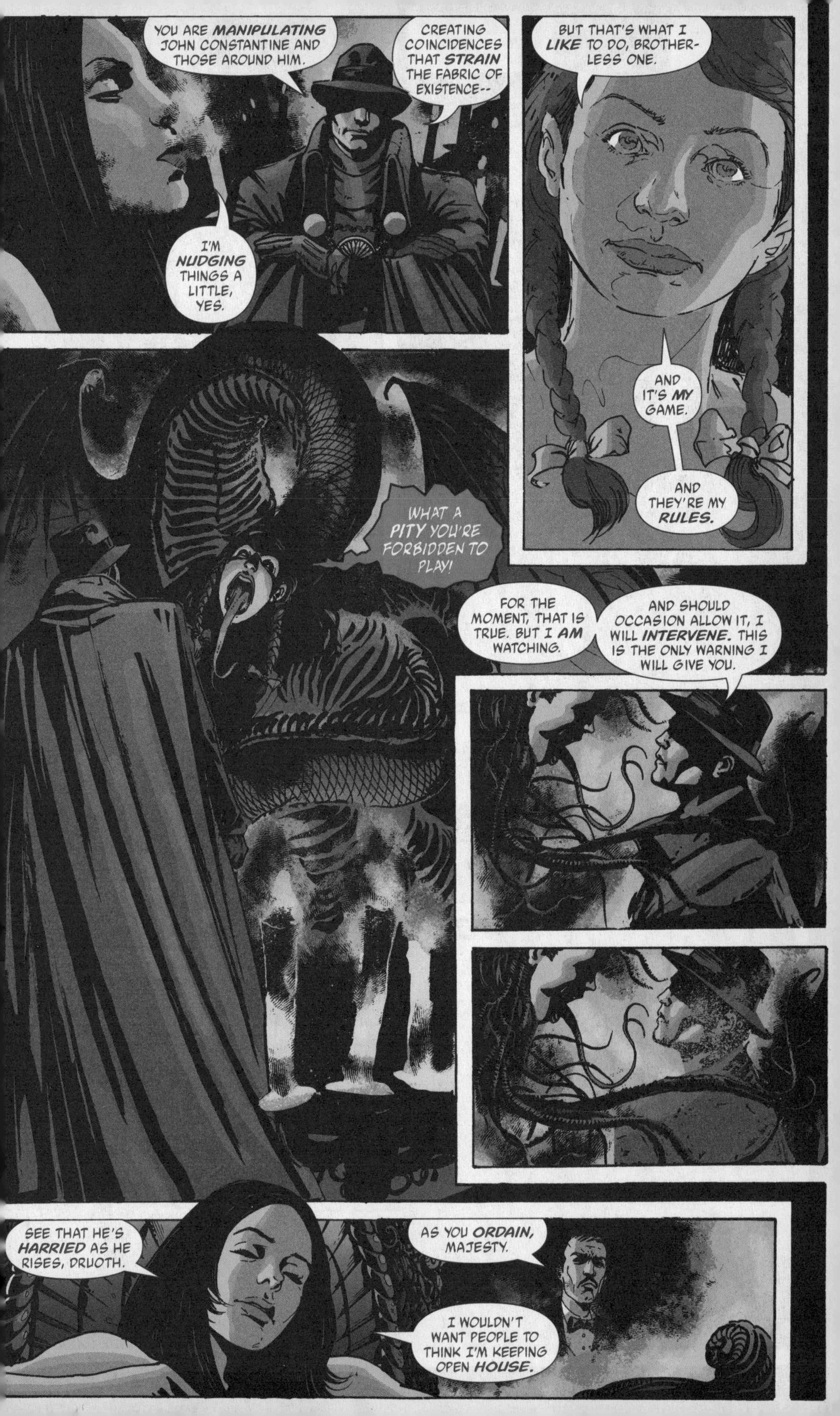
YOU ARE MANIPULATING JOHN CONSTANTINE AND THOSE AROUND HIM.
CREATING COINCIDENCES THAT STRAIN THE FABRIC OF EXISTENCE--
I'M NUDGING THINGS A LITTLE, YES.
BUT THAT'S WHAT I LIKE TO DO, BROTHER-LESS ONE.
AND IT'S MY GAME.
AND THEY'RE MY RULES.
WHAT A PITY YOU'RE FORBIDDEN TO PLAY!
FOR THE MOMENT, THAT IS TRUE. BUT I AM WATCHING.
AND SHOULD OCCASION ALLOW IT, I WILL INTERVENE. THIS IS THE ONLY WARNING I WILL GIVE YOU.
SEE THAT HE'S HARRIED AS HE RISES, DRUOTH.
AS YOU ORDAIN, MAJESTY.
I WOULDN'T WANT PEOPLE TO THINK I'M KEEPING OPEN HOUSE.

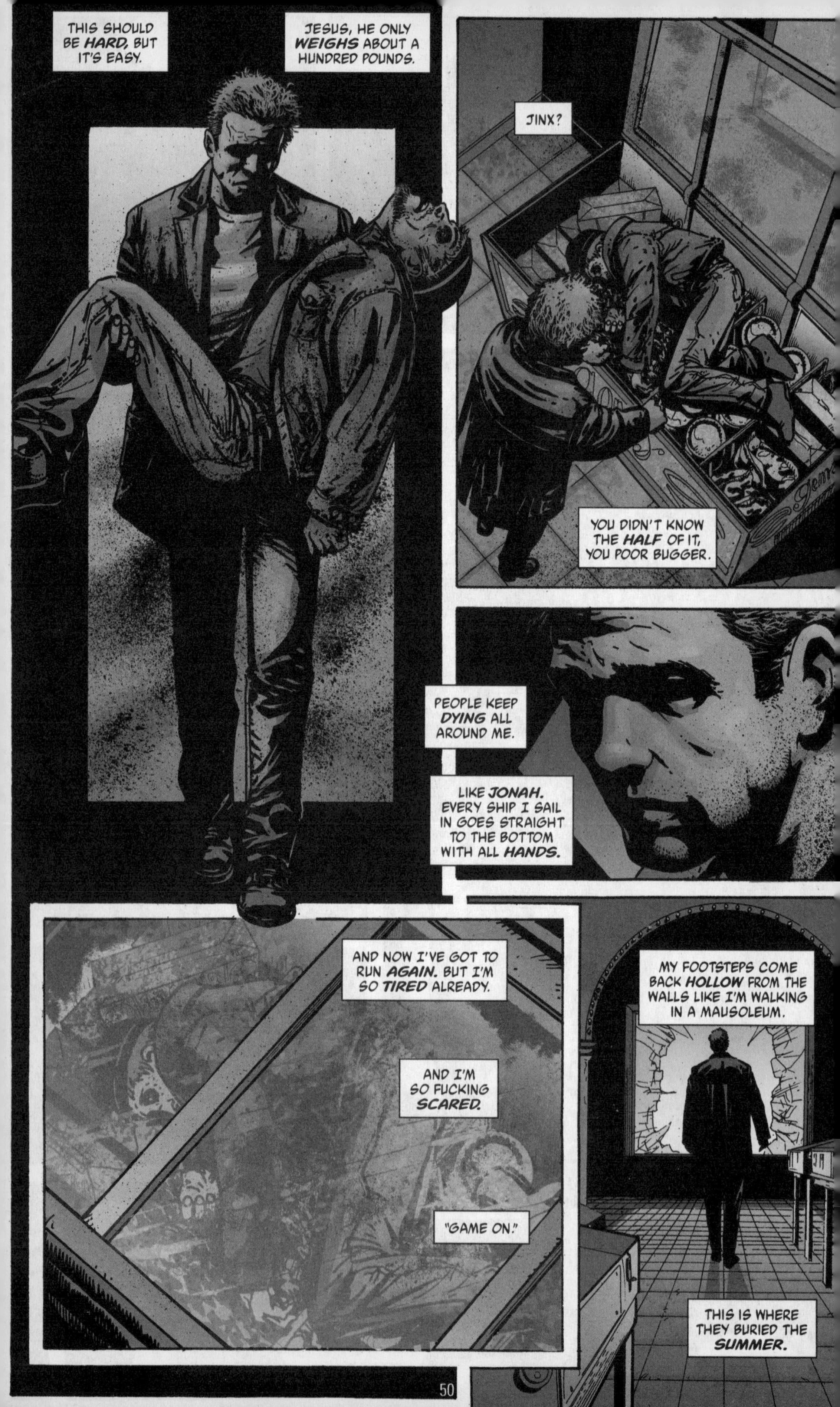

THIS SHOULD BE HARD, BUT IT'S EASY.
JESUS, HE ONLY WEIGHS ABOUT A HUNDRED POUNDS.
JINX?
YOU DIDN'T KNOW THE HALF OF IT, YOU POOR BUGGER.
PEOPLE KEEP DYING ALL AROUND ME.
LIKE JONAH. EVERY SHIP I SAIL IN GOES STRAIGHT TO THE BOTTOM WITH ALL HANDS.
AND NOW I'VE GOT TO RUN AGAIN. BUT I'M SO TIRED ALREADY.
AND I'M SO FUCKING SCARED.
"GAME ON."
MY FOOTSTEPS COME BACK HOLLOW FROM THE WALLS LIKE I'M WALKING IN A MAUSOLEUM.
THIS IS WHERE THEY BURIED THE SUMMER.

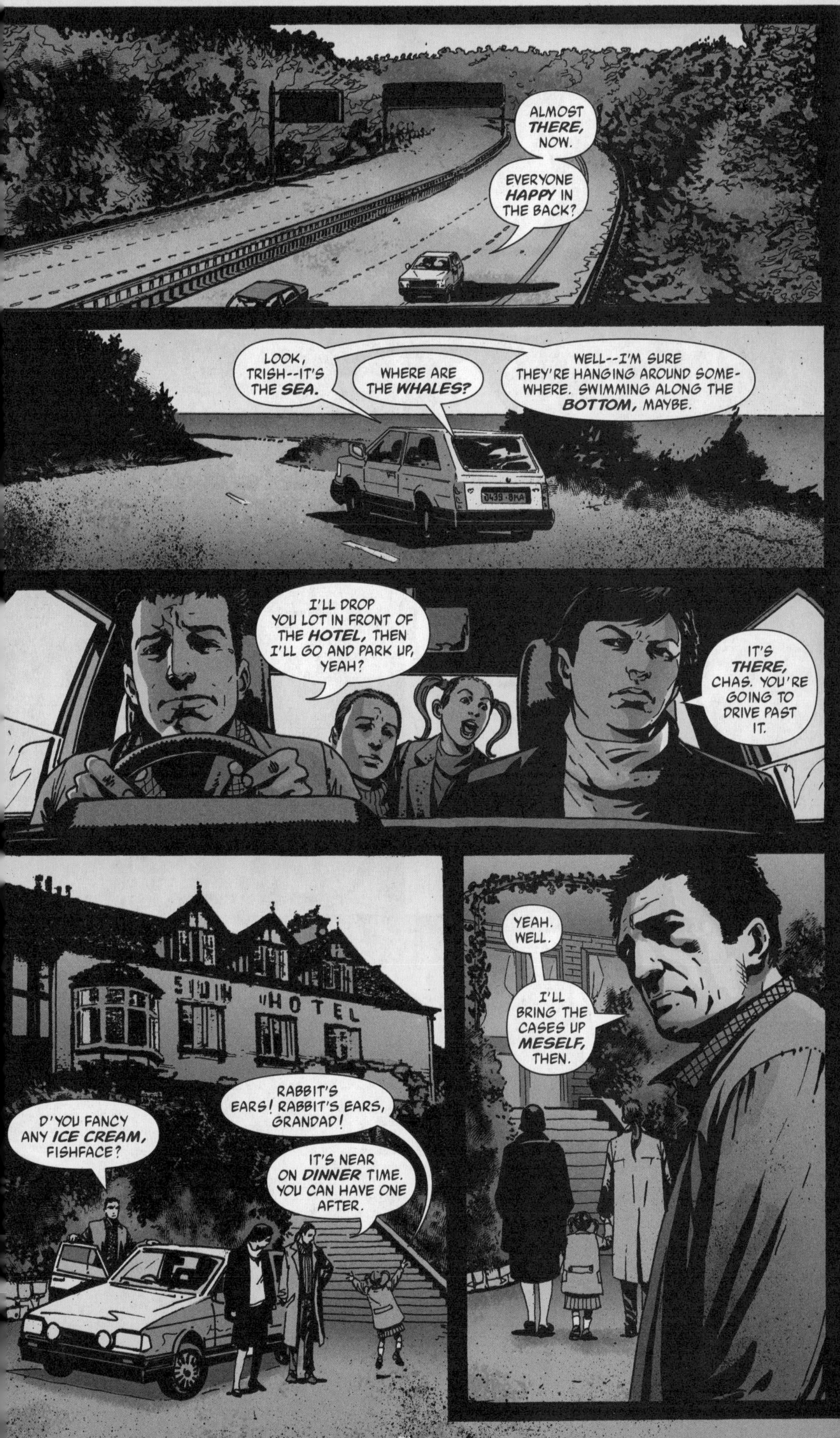
ALMOST THERE, NOW.
EVERYONE HAPPY IN THE BACK?
LOOK, TRISH--IT'S THE SEA.
WHERE ARE THE WHALES?
WELL--I'M SURE THEY'RE HANGING AROUND SOMEWHERE. SWIMMING ALONG THE BOTTOM, MAYBE.
I'LL DROP YOU LOT IN FRONT OF THE HOTEL, THEN I'LL GO AND PARK UP, YEAH?
IT'S THERE, CHAS. YOU'RE GOING TO DRIVE PAST IT.
HOTEL
D'YOU FANCY ANY ICE CREAM, FISHFACE?
RABBIT'S EARS! RABBIT'S EARS, GRANDAD!
IT'S NEAR ON DINNER TIME. YOU CAN HAVE ONE AFTER.
YEAH. WELL.
I'LL BRING THE CASES UP MESELF, THEN.

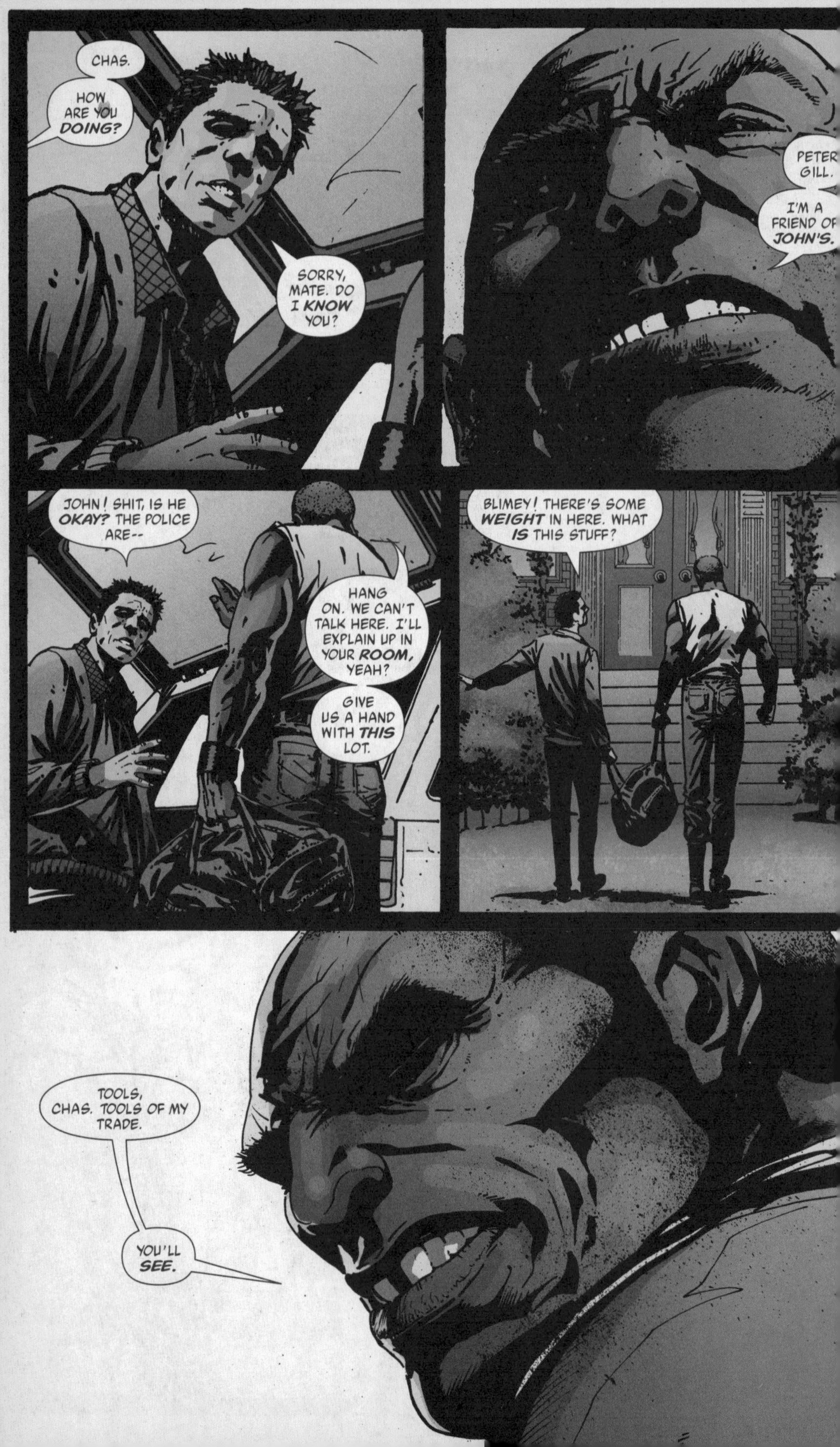

CHAS.
HOW ARE YOU DOING?
SORRY, MATE. DO I KNOW YOU?
PETER GILL.
I'M A FRIEND OF JOHN'S.
JOHN! SHIT, IS HE OKAY? THE POLICE ARE--
HANG ON. WE CAN'T TALK HERE. I'LL EXPLAIN UP IN YOUR ROOM, YEAH?
GIVE US A HAND WITH THIS LOT.
BLIMEY! THERE'S SOME WEIGHT IN HERE. WHAT IS THIS STUFF?
TOOLS, CHAS. TOOLS OF MY TRADE.
YOU'LL SEE.

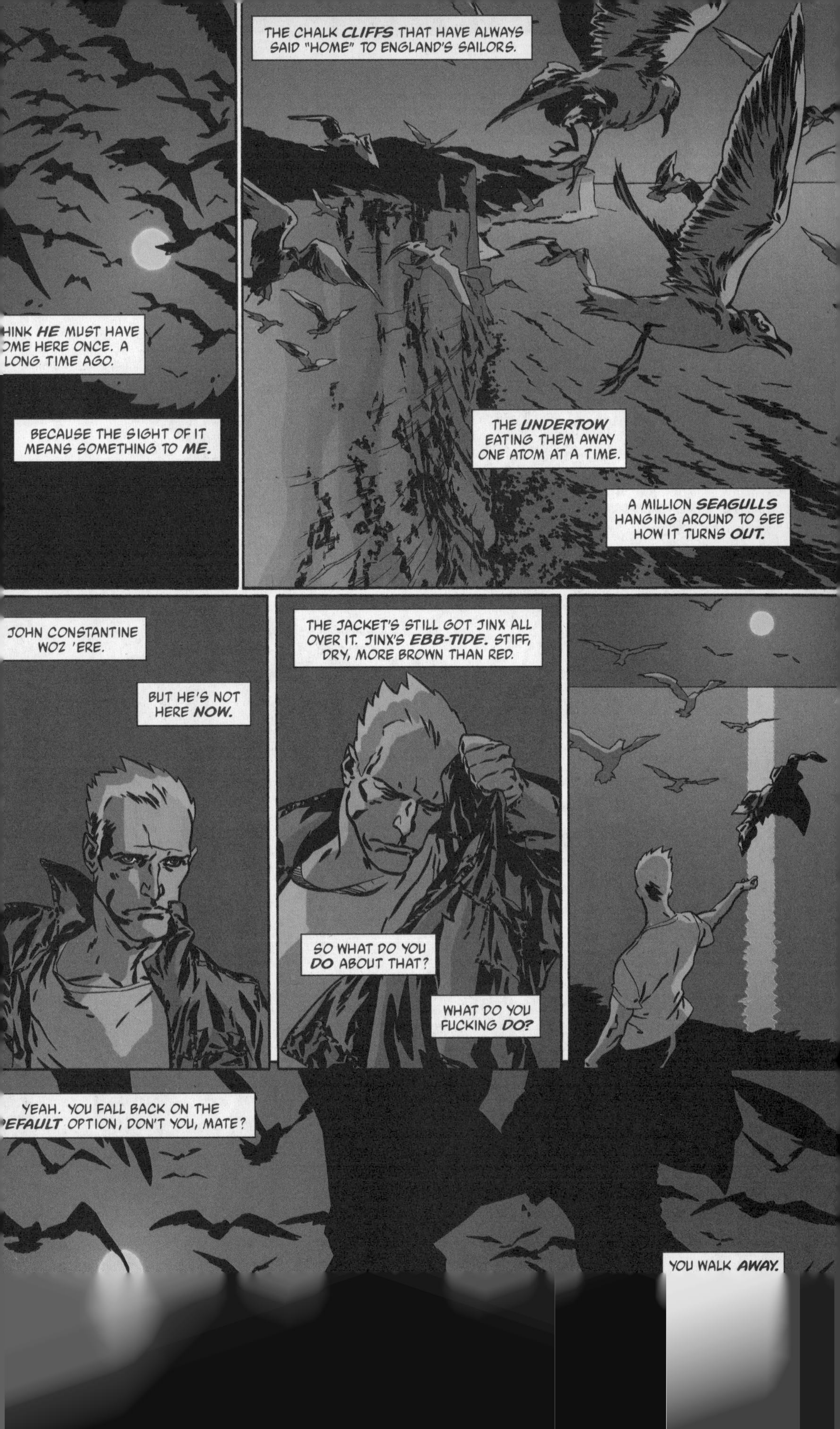

HINK HE MUST HAVE
OME HERE ONCE. A LONG TIME AGO.
BECAUSE THE SIGHT OF IT MEANS SOMETHING TO ME.
THE CHALK CLIFFS THAT HAVE ALWAYS SAID "HOME" TO ENGLAND'S SAILORS.
THE UNDERTOW EATING THEM AWAY ONE ATOM AT A TIME.
A MILLION SEAGULLS HANGING AROUND TO SEE HOW IT TURNS OUT.
JOHN CONSTANTINE WOZ 'ERE.
BUT HE'S NOT HERE NOW.
THE JACKET'S STILL GOT JINX ALL OVER IT. JINX'S EBB-TIDE. STIFF, DRY, MORE BROWN THAN RED.
SO WHAT DO YOU DO ABOUT THAT?
WHAT DO YOU FUCKING DO?
YEAH. YOU FALL BACK ON THE
EFAULT OPTION, DON'T YOU, MATE?
YOU WALK AWAY.

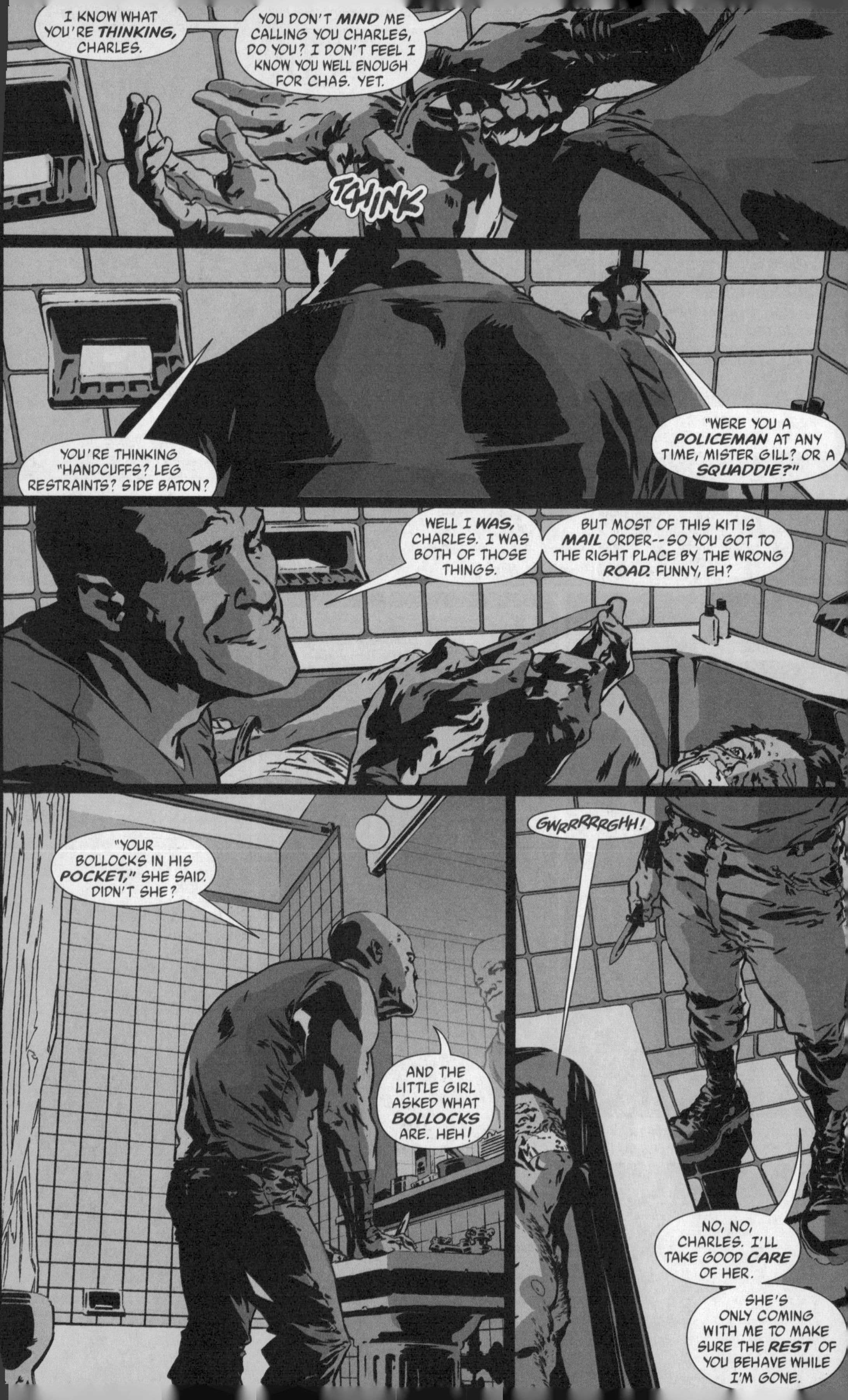
I KNOW WHAT YOU'RE THINKING, CHARLES.
YOU DON'T MIND ME CALLING YOU CHARLES, DO YOU? I DON'T FEEL I KNOW YOU WELL ENOUGH FOR CHAS. YET.
TCHINK
YOU'RE THINKING "HANDCUFFS? LEG RESTRAINTS? SIDE BATON?
"WERE YOU A POLICEMAN AT ANY TIME, MISTER GILL? OR A SQUADDIE?"
WELL I WAS, CHARLES. I WAS BOTH OF THOSE THINGS.
BUT MOST OF THIS KIT IS MAIL ORDER--SO YOU GOT TO THE RIGHT PLACE BY THE WRONG ROAD. FUNNY, EH?
"YOUR BOLLOCKS IN HIS POCKET," SHE SAID. DIDN'T SHE?
AND THE LITTLE GIRL ASKED WHAT BOLLOCKS ARE. HEH!
GWRRRRRGHH!
NO, NO, CHARLES. I'LL TAKE GOOD CARE OF HER.
SHE'S ONLY COMING WITH ME TO MAKE SURE THE REST OF YOU BEHAVE WHILE I'M GONE.

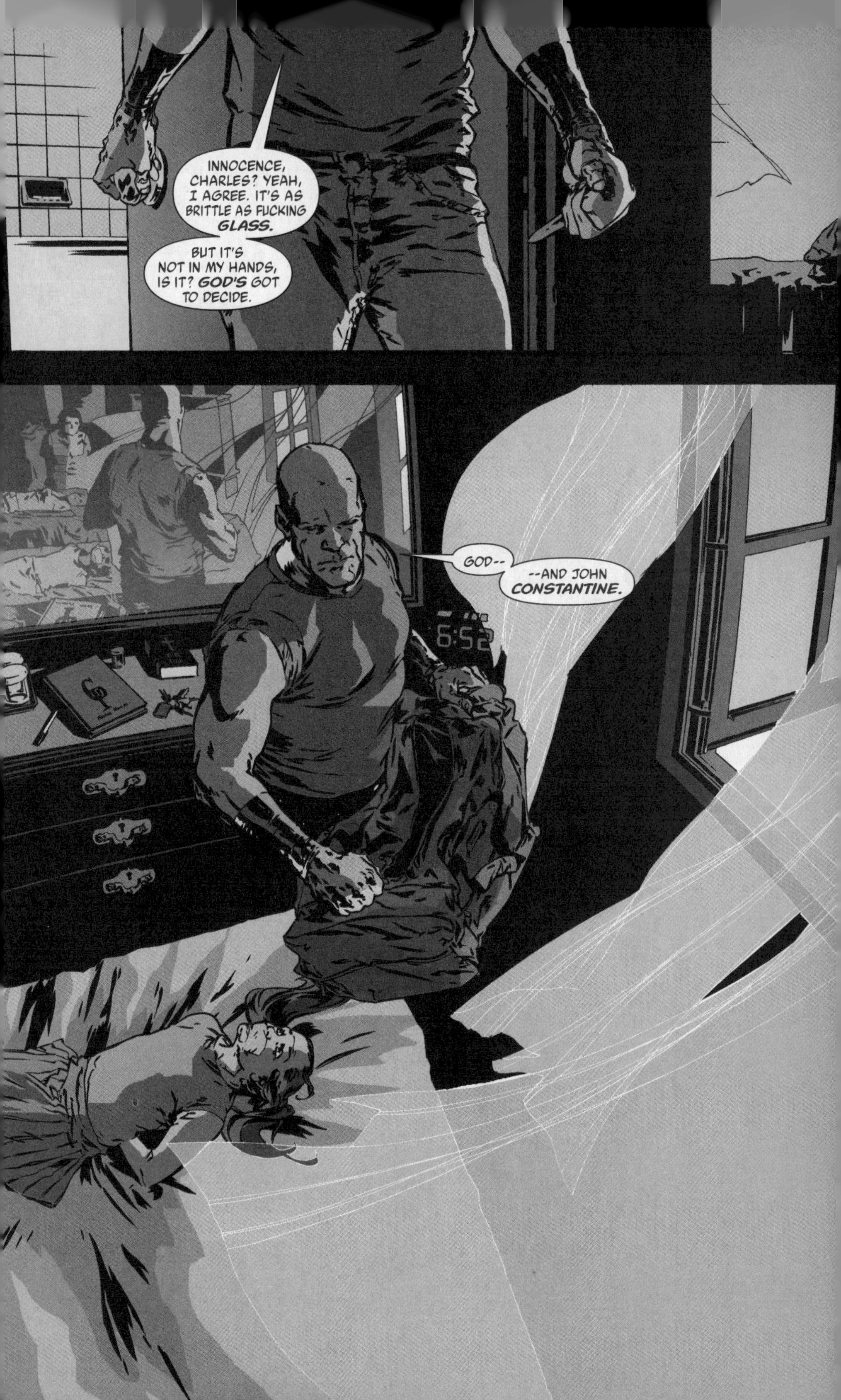
INNOCENCE, CHARLES? YEAH, I AGREE. IT'S AS BRITTLE AS FUCKING GLASS.
BUT IT'S NOT IN MY HANDS, IS IT? GOD'S GOT TO DECIDE.
GOD--
--AND JOHN CONSTANTINE.
6:52

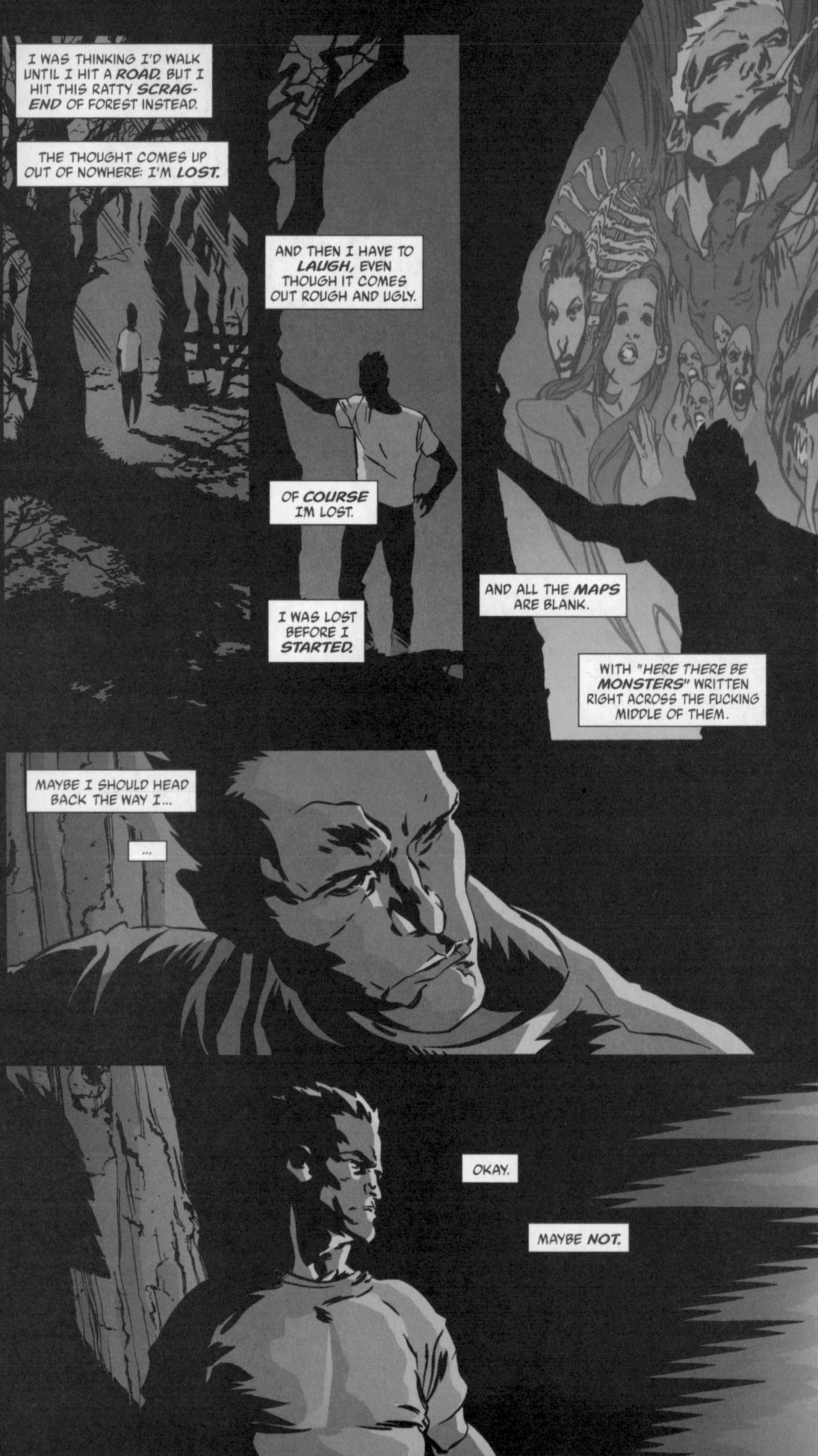
I WAS THINKING I'D WALK UNTIL I HIT A ROAD. BUT I HIT THIS RATTY SCRAG-END OF FOREST INSTEAD.
THE THOUGHT COMES UP OUT OF NOWHERE: I'M LOST.
AND THEN I HAVE TO LAUGH, EVEN THOUGH IT COMES OUT ROUGH AND UGLY.
OF COURSE I'M LOST.
I WAS LOST BEFORE I STARTED.
AND ALL THE MAPS ARE BLANK.
WITH "HERE THERE BE MONSTERS" WRITTEN RIGHT ACROSS THE FUCKING MIDDLE OF THEM.
MAYBE I SHOULD HEAD BACK THE WAY I...
...
OKAY.
MAYBE NOT.

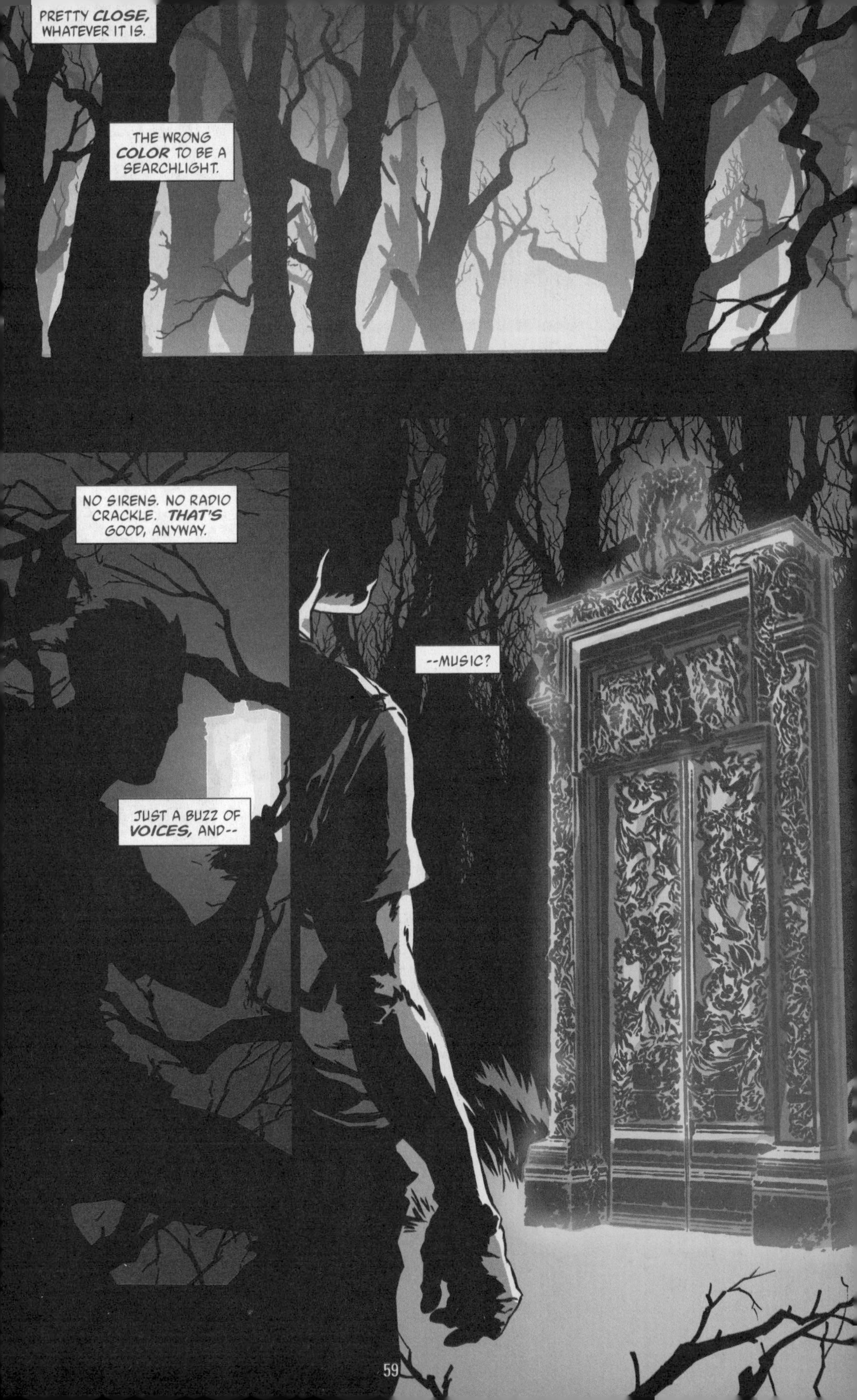
PRETTY CLOSE, WHATEVER IT IS.
THE WRONG COLOR TO BE A SEARCHLIGHT.
NO SIRENS. NO RADIO CRACKLE. THAT'S GOOD, ANYWAY.
JUST A BUZZ OF VOICES, AND--
--MUSIC?

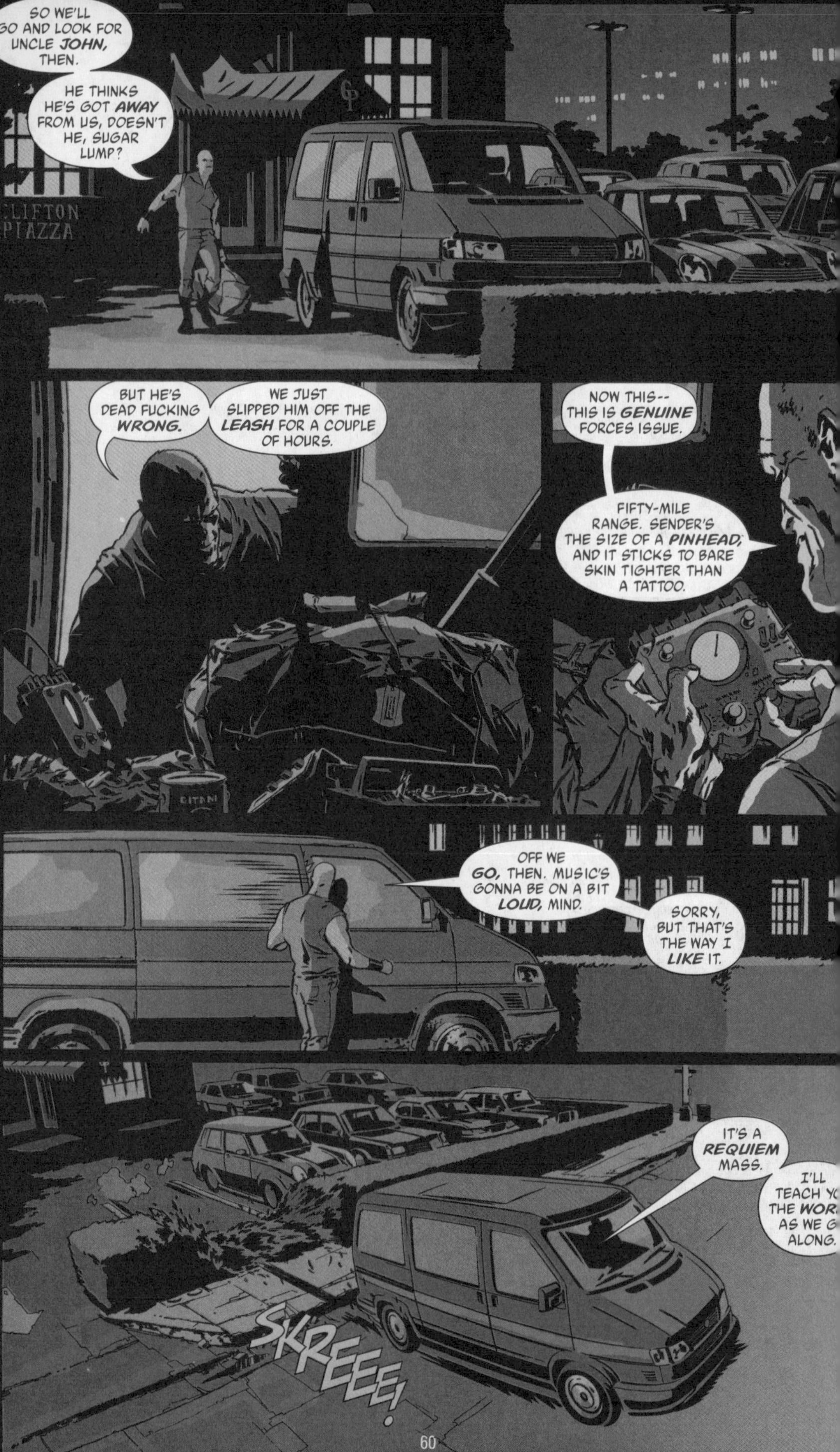
SO WE'LL GO AND LOOK FOR UNCLE JOHN, THEN.
HE THINKS HE'S GOT AWAY FROM US, DOESN'T HE, SUGAR LUMP?
CLIFTON PIAZZA
BUT HE'S DEAD FUCKING WRONG.
WE JUST SLIPPED HIM OFF THE LEASH FOR A COUPLE OF HOURS.
NOW THIS-- THIS IS GENUINE FORCES ISSUE.
FIFTY-MILE RANGE. SENDER'S THE SIZE OF A PINHEAD, AND IT STICKS TO BARE SKIN TIGHTER THAN A TATTOO.
OFF WE GO, THEN. MUSIC'S GONNA BE ON A BIT LOUD, MIND.
SORRY, BUT THAT'S THE WAY I LIKE IT.
IT'S A REQUIEM MASS.
I'LL TEACH YO THE WOR AS WE G ALONG.
SKREEEE!

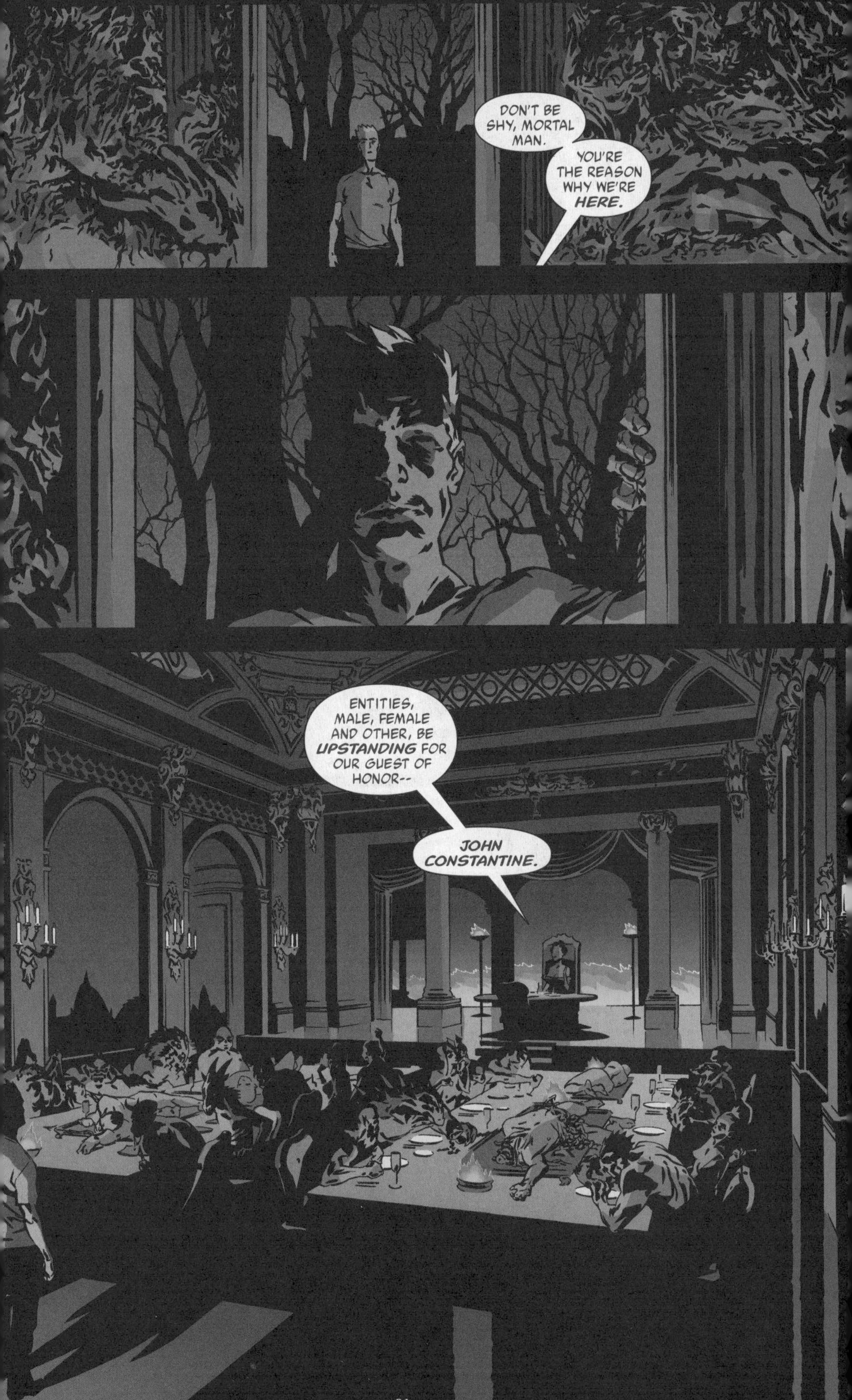
DON'T BE SHY, MORTAL MAN.
YOU'RE THE REASON WHY WE'RE *HERE.*
ENTITIES, MALE, FEMALE AND OTHER, BE *UPSTANDING* FOR OUR GUEST OF HONOR--
JOHN CONSTANTINE.

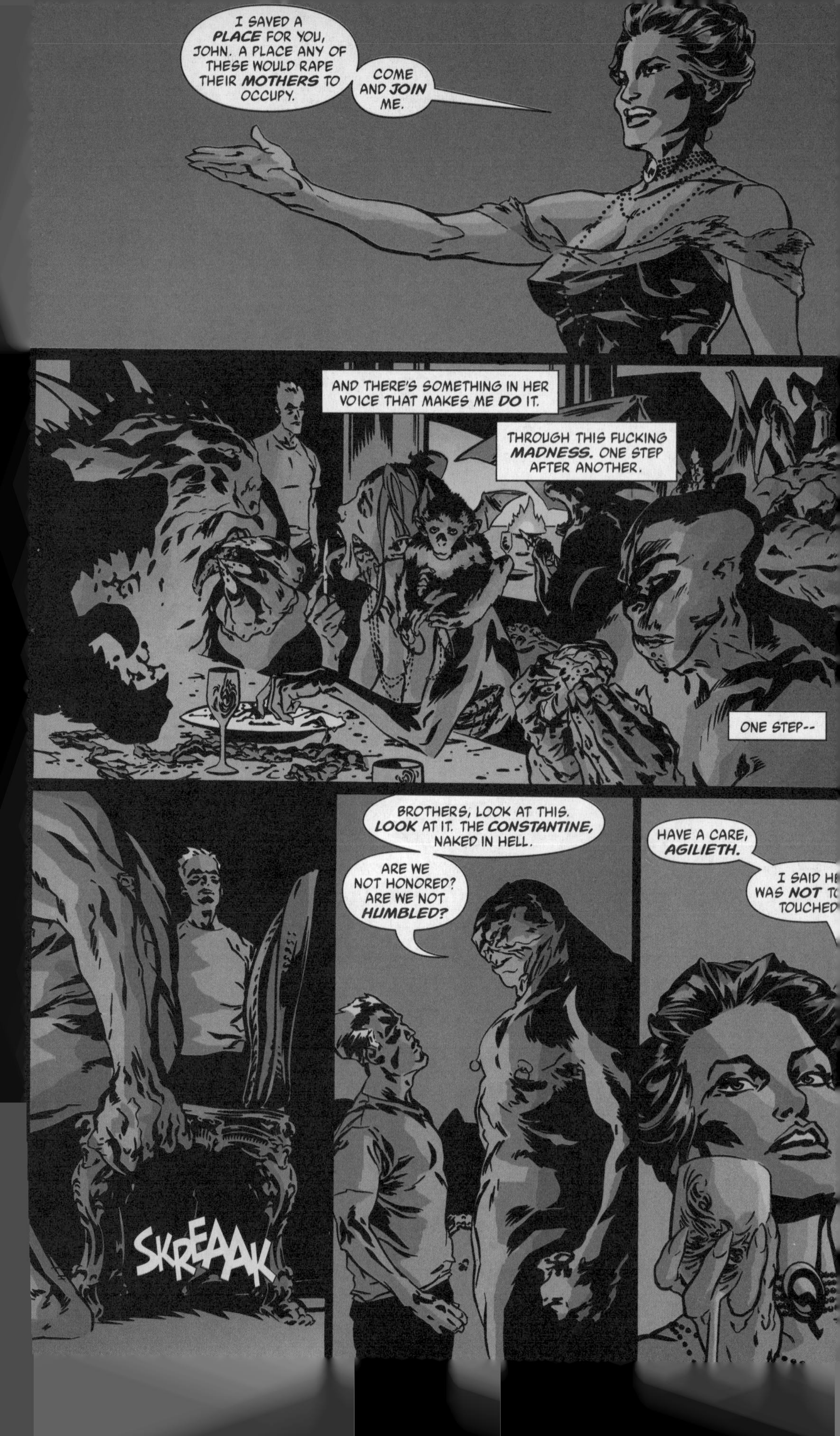
I SAVED A PLACE FOR YOU, JOHN. A PLACE ANY OF THESE WOULD RAPE THEIR MOTHERS TO OCCUPY.
COME AND JOIN ME.
AND THERE'S SOMETHING IN HER VOICE THAT MAKES ME DO IT.
THROUGH THIS FUCKING MADNESS. ONE STEP AFTER ANOTHER.
ONE STEP--
SKREAAAK
BROTHERS, LOOK AT THIS. LOOK AT IT. THE CONSTANTINE, NAKED IN HELL.
ARE WE NOT HONORED? ARE WE NOT HUMBLED?
HAVE A CARE, AGILIETH.

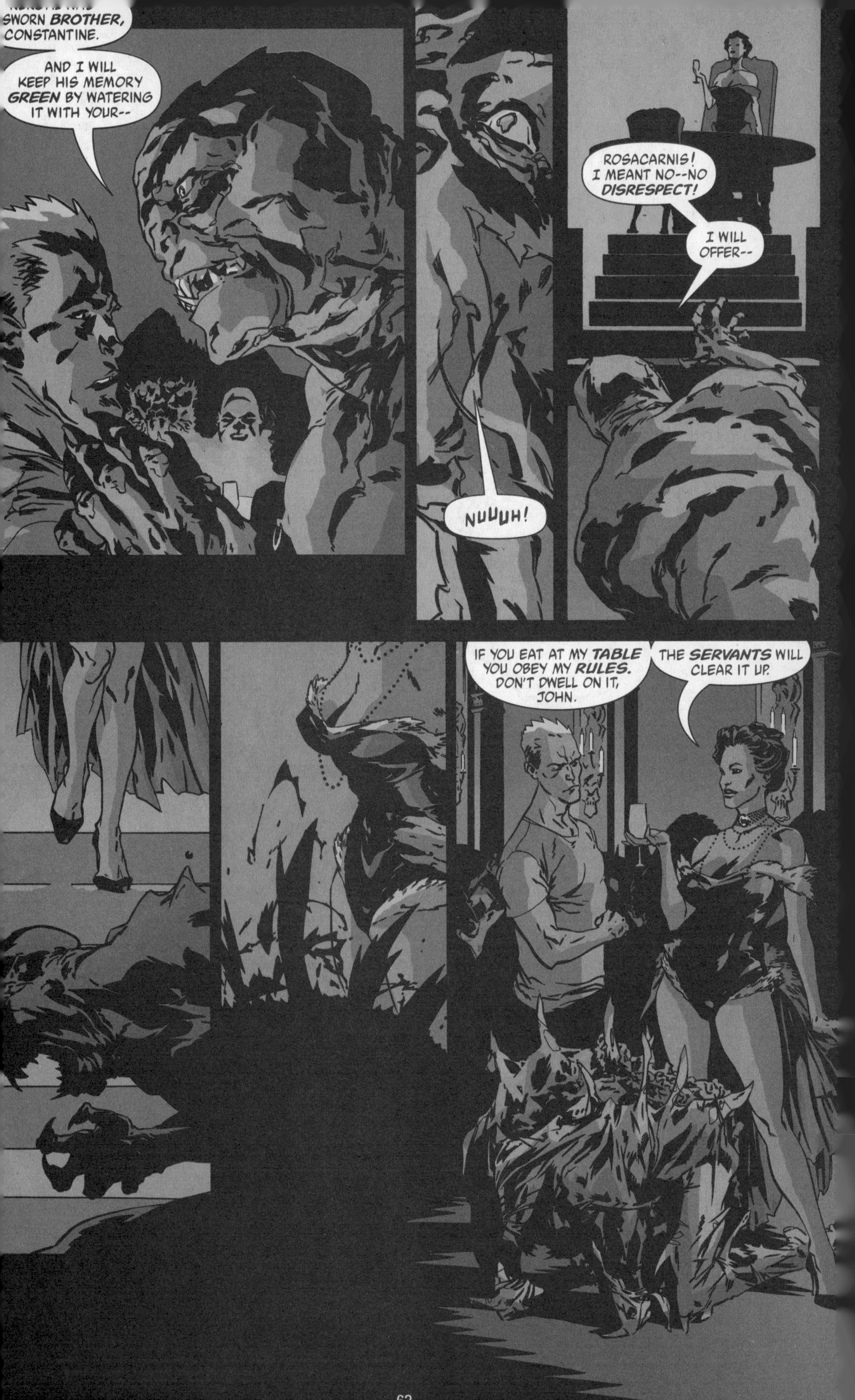
SWORN BROTHER, CONSTANTINE.
AND I WILL KEEP HIS MEMORY GREEN BY WATERING IT WITH YOUR--
NUUUH!
ROSACARNIS! I MEANT NO--NO DISRESPECT!
I WILL OFFER--
IF YOU EAT AT MY TABLE YOU OBEY MY RULES. DON'T DWELL ON IT, JOHN.
THE SERVANTS WILL CLEAR IT UP.

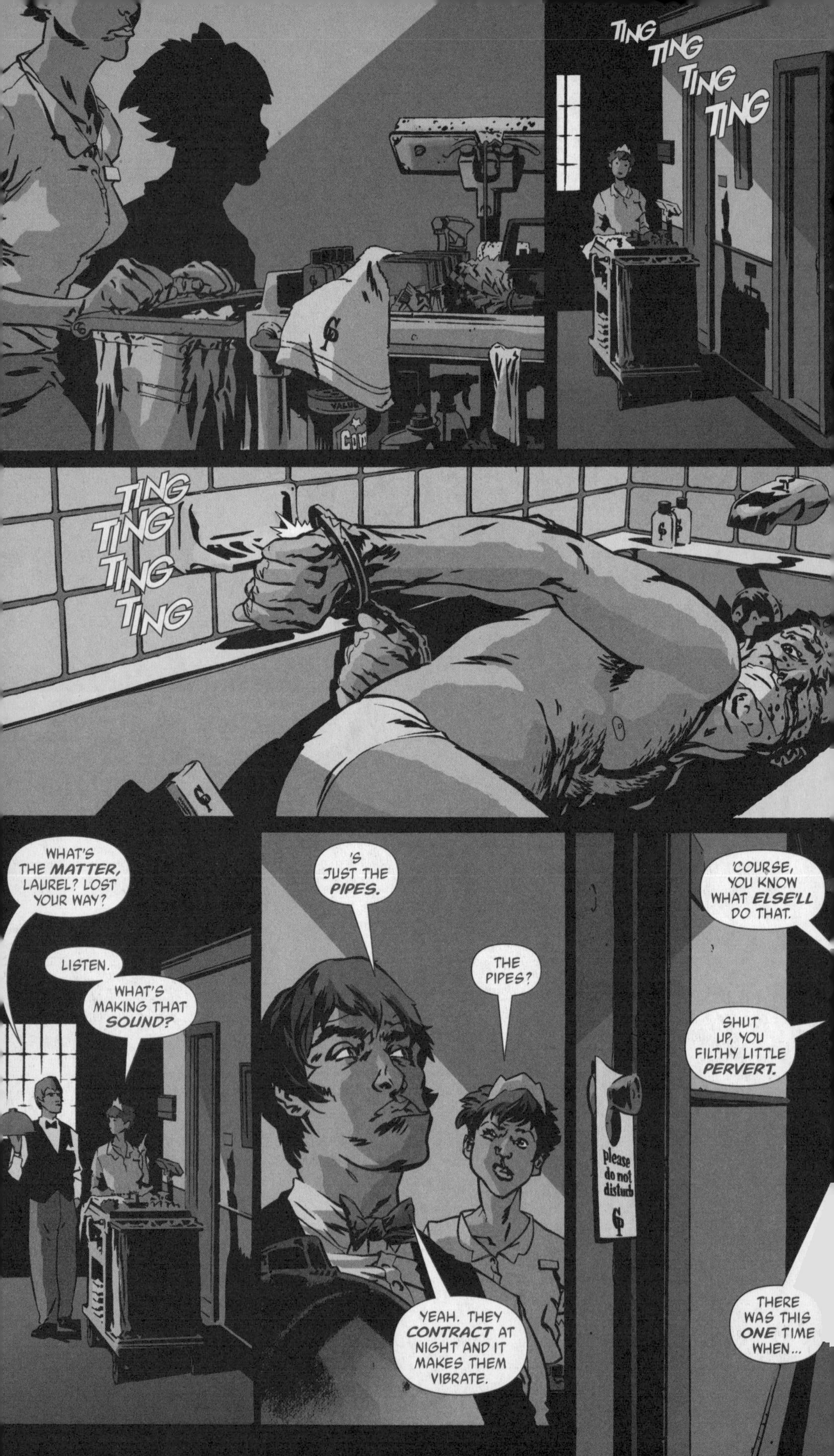

TING TING TING TING
TING TING TING TING
WHAT'S THE MATTER, LAUREL? LOST YOUR WAY?
LISTEN.
WHAT'S MAKING THAT SOUND?
'S JUST THE PIPES.
THE PIPES?
YEAH. THEY CONTRACT AT NIGHT AND IT MAKES THEM VIBRATE.
please do not disturb
'COURSE, YOU KNOW WHAT ELSE'LL DO THAT.
SHUT UP, YOU FILTHY LITTLE PERVERT.
THERE WAS THIS ONE TIME WHEN...

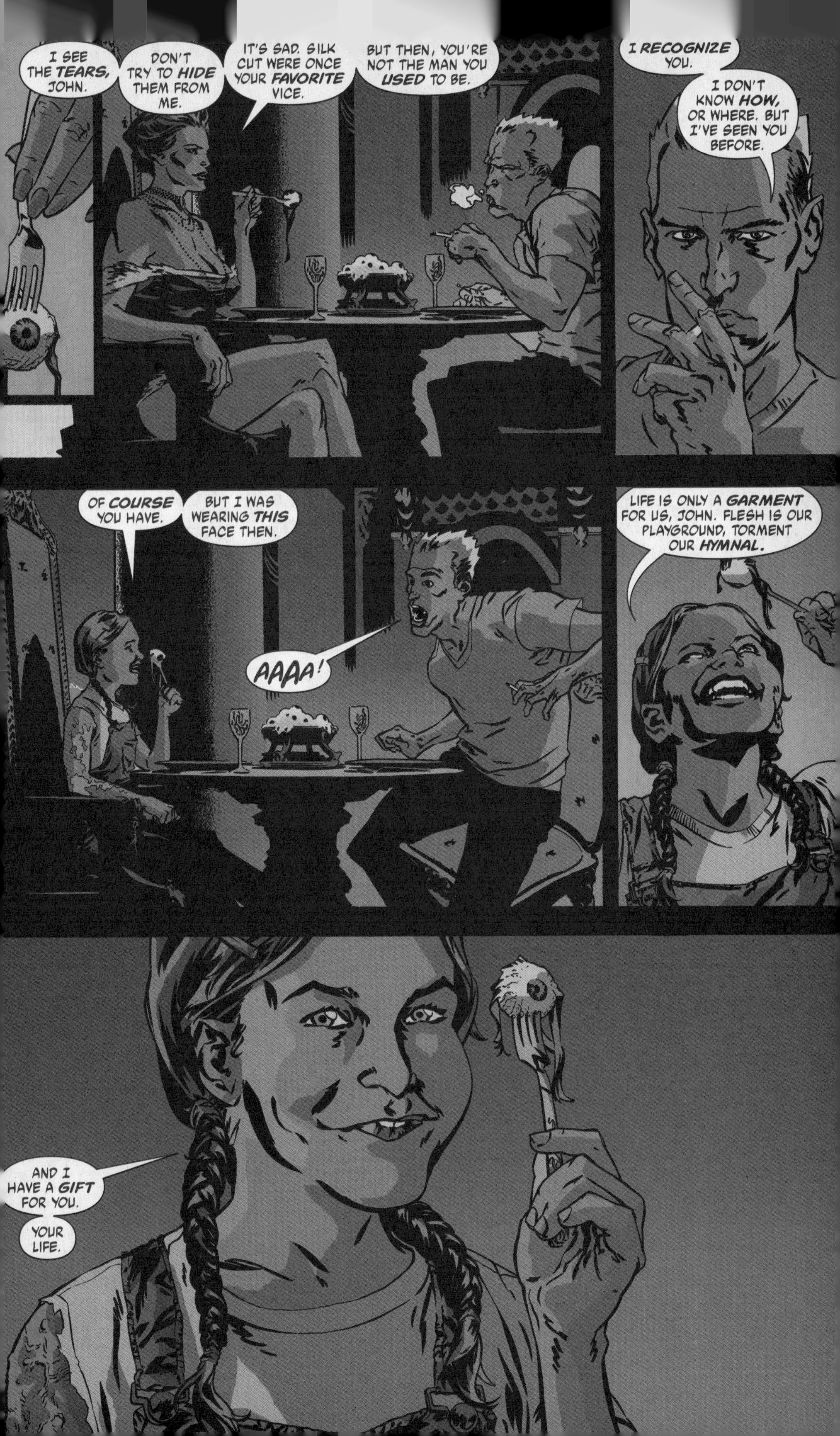
I SEE THE TEARS, JOHN.
DON'T TRY TO HIDE THEM FROM ME.
IT'S SAD. SILK CUT WERE ONCE YOUR FAVORITE VICE.
BUT THEN, YOU'RE NOT THE MAN YOU USED TO BE.
I RECOGNIZE YOU.
I DON'T KNOW HOW, OR WHERE. BUT I'VE SEEN YOU BEFORE.
OF COURSE YOU HAVE.
BUT I WAS WEARING THIS FACE THEN.
AAAA!
LIFE IS ONLY A GARMENT FOR US, JOHN. FLESH IS OUR PLAYGROUND, TORMENT OUR HYMNAL.
AND I HAVE A GIFT FOR YOU.
YOUR LIFE.

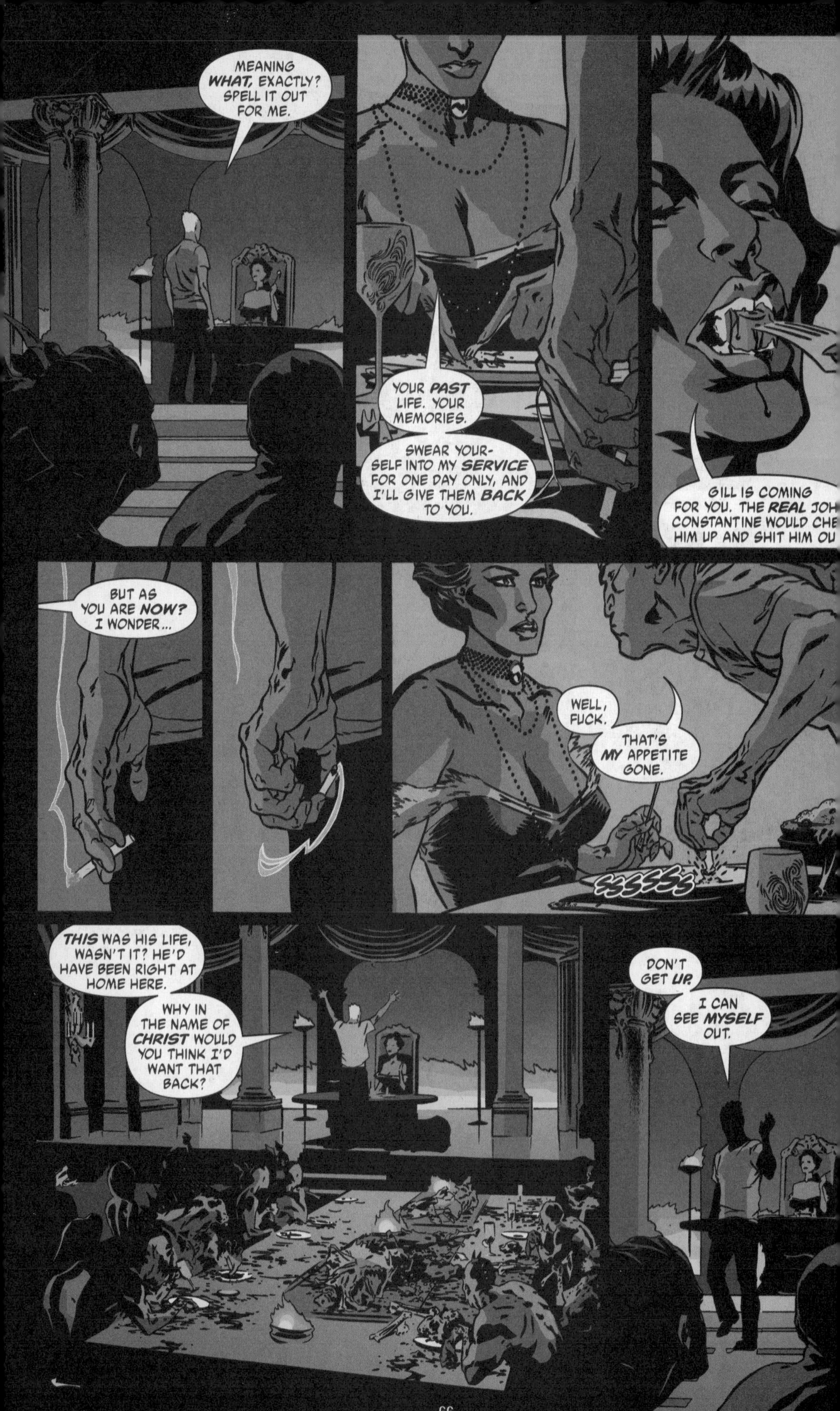
MEANING WHAT, EXACTLY? SPELL IT OUT FOR ME.
YOUR PAST LIFE. YOUR MEMORIES.
SWEAR YOURSELF INTO MY SERVICE FOR ONE DAY ONLY, AND I'LL GIVE THEM BACK TO YOU.
GILL IS COMING FOR YOU. THE REAL JOH
CONSTANTINE WOULD CHE
HIM UP AND SHIT HIM OU
BUT AS YOU ARE NOW? I WONDER...
WELL, FUCK.
THAT'S MY APPETITE GONE.
SSSSSS
THIS WAS HIS LIFE, WASN'T IT? HE'D HAVE BEEN RIGHT AT HOME HERE.
WHY IN THE NAME OF CHRIST WOULD YOU THINK I'D WANT THAT BACK?
DON'T GET UP.
I CAN SEE MYSELF OUT.

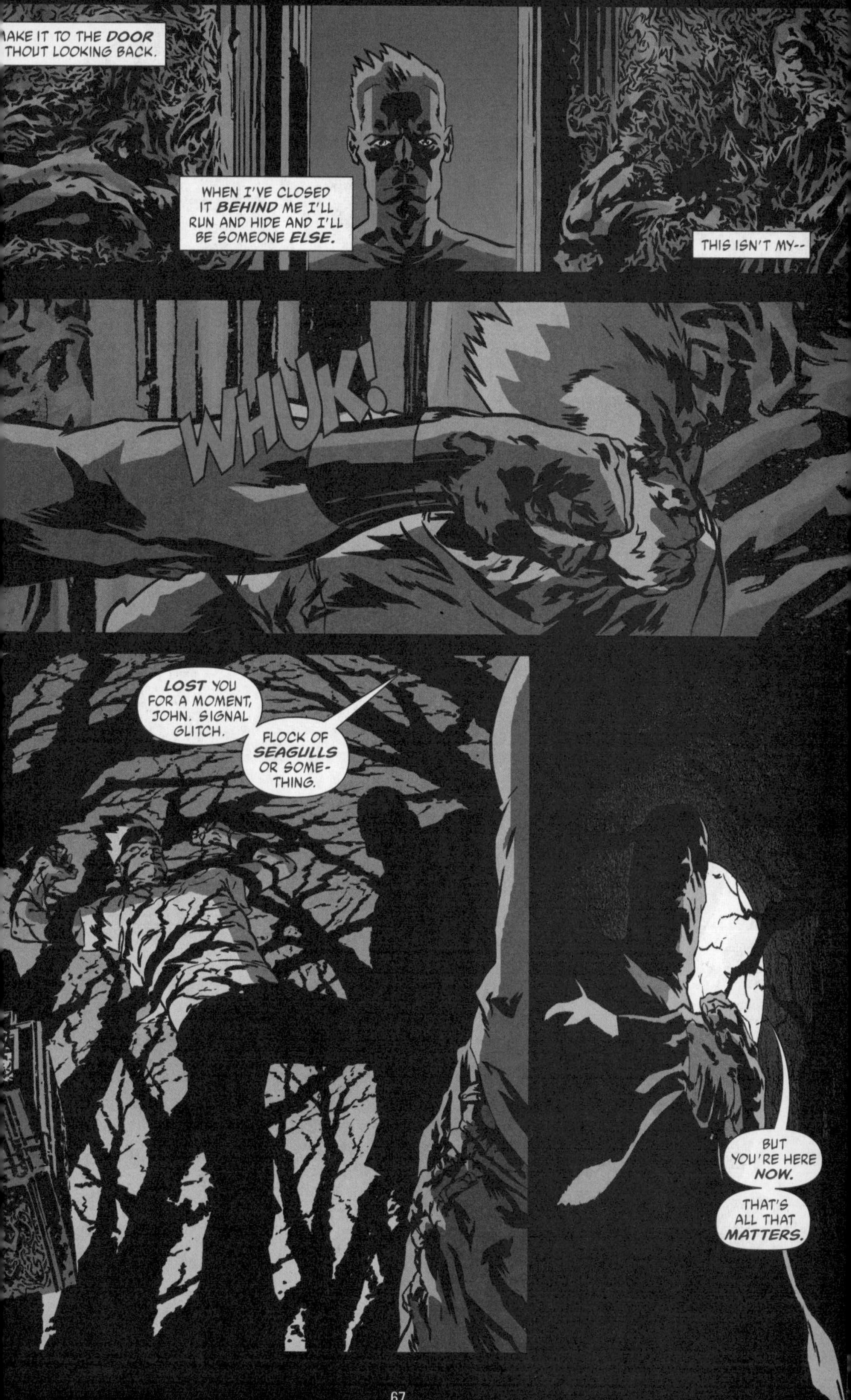

AKE IT TO THE DOOR THOUT LOOKING BACK.
WHEN I'VE CLOSED IT BEHIND ME I'LL RUN AND HIDE AND I'LL BE SOMEONE ELSE.
THIS ISN'T MY--
WHUK!
LOST YOU FOR A MOMENT, JOHN. SIGNAL GLITCH.
FLOCK OF SEAGULLS OR SOME-THING.
BUT YOU'RE HERE NOW.
THAT'S ALL THAT MATTERS.

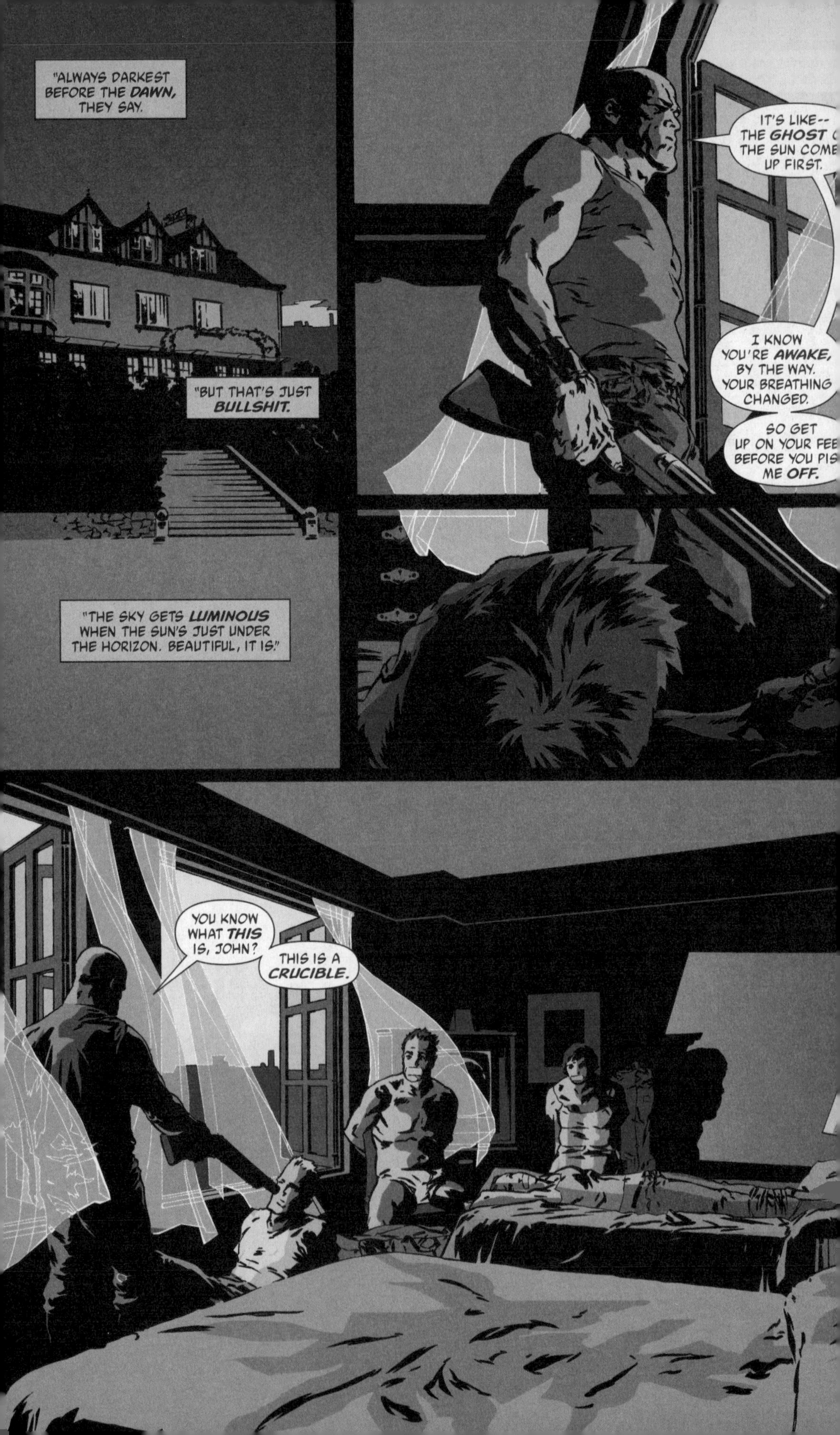
"ALWAYS DARKEST BEFORE THE DAWN, THEY SAY.
IT'S LIKE-- THE GHOST THE SUN COME UP FIRST.
"BUT THAT'S JUST BULLSHIT.
I KNOW YOU'RE AWAKE, BY THE WAY. YOUR BREATHING CHANGED.
SO GET UP ON YOUR FEE BEFORE YOU PIS ME OFF.
"THE SKY GETS LUMINOUS WHEN THE SUN'S JUST UNDER THE HORIZON. BEAUTIFUL, IT IS."
YOU KNOW WHAT THIS IS, JOHN?
THIS IS A CRUCIBLE.

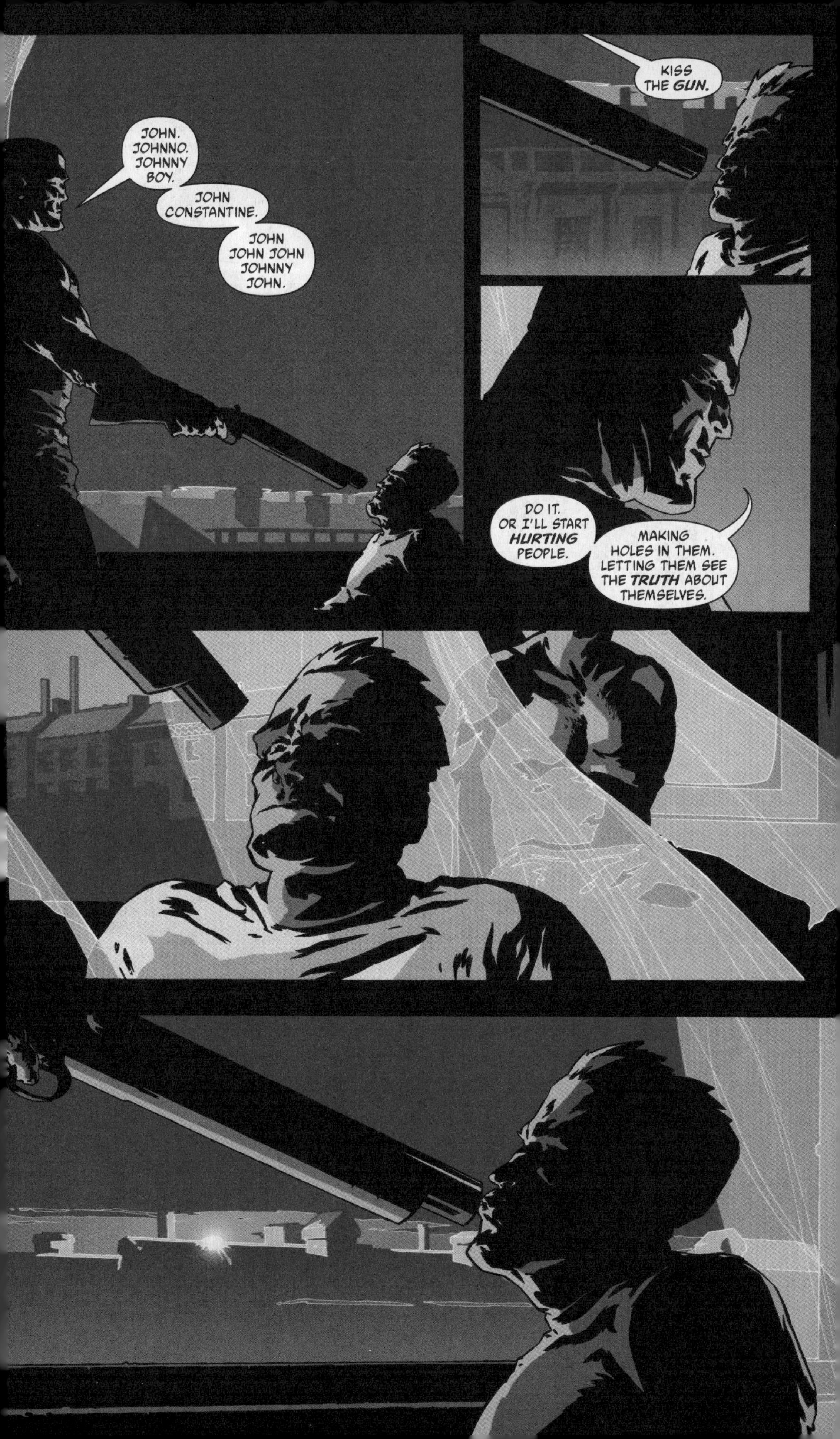
JOHN. JOHNNO. JOHNNY BOY.
JOHN CONSTANTINE.
JOHN JOHN JOHN JOHNNY JOHN.
KISS THE **GUN.**
DO IT. OR I'LL START **HURTING** PEOPLE.
MAKING HOLES IN THEM. LETTING THEM SEE THE **TRUTH** ABOUT THEMSELVES.

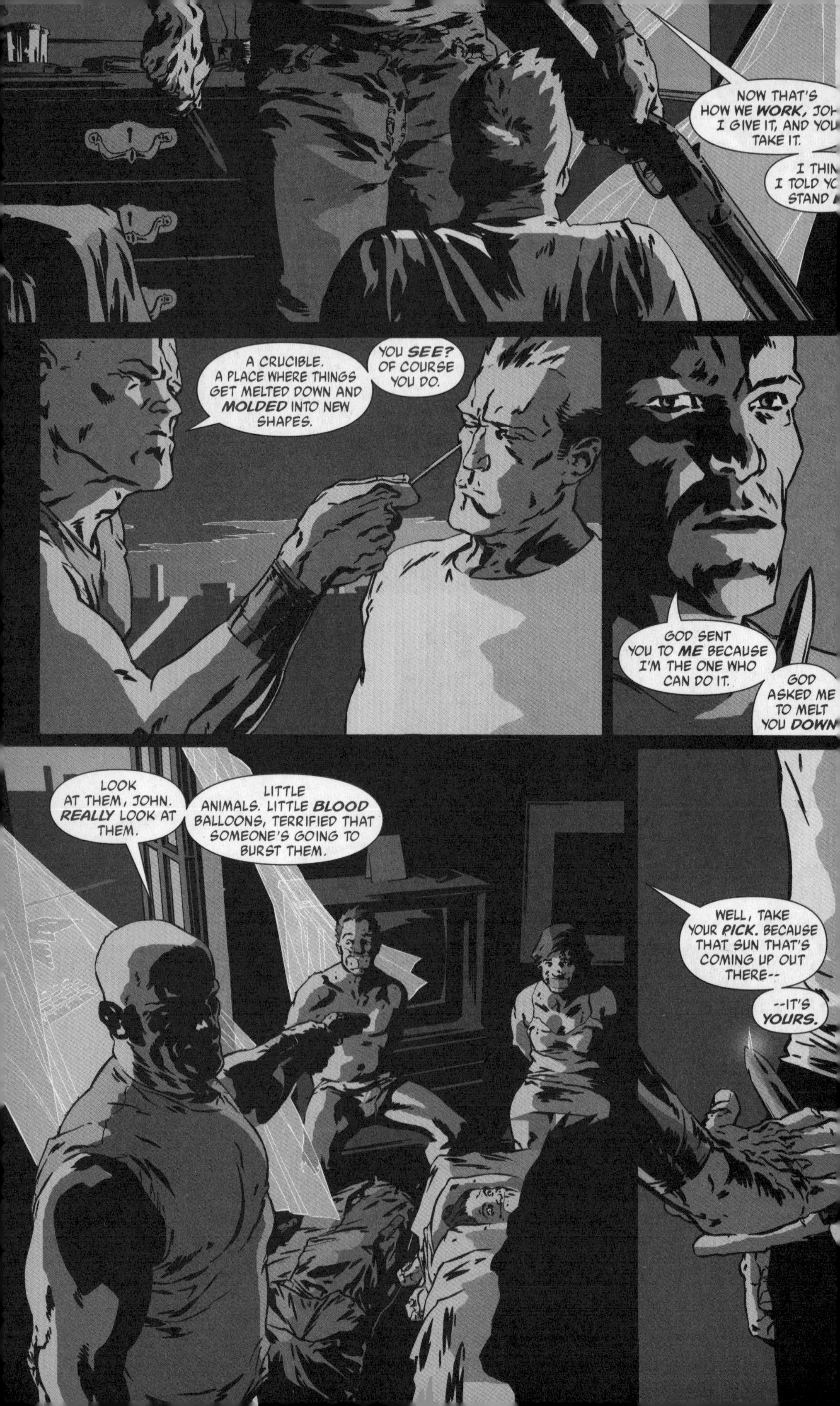

NOW THAT'S HOW WE **WORK,** JOH I GIVE IT, AND YOU TAKE IT.
I THIN I TOLD YO STAND
A CRUCIBLE. A PLACE WHERE THINGS GET MELTED DOWN AND **MOLDED** INTO NEW SHAPES.
YOU **SEE?** OF COURSE YOU DO.
GOD SENT YOU TO **ME** BECAUSE I'M THE ONE WHO CAN DO IT.
GOD ASKED ME TO MELT YOU **DOWN**
LOOK AT THEM, JOHN. **REALLY** LOOK AT THEM.
LITTLE ANIMALS. LITTLE **BLOOD** BALLOONS, TERRIFIED THAT SOMEONE'S GOING TO BURST THEM.
WELL, TAKE YOUR **PICK.** BECAUSE THAT SUN THAT'S COMING UP OUT THERE--
--IT'S **YOURS.**

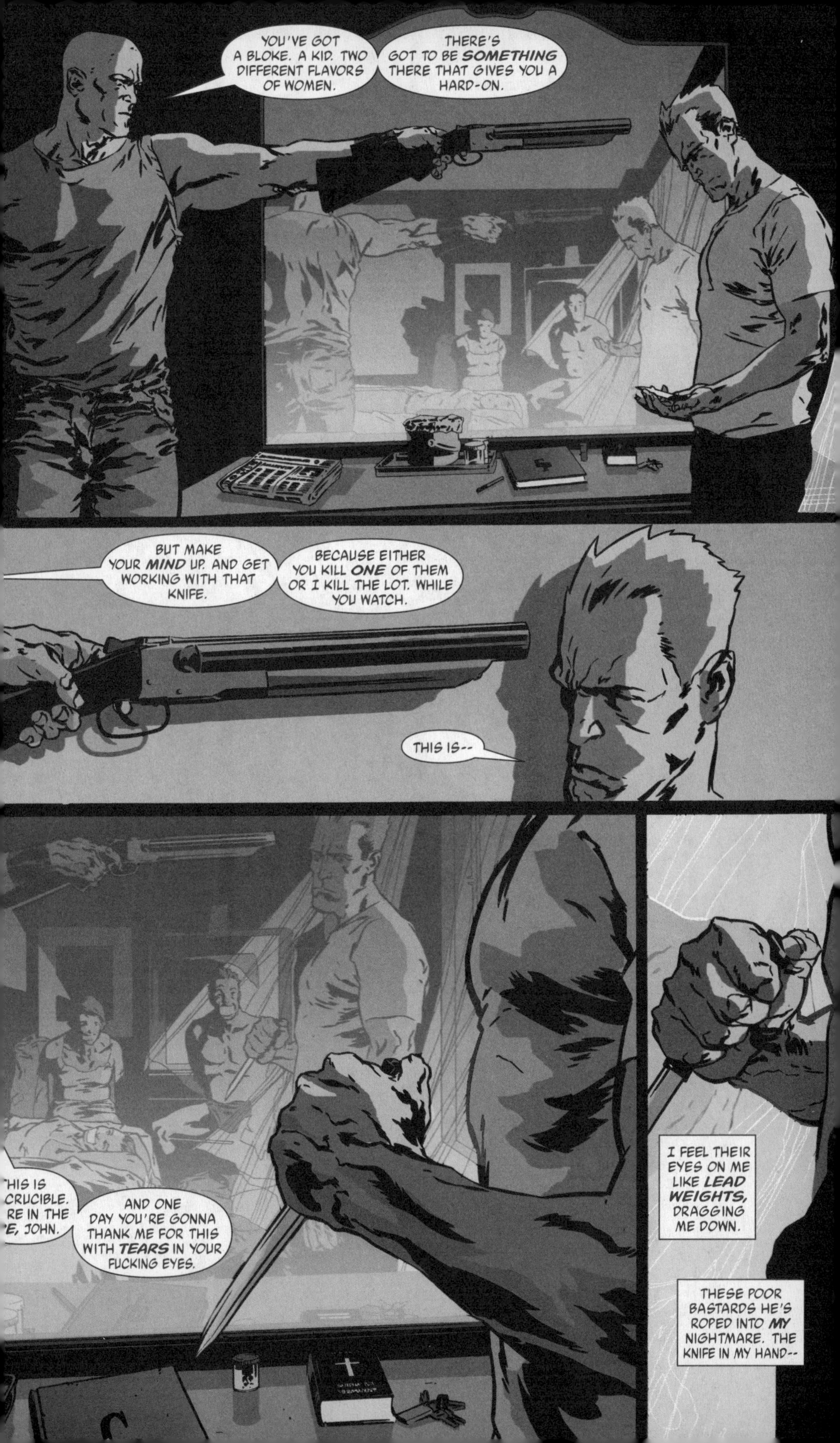
YOU'VE GOT A BLOKE. A KID. TWO DIFFERENT FLAVORS OF WOMEN.
THERE'S GOT TO BE SOMETHING THERE THAT GIVES YOU A HARD-ON.
BUT MAKE YOUR MIND UP. AND GET WORKING WITH THAT KNIFE.
BECAUSE EITHER YOU KILL ONE OF THEM OR I KILL THE LOT. WHILE YOU WATCH.
THIS IS--
HIS IS CRUCIBLE. RE IN THE E, JOHN.
AND ONE DAY YOU'RE GONNA THANK ME FOR THIS WITH TEARS IN YOUR FUCKING EYES.
I FEEL THEIR EYES ON ME LIKE LEAD WEIGHTS, DRAGGING ME DOWN.
THESE POOR BASTARDS HE'S ROPED INTO MY NIGHTMARE. THE KNIFE IN MY HAND--

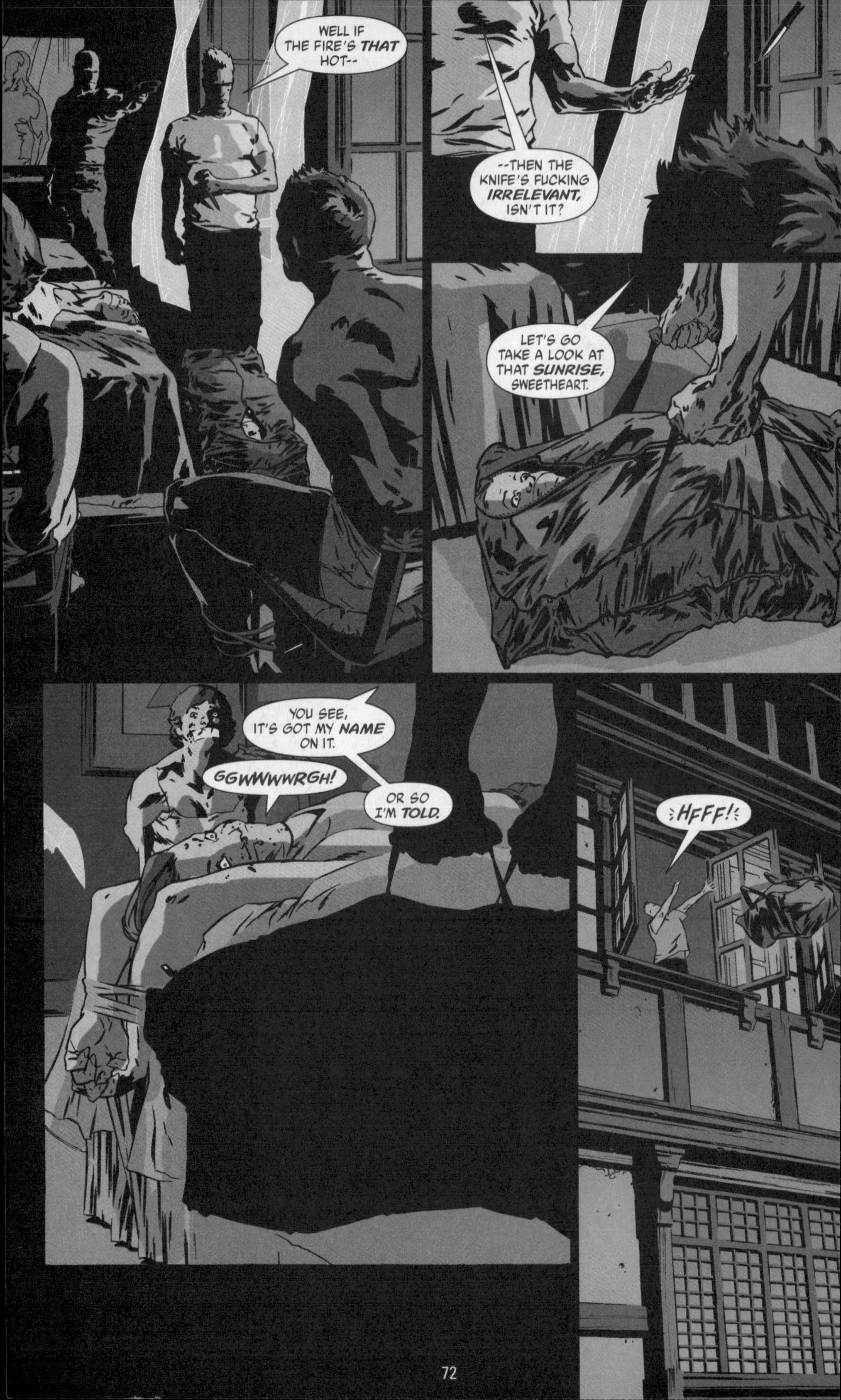
WELL IF THE FIRE'S THAT HOT--
--THEN THE KNIFE'S FUCKING IRRELEVANT, ISN'T IT?
LET'S GO TAKE A LOOK AT THAT SUNRISE, SWEETHEART.
YOU SEE, IT'S GOT MY NAME ON IT.
GGWWWWRGH!
OR SO I'M TOLD.
HFFF!

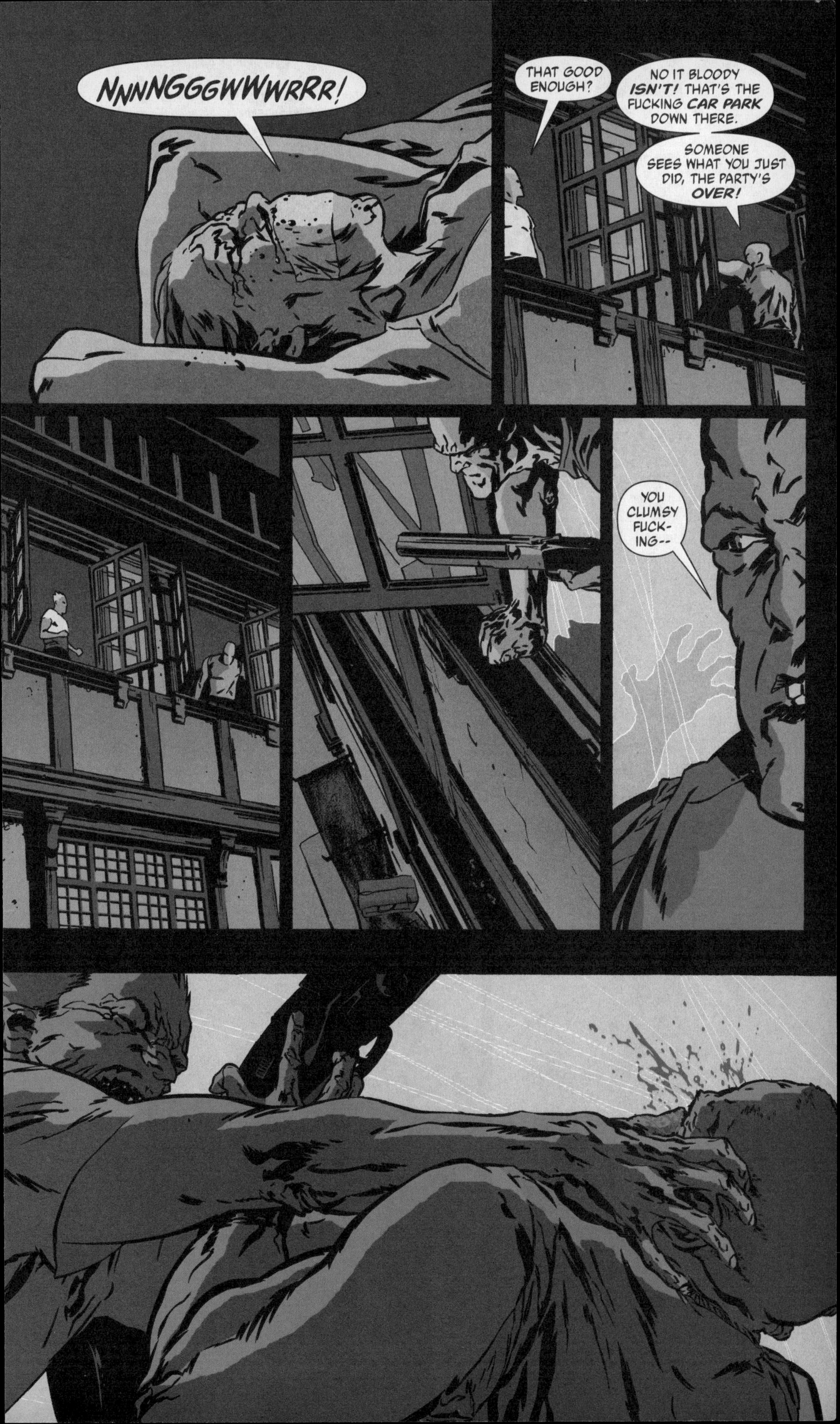
NNNNGGGWWWRRRR!
THAT GOOD ENOUGH?
NO IT BLOODY ISN'T! THAT'S THE FUCKING CAR PARK DOWN THERE.
SOMEONE SEES WHAT YOU JUST DID, THE PARTY'S OVER!
YOU CLUMSY FUCK-ING--

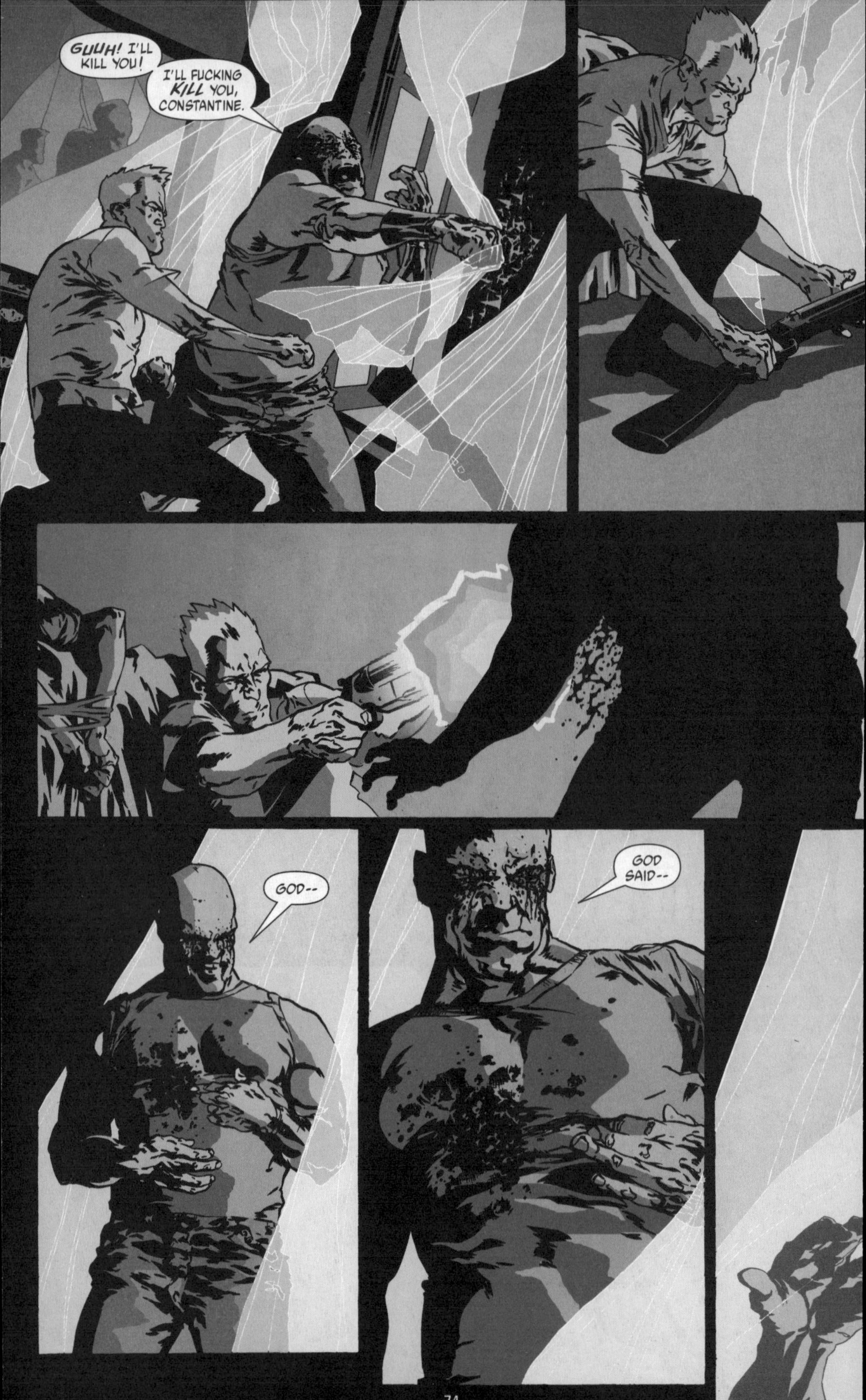
GUUH! I'LL KILL YOU!
I'LL FUCKING KILL YOU, CONSTANTINE.
GOD--
GOD SAID--

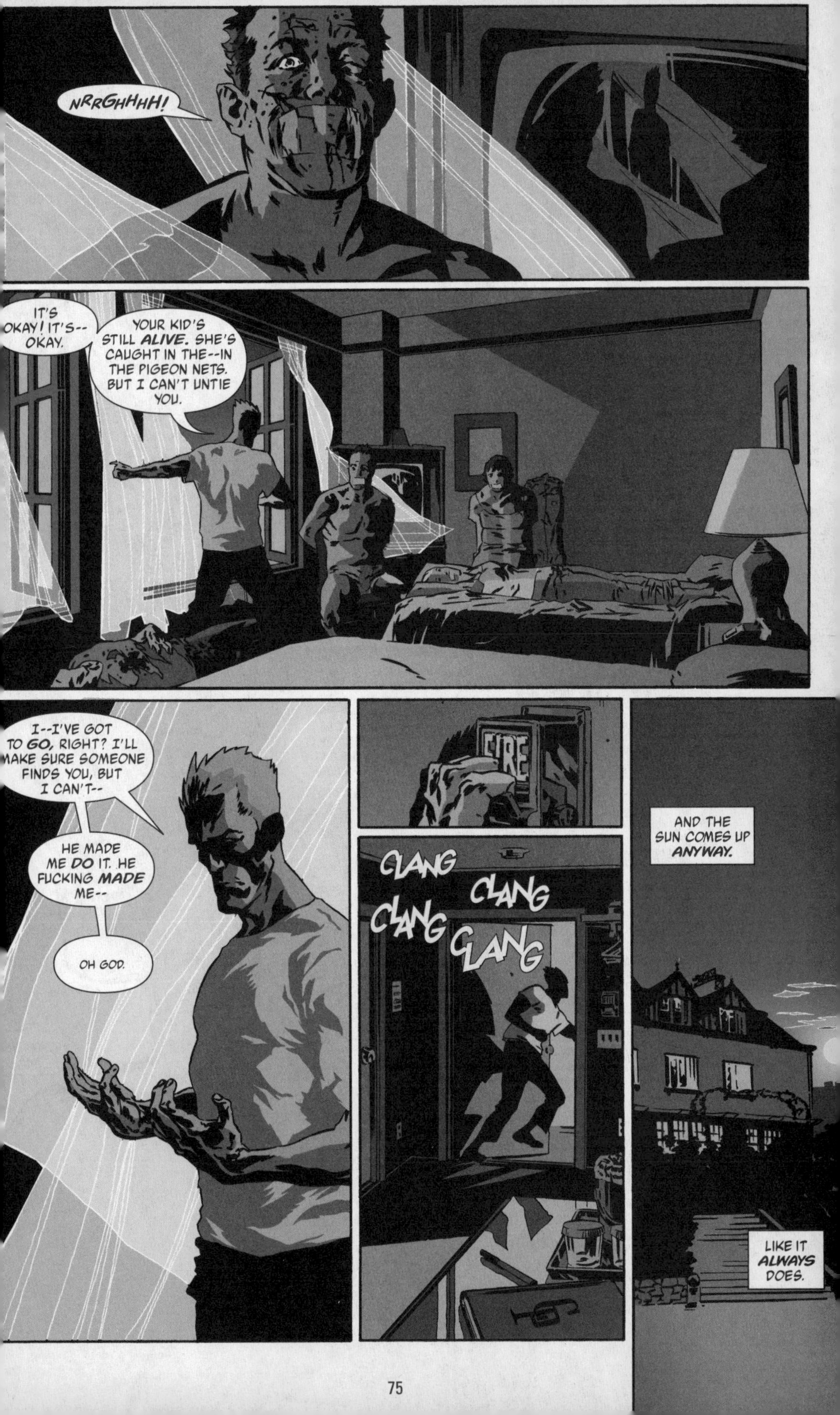
NRRGHHHH!
IT'S OKAY! IT'S-- OKAY.
YOUR KID'S STILL ALIVE. SHE'S CAUGHT IN THE--IN THE PIGEON NETS. BUT I CAN'T UNTIE YOU.
I--I'VE GOT TO GO, RIGHT? I'LL MAKE SURE SOMEONE FINDS YOU, BUT I CAN'T--
HE MADE ME DO IT. HE FUCKING MADE ME--
OH GOD.
FIRE
CLANG
CLANG
CLANG
CLANG
AND THE SUN COMES UP ANYWAY.
LIKE IT ALWAYS DOES.

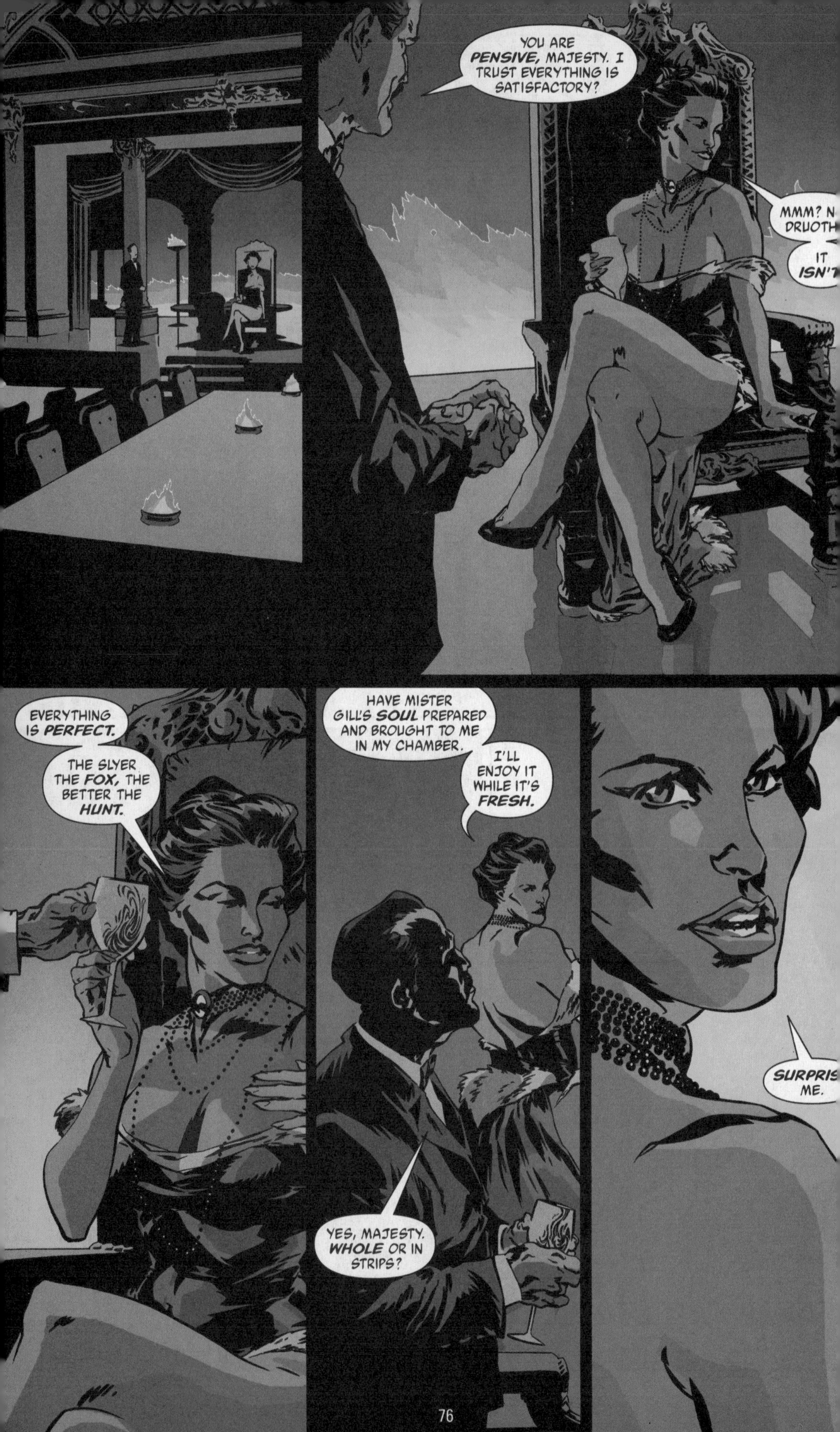
YOU ARE PENSIVE, MAJESTY. I TRUST EVERYTHING IS SATISFACTORY?
MMM? N
DRUOTH
IT
ISN'T
EVERYTHING IS PERFECT.
THE SLYER THE FOX, THE BETTER THE HUNT.
HAVE MISTER GILL'S SOUL PREPARED AND BROUGHT TO ME IN MY CHAMBER.
I'LL ENJOY IT WHILE IT'S FRESH.
YES, MAJESTY. WHOLE OR IN STRIPS?
SURPRIS
ME.

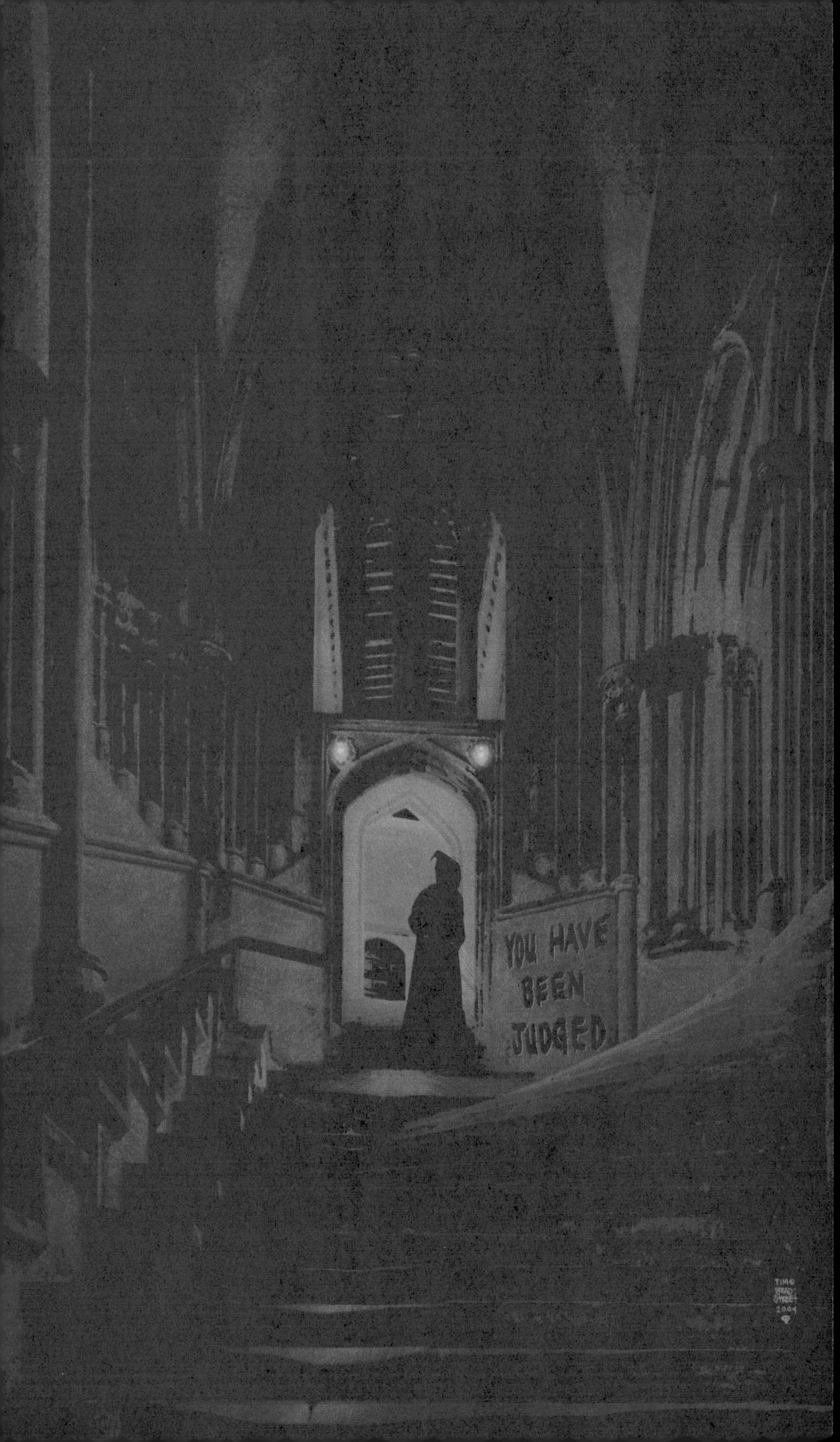
YOU HAVE BEEN JUDGED.
TIMO READ STREET 2004

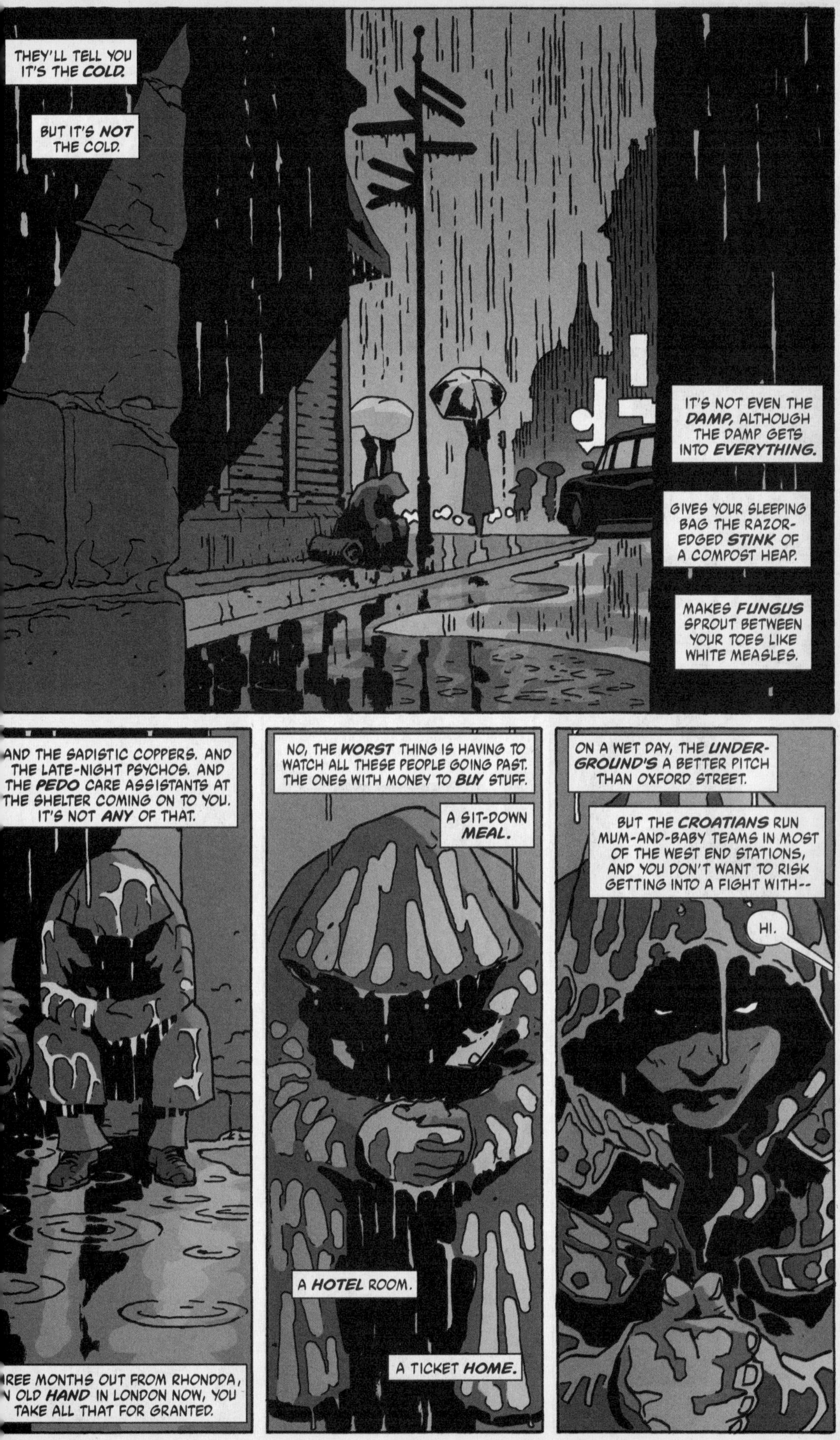
THEY'LL TELL YOU IT'S THE COLD.
BUT IT'S NOT THE COLD.
IT'S NOT EVEN THE DAMP, ALTHOUGH THE DAMP GETS INTO EVERYTHING.
GIVES YOUR SLEEPING BAG THE RAZOR-EDGED STINK OF A COMPOST HEAP.
MAKES FUNGUS SPROUT BETWEEN YOUR TOES LIKE WHITE MEASLES.
AND THE SADISTIC COPPERS. AND THE LATE-NIGHT PSYCHOS. AND THE PEDO CARE ASSISTANTS AT THE SHELTER COMING ON TO YOU. IT'S NOT ANY OF THAT.
REE MONTHS OUT FROM RHONDDA, N OLD HAND IN LONDON NOW, YOU TAKE ALL THAT FOR GRANTED.
NO, THE WORST THING IS HAVING TO WATCH ALL THESE PEOPLE GOING PAST. THE ONES WITH MONEY TO BUY STUFF.
A SIT-DOWN MEAL.
A HOTEL ROOM.
A TICKET HOME.
ON A WET DAY, THE UNDER-GROUND'S A BETTER PITCH THAN OXFORD STREET.
BUT THE CROATIANS RUN MUM-AND-BABY TEAMS IN MOST OF THE WEST END STATIONS, AND YOU DON'T WANT TO RISK GETTING INTO A FIGHT WITH--
HI.

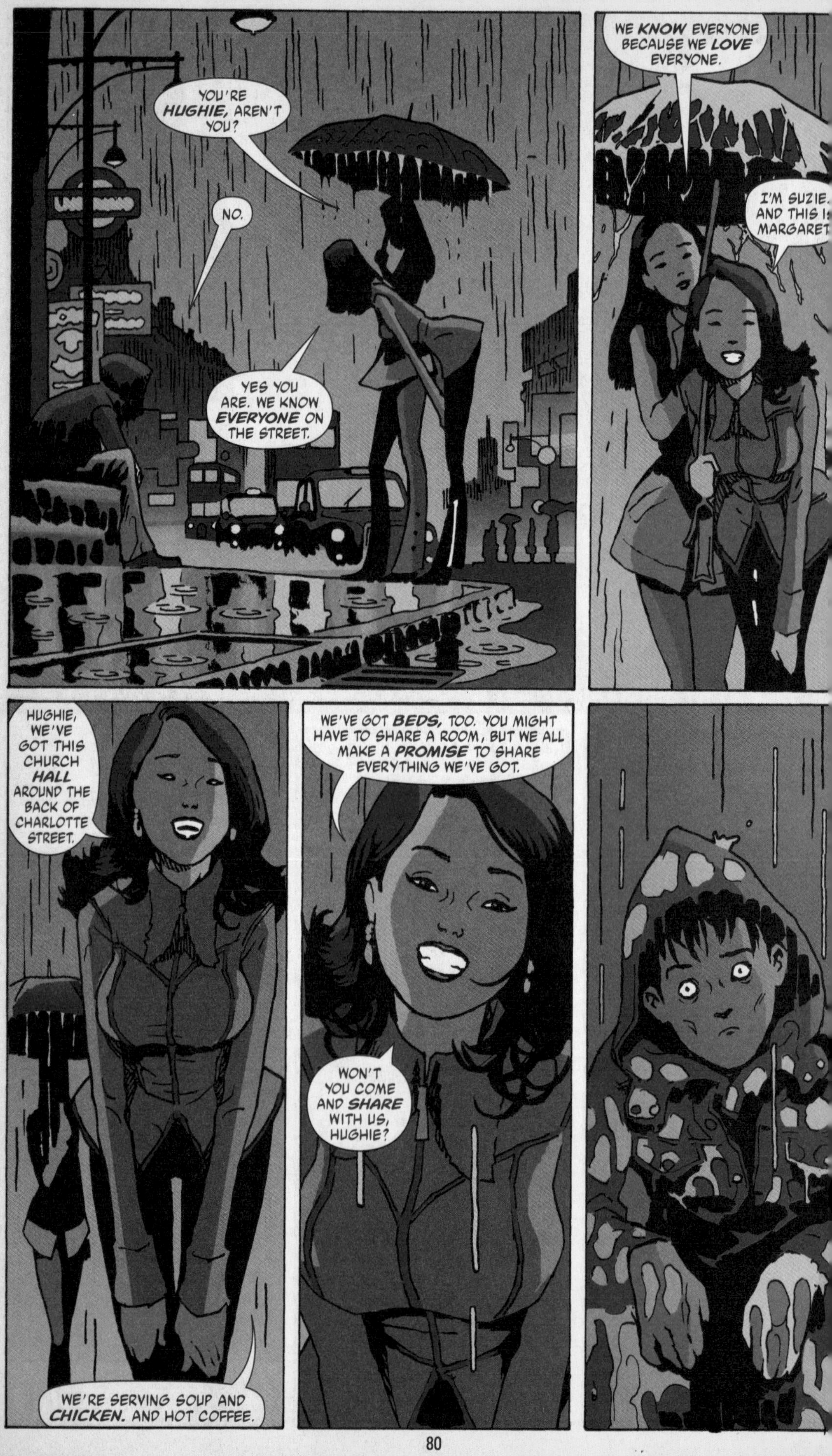

YOU'RE HUGHIE, AREN'T YOU?
NO.
YES YOU ARE. WE KNOW EVERYONE ON THE STREET.
WE KNOW EVERYONE BECAUSE WE LOVE EVERYONE.
I'M SUZIE. AND THIS IS MARGARET.
HUGHIE, WE'VE GOT THIS CHURCH HALL AROUND THE BACK OF CHARLOTTE STREET.
WE'RE SERVING SOUP AND CHICKEN. AND HOT COFFEE.
WE'VE GOT BEDS, TOO. YOU MIGHT HAVE TO SHARE A ROOM, BUT WE ALL MAKE A PROMISE TO SHARE EVERYTHING WE'VE GOT.
WON'T YOU COME AND SHARE WITH US, HUGHIE?

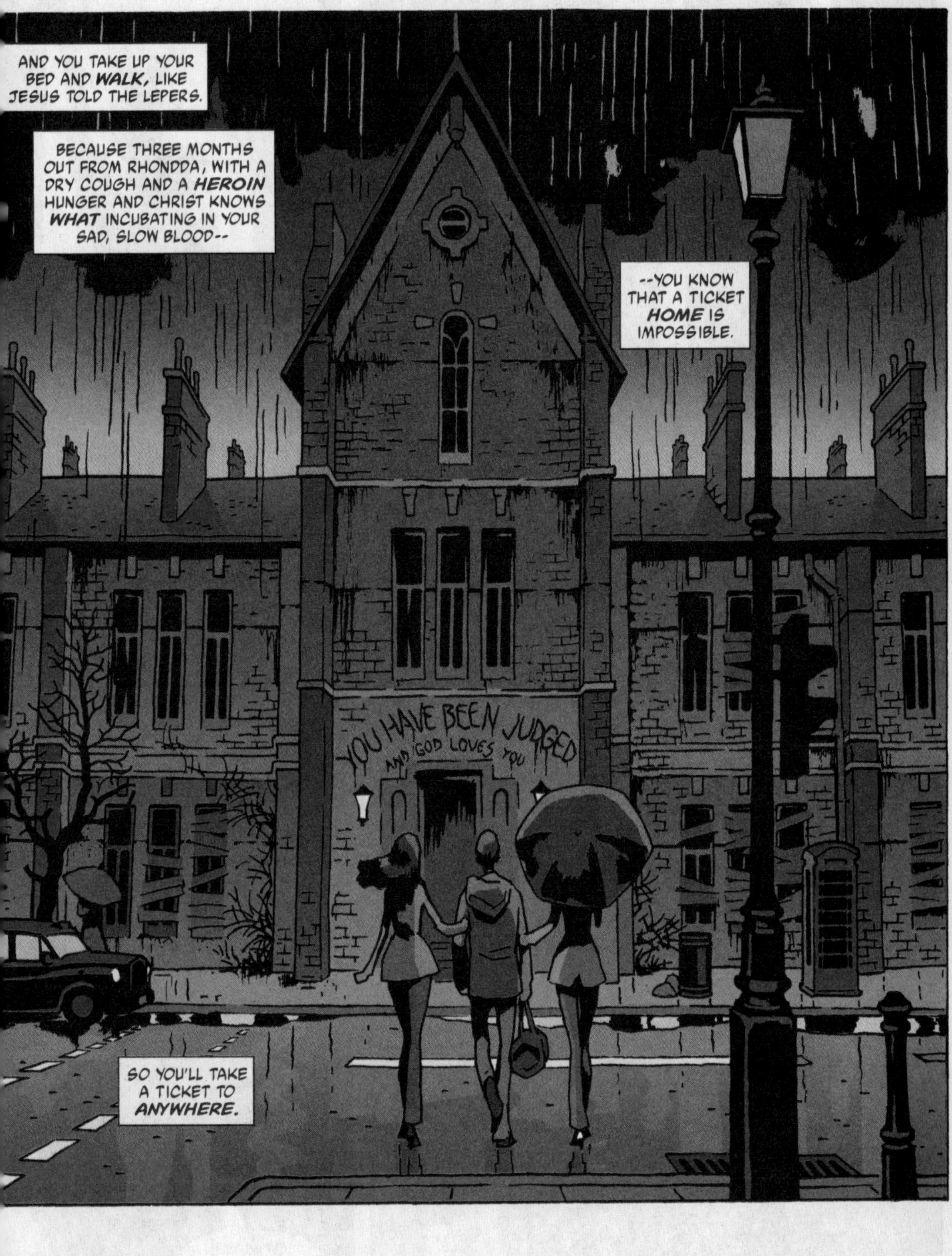
AND YOU TAKE UP YOUR BED AND WALK, LIKE JESUS TOLD THE LEPERS.
BECAUSE THREE MONTHS OUT FROM RHONDDA, WITH A DRY COUGH AND A HEROIN HUNGER AND CHRIST KNOWS WHAT INCUBATING IN YOUR SAD, SLOW BLOOD--
--YOU KNOW THAT A TICKET HOME IS IMPOSSIBLE.
YOU HAVE BEEN JUDGED
AND GOD LOVES YOU
SO YOU'LL TAKE A TICKET TO ANYWHERE.

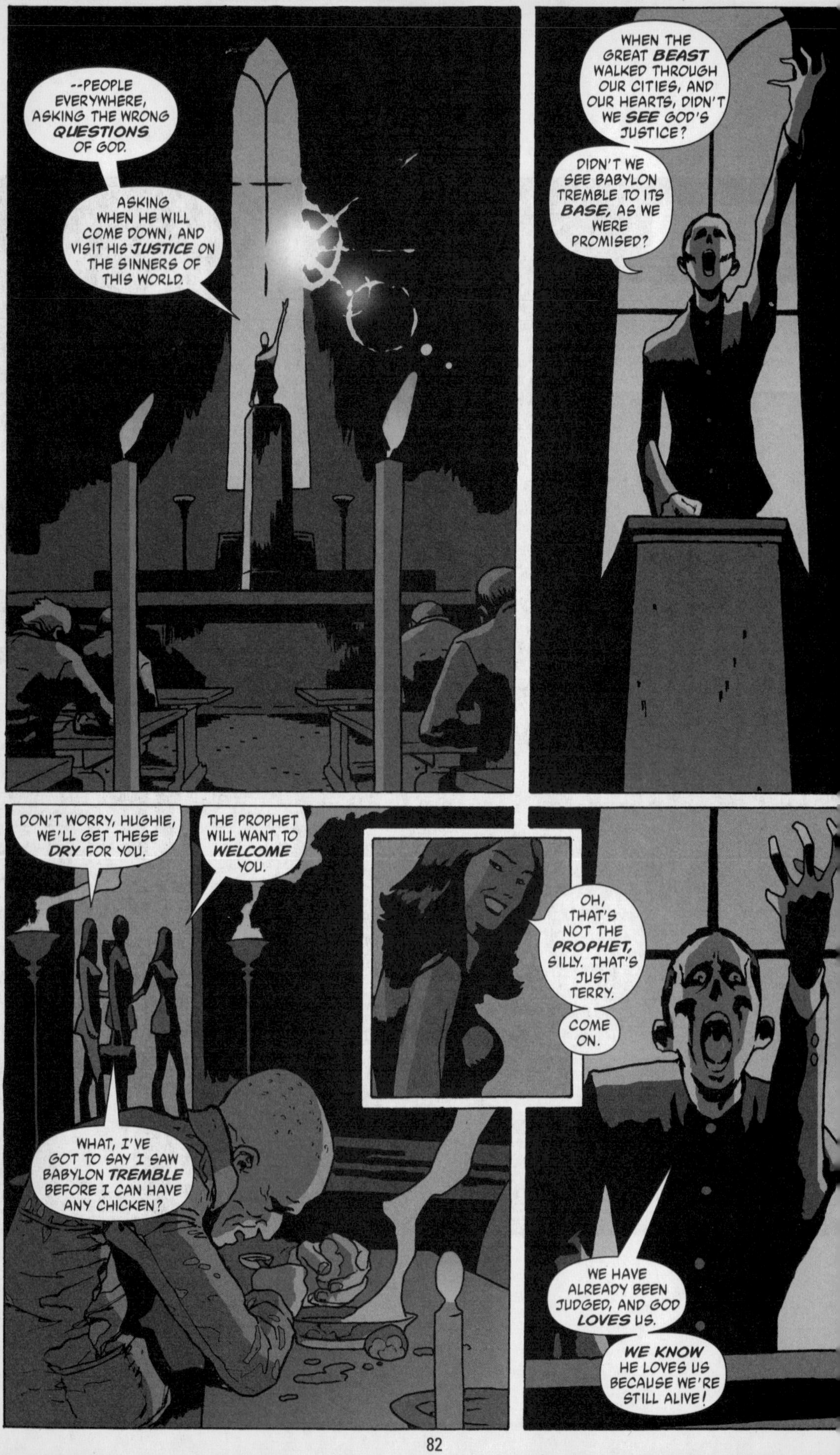
--PEOPLE EVERYWHERE, ASKING THE WRONG QUESTIONS OF GOD.
ASKING WHEN HE WILL COME DOWN, AND VISIT HIS JUSTICE ON THE SINNERS OF THIS WORLD.
WHEN THE GREAT BEAST WALKED THROUGH OUR CITIES, AND OUR HEARTS, DIDN'T WE SEE GOD'S JUSTICE?
DIDN'T WE SEE BABYLON TREMBLE TO ITS BASE, AS WE WERE PROMISED?
DON'T WORRY, HUGHIE, WE'LL GET THESE DRY FOR YOU.
THE PROPHET WILL WANT TO WELCOME YOU.
WHAT, I'VE GOT TO SAY I SAW BABYLON TREMBLE BEFORE I CAN HAVE ANY CHICKEN?
OH, THAT'S NOT THE PROPHET, SILLY. THAT'S JUST TERRY.
COME ON.
WE HAVE ALREADY BEEN JUDGED, AND GOD LOVES US.
WE KNOW HE LOVES US BECAUSE WE'RE STILL ALIVE!

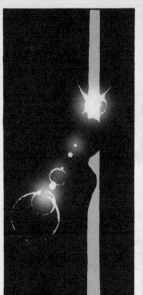

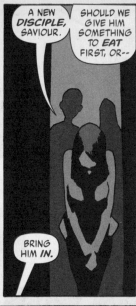

A NEW *DISCIPLE*, SAVIOUR.

SHOULD WE GIVE HIM SOMETHING TO *EAT* FIRST, OR--

BRING HIM *IN*.

JUST BE *YOUR-SELF*, HUGHIE, AND YOU'LL BE FINE.

WE'LL SEE YOU *LATER*, IN THE KITCHEN.

AND MAYBE IN THE *DORMITORY*.

N, E THE R.

ETTER OCK IT, TOO.

SALVATION IS A VERY *PRIVATE* THING.

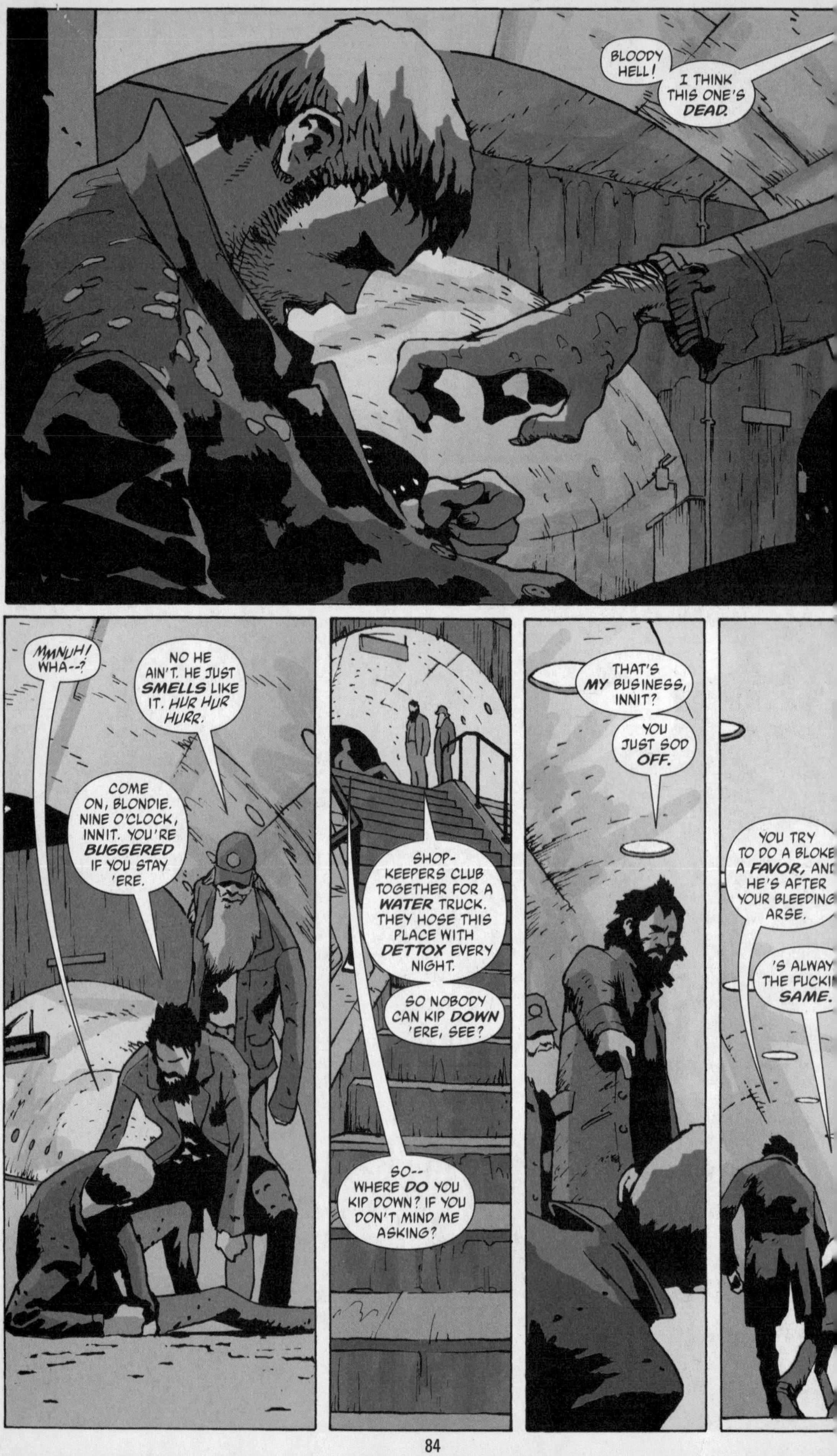
BLOODY HELL!
I THINK THIS ONE'S DEAD.
MMNUH! WHA--?
NO HE AIN'T. HE JUST SMELLS LIKE IT. HUR HUR HURR.
COME ON, BLONDIE. NINE O'CLOCK, INNIT. YOU'RE BUGGERED IF YOU STAY 'ERE.
SHOP-KEEPERS CLUB TOGETHER FOR A WATER TRUCK. THEY HOSE THIS PLACE WITH DETTOX EVERY NIGHT.
SO NOBODY CAN KIP DOWN 'ERE, SEE?
SO-- WHERE DO YOU KIP DOWN? IF YOU DON'T MIND ME ASKING?
THAT'S MY BUSINESS, INNIT?
YOU JUST SOD OFF.
YOU TRY TO DO A BLOKE A FAVOR, AND HE'S AFTER YOUR BLEEDING ARSE.
'S ALWAY THE FUCKI SAME.

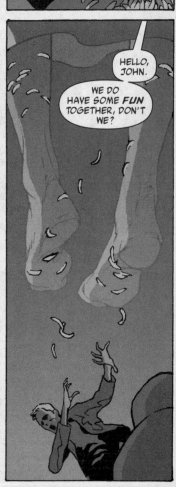

HELLO, JOHN.

WE DO HAVE SOME *FUN* TOGETHER, DON'T WE?

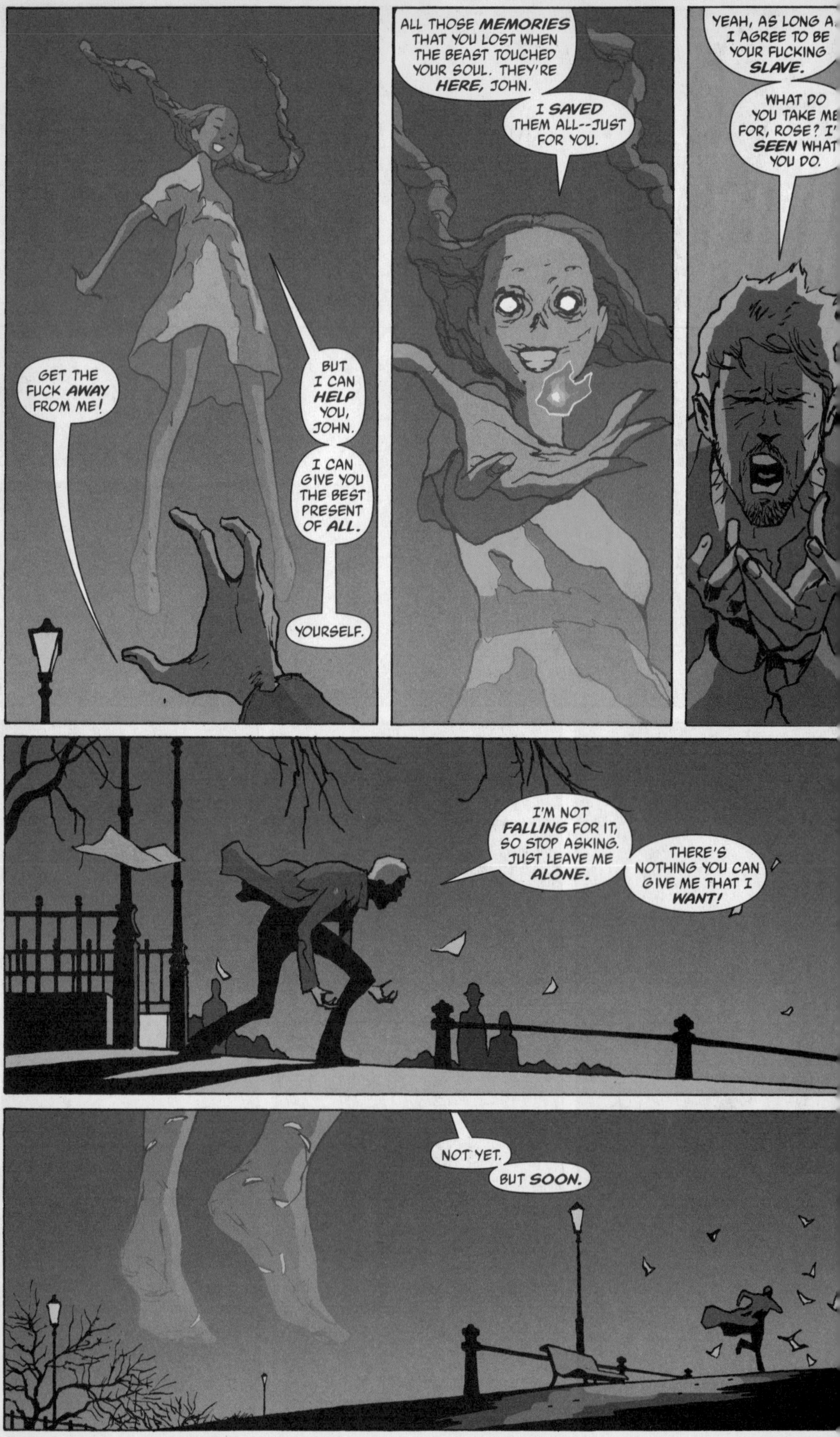
GET THE FUCK AWAY FROM ME!
BUT I CAN HELP YOU, JOHN.
I CAN GIVE YOU THE BEST PRESENT OF ALL.
YOURSELF.
ALL THOSE MEMORIES THAT YOU LOST WHEN THE BEAST TOUCHED YOUR SOUL. THEY'RE HERE, JOHN.
I SAVED THEM ALL--JUST FOR YOU.
YEAH, AS LONG A I AGREE TO BE YOUR FUCKING SLAVE.
WHAT DO YOU TAKE ME FOR, ROSE? I' SEEN WHAT YOU DO.
I'M NOT FALLING FOR IT, SO STOP ASKING. JUST LEAVE ME ALONE.
THERE'S NOTHING YOU CAN GIVE ME THAT I WANT!
NOT YET.
BUT SOON.

"THE SOUL AS *PRODUCT*. THE BODY AS *PACKAGING*.

"CELESTIAL *ECONOMICS*. YOU SEE? YOU SEE?"

NO.

LOOK, THOSE GIRLS SAID THERE WAS *FOOD*--

AND THERE *IS*. OH YES.

THE *TRUTH* IS FOOD. FOOD FOR THE *SOUL*.

TRUTH IS, I TRY TO *CONTROL* MYSELF. I MANAGE. *MOST* OF THE TIME.

BUT TODAY'S BEEN A BAD DAY.

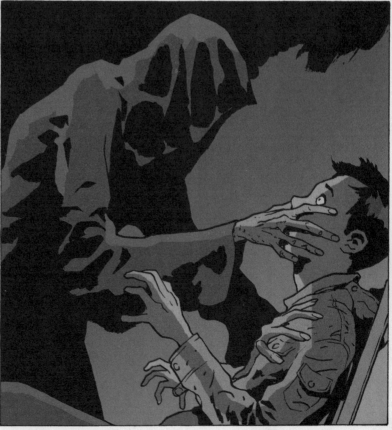

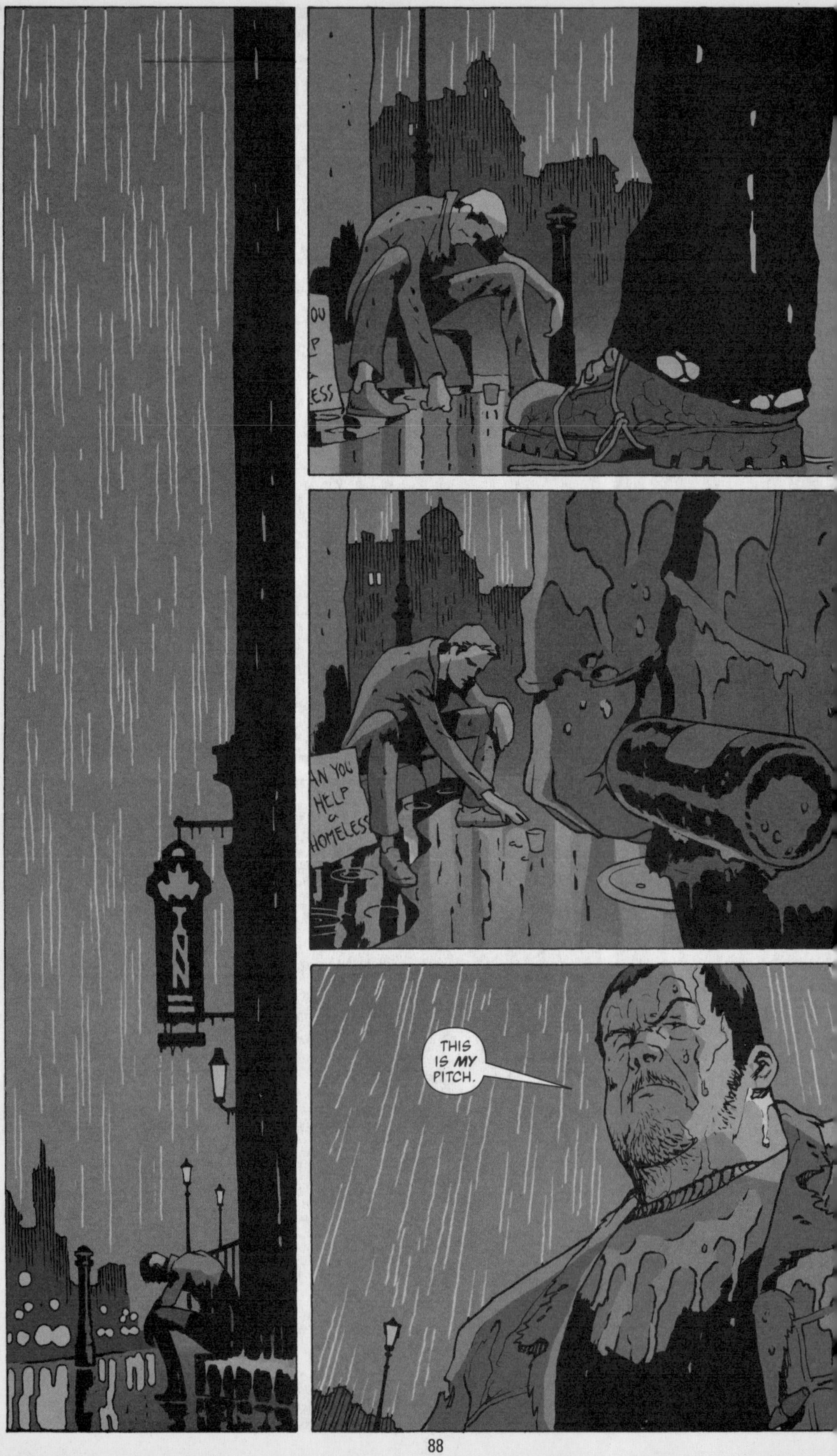
AN YOU
HELP
a
HOMELESS
THIS IS MY PITCH.

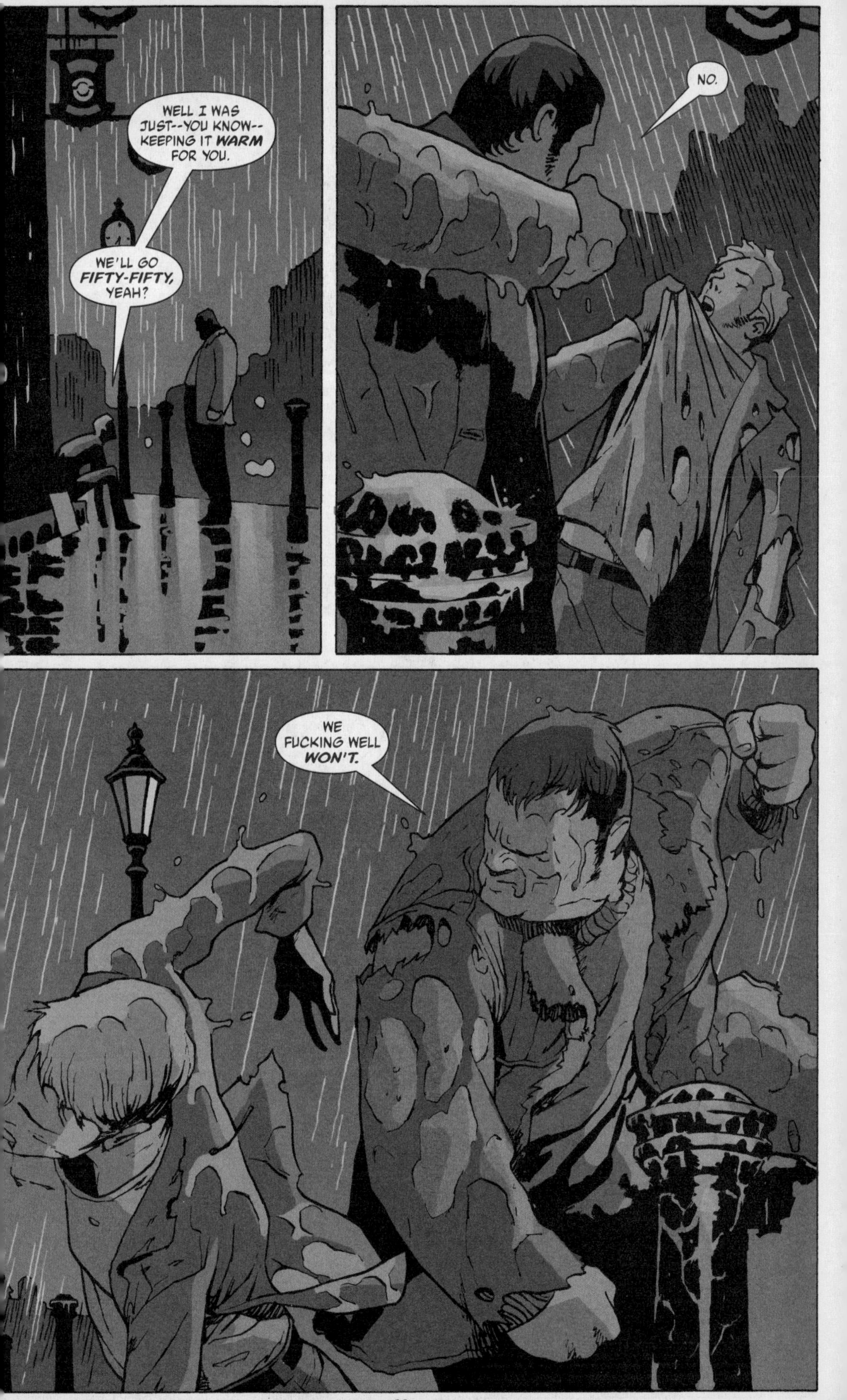
WELL I WAS JUST--YOU KNOW--KEEPING IT WARM FOR YOU.
WE'LL GO FIFTY-FIFTY, YEAH?
NO.
WE FUCKING WELL WON'T.

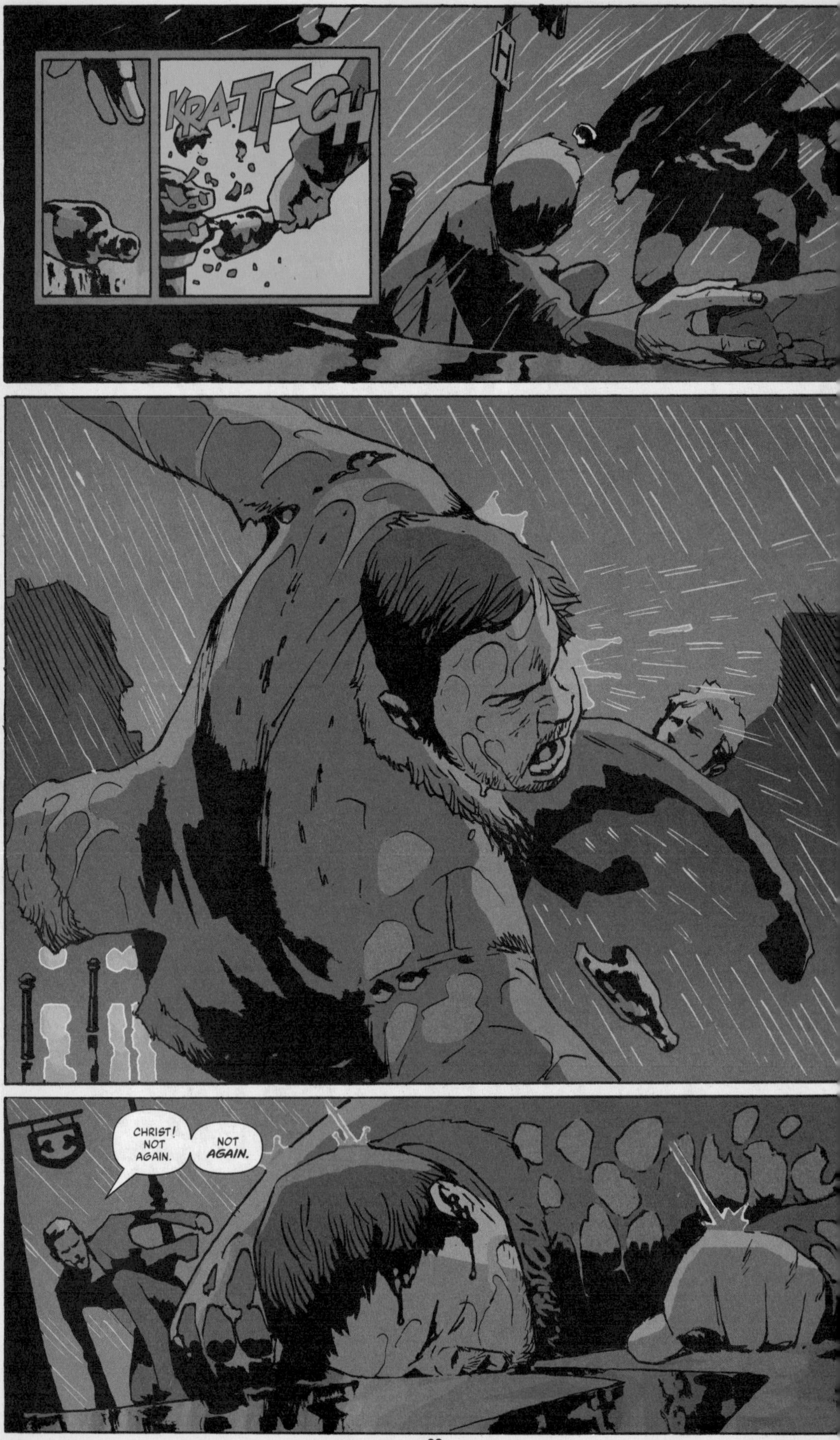
KRATISCH
CHRIST! NOT AGAIN.
NOT AGAIN.

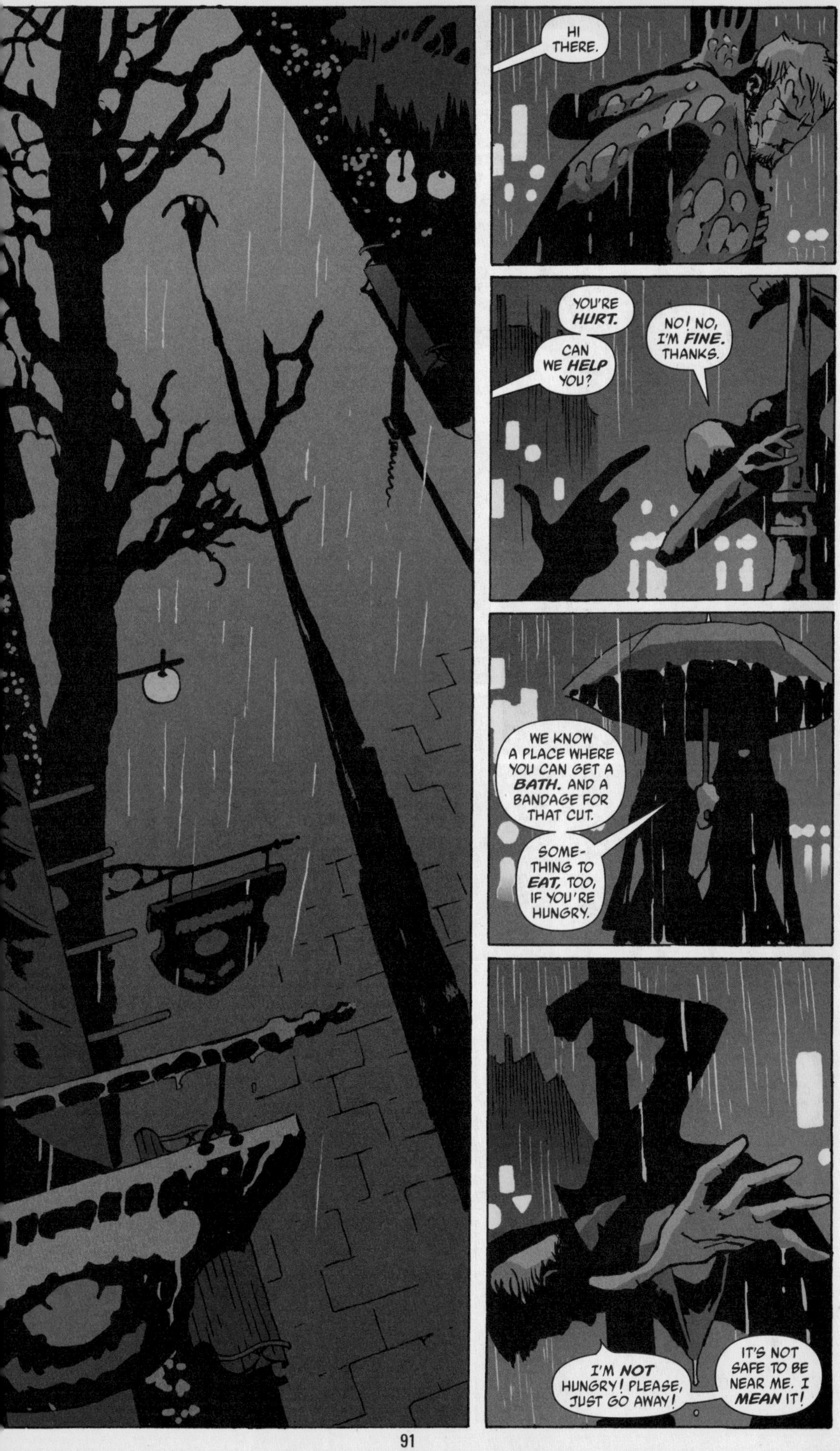
HI THERE.
YOU'RE HURT.
CAN WE HELP YOU?
NO! NO, I'M FINE. THANKS.
WE KNOW A PLACE WHERE YOU CAN GET A BATH. AND A BANDAGE FOR THAT CUT.
SOME-THING TO EAT, TOO, IF YOU'RE HUNGRY.
I'M NOT HUNGRY! PLEASE, JUST GO AWAY!
IT'S NOT SAFE TO BE NEAR ME. I MEAN IT!

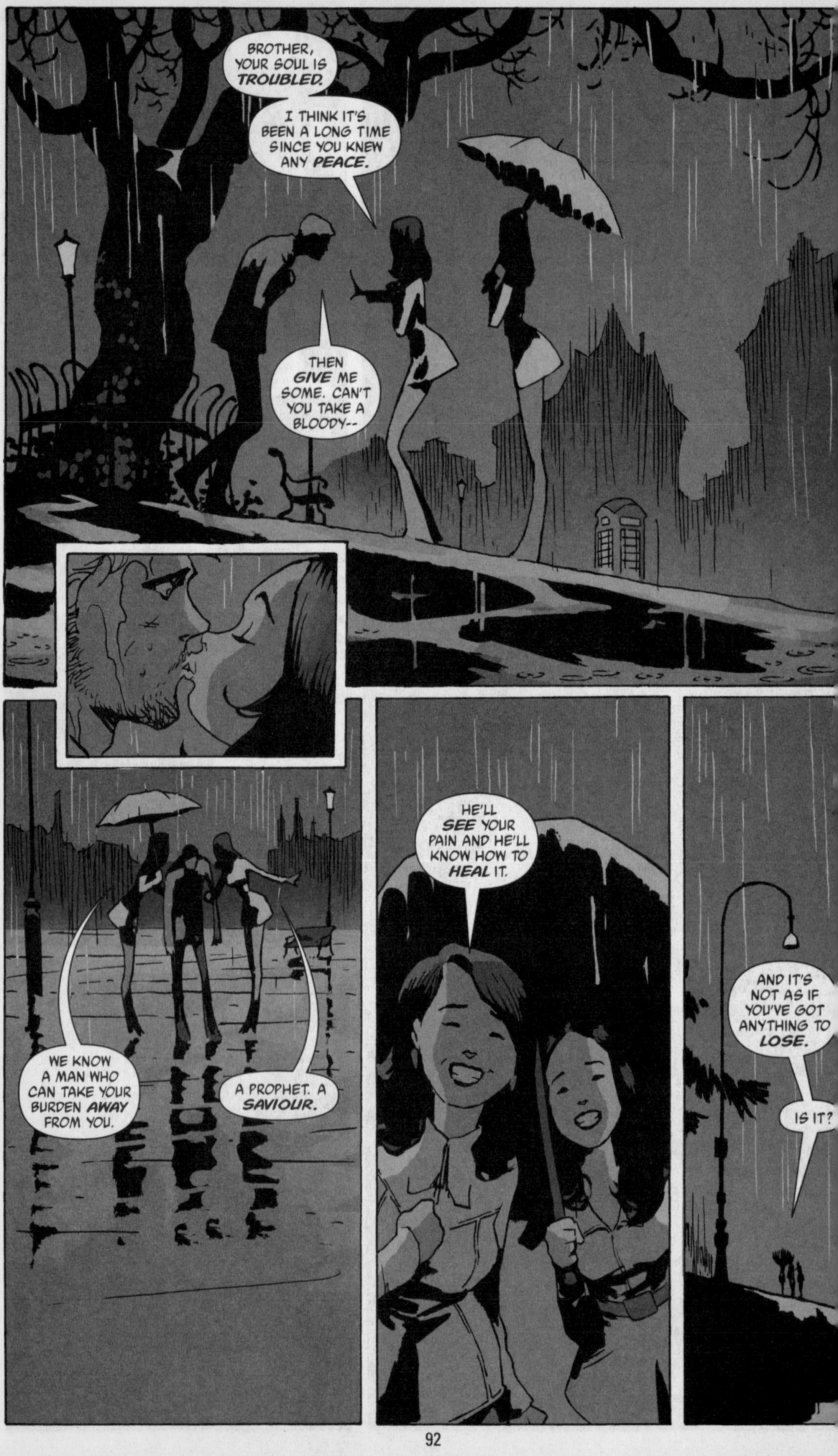
BROTHER, YOUR SOUL IS TROUBLED.
I THINK IT'S BEEN A LONG TIME SINCE YOU KNEW ANY PEACE.
THEN GIVE ME SOME. CAN'T YOU TAKE A BLOODY--
WE KNOW A MAN WHO CAN TAKE YOUR BURDEN AWAY FROM YOU.
A PROPHET. A SAVIOUR.
HE'LL SEE YOUR PAIN AND HE'LL KNOW HOW TO HEAL IT.
AND IT'S NOT AS IF YOU'VE GOT ANYTHING TO LOSE.
IS IT?

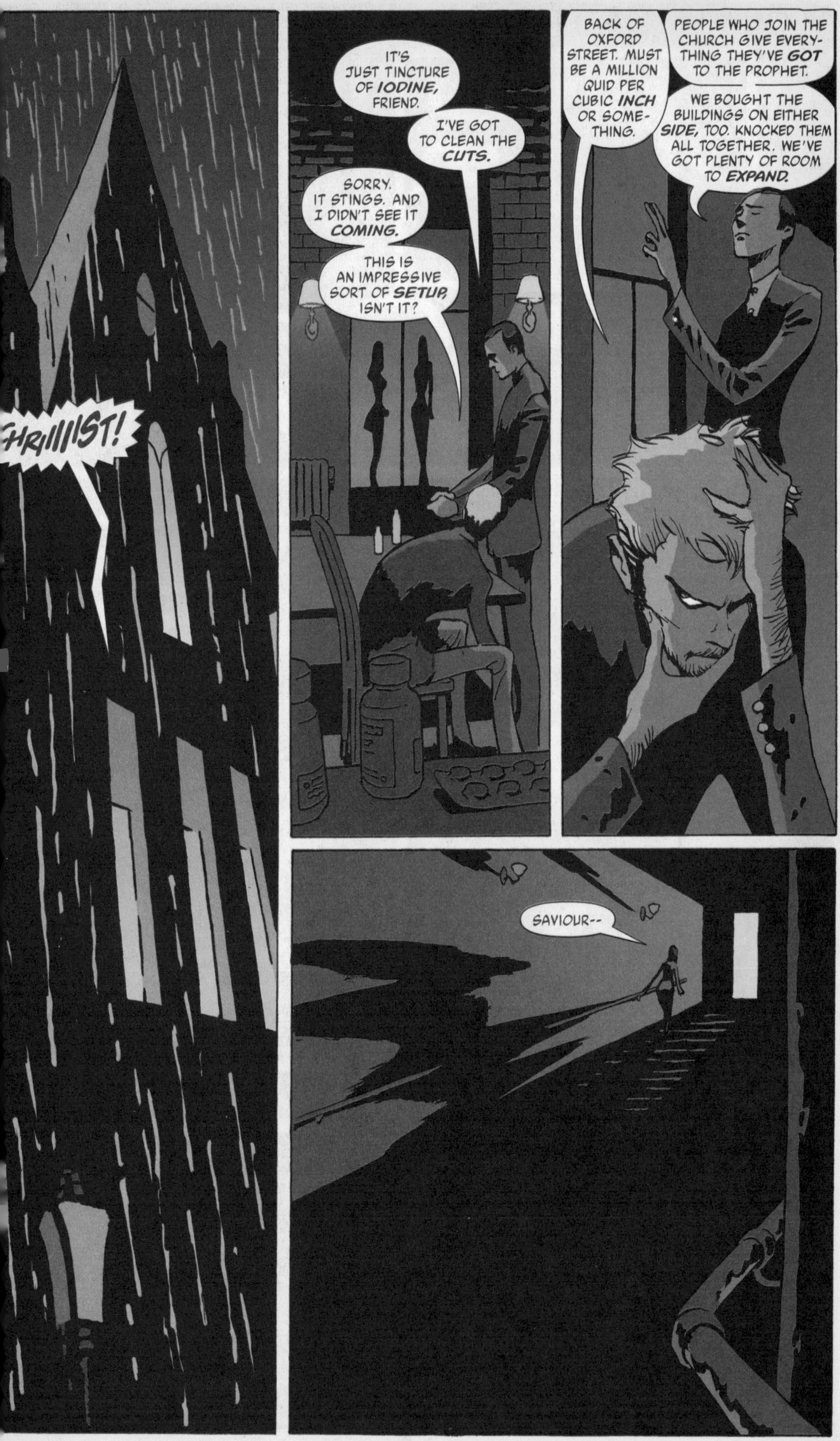
CHRIIIIST!
IT'S JUST TINCTURE OF IODINE, FRIEND.
I'VE GOT TO CLEAN THE CUTS.
SORRY. IT STINGS. AND I DIDN'T SEE IT COMING.
THIS IS AN IMPRESSIVE SORT OF SETUP, ISN'T IT?
BACK OF OXFORD STREET. MUST BE A MILLION QUID PER CUBIC INCH OR SOMETHING.
PEOPLE WHO JOIN THE CHURCH GIVE EVERYTHING THEY'VE GOT TO THE PROPHET.
WE BOUGHT THE BUILDINGS ON EITHER SIDE, TOO. KNOCKED THEM ALL TOGETHER. WE'VE GOT PLENTY OF ROOM TO EXPAND.
SAVIOUR--

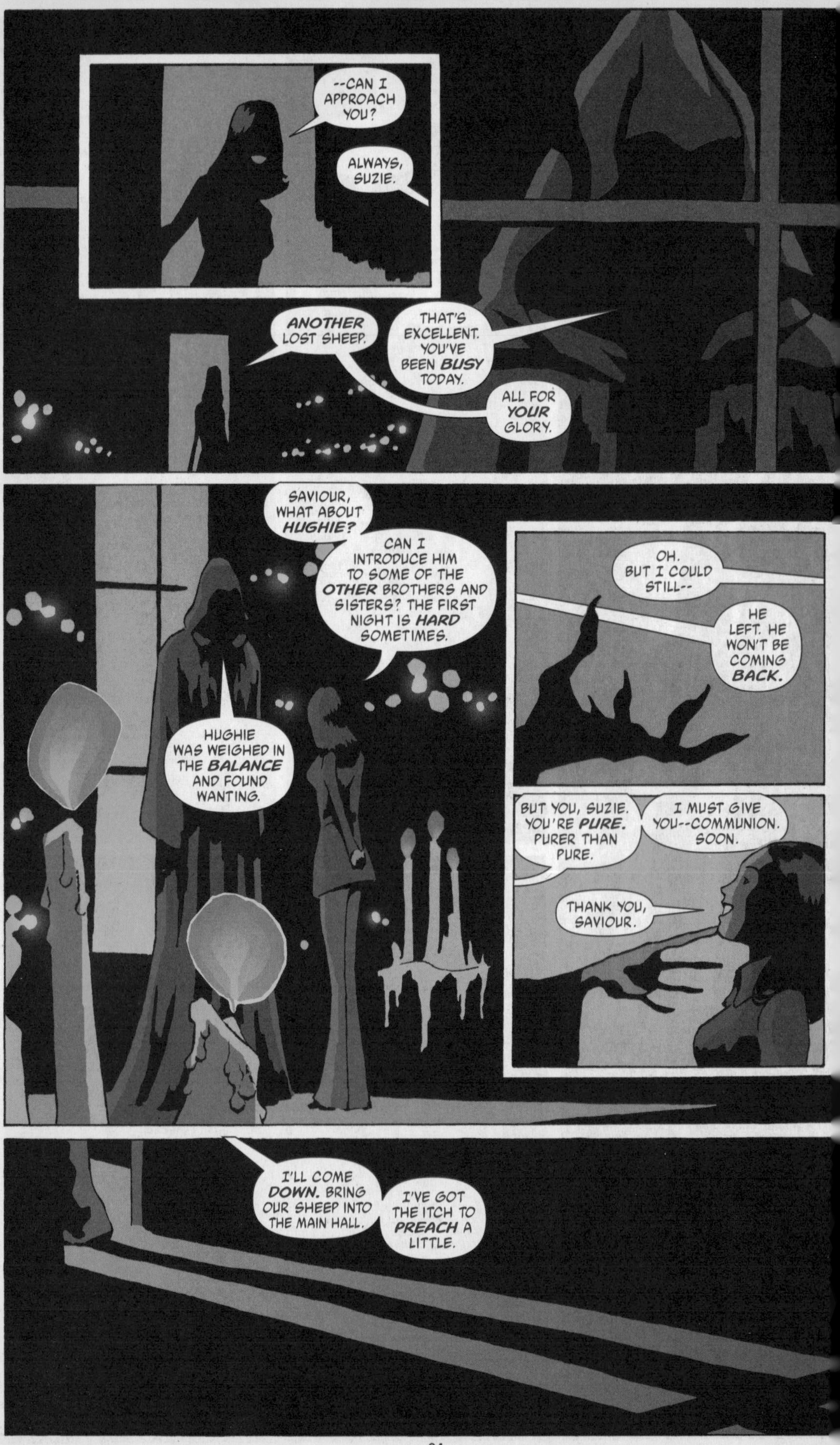
--CAN I APPROACH YOU?
ALWAYS, SUZIE.
ANOTHER LOST SHEEP.
THAT'S EXCELLENT. YOU'VE BEEN BUSY TODAY.
ALL FOR YOUR GLORY.
SAVIOUR, WHAT ABOUT HUGHIE?
CAN I INTRODUCE HIM TO SOME OF THE OTHER BROTHERS AND SISTERS? THE FIRST NIGHT IS HARD SOMETIMES.
HUGHIE WAS WEIGHED IN THE BALANCE AND FOUND WANTING.
OH. BUT I COULD STILL--
HE LEFT. HE WON'T BE COMING BACK.
BUT YOU, SUZIE. YOU'RE PURE. PURER THAN PURE.
I MUST GIVE YOU--COMMUNION. SOON.
THANK YOU, SAVIOUR.
I'LL COME DOWN. BRING OUR SHEEP INTO THE MAIN HALL.
I'VE GOT THE ITCH TO PREACH A LITTLE.

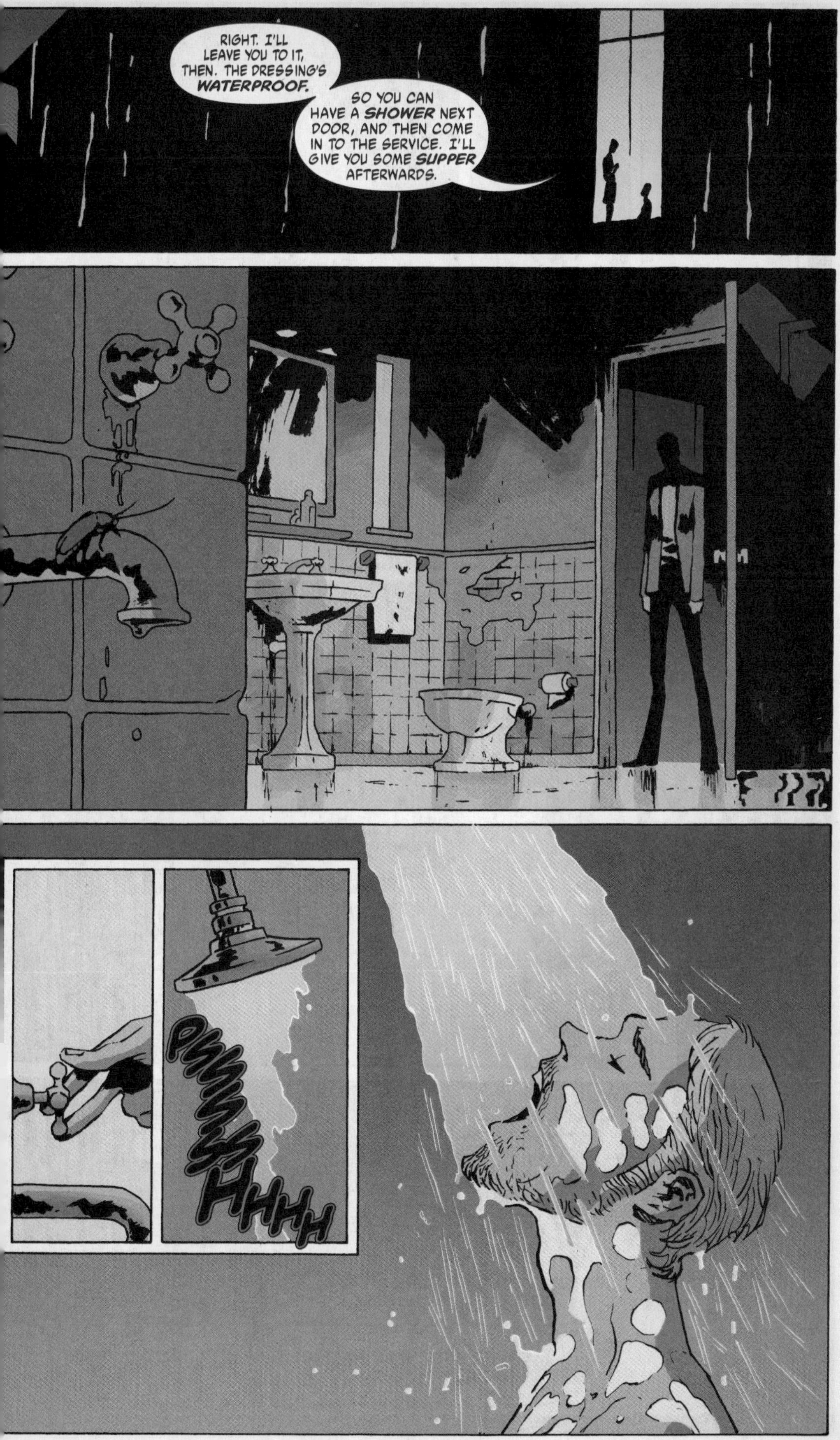
RIGHT. I'LL LEAVE YOU TO IT, THEN. THE DRESSING'S WATERPROOF.
SO YOU CAN HAVE A SHOWER NEXT DOOR, AND THEN COME IN TO THE SERVICE. I'LL GIVE YOU SOME SUPPER AFTERWARDS.
PWSSSSHHHH

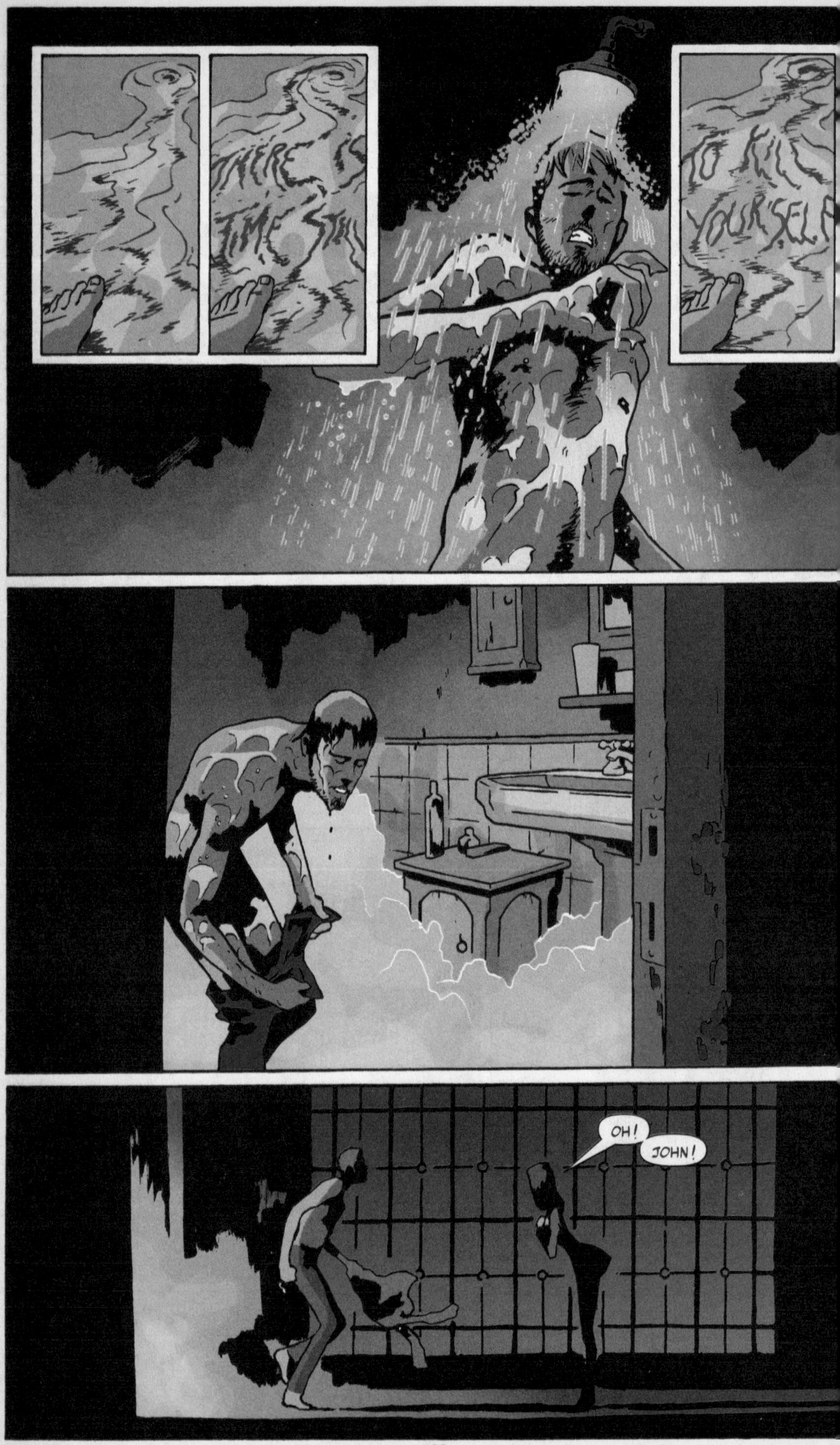
THERE IS
TIME STILL
TO KILL
YOURSELF
OH!
JOHN!

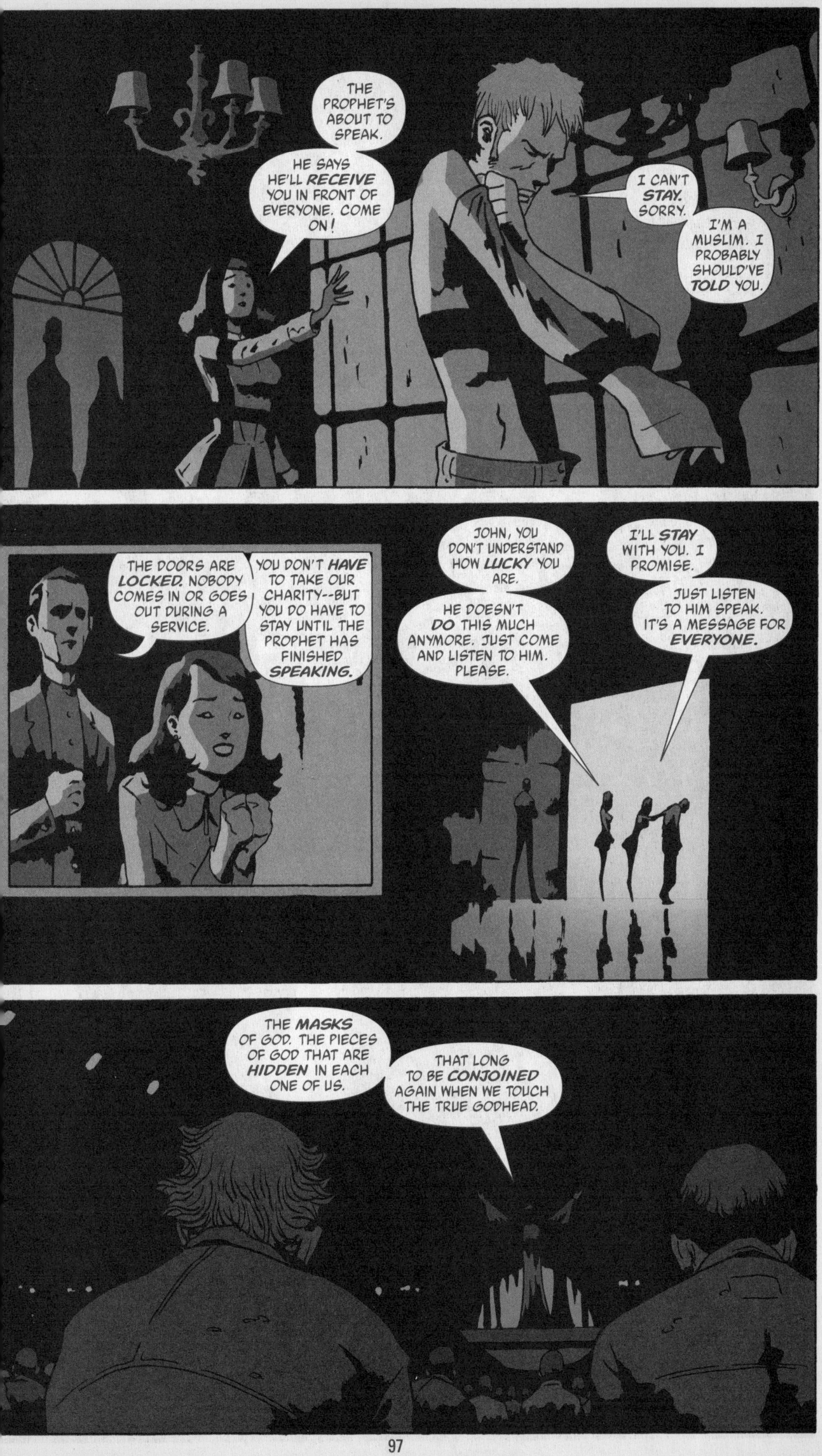
THE PROPHET'S ABOUT TO SPEAK.
HE SAYS HE'LL **RECEIVE** YOU IN FRONT OF EVERYONE. COME ON!
I CAN'T **STAY.** SORRY.
I'M A MUSLIM. I PROBABLY SHOULD'VE **TOLD** YOU.
THE DOORS ARE **LOCKED.** NOBODY COMES IN OR GOES OUT DURING A SERVICE.
YOU DON'T **HAVE** TO TAKE OUR CHARITY--BUT YOU DO HAVE TO STAY UNTIL THE PROPHET HAS FINISHED **SPEAKING.**
JOHN, YOU DON'T UNDERSTAND HOW **LUCKY** YOU ARE.
HE DOESN'T **DO** THIS MUCH ANYMORE. JUST COME AND LISTEN TO HIM. PLEASE.
I'LL **STAY** WITH YOU. I PROMISE.
JUST LISTEN TO HIM SPEAK. IT'S A MESSAGE FOR **EVERYONE.**
THE **MASKS** OF GOD. THE PIECES OF GOD THAT ARE **HIDDEN** IN EACH ONE OF US.
THAT LONG TO BE **CONJOINED** AGAIN WHEN WE TOUCH THE TRUE GODHEAD.

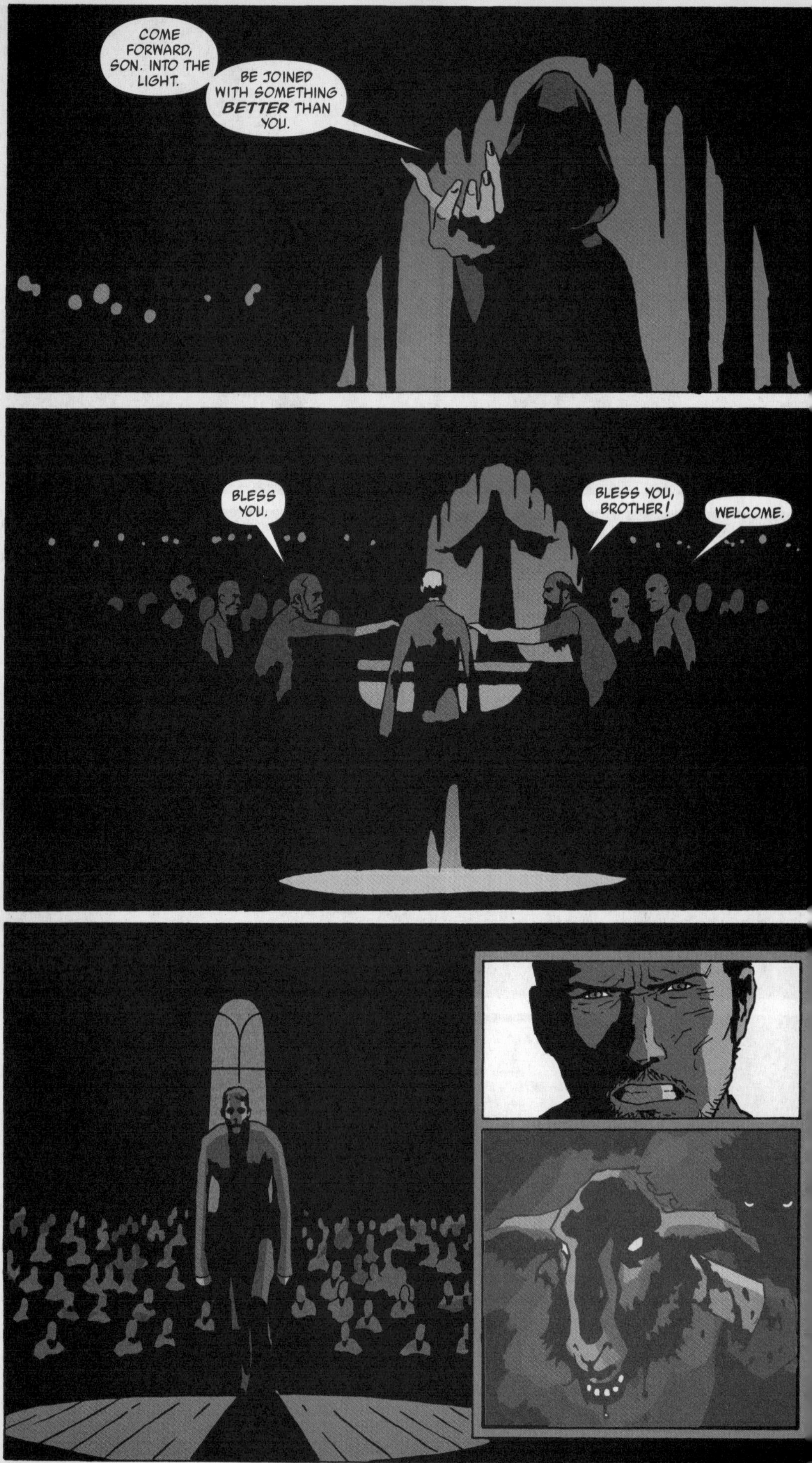
COME FORWARD, SON. INTO THE LIGHT.
BE JOINED WITH SOMETHING BETTER THAN YOU.
BLESS YOU.
BLESS YOU, BROTHER!
WELCOME.

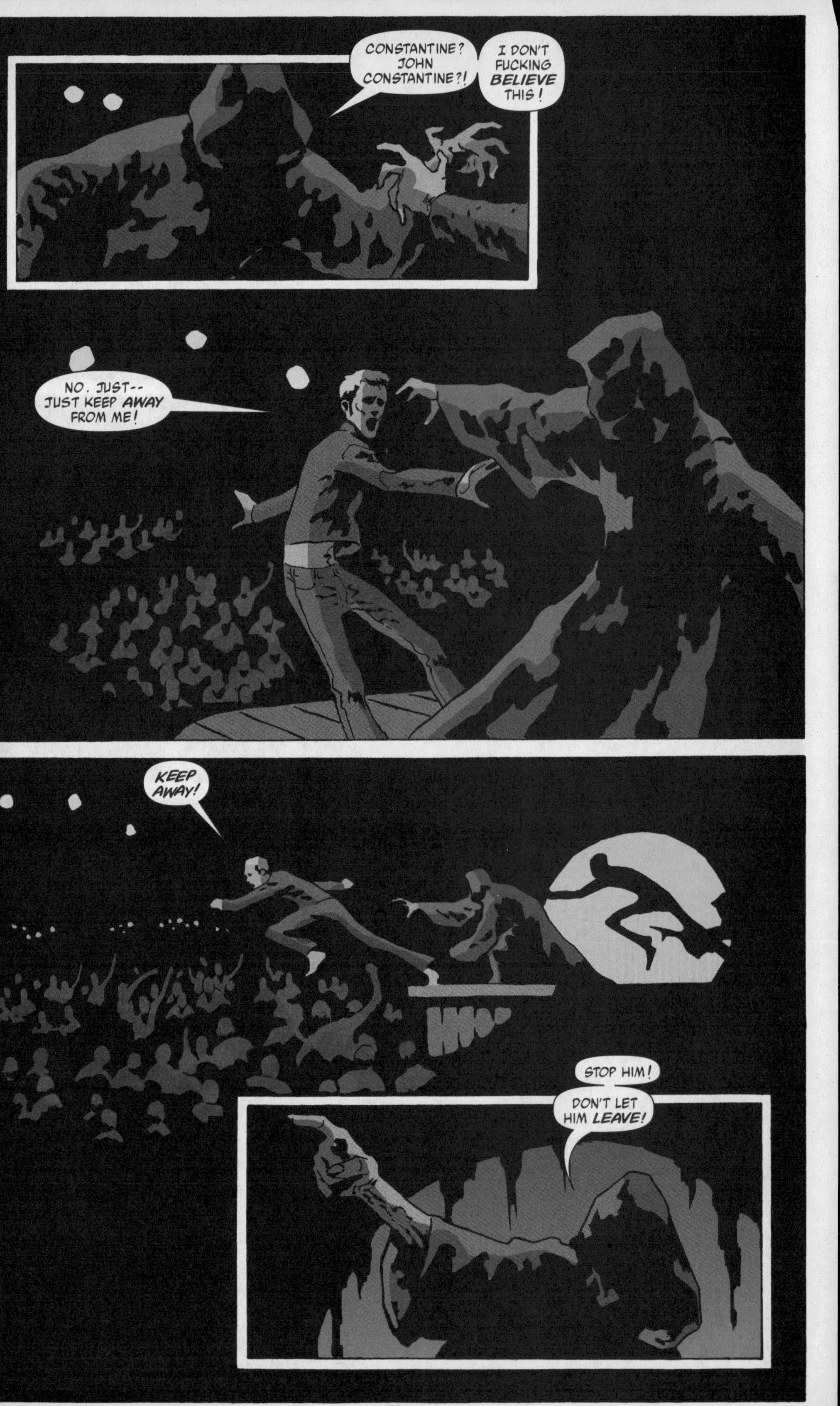
CONSTANTINE? JOHN CONSTANTINE?!
I DON'T FUCKING BELIEVE THIS!
NO. JUST-- JUST KEEP AWAY FROM ME!
KEEP AWAY!
STOP HIM!
DON'T LET HIM LEAVE!

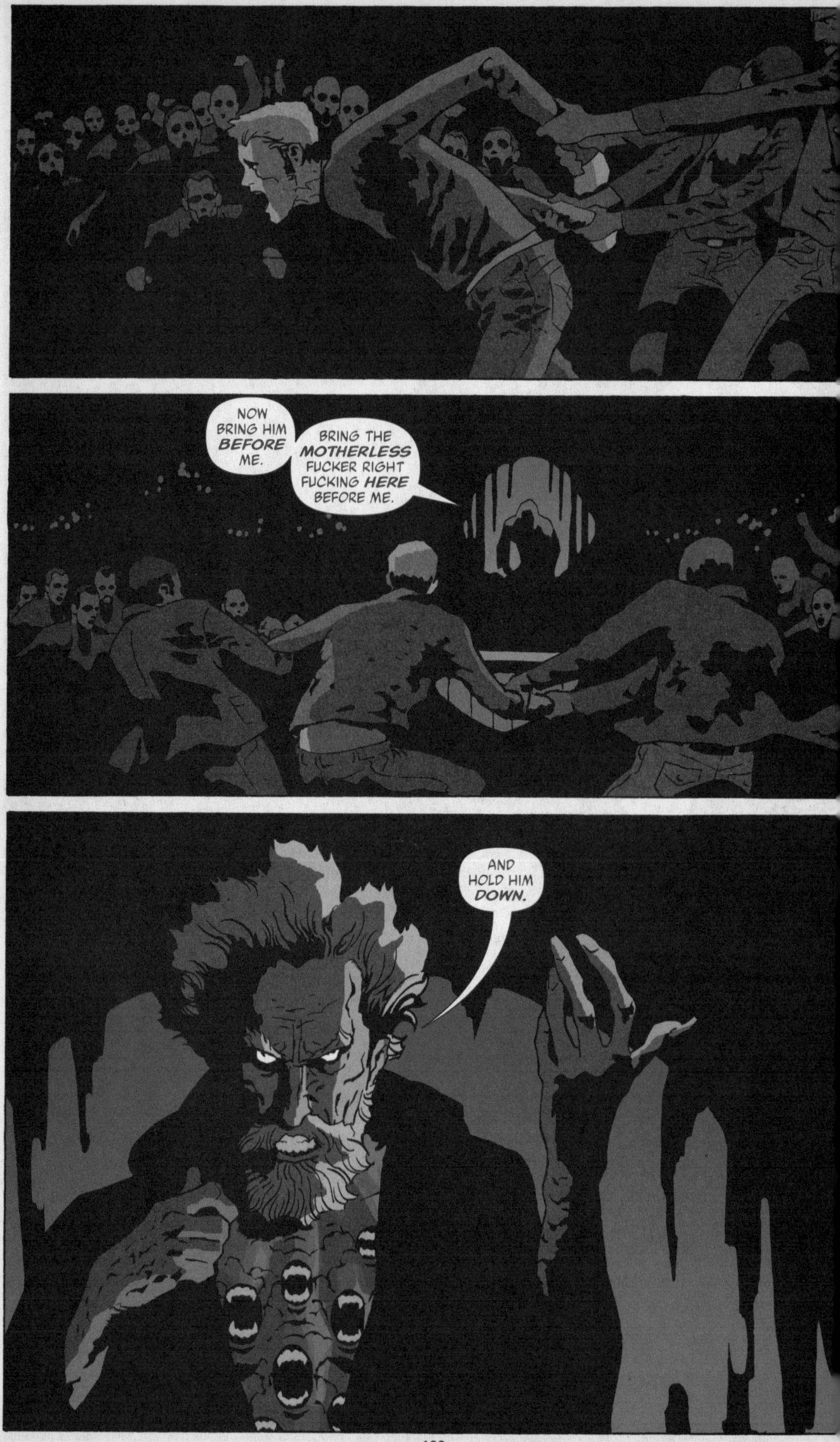
NOW BRING HIM BEFORE ME.
BRING THE MOTHERLESS FUCKER RIGHT FUCKING HERE BEFORE ME.
AND HOLD HIM DOWN.

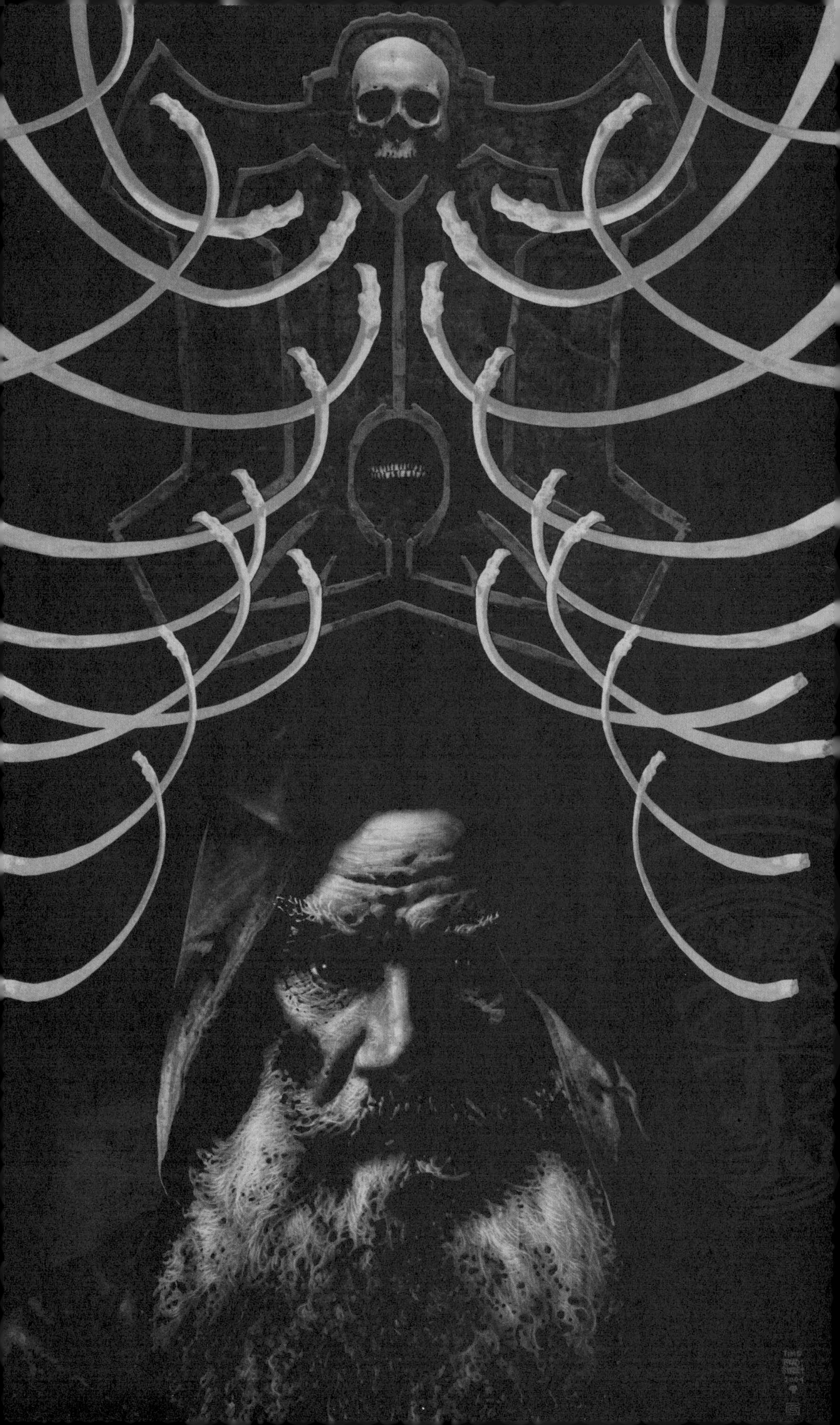

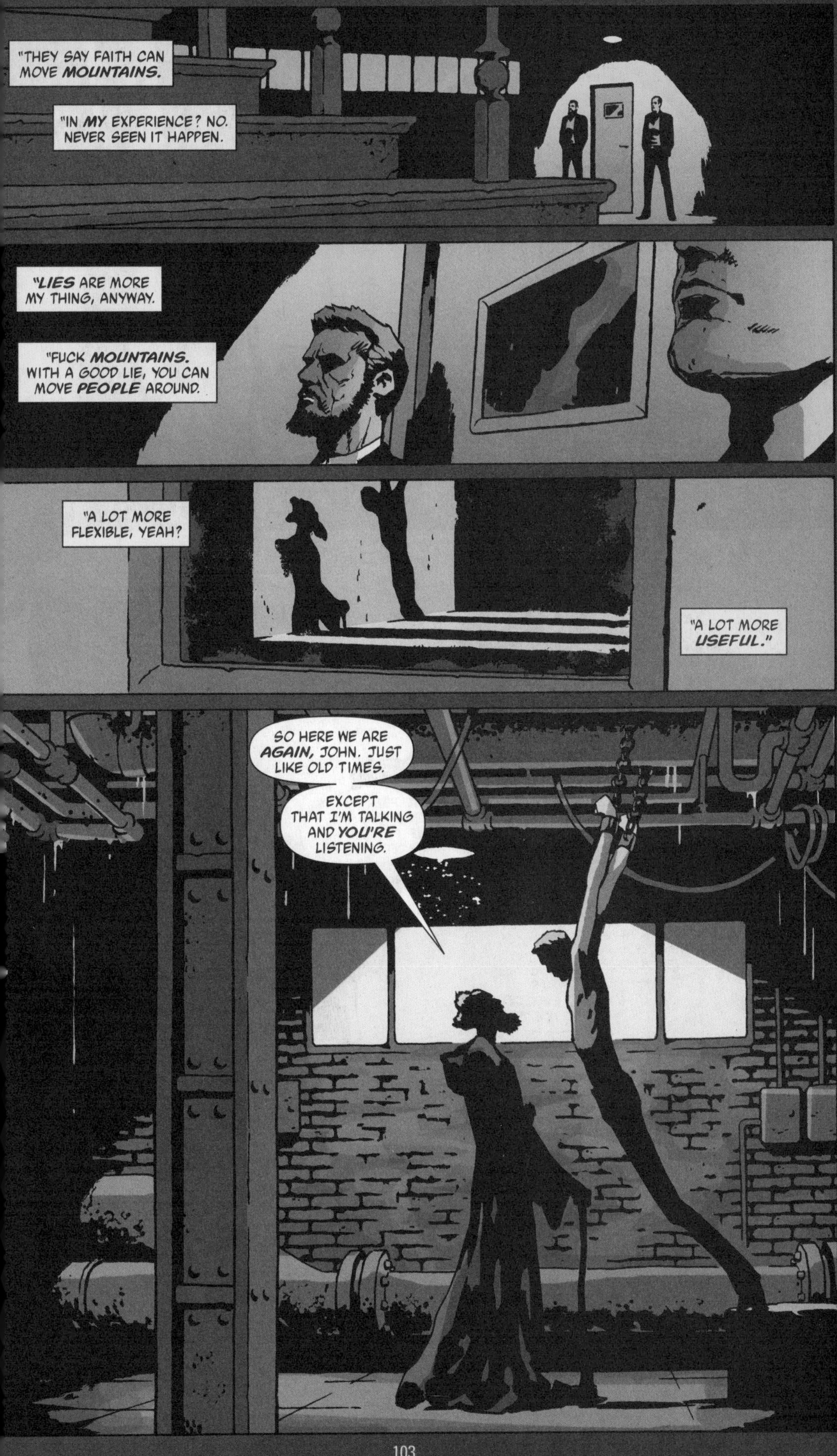
"THEY SAY FAITH CAN MOVE MOUNTAINS.
"IN MY EXPERIENCE? NO. NEVER SEEN IT HAPPEN.
"LIES ARE MORE MY THING, ANYWAY.
"FUCK MOUNTAINS. WITH A GOOD LIE, YOU CAN MOVE PEOPLE AROUND.
"A LOT MORE FLEXIBLE, YEAH?
"A LOT MORE USEFUL."
SO HERE WE ARE AGAIN, JOHN. JUST LIKE OLD TIMES.
EXCEPT THAT I'M TALKING AND YOU'RE LISTENING.

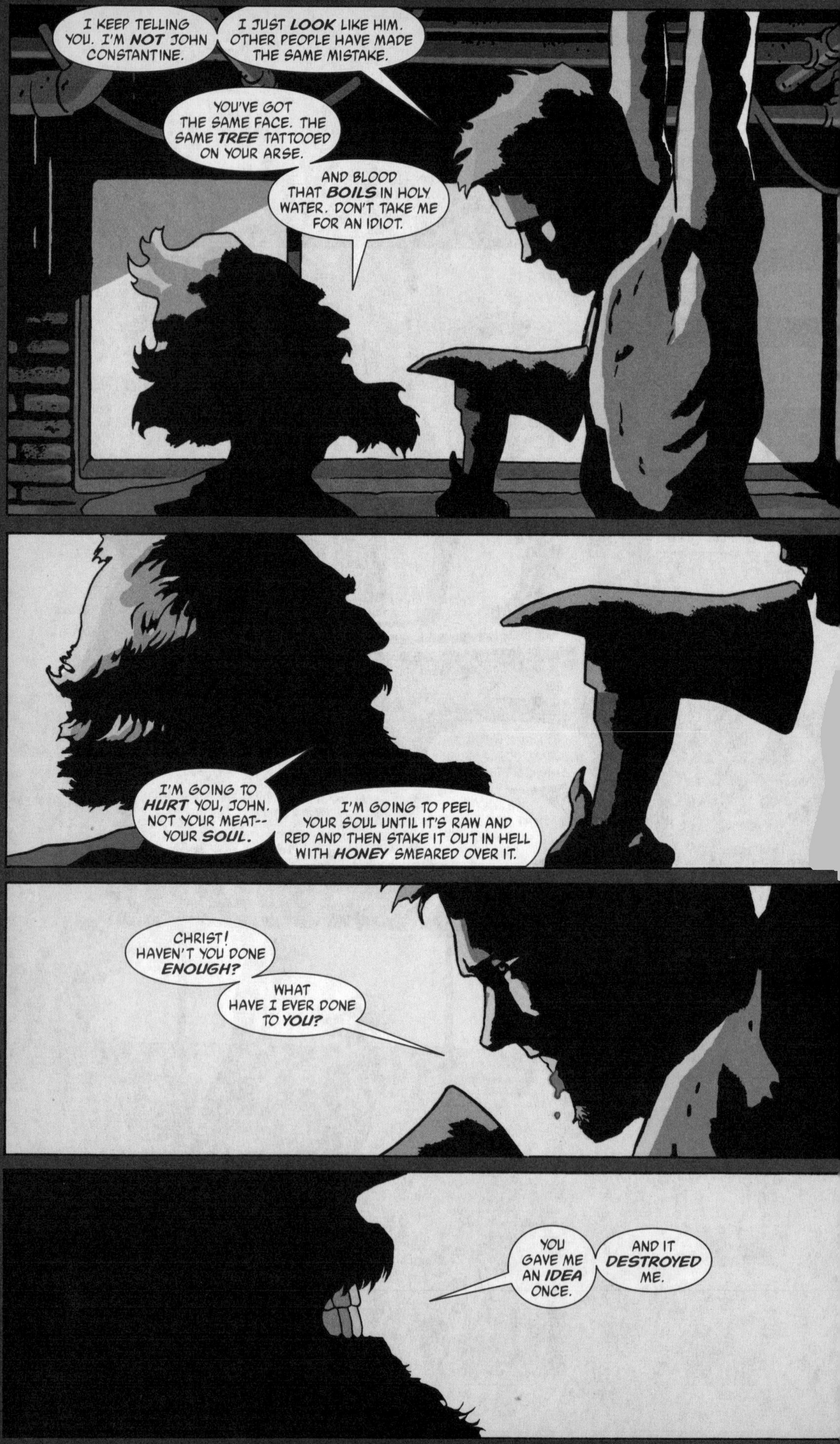
I KEEP TELLING YOU. I'M NOT JOHN CONSTANTINE.
I JUST LOOK LIKE HIM. OTHER PEOPLE HAVE MADE THE SAME MISTAKE.
YOU'VE GOT THE SAME FACE. THE SAME TREE TATTOOED ON YOUR ARSE.
AND BLOOD THAT BOILS IN HOLY WATER. DON'T TAKE ME FOR AN IDIOT.
I'M GOING TO HURT YOU, JOHN. NOT YOUR MEAT-- YOUR SOUL.
I'M GOING TO PEEL YOUR SOUL UNTIL IT'S RAW AND RED AND THEN STAKE IT OUT IN HELL WITH HONEY SMEARED OVER IT.
CHRIST! HAVEN'T YOU DONE ENOUGH?
WHAT HAVE I EVER DONE TO YOU?
YOU GAVE ME AN IDEA ONCE.
AND IT DESTROYED ME.

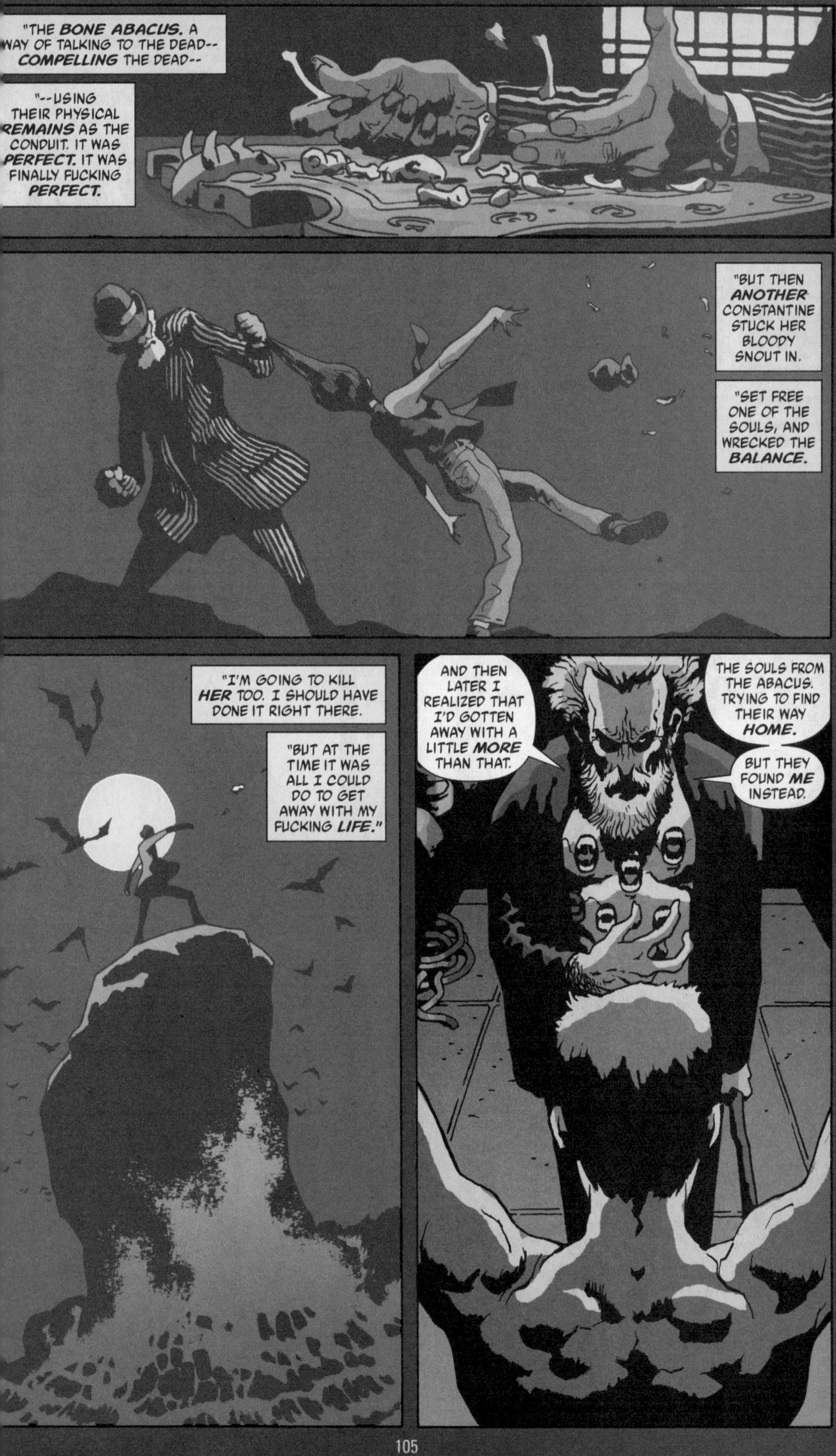
"THE BONE ABACUS. A WAY OF TALKING TO THE DEAD-- COMPELLING THE DEAD--
"--USING THEIR PHYSICAL REMAINS AS THE CONDUIT. IT WAS PERFECT. IT WAS FINALLY FUCKING PERFECT.
"BUT THEN ANOTHER CONSTANTINE STUCK HER BLOODY SNOUT IN.
"SET FREE ONE OF THE SOULS, AND WRECKED THE BALANCE.
"I'M GOING TO KILL HER TOO. I SHOULD HAVE DONE IT RIGHT THERE.
"BUT AT THE TIME IT WAS ALL I COULD DO TO GET AWAY WITH MY FUCKING LIFE."
AND THEN LATER I REALIZED THAT I'D GOTTEN AWAY WITH A LITTLE MORE THAN THAT.
THE SOULS FROM THE ABACUS. TRYING TO FIND THEIR WAY HOME.
BUT THEY FOUND ME INSTEAD.

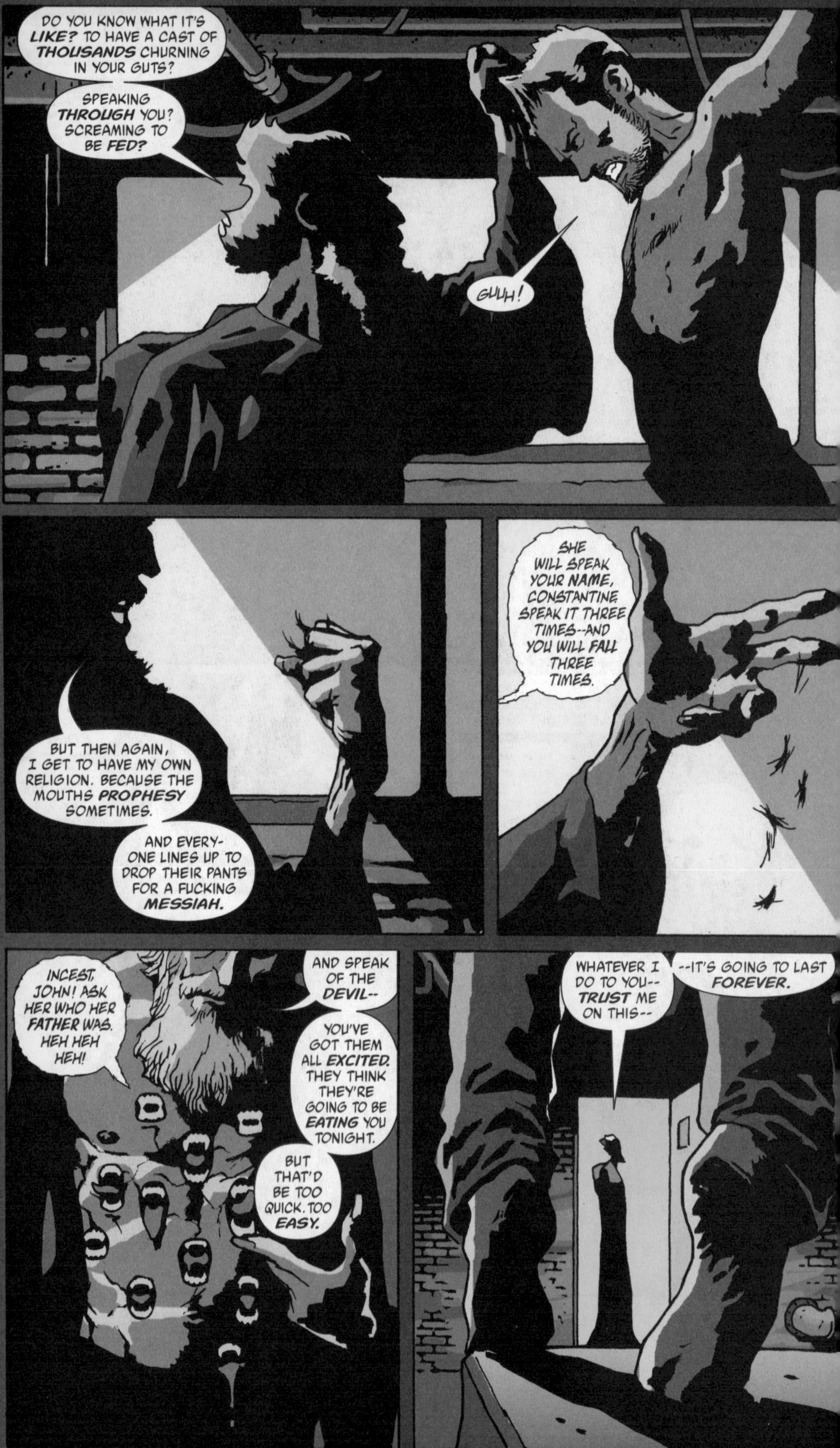
DO YOU KNOW WHAT IT'S LIKE? TO HAVE A CAST OF THOUSANDS CHURNING IN YOUR GUTS?
SPEAKING THROUGH YOU? SCREAMING TO BE FED?
GUUH!
BUT THEN AGAIN, I GET TO HAVE MY OWN RELIGION. BECAUSE THE MOUTHS PROPHESY SOMETIMES.
AND EVERY-ONE LINES UP TO DROP THEIR PANTS FOR A FUCKING MESSIAH.
SHE WILL SPEAK YOUR NAME, CONSTANTINE. SPEAK IT THREE TIMES--AND YOU WILL FALL THREE TIMES.
INCEST, JOHN! ASK HER WHO HER FATHER WAS. HEH HEH HEH!
AND SPEAK OF THE DEVIL--
YOU'VE GOT THEM ALL EXCITED. THEY THINK THEY'RE GOING TO BE EATING YOU TONIGHT.
BUT THAT'D BE TOO QUICK. TOO EASY.
WHATEVER I DO TO YOU-- TRUST ME ON THIS--
--IT'S GOING TO LAST FOREVER.

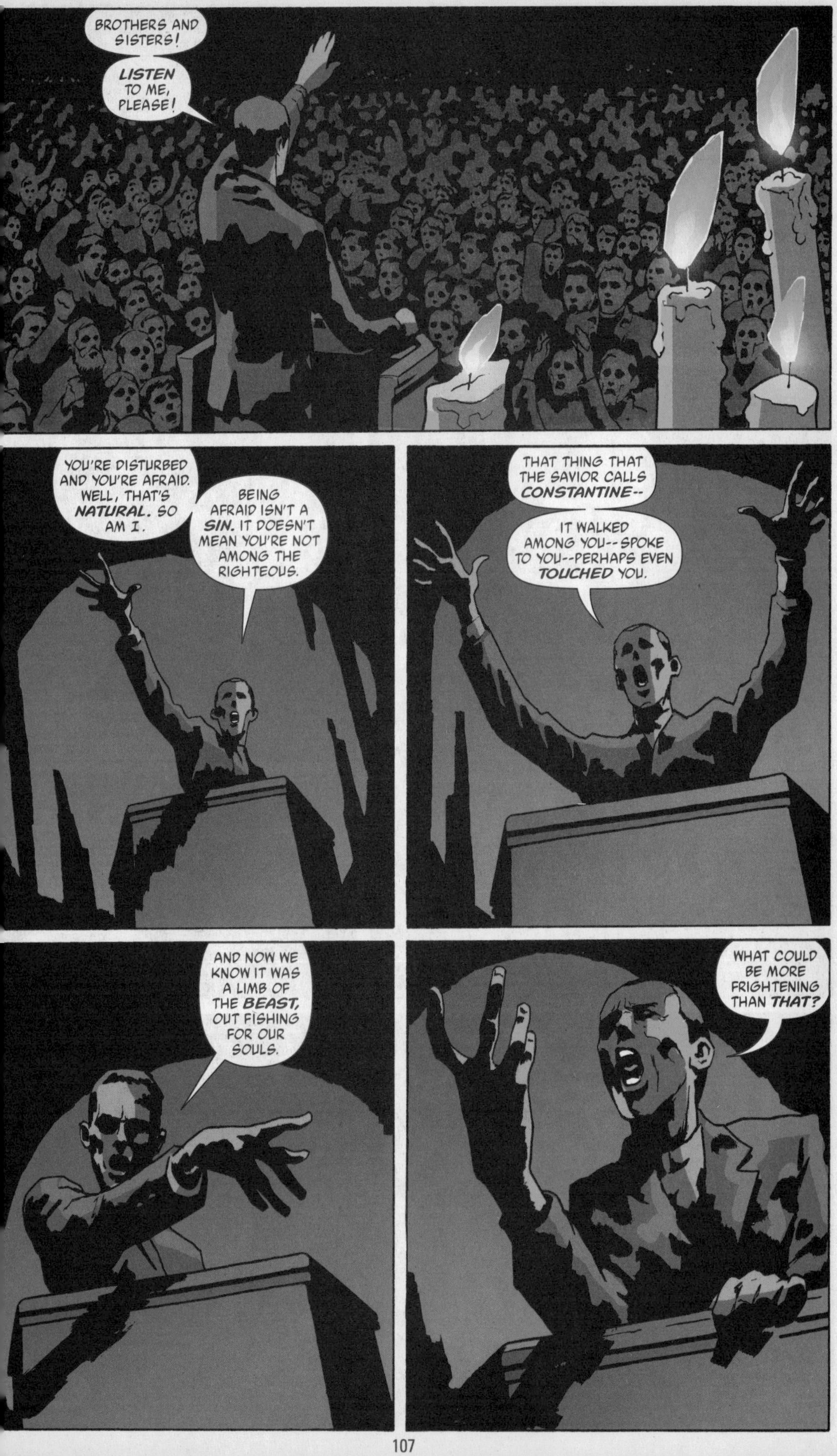
BROTHERS AND SISTERS!
LISTEN TO ME, PLEASE!
YOU'RE DISTURBED AND YOU'RE AFRAID. WELL, THAT'S NATURAL. SO AM I.
BEING AFRAID ISN'T A SIN. IT DOESN'T MEAN YOU'RE NOT AMONG THE RIGHTEOUS.
THAT THING THAT THE SAVIOR CALLS CONSTANTINE--
IT WALKED AMONG YOU--SPOKE TO YOU--PERHAPS EVEN TOUCHED YOU.
AND NOW WE KNOW IT WAS A LIMB OF THE BEAST, OUT FISHING FOR OUR SOULS.
WHAT COULD BE MORE FRIGHTENING THAN THAT?

THE SAVIOR HAS FOUGHT IT *BEFORE.*

THINK OF *THAT.* THINK OF WHAT THAT MEANS.

AN EVIL SO POWERFUL--

--IT CONTENDED AGAINST THE *SAVIOR* AND IT LIVED TO WALK AWAY.

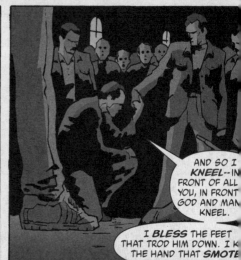

AND SO I *KNEEL*--IN FRONT OF ALL YOU, IN FRONT GOD AND MAN KNEEL.

I *BLESS* THE FEET THAT TROD HIM DOWN. I K THE HAND THAT *SMOTE*

FOR HOW ELS WILL TH SOULS TH FELL TO T BEAST F THEIR W *HOME* AGAIN--

--SAVE BY WALKING THE ROAD OF ITS FOUL *BLOOD?*

AMEN!

AMEN!

AMEN!

AMEN!

AMEN!

AMEN!

AMEN!

AMEN!

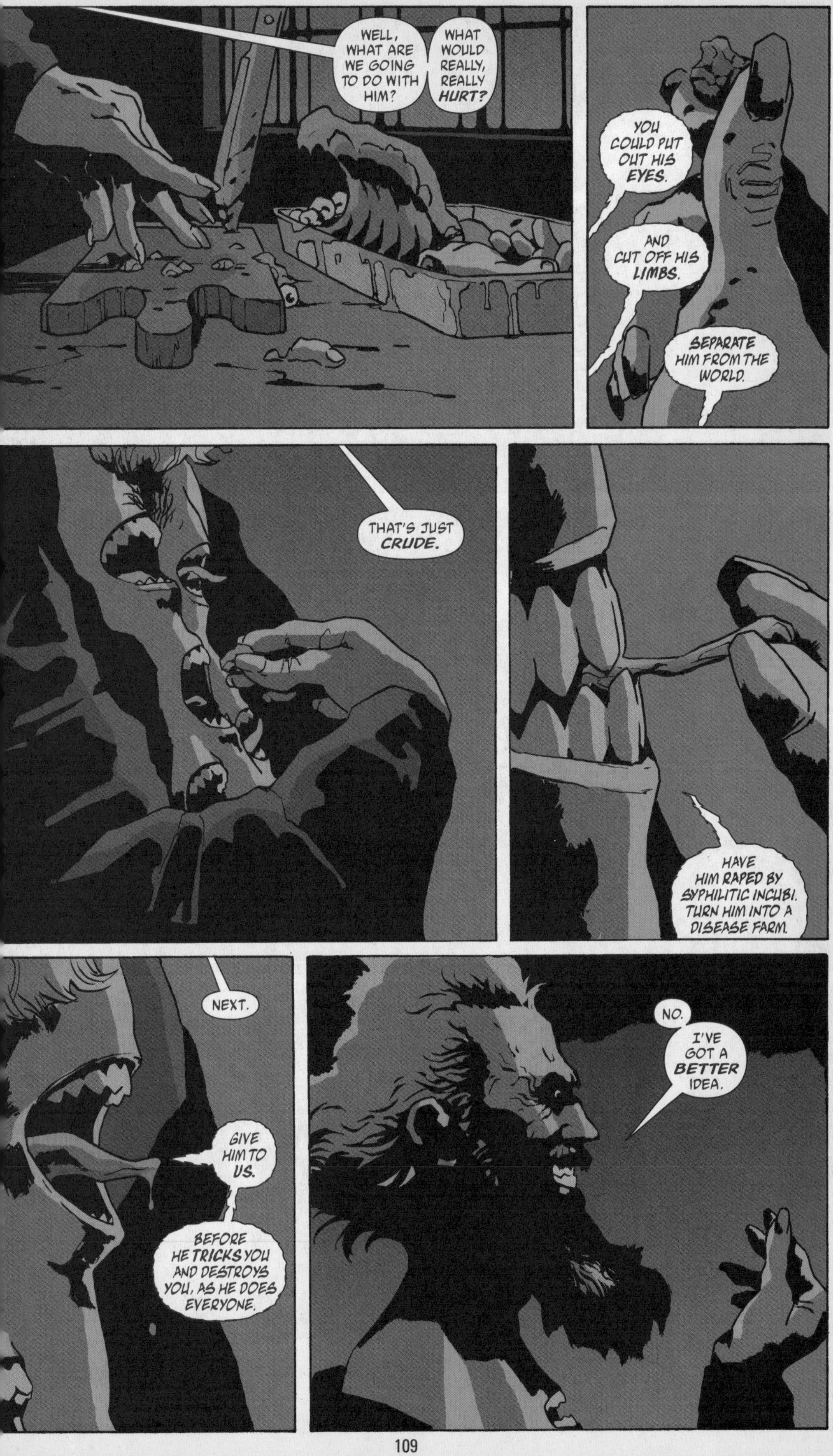

WELL, WHAT ARE WE GOING TO DO WITH HIM?
WHAT WOULD REALLY, REALLY HURT?
YOU COULD PUT OUT HIS EYES.
AND CUT OFF HIS LIMBS.
SEPARATE HIM FROM THE WORLD.
THAT'S JUST CRUDE.
HAVE HIM RAPED BY SYPHILITIC INCUBI. TURN HIM INTO A DISEASE FARM.
NEXT.
GIVE HIM TO US.
BEFORE HE TRICKS YOU AND DESTROYS YOU, AS HE DOES EVERYONE.
NO.
I'VE GOT A BETTER IDEA.

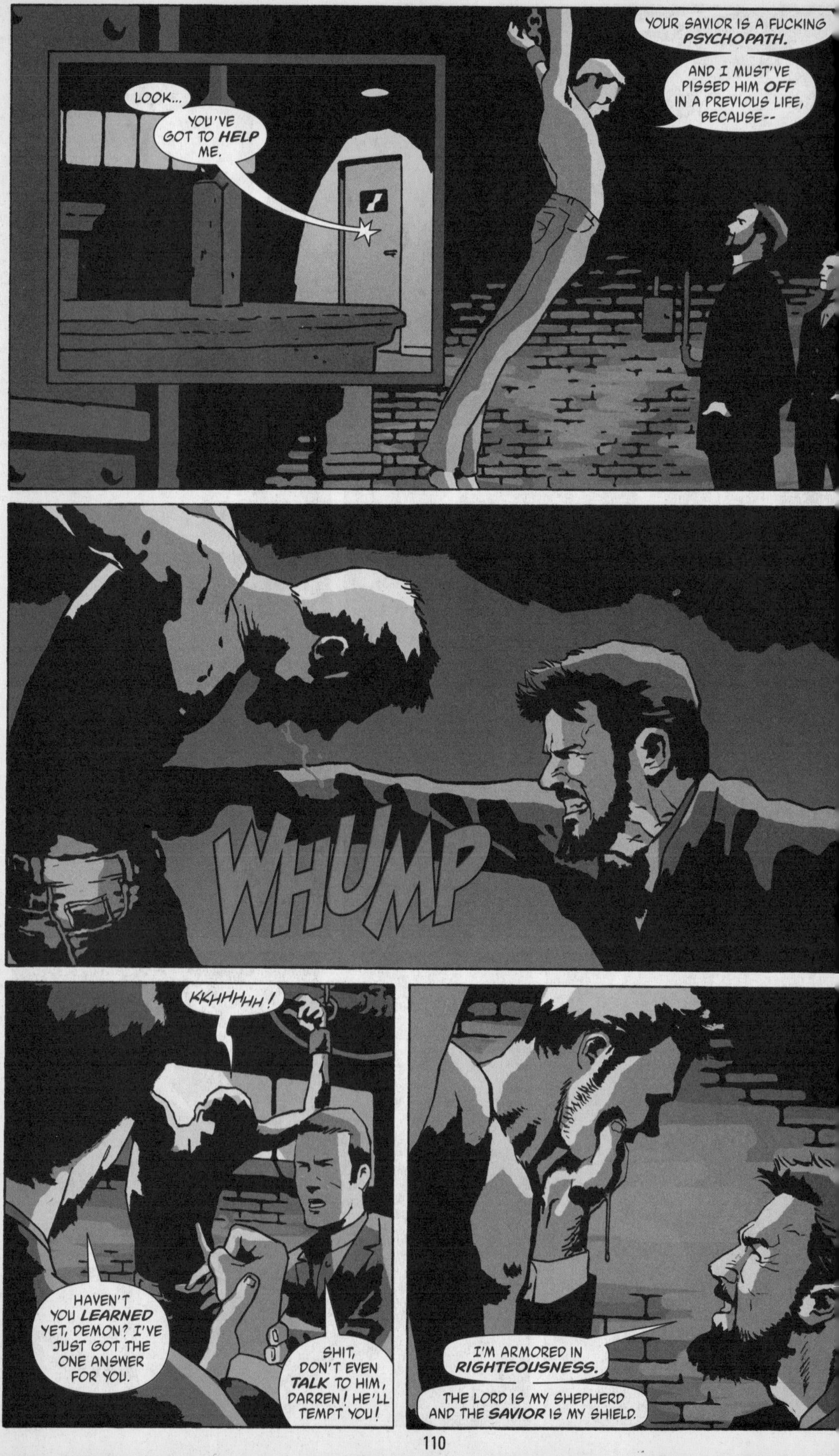
YOUR SAVIOR IS A FUCKING PSYCHOPATH.
AND I MUST'VE PISSED HIM OFF IN A PREVIOUS LIFE, BECAUSE--
LOOK...
YOU'VE GOT TO HELP ME.
WHUMP
KKHHHHH!
HAVEN'T YOU LEARNED YET, DEMON? I'VE JUST GOT THE ONE ANSWER FOR YOU.
SHIT, DON'T EVEN TALK TO HIM, DARREN! HE'LL TEMPT YOU!
I'M ARMORED IN RIGHTEOUSNESS.
THE LORD IS MY SHEPHERD AND THE SAVIOR IS MY SHIELD.

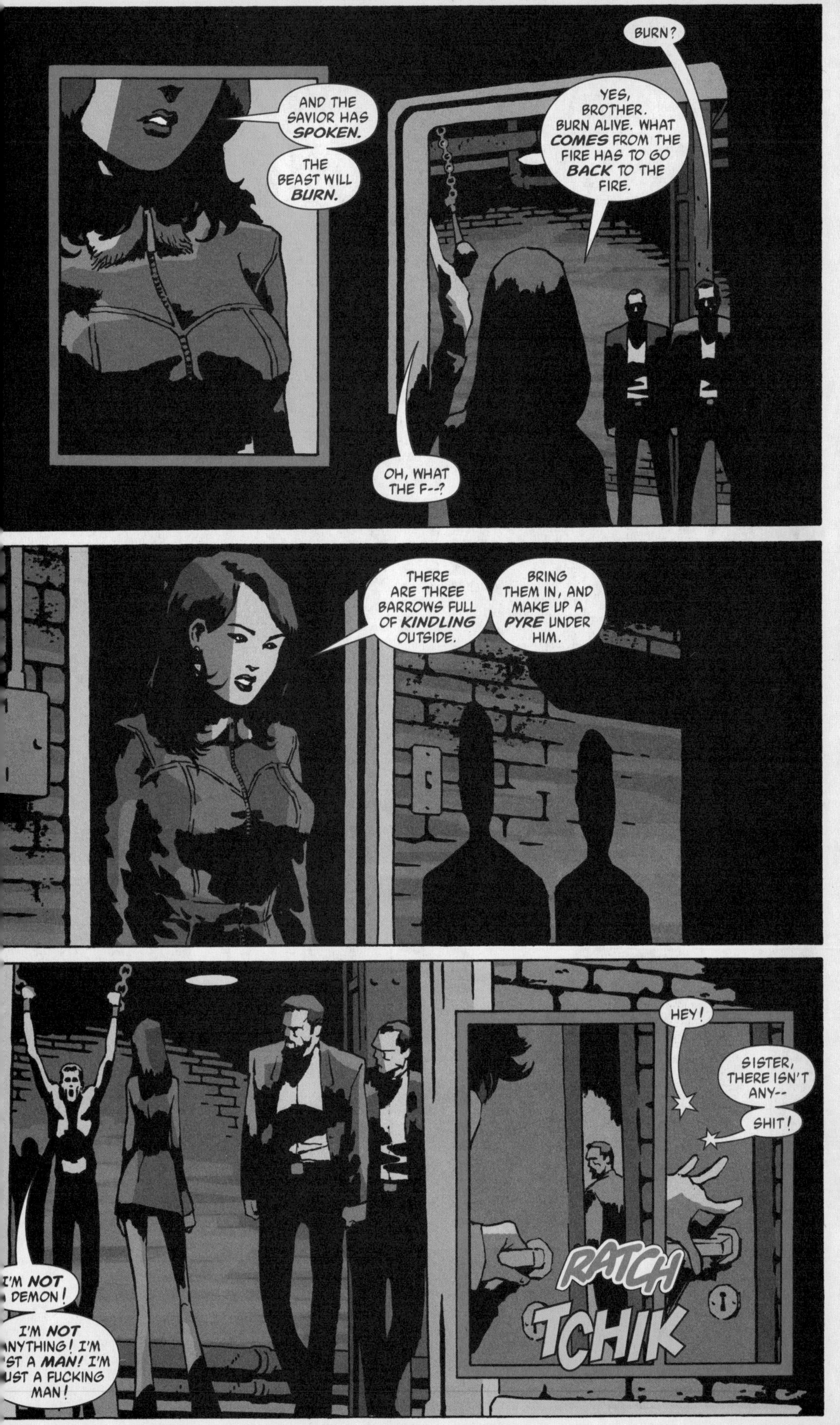
AND THE SAVIOR HAS SPOKEN.
THE BEAST WILL BURN.
BURN?
YES, BROTHER. BURN ALIVE. WHAT COMES FROM THE FIRE HAS TO GO BACK TO THE FIRE.
OH, WHAT THE F--?
THERE ARE THREE BARROWS FULL OF KINDLING OUTSIDE.
BRING THEM IN, AND MAKE UP A PYRE UNDER HIM.
I'M NOT DEMON!
I'M NOT NYTHING! I'M ST A MAN! I'M UST A FUCKING MAN!
HEY!
SISTER, THERE ISN'T ANY--
SHIT!
RATCH
TCHIK

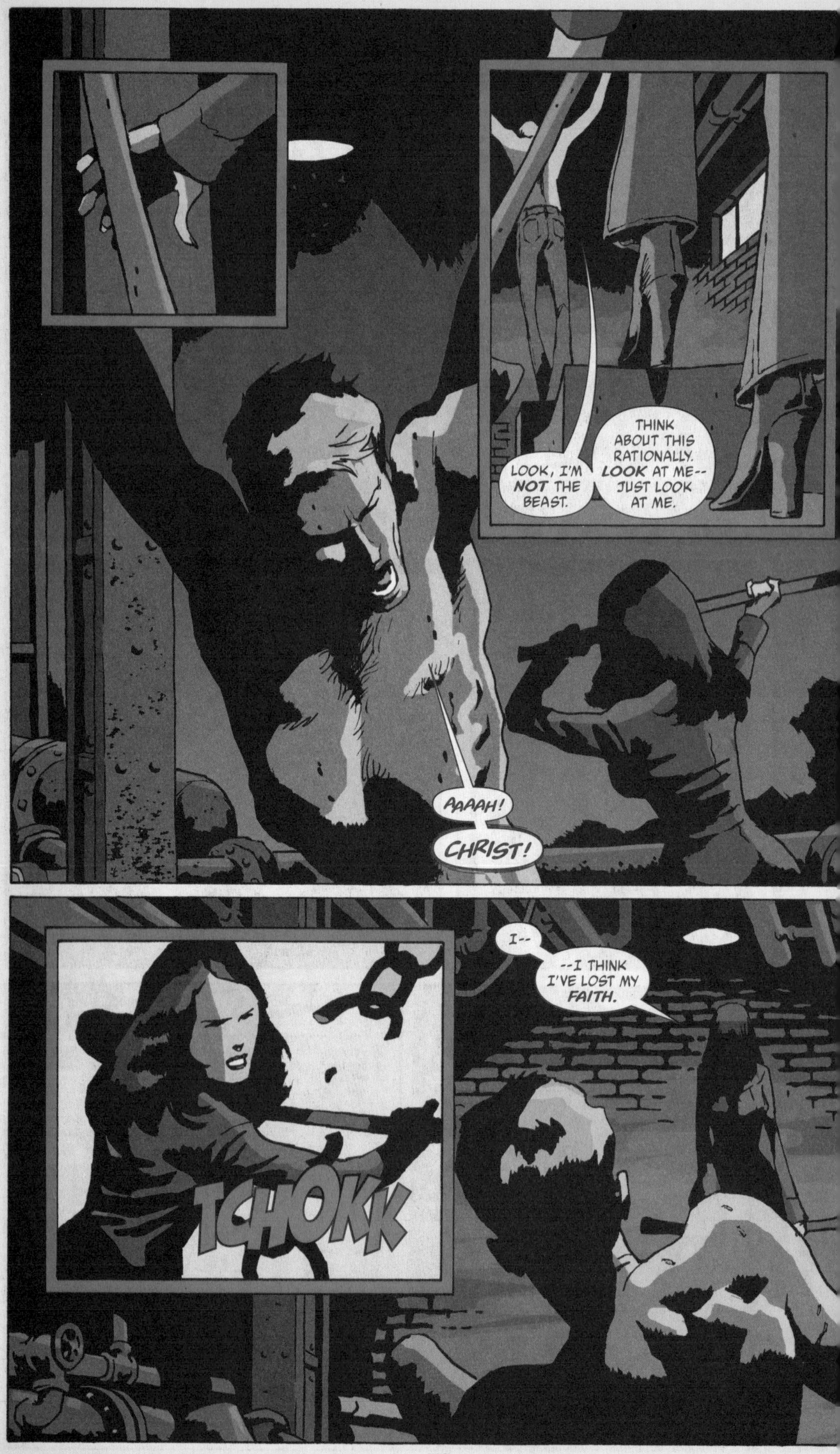
LOOK, I'M NOT THE BEAST.
THINK ABOUT THIS RATIONALLY. LOOK AT ME-- JUST LOOK AT ME.
AAAAH!
CHRIST!
TCHOKK
I--
--I THINK I'VE LOST MY FAITH.

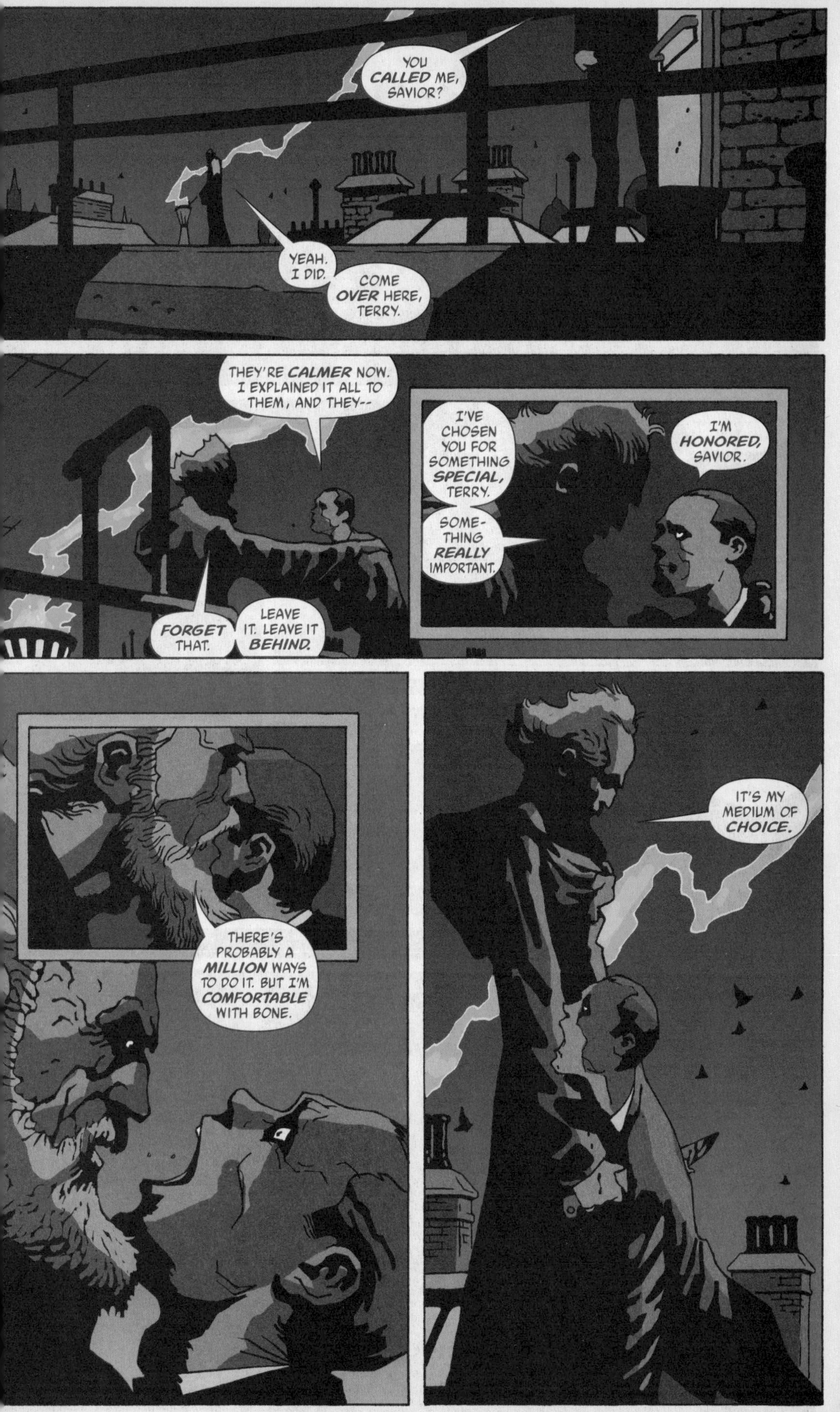
YOU CALLED ME, SAVIOR?
YEAH. I DID.
COME OVER HERE, TERRY.
THEY'RE CALMER NOW. I EXPLAINED IT ALL TO THEM, AND THEY--
FORGET THAT.
LEAVE IT. LEAVE IT BEHIND.
I'VE CHOSEN YOU FOR SOMETHING SPECIAL, TERRY.
SOME-THING REALLY IMPORTANT.
I'M HONORED, SAVIOR.
THERE'S PROBABLY A MILLION WAYS TO DO IT. BUT I'M COMFORTABLE WITH BONE.
IT'S MY MEDIUM OF CHOICE.

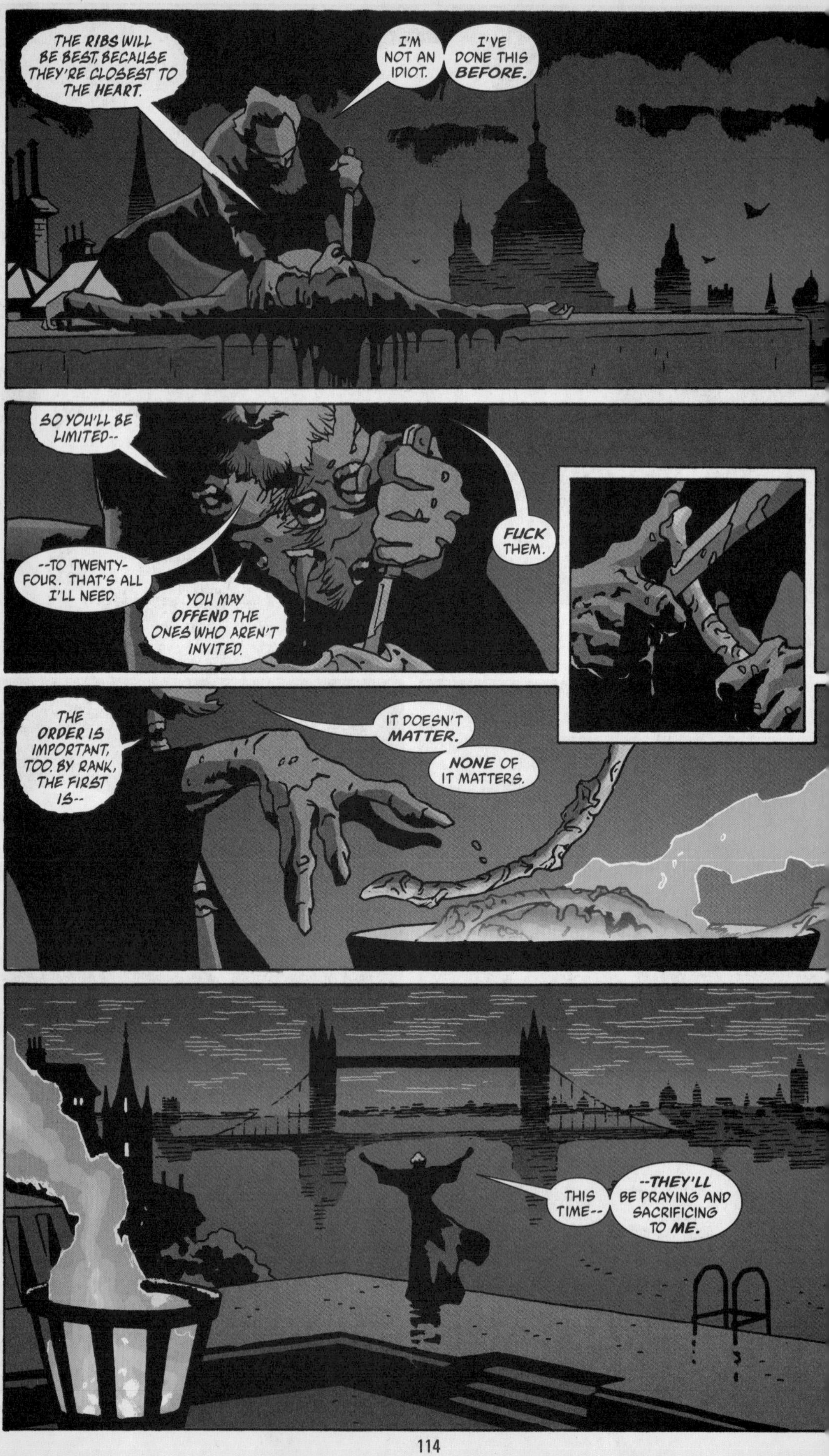
THE RIBS WILL BE BEST, BECAUSE THEY'RE CLOSEST TO THE HEART.
I'M NOT AN IDIOT.
I'VE DONE THIS BEFORE.
SO YOU'LL BE LIMITED--
--TO TWENTY-FOUR. THAT'S ALL I'LL NEED.
YOU MAY OFFEND THE ONES WHO AREN'T INVITED.
FUCK THEM.
THE ORDER IS IMPORTANT, TOO. BY RANK, THE FIRST IS--
IT DOESN'T MATTER.
NONE OF IT MATTERS.
THIS TIME--
--THEY'LL BE PRAYING AND SACRIFICING TO ME.

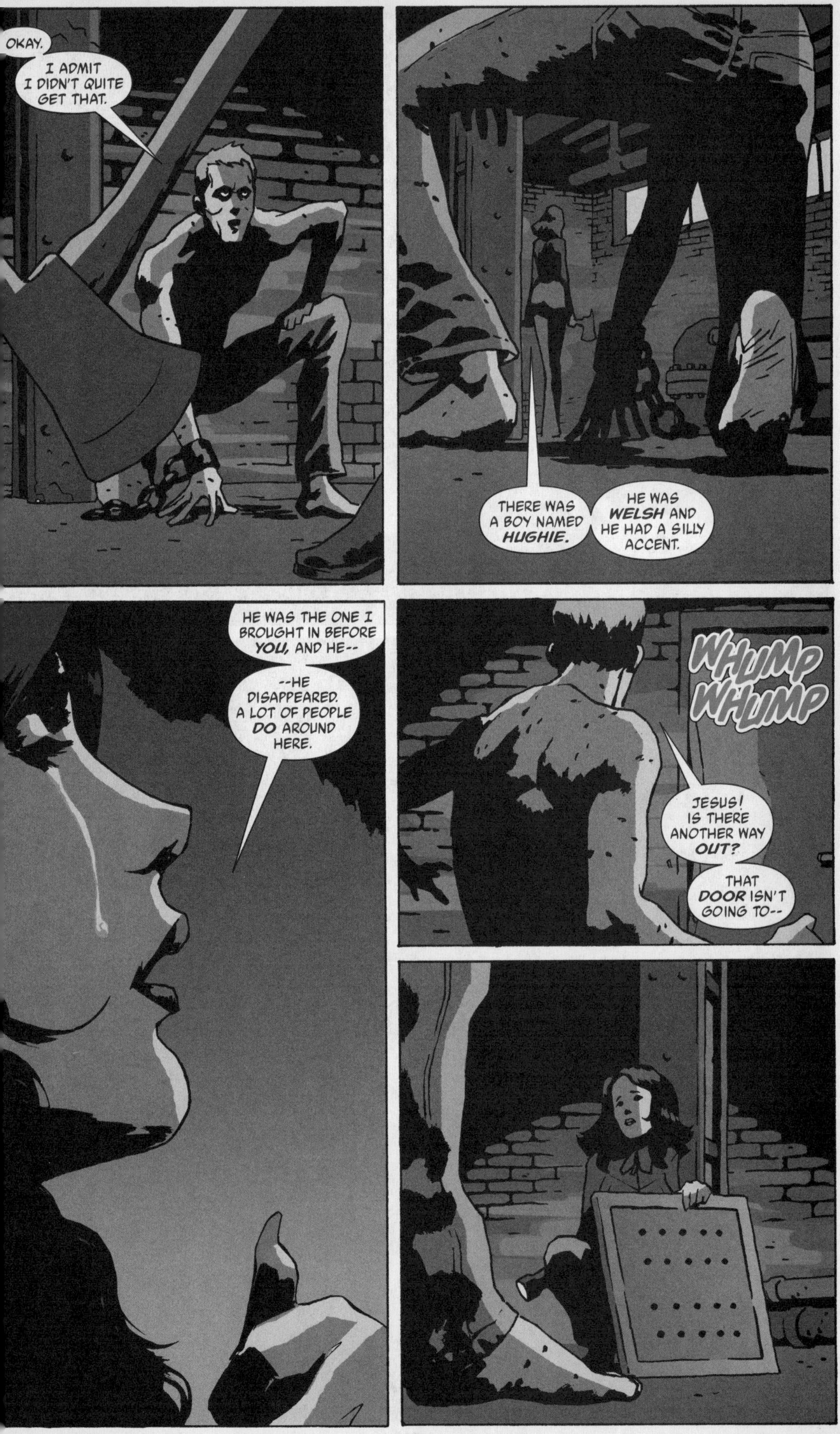
OKAY.
I ADMIT I DIDN'T QUITE GET THAT.
THERE WAS A BOY NAMED HUGHIE.
HE WAS WELSH AND HE HAD A SILLY ACCENT.
HE WAS THE ONE I BROUGHT IN BEFORE YOU, AND HE--
--HE DISAPPEARED. A LOT OF PEOPLE DO AROUND HERE.
WHUMP WHUMP
JESUS! IS THERE ANOTHER WAY OUT?
THAT DOOR ISN'T GOING TO--

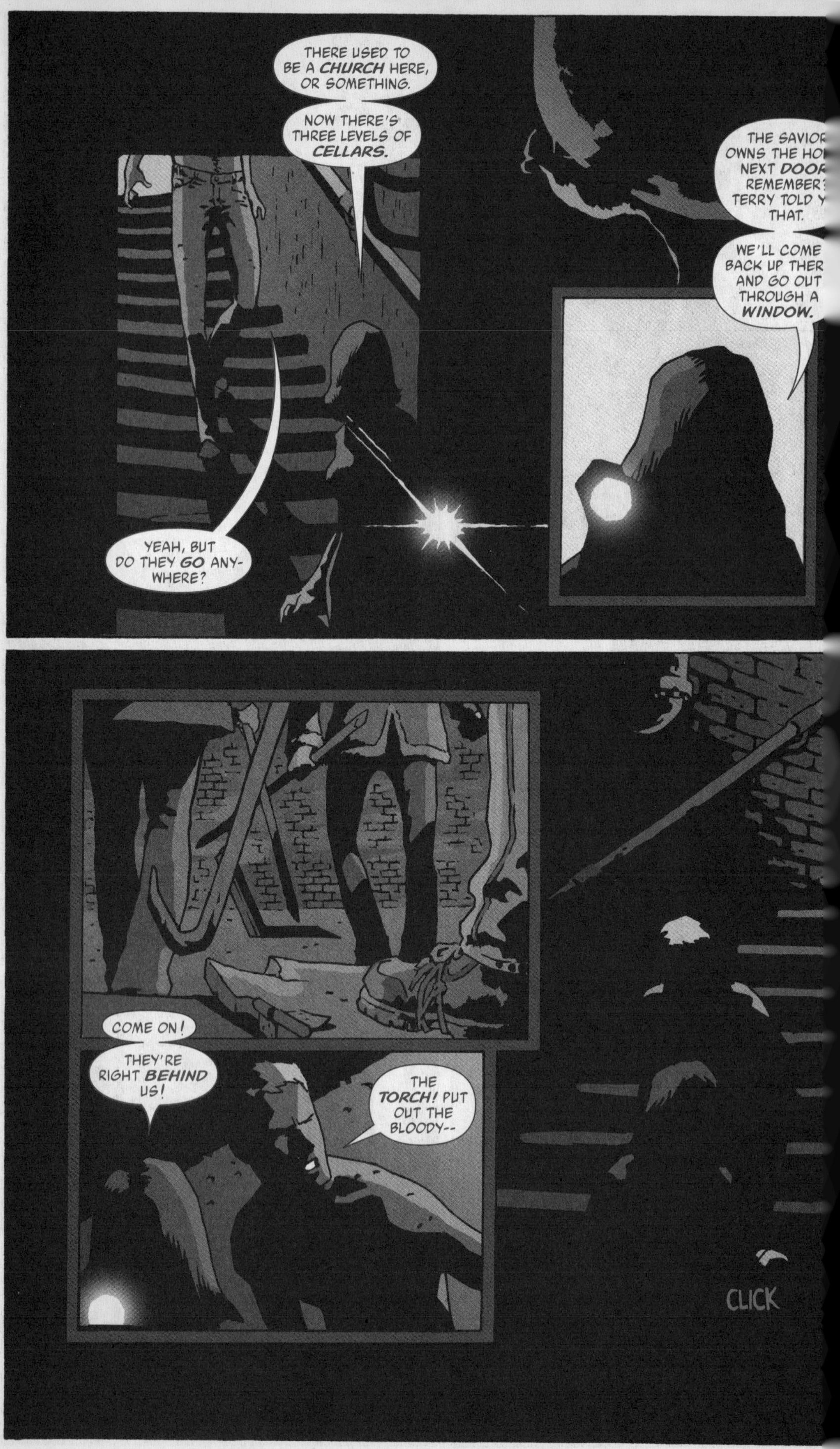
THERE USED TO BE A **CHURCH** HERE, OR SOMETHING.
NOW THERE'S THREE LEVELS OF **CELLARS.**
YEAH, BUT DO THEY **GO** ANY-WHERE?
THE SAVIOR OWNS THE HO NEXT **DOOR** REMEMBER? TERRY TOLD Y THAT.
WE'LL COME BACK UP THER AND GO OUT THROUGH A **WINDOW.**
COME ON!
THEY'RE RIGHT **BEHIND** US!
THE **TORCH!** PUT OUT THE BLOODY--
CLICK

OH.
THIS-- THIS ISN'T THE RIGHT WAY.
WELL, WE CAN'T GO BACK. WE'LL HAVE TO TRY THE LOWER LEVELS.
BUT I DON'T KNOW THEM!
THIS WAY!
TAKE IT SLOW, WE'LL GET THEM.
THAT BITCH IS GOING TO BURN FOR THIS!

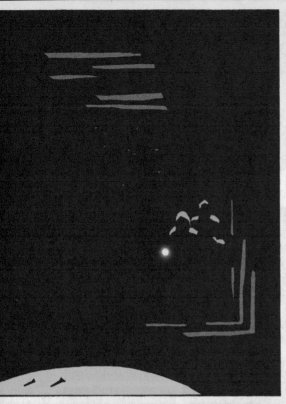

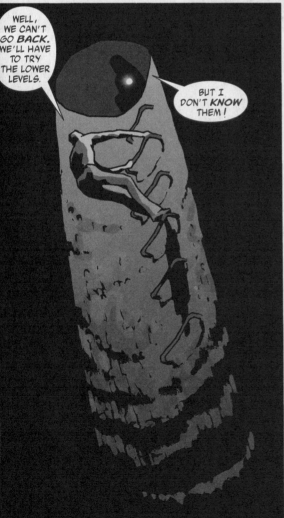

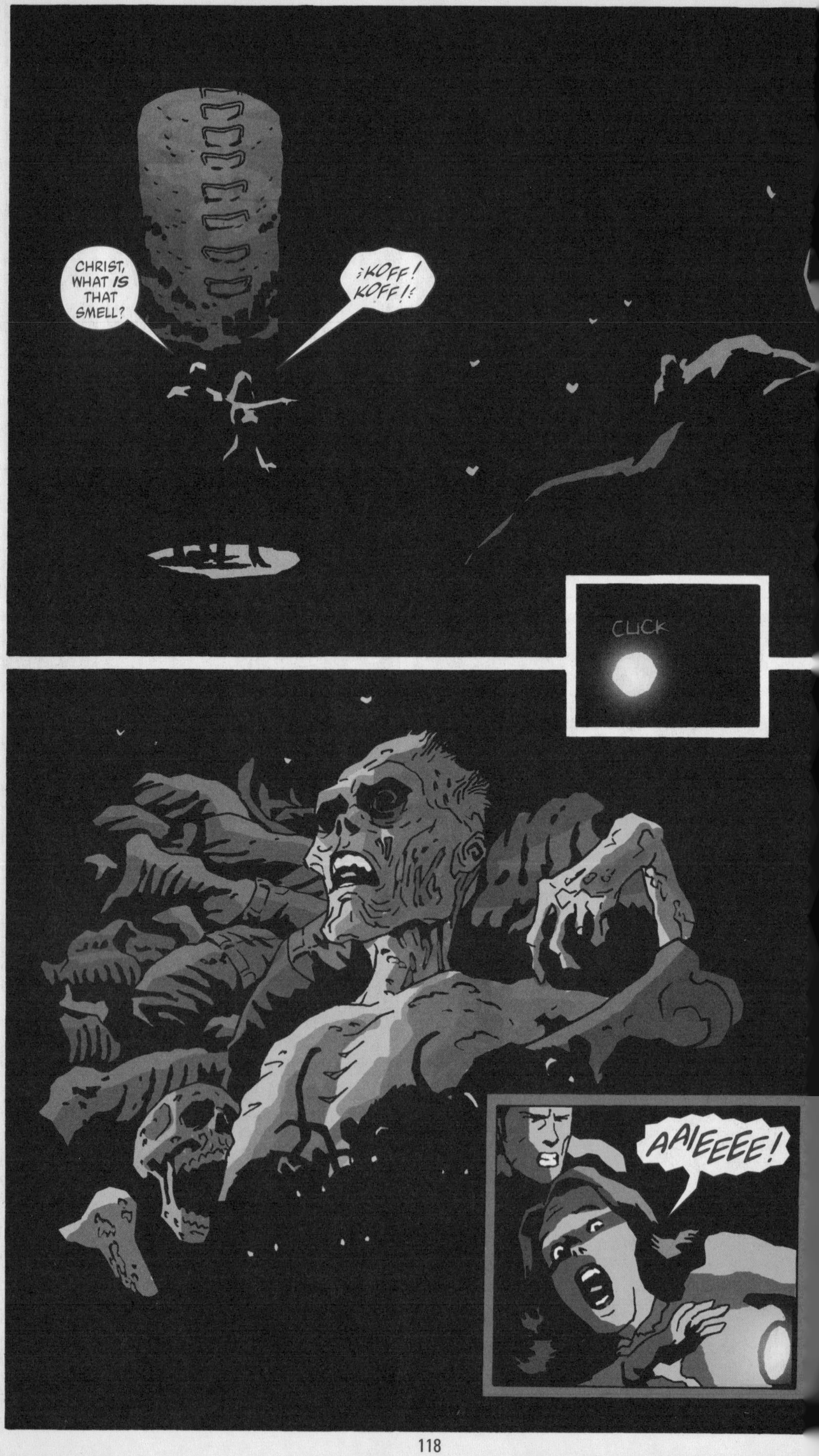
CHRIST, WHAT IS THAT SMELL?
KOFF! KOFF!
CLICK
AAIEEEE!

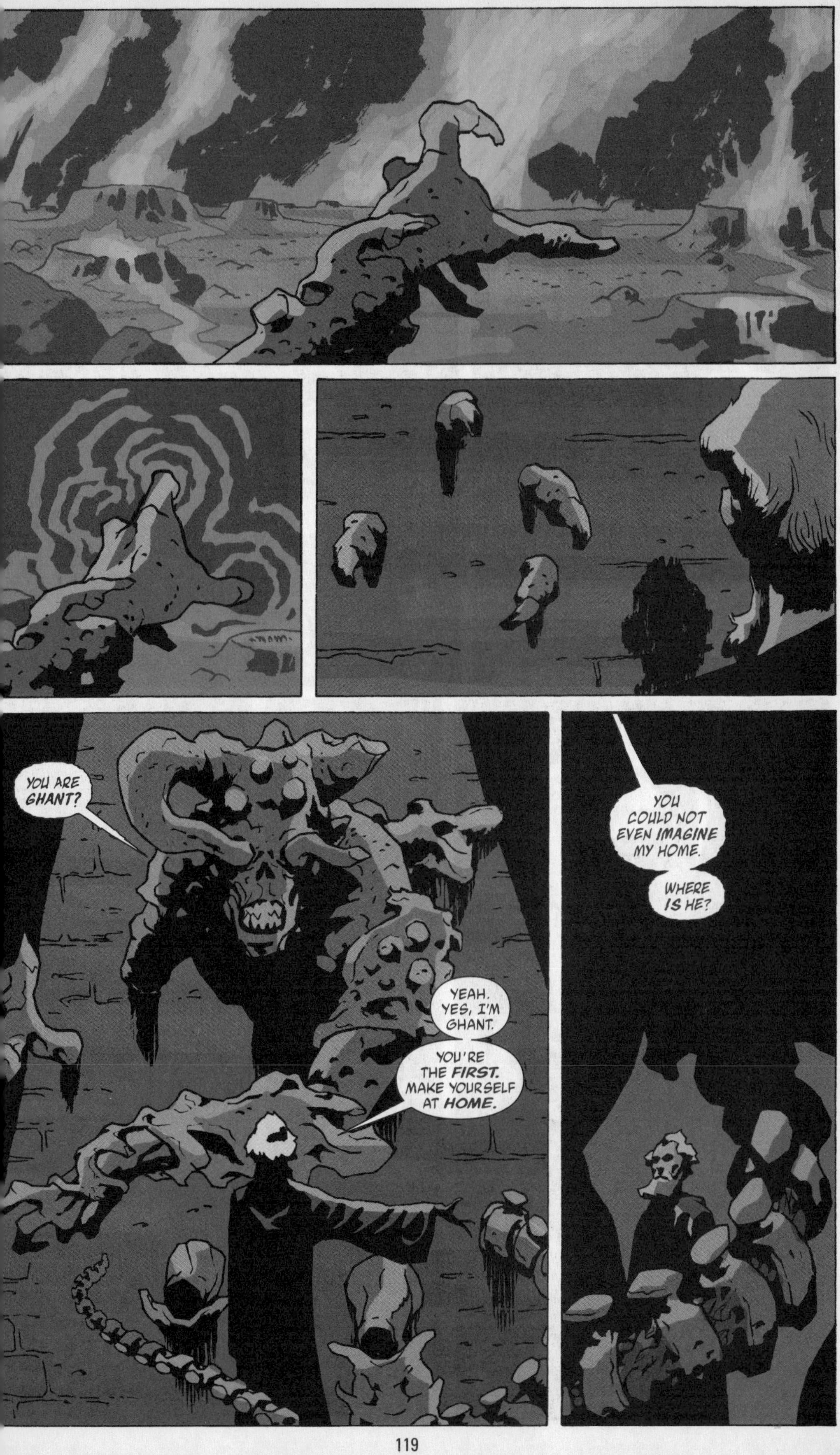
YOU ARE GHANT?
YEAH. YES, I'M GHANT.
YOU'RE THE FIRST. MAKE YOURSELF AT HOME.
YOU COULD NOT EVEN IMAGINE MY HOME.
WHERE IS HE?

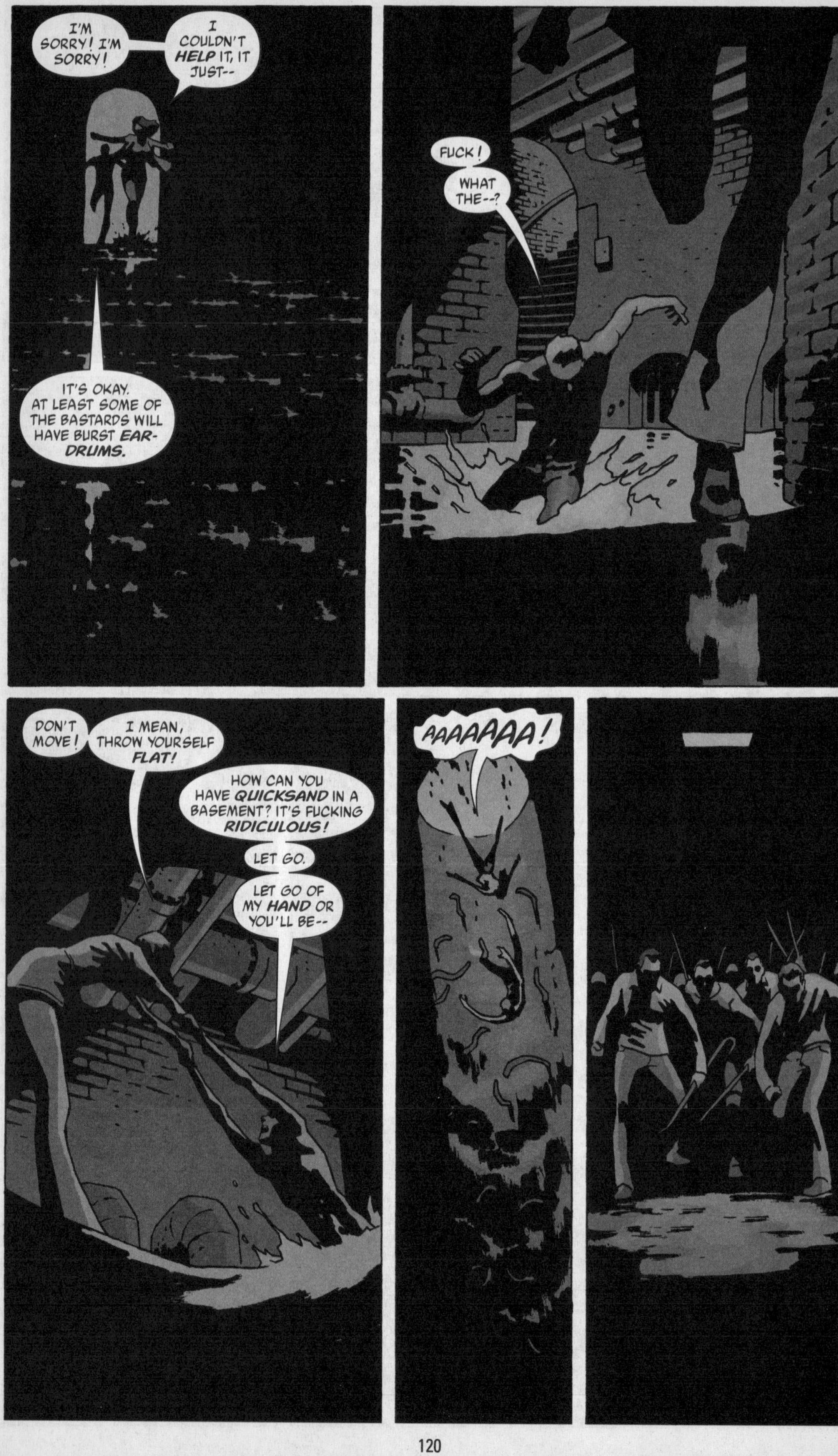
I'M SORRY! I'M SORRY!
I COULDN'T HELP IT, IT JUST--
IT'S OKAY. AT LEAST SOME OF THE BASTARDS WILL HAVE BURST EAR-DRUMS.
FUCK!
WHAT THE--?
DON'T MOVE!
I MEAN, THROW YOURSELF FLAT!
HOW CAN YOU HAVE QUICKSAND IN A BASEMENT? IT'S FUCKING RIDICULOUS!
LET GO.
LET GO OF MY HAND OR YOU'LL BE--
AAAAAAA!

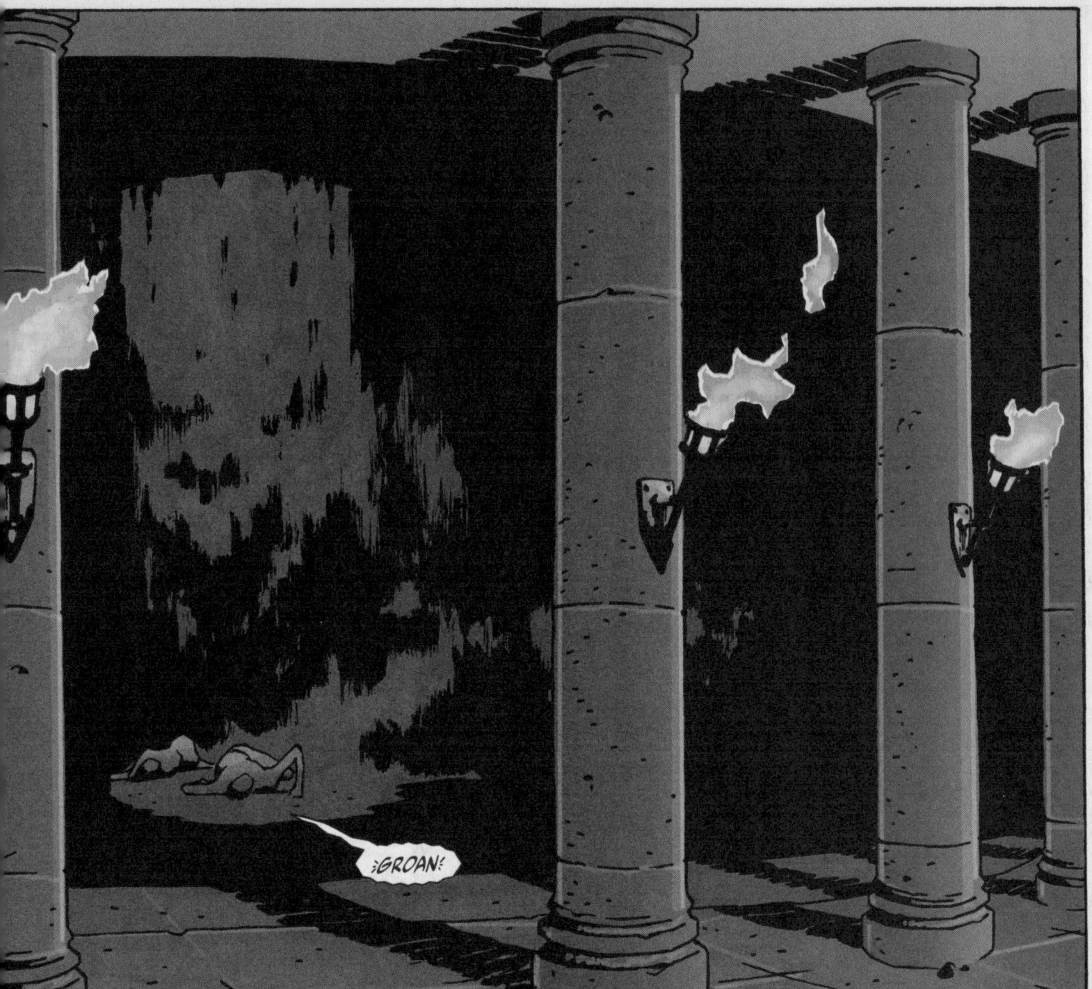
GROAN

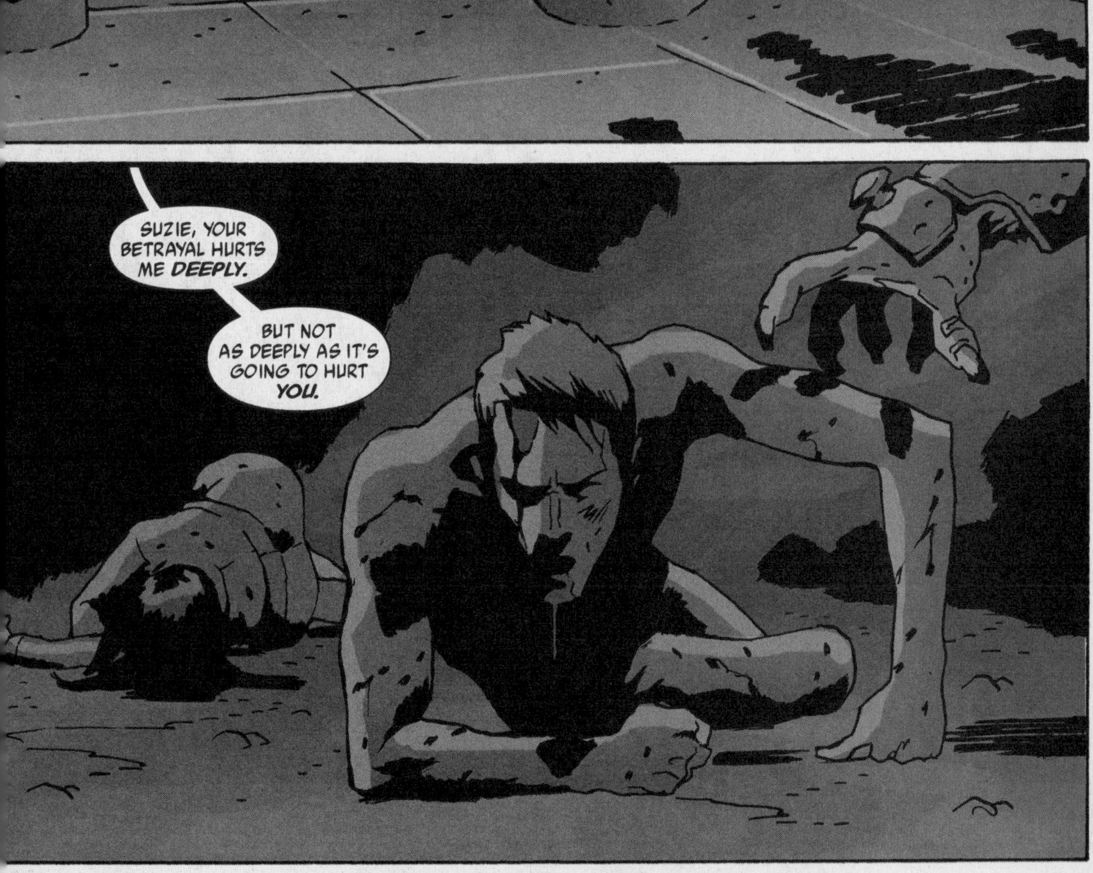
SUZIE, YOUR BETRAYAL HURTS ME DEEPLY.
BUT NOT AS DEEPLY AS IT'S GOING TO HURT YOU.

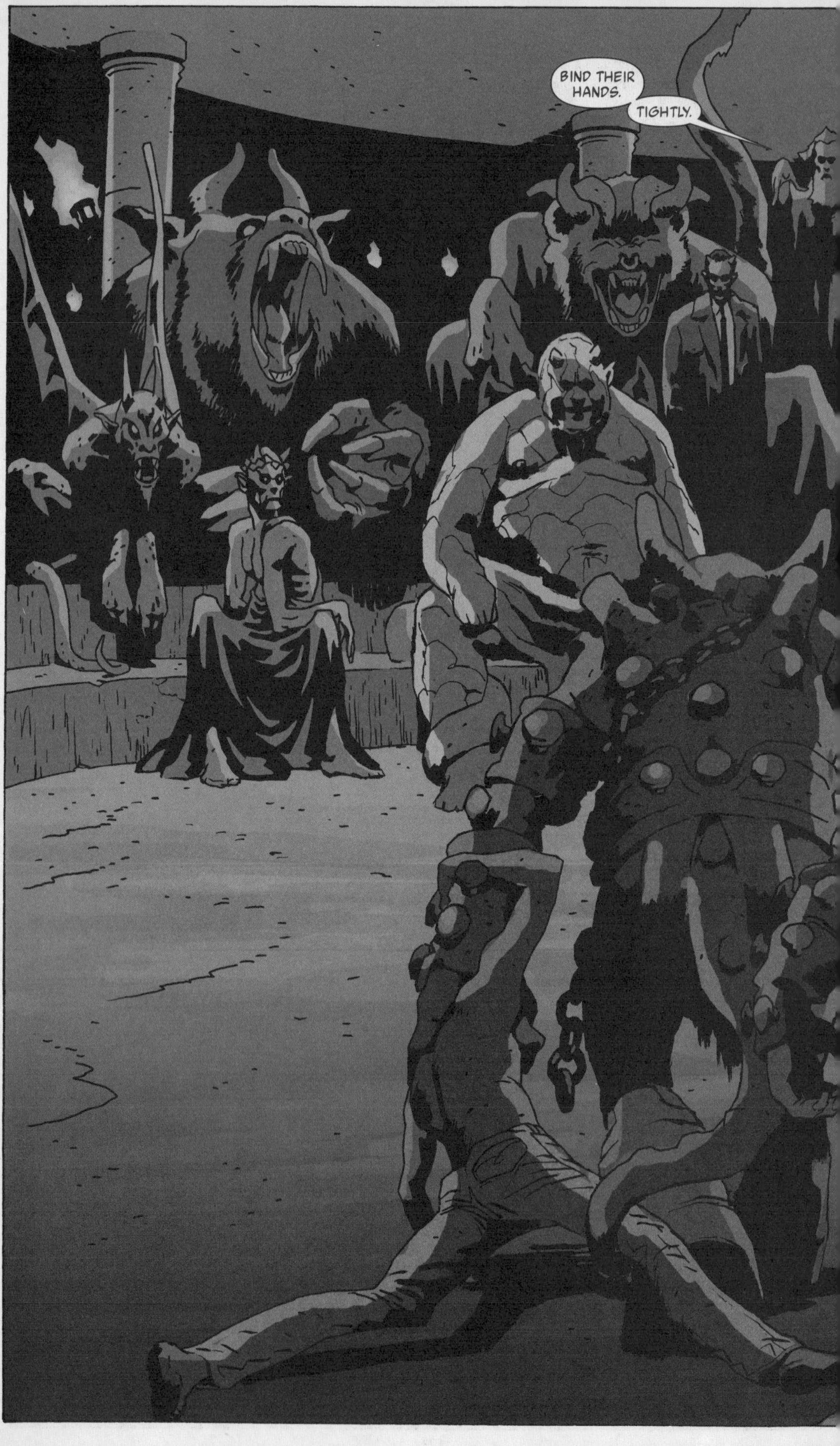

BIND THEIR HANDS.
TIGHTLY.

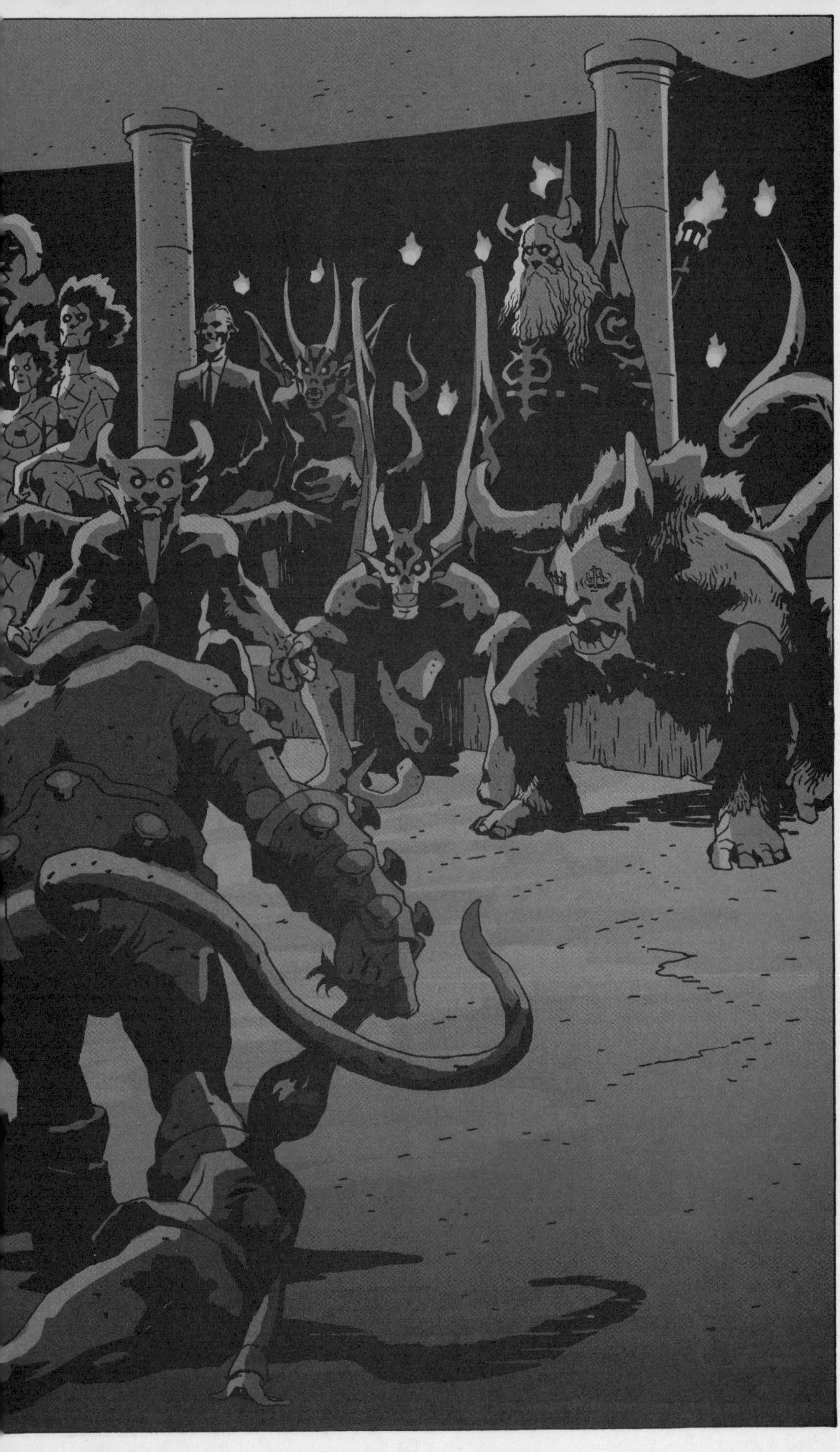

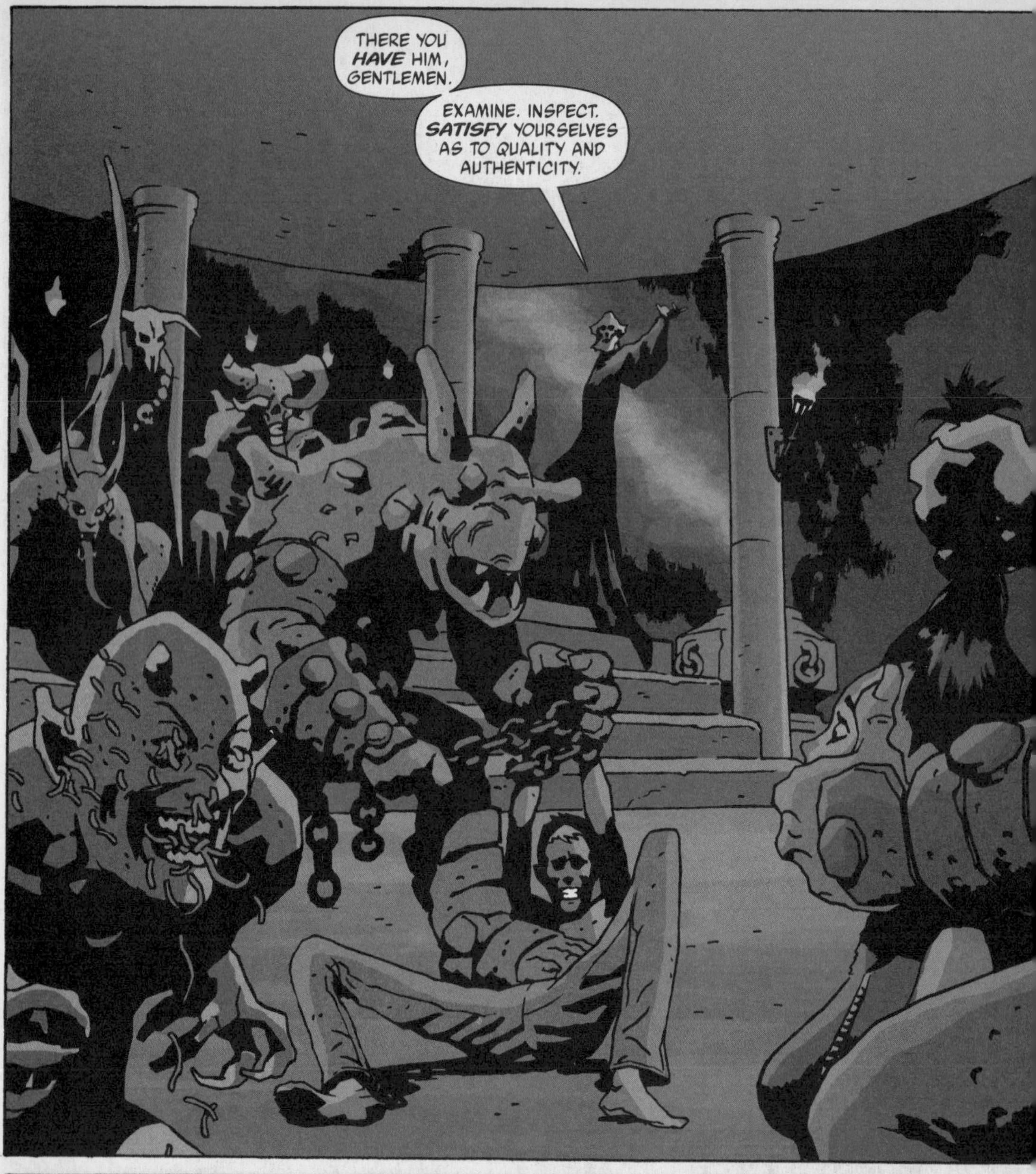
THERE YOU **HAVE** HIM, GENTLEMEN.
EXAMINE. INSPECT. **SATISFY** YOURSELVES AS TO QUALITY AND AUTHENTICITY.

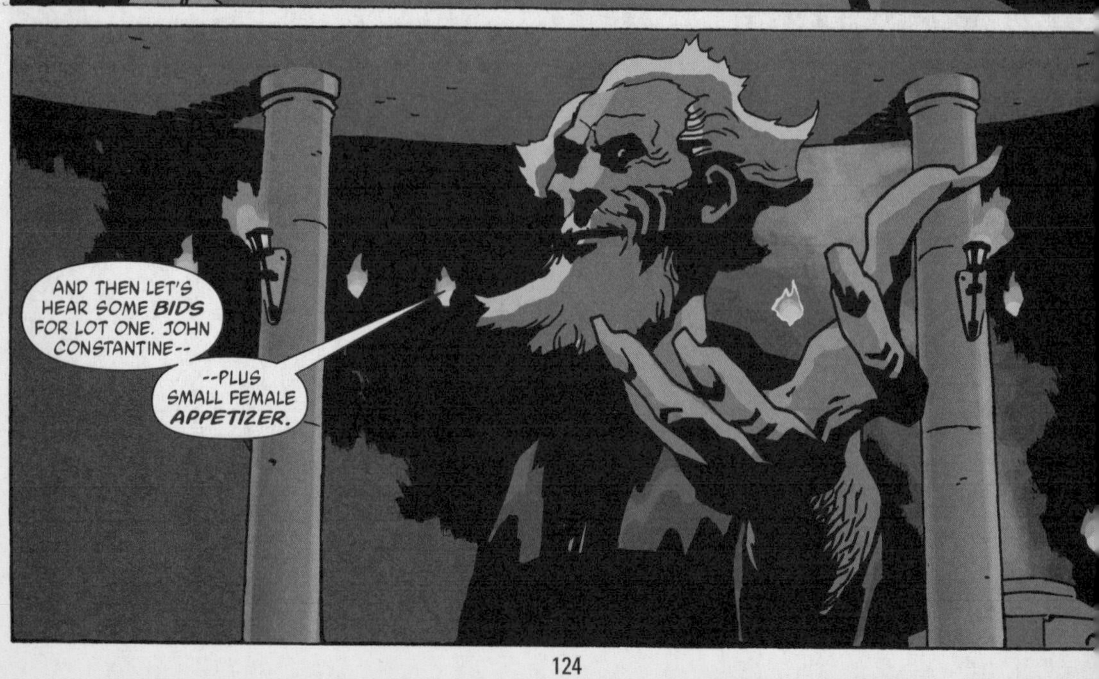
AND THEN LET'S HEAR SOME **BIDS** FOR LOT ONE. JOHN CONSTANTINE--
--PLUS SMALL FEMALE **APPETIZER.**

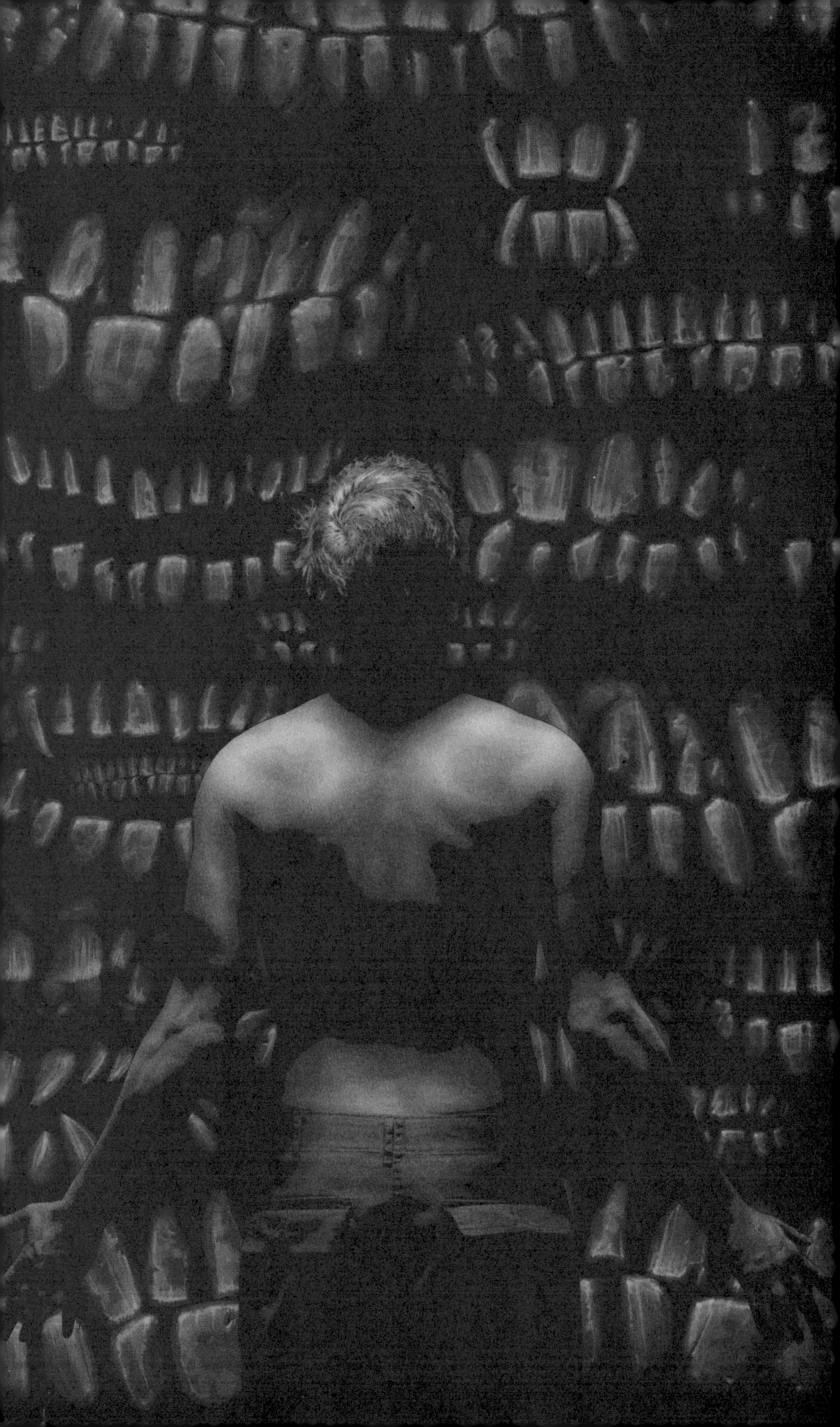

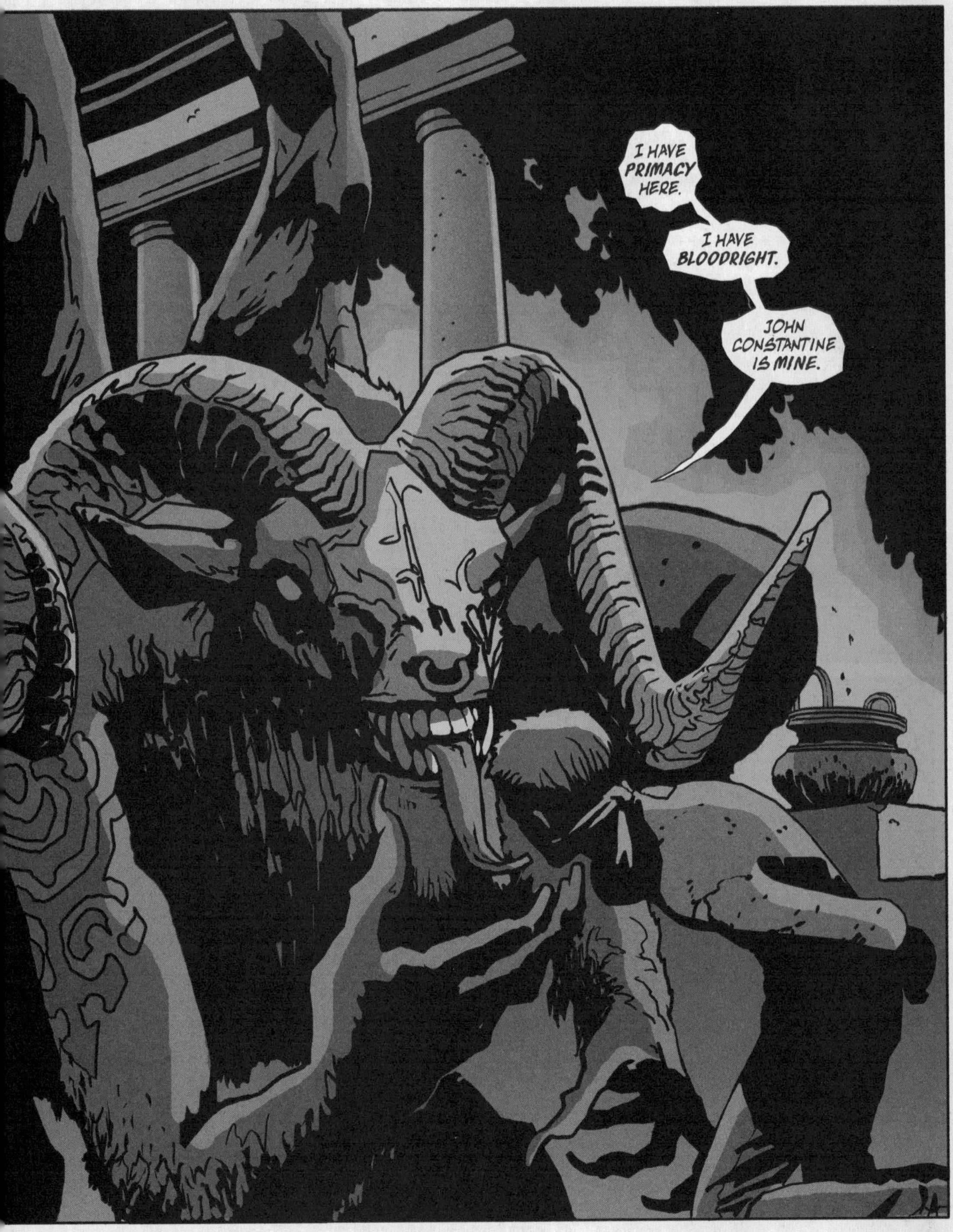
I HAVE PRIMACY HERE.
I HAVE BLOODRIGHT.
JOHN CONSTANTINE IS MINE.

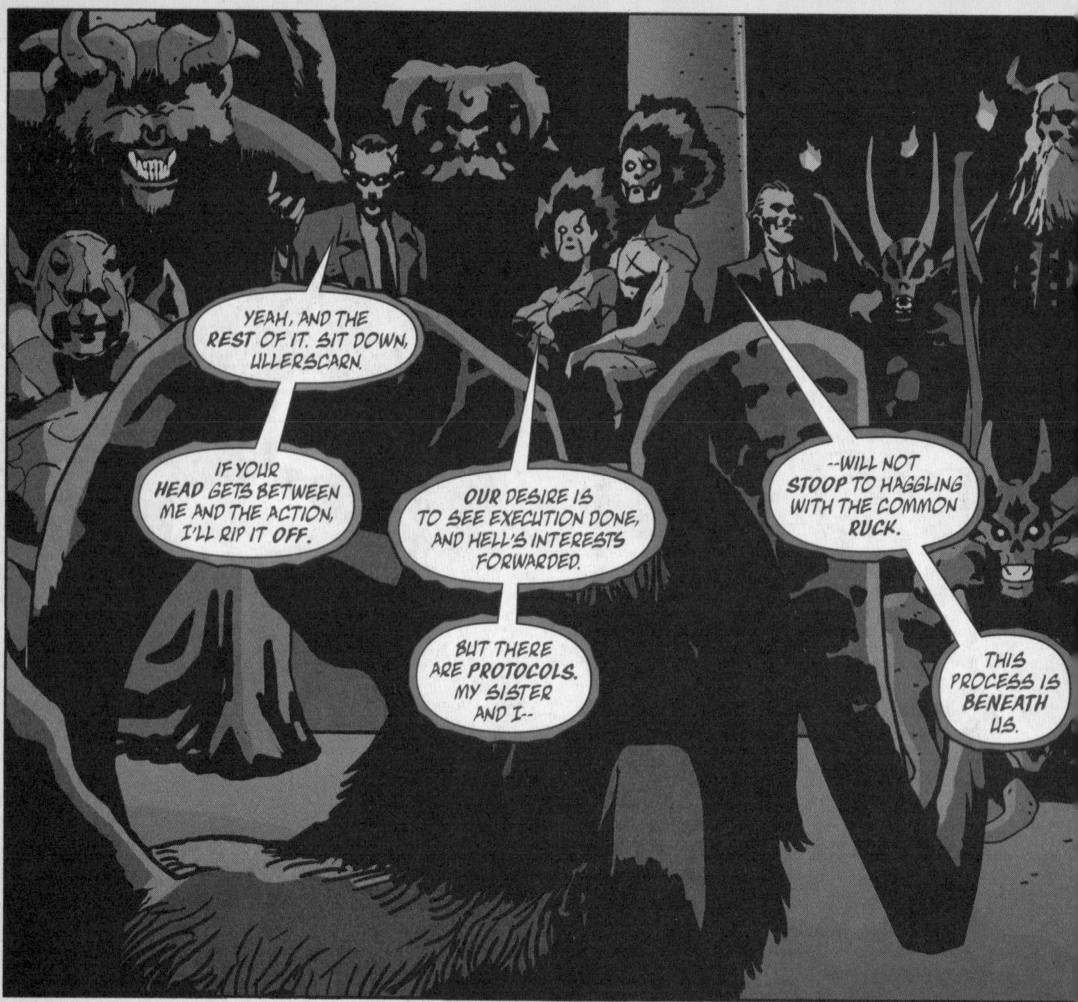
YEAH, AND THE REST OF IT. SIT DOWN, ULLERSCARN.
IF YOUR HEAD GETS BETWEEN ME AND THE ACTION, I'LL RIP IT OFF.
OUR DESIRE IS TO SEE EXECUTION DONE, AND HELL'S INTERESTS FORWARDED.
BUT THERE ARE PROTOCOLS. MY SISTER AND I--
--WILL NOT STOOP TO HAGGLING WITH THE COMMON RUCK.
THIS PROCESS IS BENEATH US.

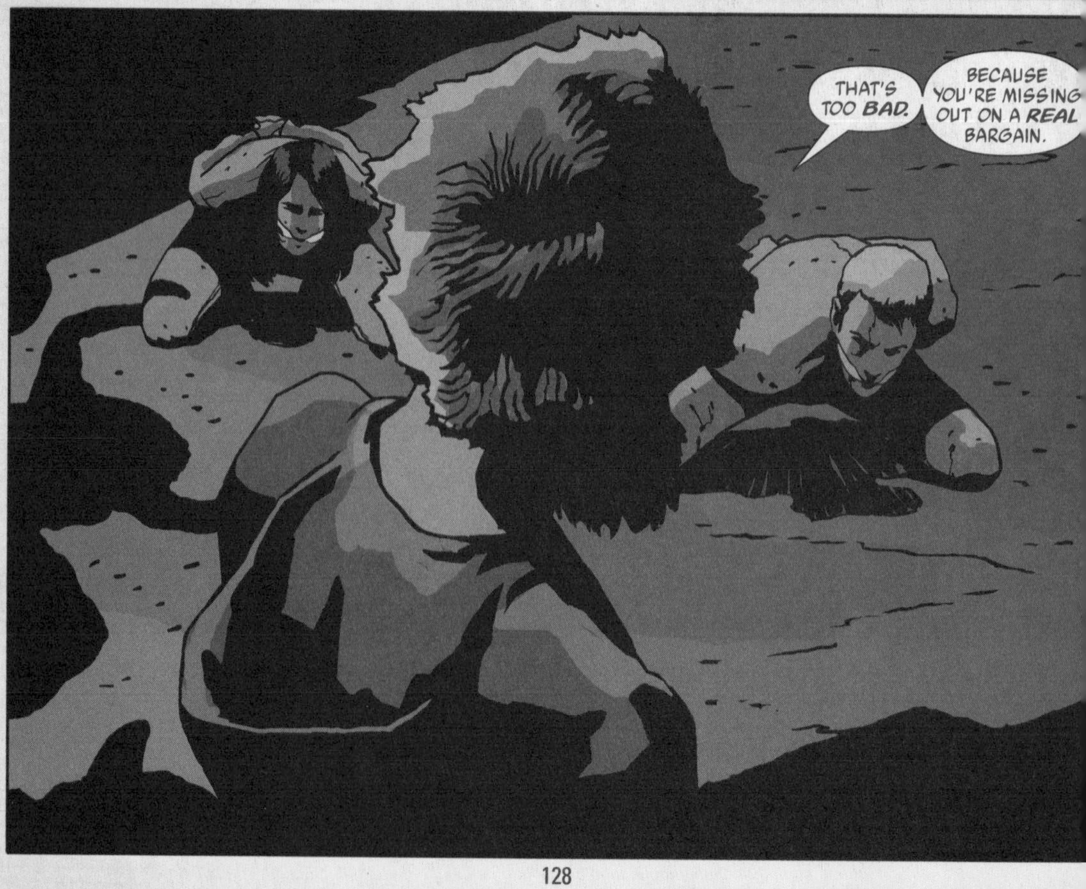
THAT'S TOO BAD.
BECAUSE YOU'RE MISSING OUT ON A REAL BARGAIN.

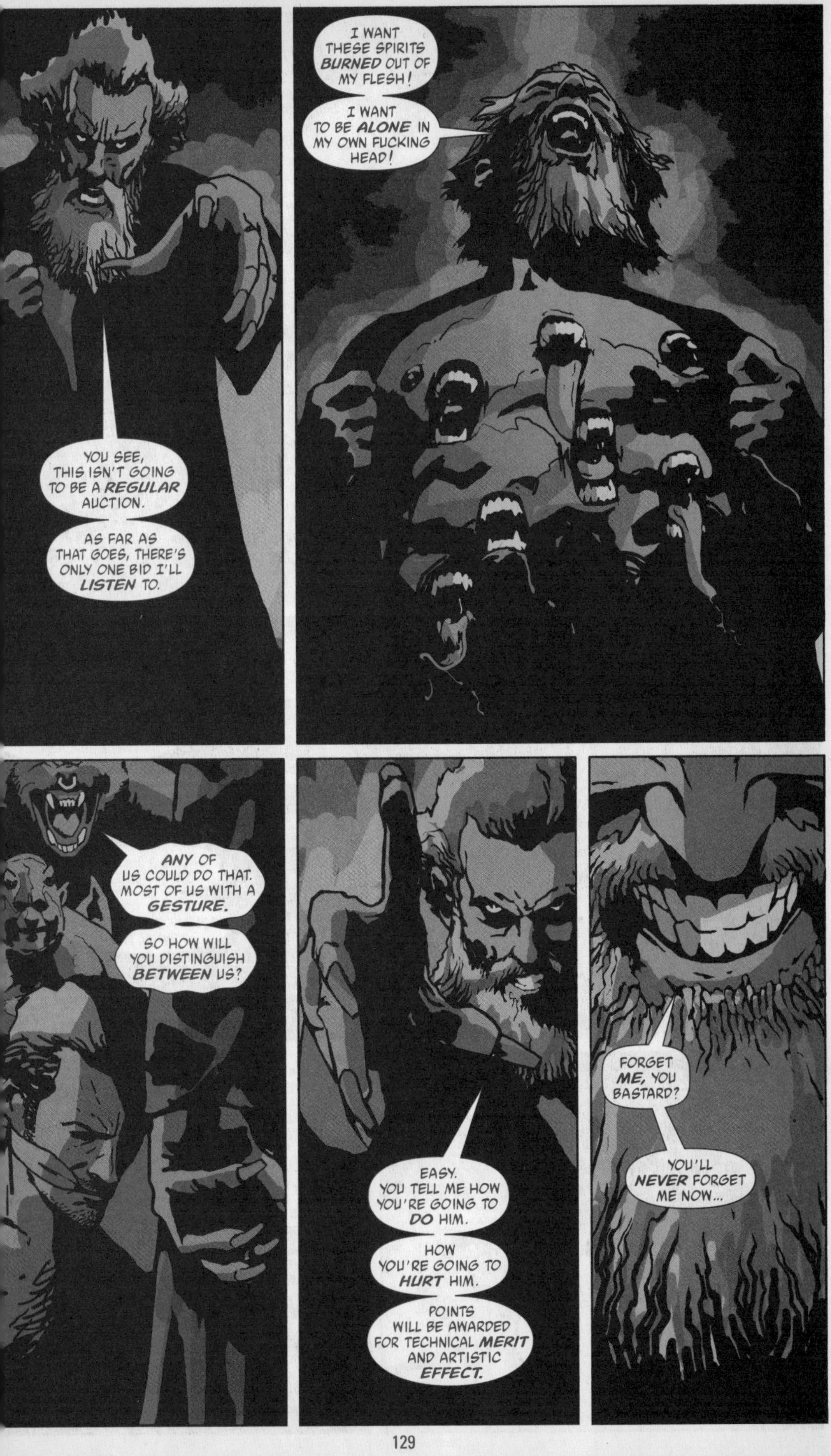
YOU SEE, THIS ISN'T GOING TO BE A REGULAR AUCTION.
AS FAR AS THAT GOES, THERE'S ONLY ONE BID I'LL LISTEN TO.
I WANT THESE SPIRITS BURNED OUT OF MY FLESH!
I WANT TO BE ALONE IN MY OWN FUCKING HEAD!
ANY OF US COULD DO THAT. MOST OF US WITH A GESTURE.
SO HOW WILL YOU DISTINGUISH BETWEEN US?
EASY. YOU TELL ME HOW YOU'RE GOING TO DO HIM.
HOW YOU'RE GOING TO HURT HIM.
POINTS WILL BE AWARDED FOR TECHNICAL MERIT AND ARTISTIC EFFECT.
FORGET ME, YOU BASTARD?
YOU'LL NEVER FORGET ME NOW...

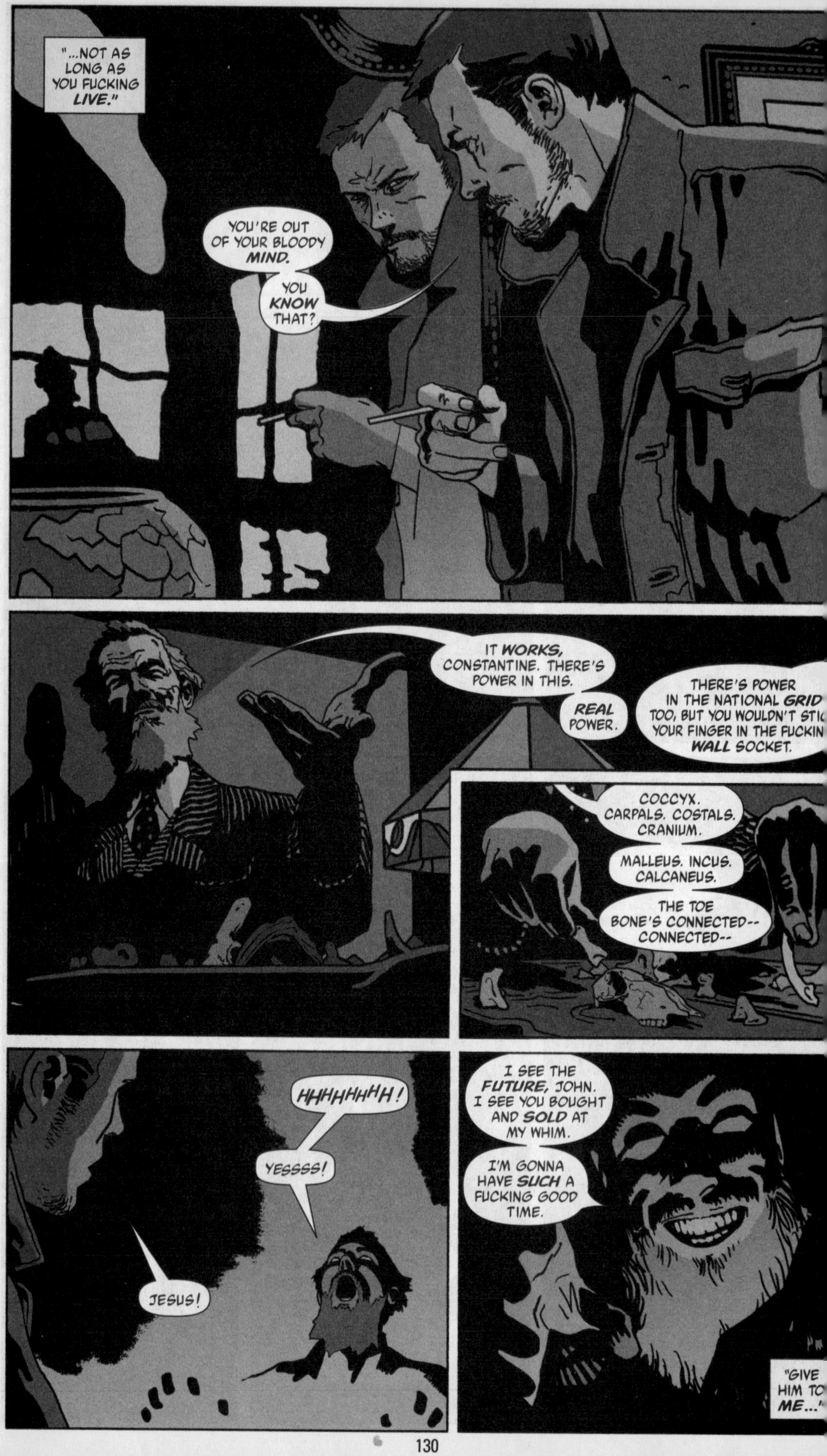
"...NOT AS LONG AS YOU FUCKING LIVE."
YOU'RE OUT OF YOUR BLOODY MIND.
YOU KNOW THAT?
IT WORKS, CONSTANTINE. THERE'S POWER IN THIS.
REAL POWER.
THERE'S POWER IN THE NATIONAL GRID TOO, BUT YOU WOULDN'T STIC YOUR FINGER IN THE FUCKIN WALL SOCKET.
COCCYX. CARPALS. COSTALS. CRANIUM.
MALLEUS. INCUS. CALCANEUS.
THE TOE BONE'S CONNECTED-- CONNECTED--
HHHHHHHH!
YESSSS!
JESUS!
I SEE THE FUTURE, JOHN. I SEE YOU BOUGHT AND SOLD AT MY WHIM.
I'M GONNA HAVE SUCH A FUCKING GOOD TIME.
"GIVE HIM TO ME..."

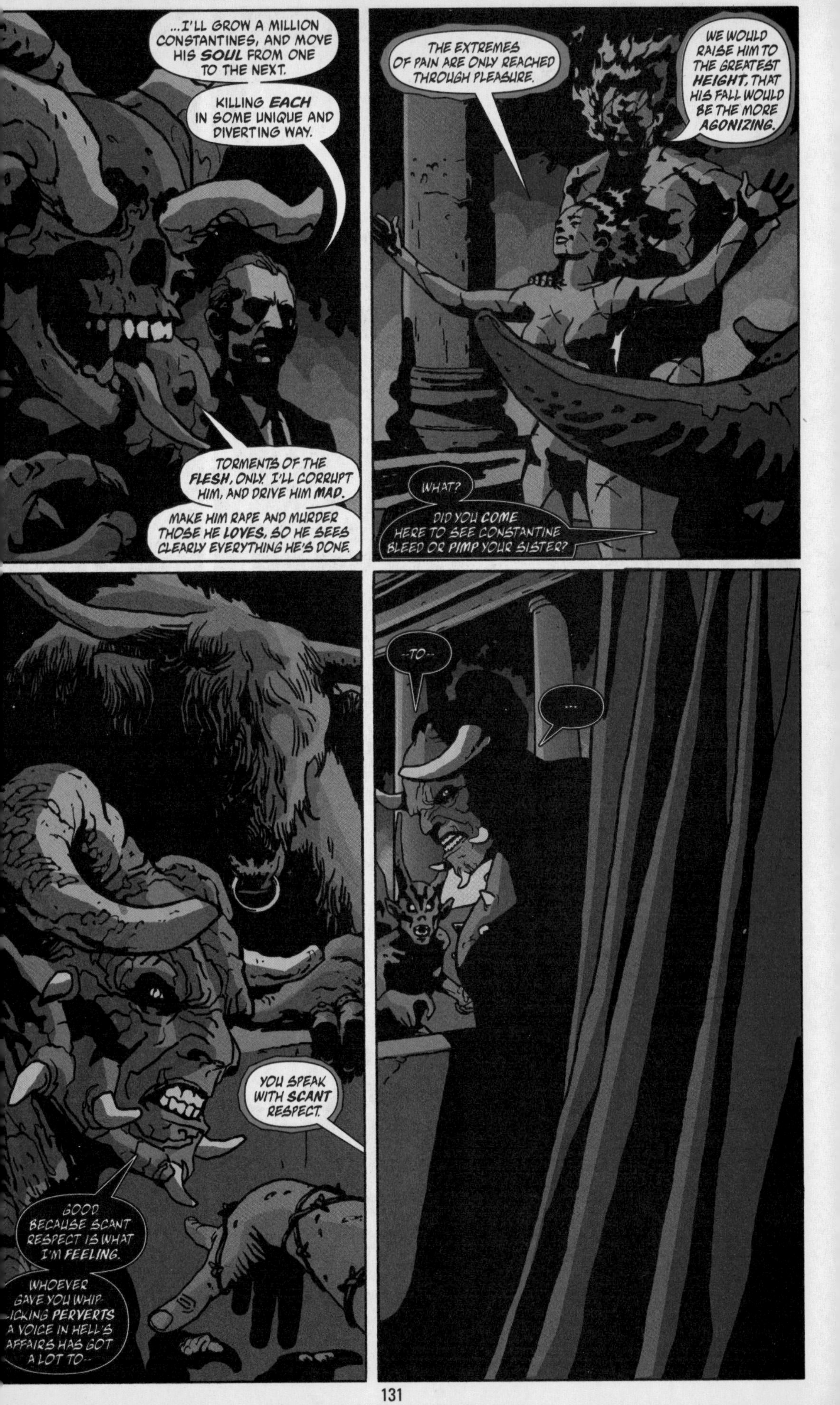
...I'LL GROW A MILLION CONSTANTINES, AND MOVE HIS SOUL FROM ONE TO THE NEXT.
KILLING EACH IN SOME UNIQUE AND DIVERTING WAY.
TORMENTS OF THE FLESH, ONLY. I'LL CORRUPT HIM, AND DRIVE HIM MAD.
MAKE HIM RAPE AND MURDER THOSE HE LOVES, SO HE SEES CLEARLY EVERYTHING HE'S DONE.
THE EXTREMES OF PAIN ARE ONLY REACHED THROUGH PLEASURE.
WE WOULD RAISE HIM TO THE GREATEST HEIGHT, THAT HIS FALL WOULD BE THE MORE AGONIZING.
WHAT?
DID YOU COME HERE TO SEE CONSTANTINE BLEED OR PIMP YOUR SISTER?
YOU SPEAK WITH SCANT RESPECT.
GOOD. BECAUSE SCANT RESPECT IS WHAT I'M FEELING.
WHOEVER GAVE YOU WHIP-LICKING PERVERTS A VOICE IN HELL'S AFFAIRS HAS GOT A LOT TO--
--TO--
...

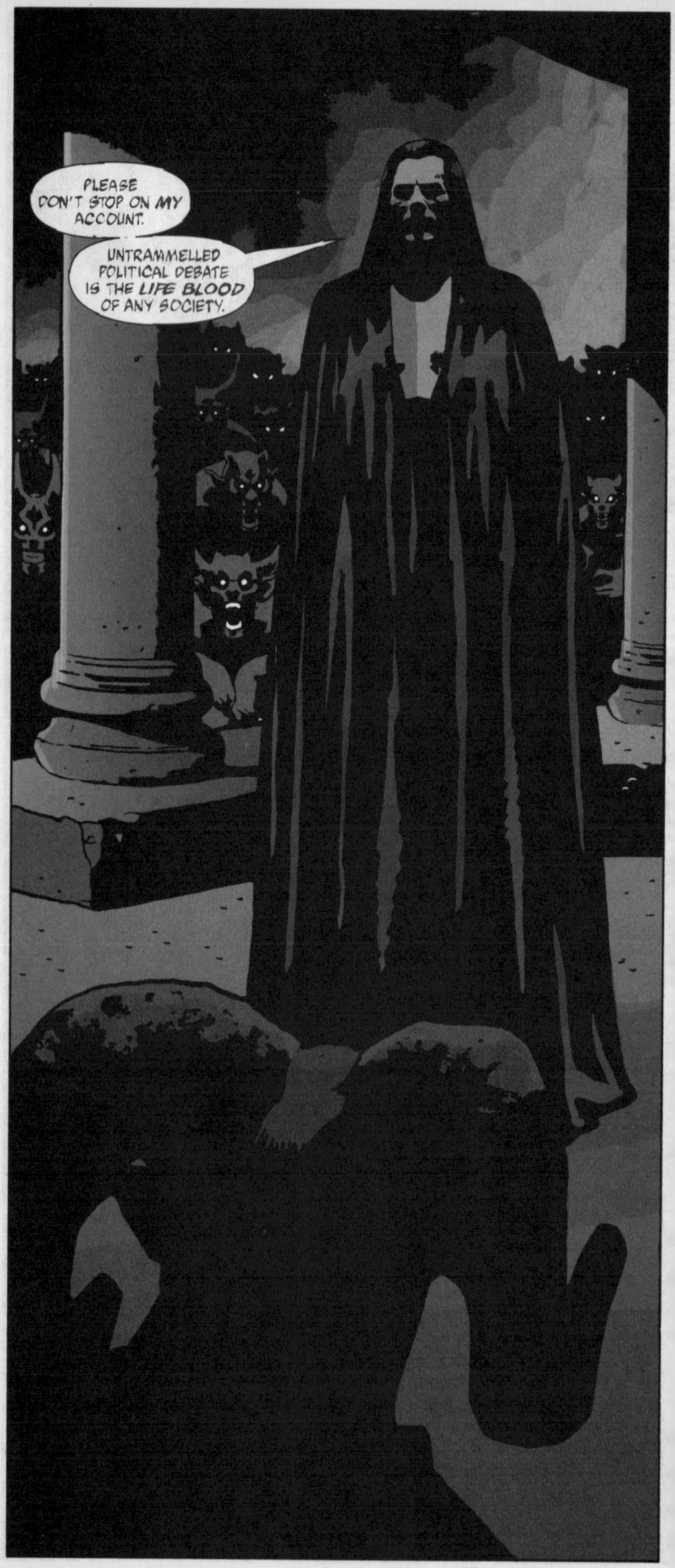
PLEASE DON'T STOP ON *MY* ACCOUNT.
UNTRAMMELLED POLITICAL DEBATE IS THE *LIFE BLOOD* OF ANY SOCIETY.

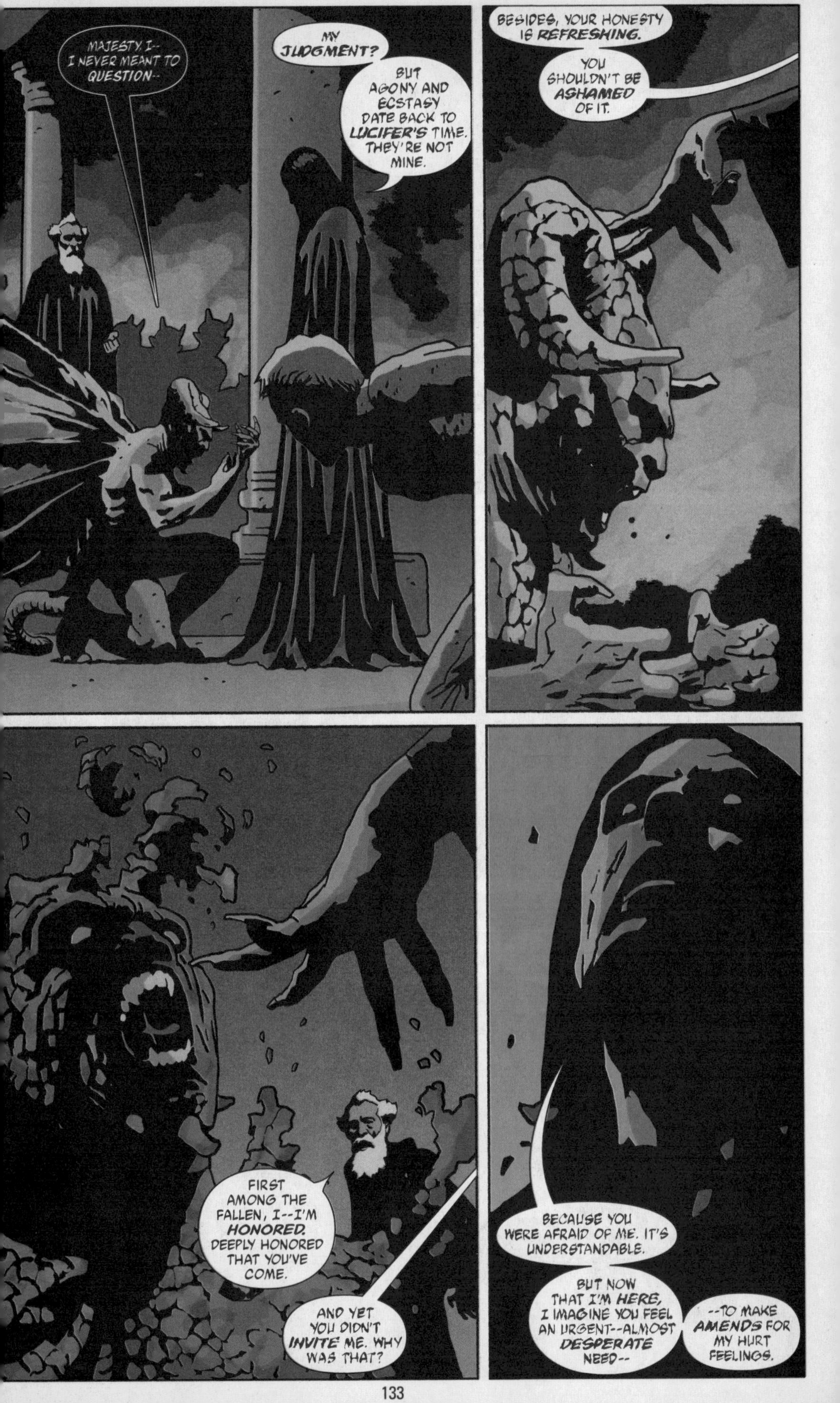
MAJESTY, I-- I NEVER MEANT TO QUESTION--
MY JUDGMENT?
BUT AGONY AND ECSTASY DATE BACK TO LUCIFER'S TIME. THEY'RE NOT MINE.
BESIDES, YOUR HONESTY IS REFRESHING.
YOU SHOULDN'T BE ASHAMED OF IT.
FIRST AMONG THE FALLEN, I--I'M HONORED. DEEPLY HONORED THAT YOU'VE COME.
AND YET YOU DIDN'T INVITE ME. WHY WAS THAT?
BECAUSE YOU WERE AFRAID OF ME. IT'S UNDERSTANDABLE.
BUT NOW THAT I'M HERE, I IMAGINE YOU FEEL AN URGENT--ALMOST DESPERATE NEED--
--TO MAKE AMENDS FOR MY HURT FEELINGS.

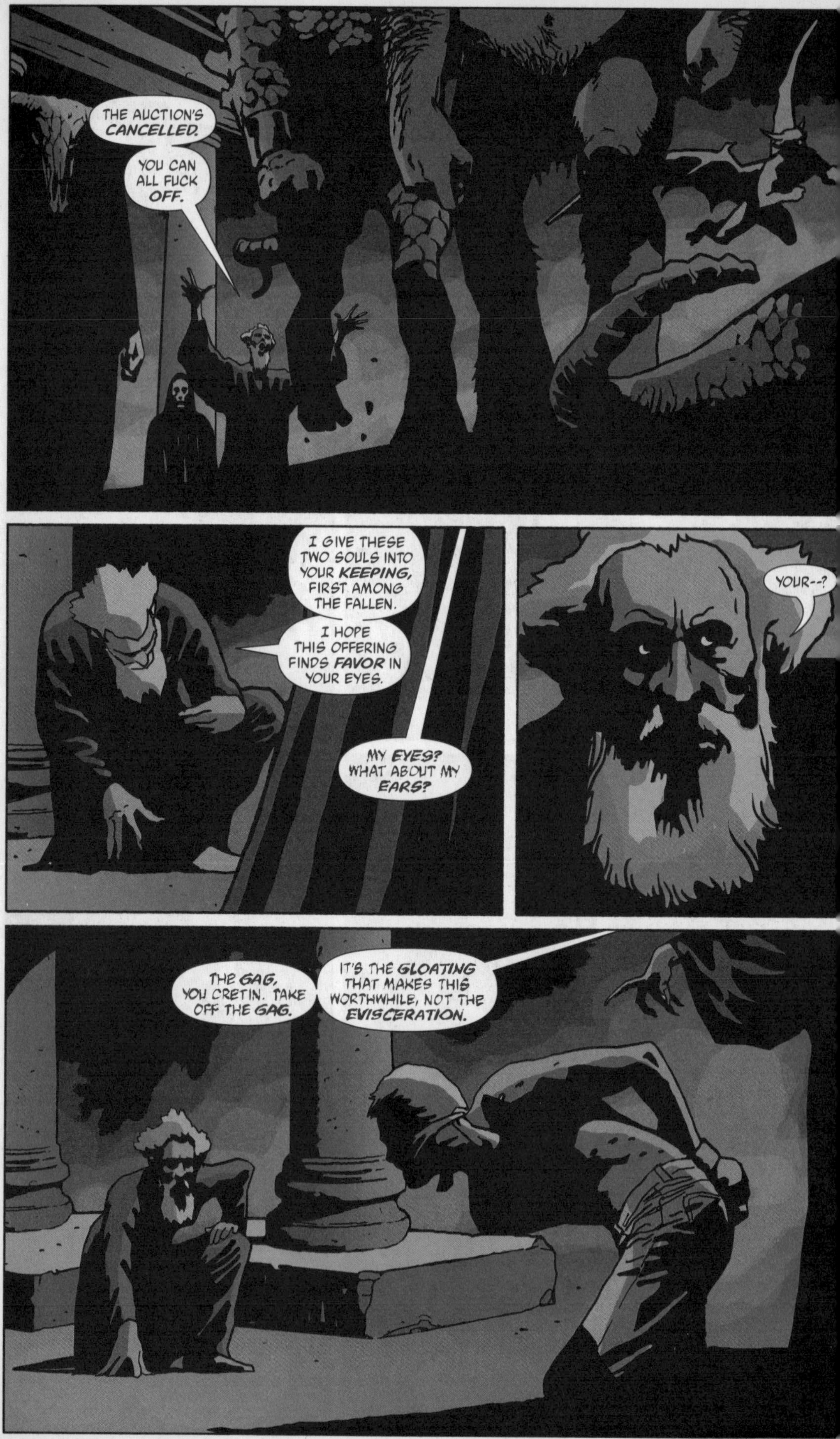
THE AUCTION'S CANCELLED.
YOU CAN ALL FUCK OFF.
I GIVE THESE TWO SOULS INTO YOUR KEEPING, FIRST AMONG THE FALLEN.
I HOPE THIS OFFERING FINDS FAVOR IN YOUR EYES.
MY EYES? WHAT ABOUT MY EARS?
YOUR--?
THE GAG, YOU CRETIN. TAKE OFF THE GAG.
IT'S THE GLOATING THAT MAKES THIS WORTHWHILE, NOT THE EVISCERATION.

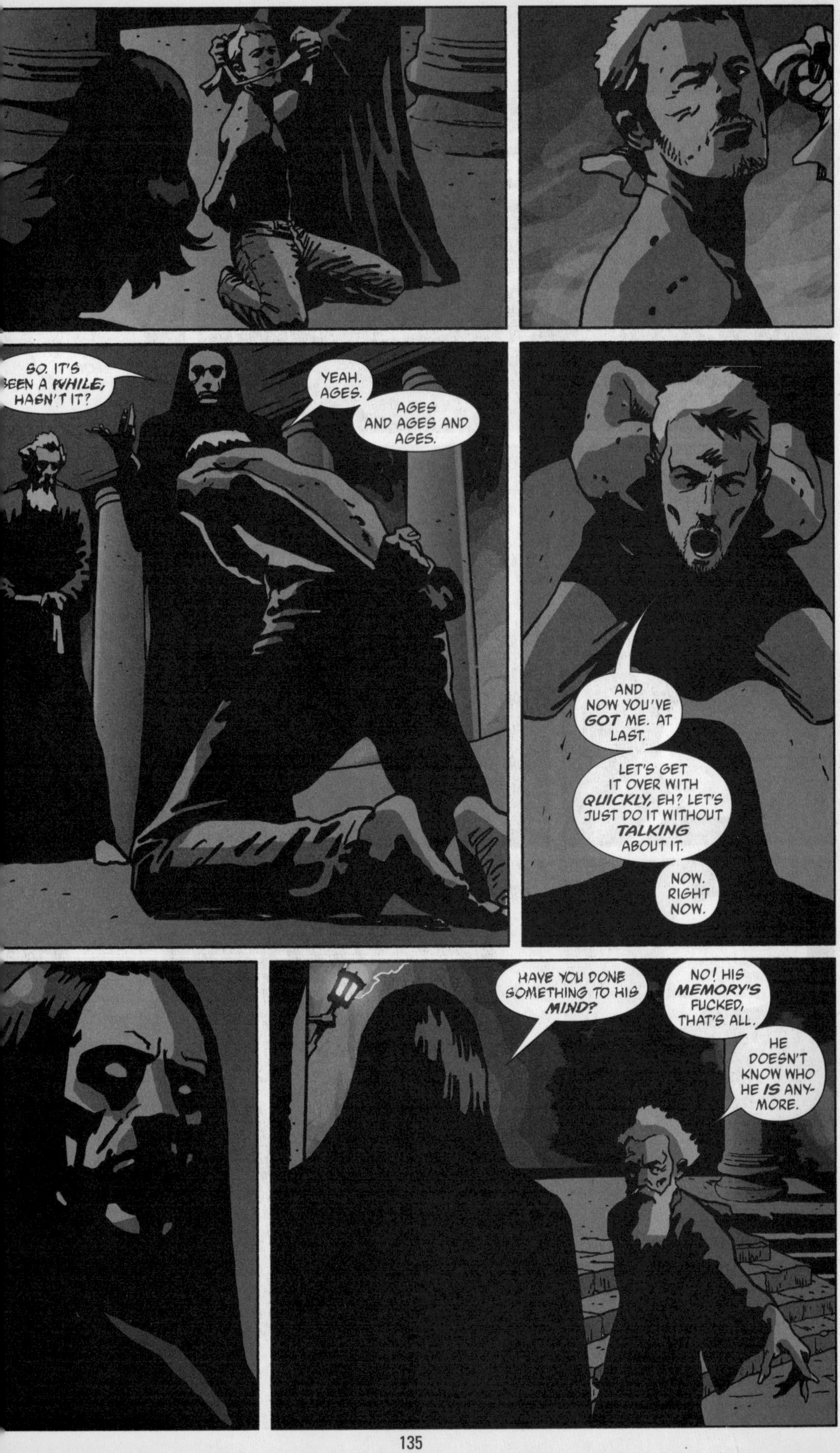
SO. IT'S BEEN A WHILE, HASN'T IT?
YEAH. AGES.
AGES AND AGES AND AGES.
AND NOW YOU'VE GOT ME. AT LAST.
LET'S GET IT OVER WITH QUICKLY, EH? LET'S JUST DO IT WITHOUT TALKING ABOUT IT.
NOW. RIGHT NOW.
HAVE YOU DONE SOMETHING TO HIS MIND?
NO! HIS MEMORY'S FUCKED, THAT'S ALL.
HE DOESN'T KNOW WHO HE IS ANY-MORE.

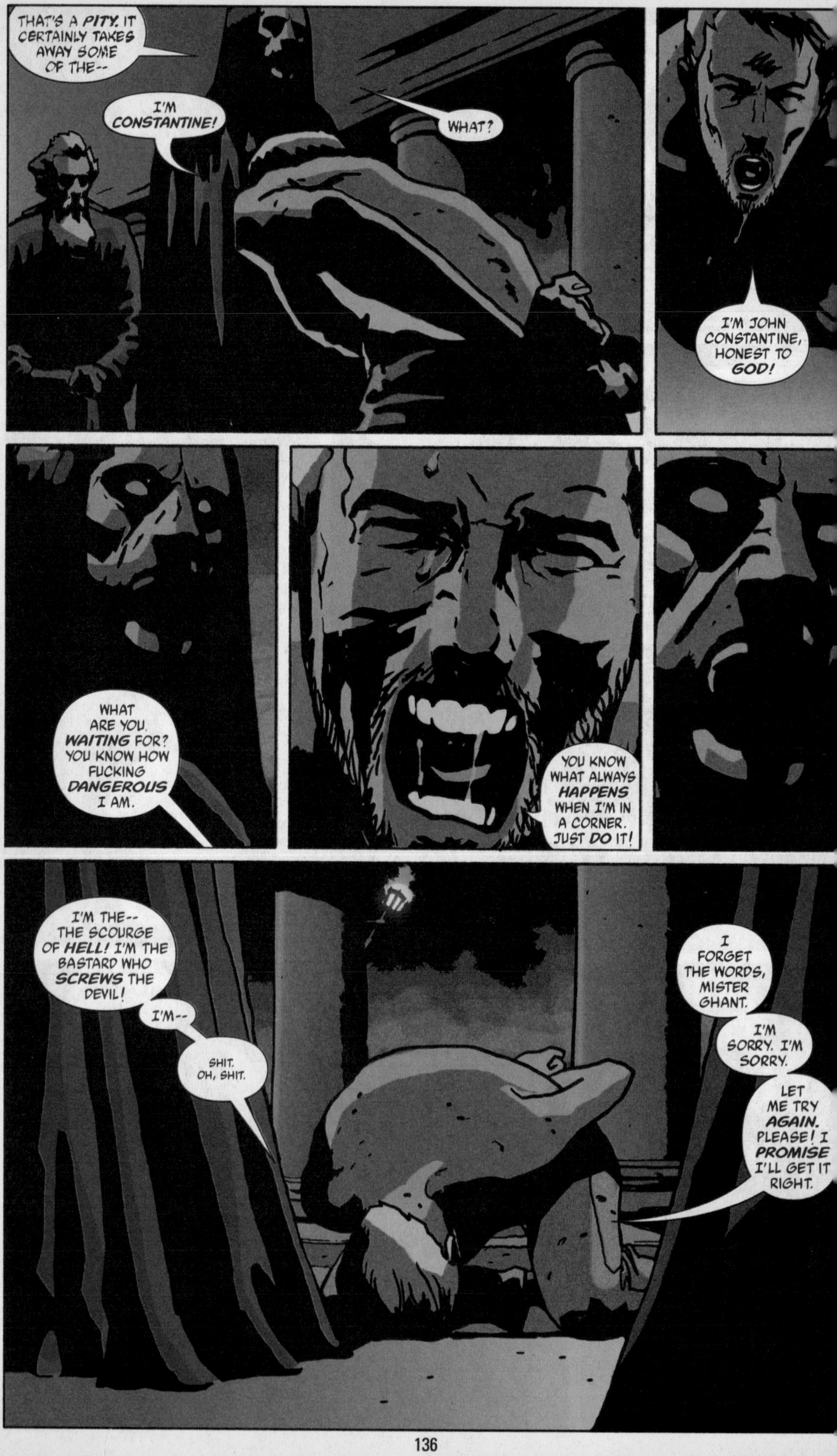
THAT'S A PITY. IT CERTAINLY TAKES AWAY SOME OF THE--
I'M CONSTANTINE!
WHAT?
I'M JOHN CONSTANTINE, HONEST TO GOD!
WHAT ARE YOU WAITING FOR? YOU KNOW HOW FUCKING DANGEROUS I AM.
YOU KNOW WHAT ALWAYS HAPPENS WHEN I'M IN A CORNER. JUST DO IT!
I'M THE-- THE SCOURGE OF HELL! I'M THE BASTARD WHO SCREWS THE DEVIL!
I'M--
SHIT. OH, SHIT.
I FORGET THE WORDS, MISTER GHANT.
I'M SORRY. I'M SORRY.
LET ME TRY AGAIN. PLEASE! I PROMISE I'LL GET IT RIGHT.

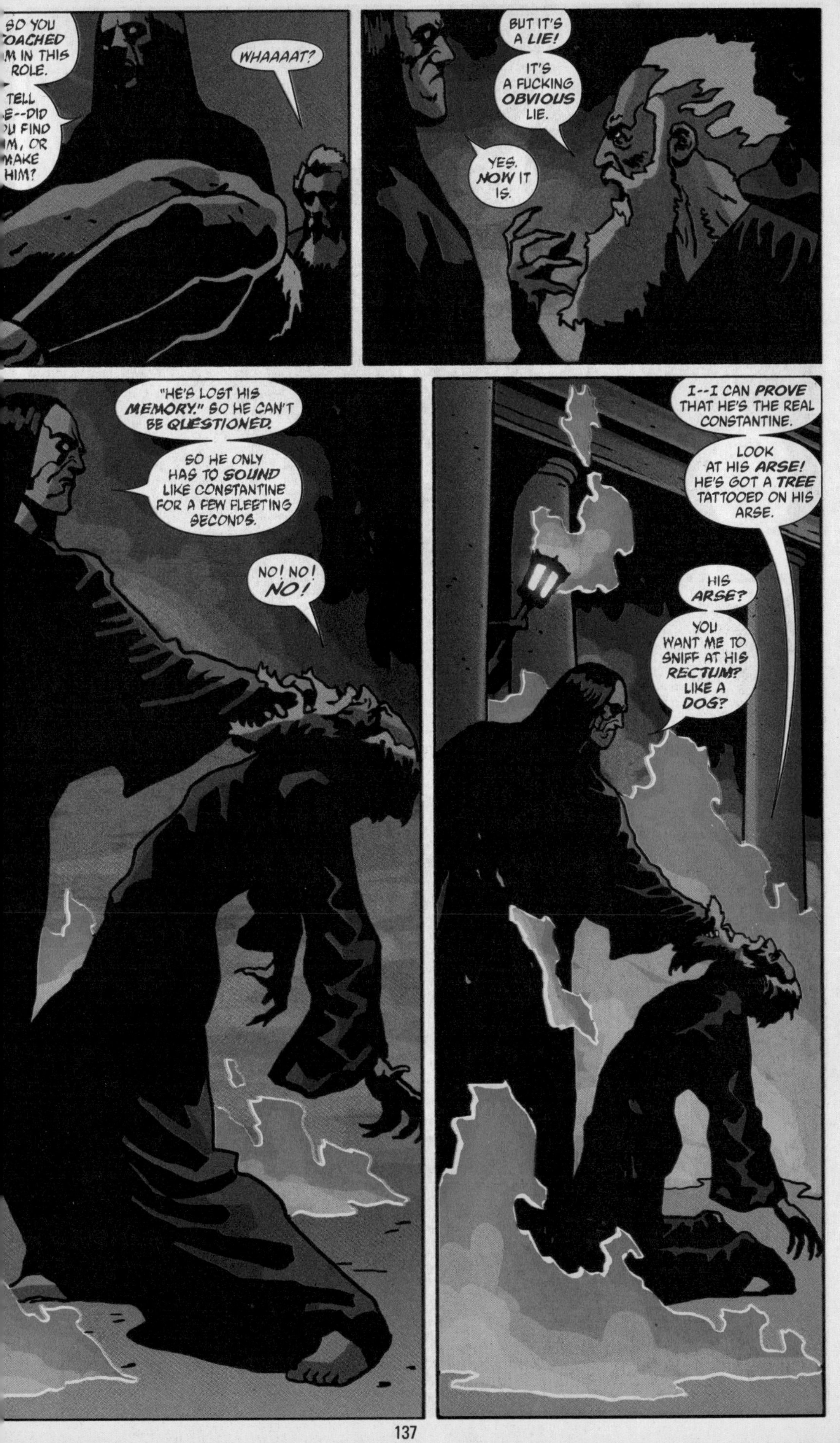

SO YOU COACHED M IN THIS ROLE.
TELL E--DID OU FIND M, OR MAKE HIM?
WHAAAAT?
BUT IT'S A LIE!
IT'S A FUCKING OBVIOUS LIE.
YES. NOW IT IS.
"HE'S LOST HIS MEMORY." SO HE CAN'T BE QUESTIONED.
SO HE ONLY HAS TO SOUND LIKE CONSTANTINE FOR A FEW FLEETING SECONDS.
NO! NO! NO!
I--I CAN PROVE THAT HE'S THE REAL CONSTANTINE.
LOOK AT HIS ARSE! HE'S GOT A TREE TATTOOED ON HIS ARSE.
HIS ARSE?
YOU WANT ME TO SNIFF AT HIS RECTUM? LIKE A DOG?

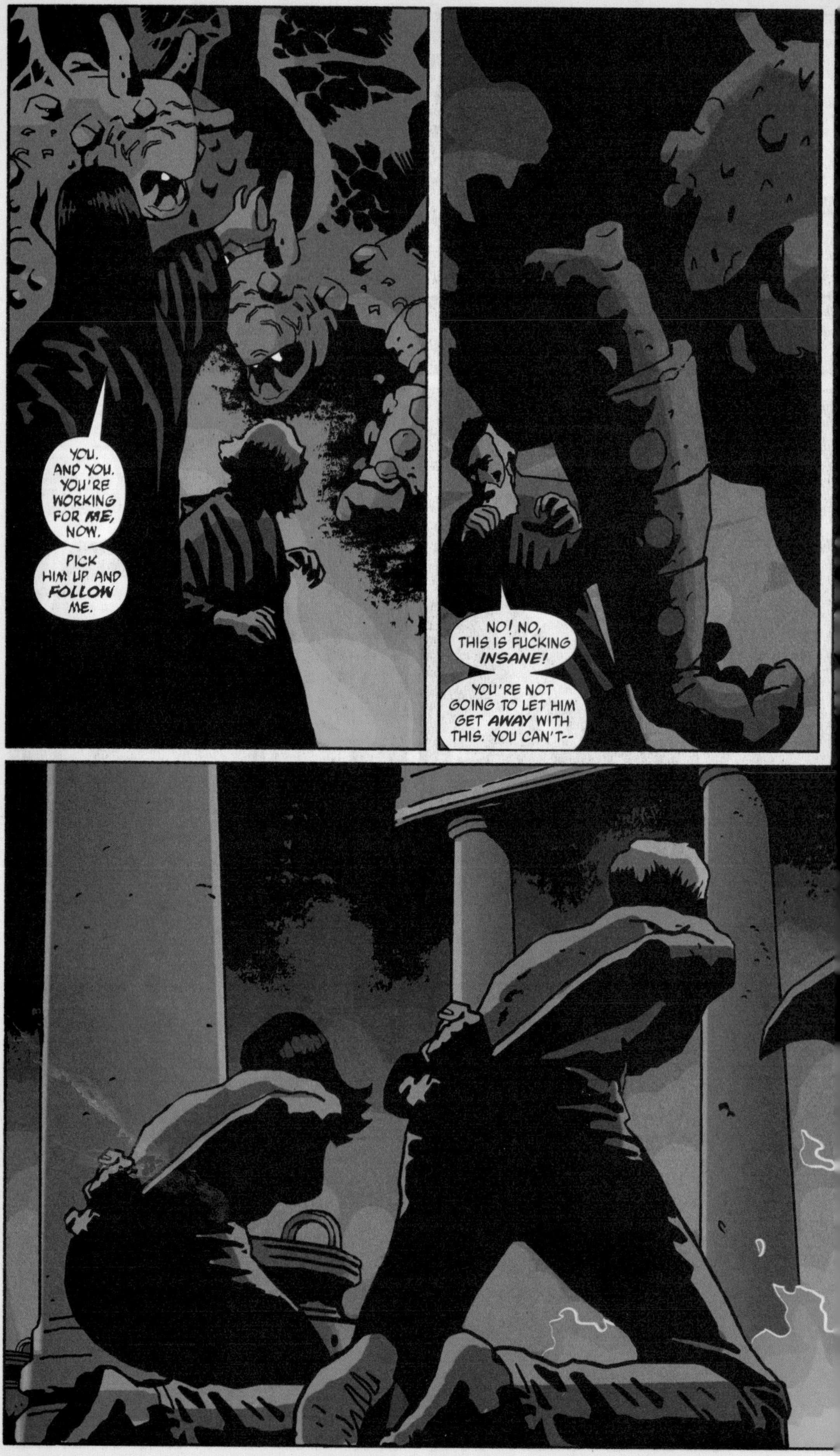
YOU. AND YOU. YOU'RE WORKING FOR ME, NOW.
PICK HIM UP AND FOLLOW ME.
NO! NO, THIS IS FUCKING INSANE!
YOU'RE NOT GOING TO LET HIM GET AWAY WITH THIS. YOU CAN'T--

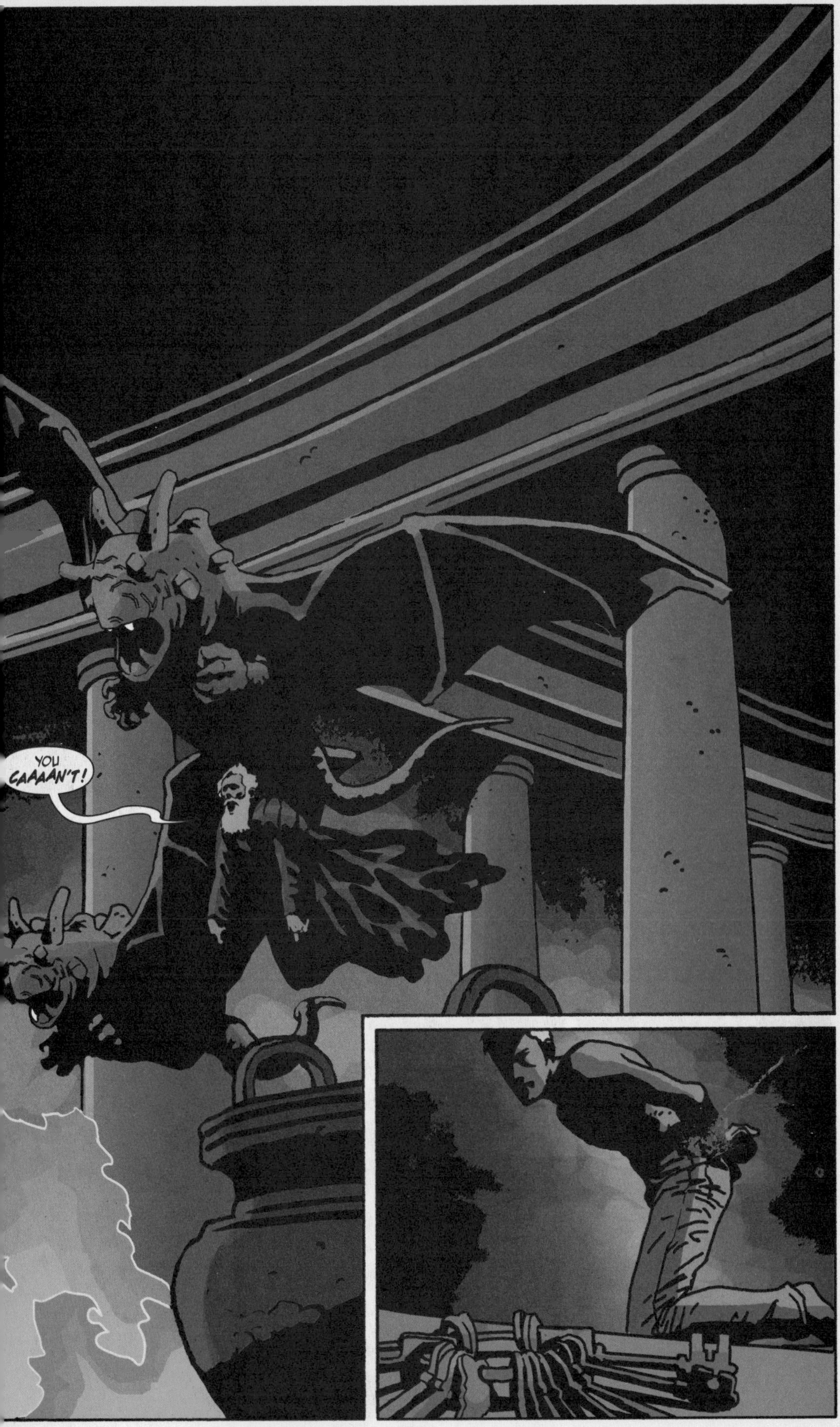
YOU CAAAAN'T!

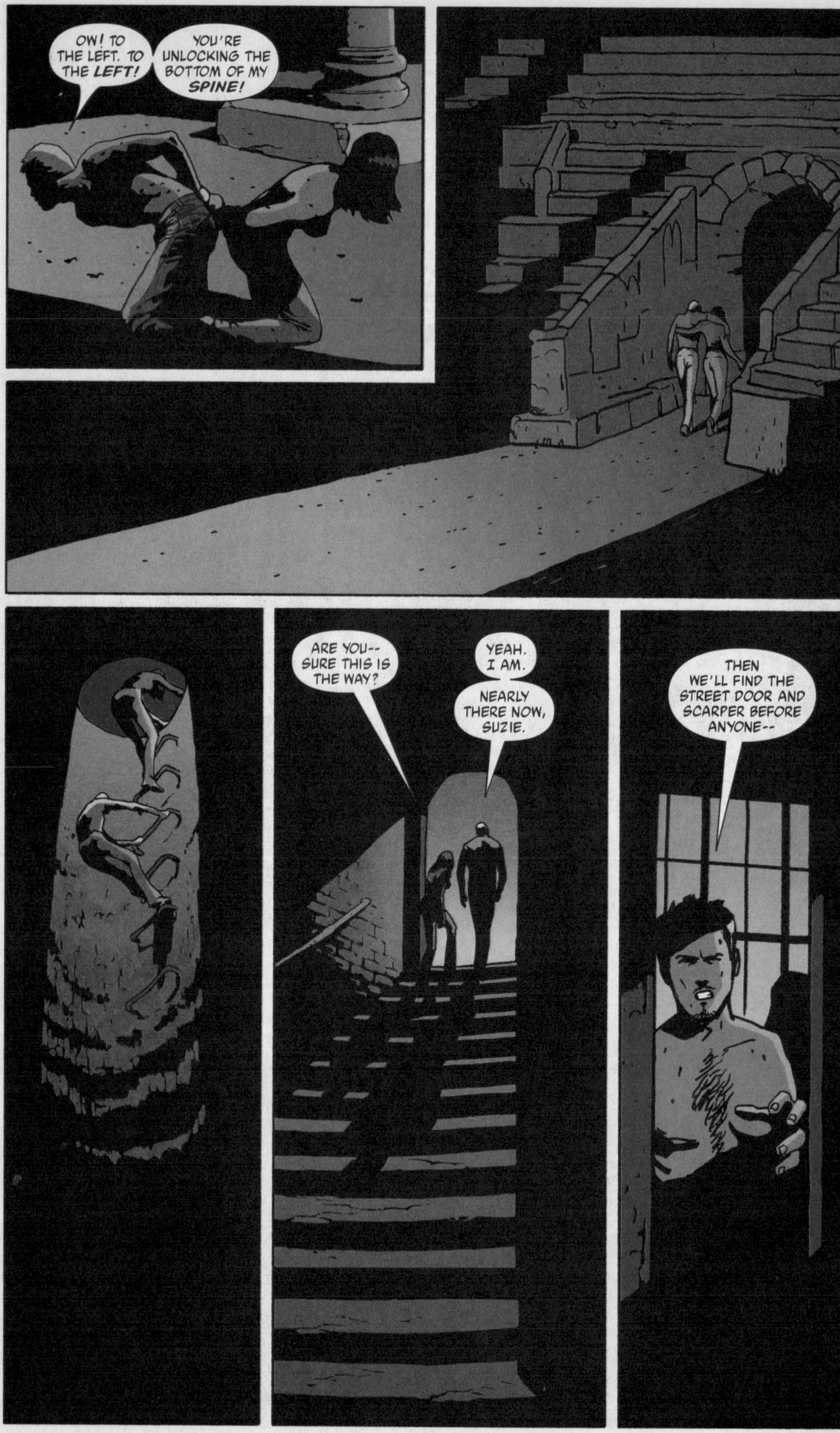
OW! TO THE LEFT. TO THE LEFT!
YOU'RE UNLOCKING THE BOTTOM OF MY SPINE!
ARE YOU-- SURE THIS IS THE WAY?
YEAH. I AM.
NEARLY THERE NOW, SUZIE.
THEN WE'LL FIND THE STREET DOOR AND SCARPER BEFORE ANYONE--

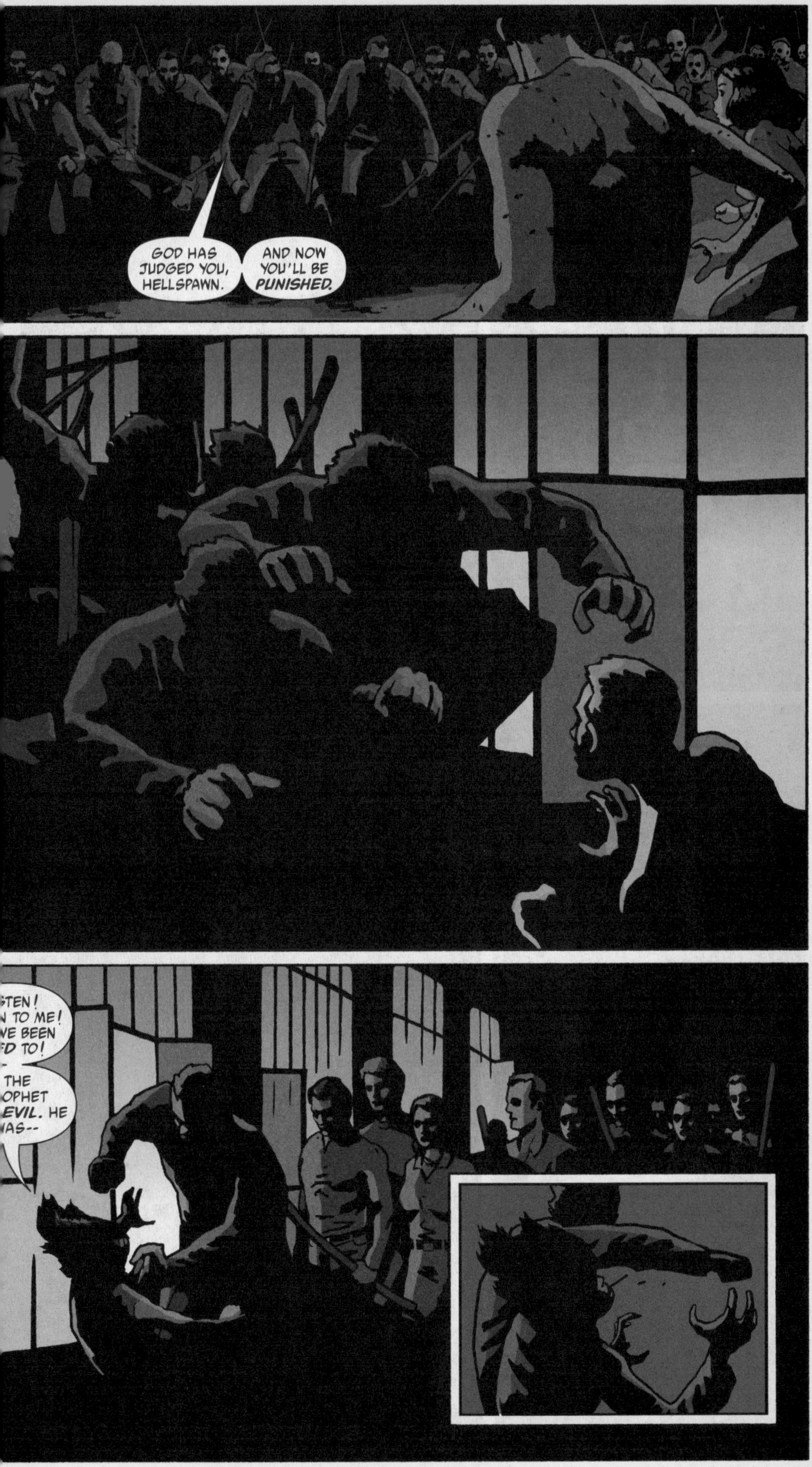
GOD HAS JUDGED YOU, HELLSPAWN.
AND NOW YOU'LL BE PUNISHED.
STEN! N TO ME! VE BEEN FD TO!
THE OPHET EVIL. HE AS--

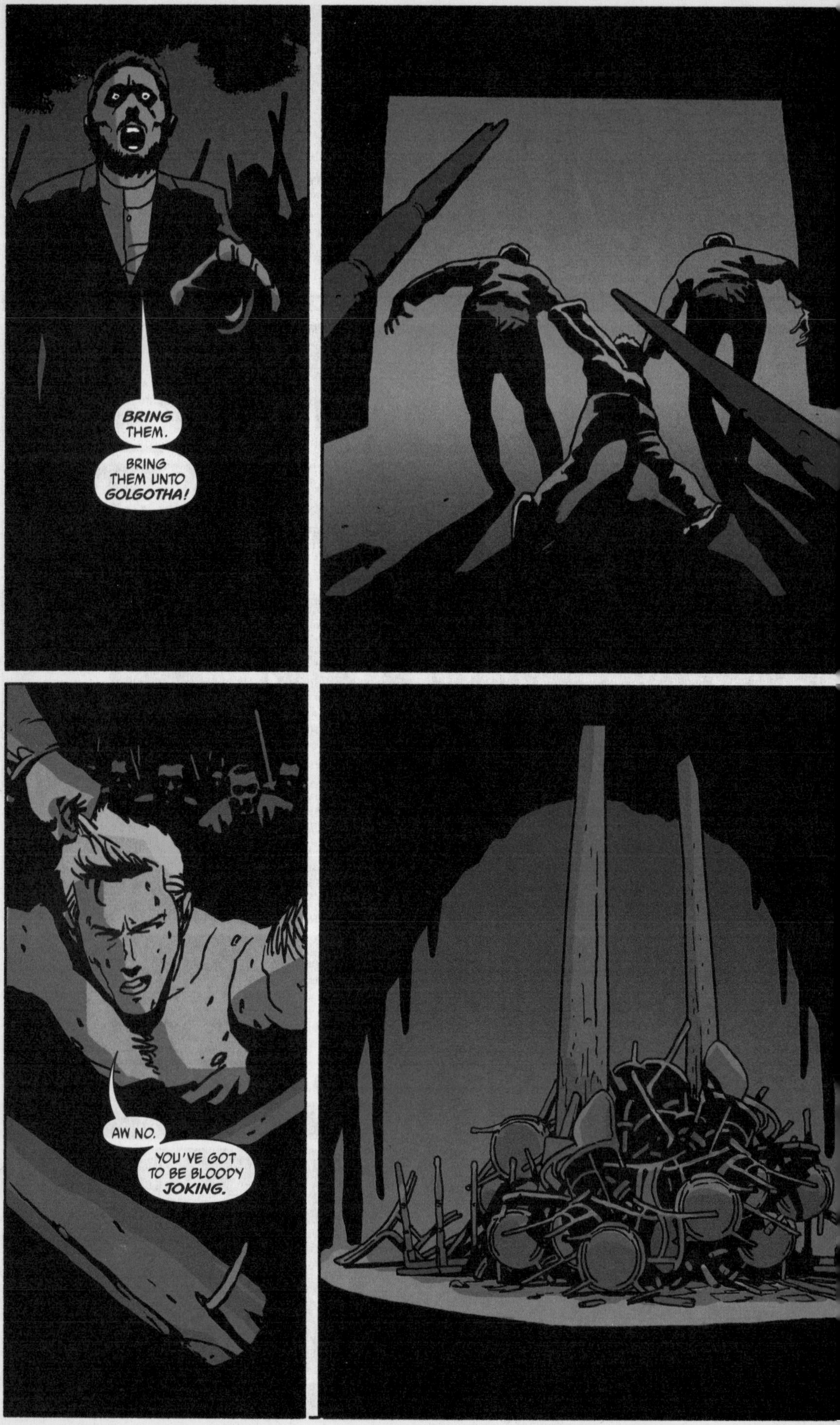

BRING THEM.
BRING THEM UNTO GOLGOTHA!
AW NO.
YOU'VE GOT TO BE BLOODY JOKING.

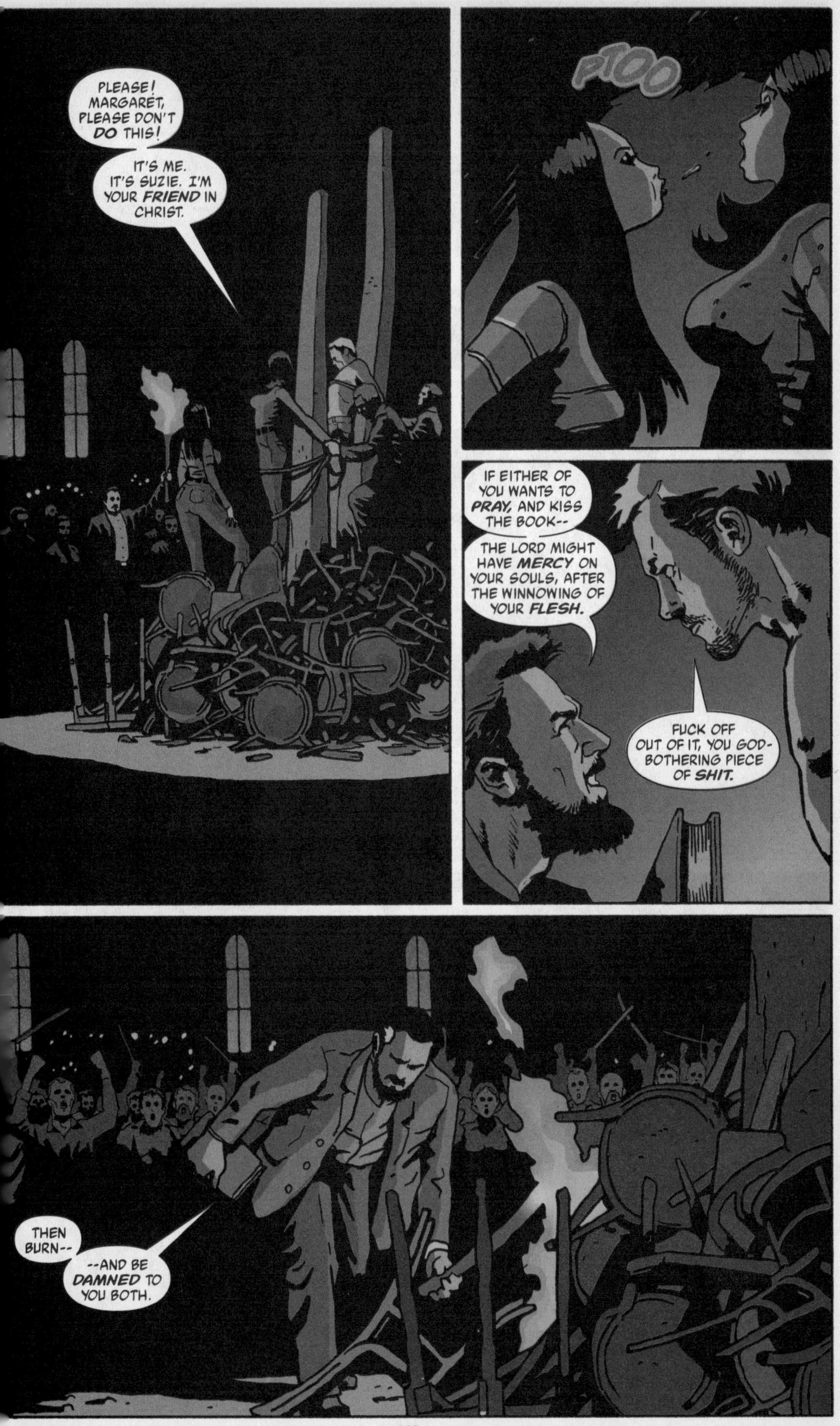
PLEASE! MARGARET, PLEASE DON'T DO THIS!
IT'S ME. IT'S SUZIE. I'M YOUR FRIEND IN CHRIST.
PTOO
IF EITHER OF YOU WANTS TO PRAY, AND KISS THE BOOK--
THE LORD MIGHT HAVE MERCY ON YOUR SOULS, AFTER THE WINNOWING OF YOUR FLESH.
FUCK OFF OUT OF IT, YOU GOD-BOTHERING PIECE OF SHIT.
THEN BURN--
--AND BE DAMNED TO YOU BOTH.

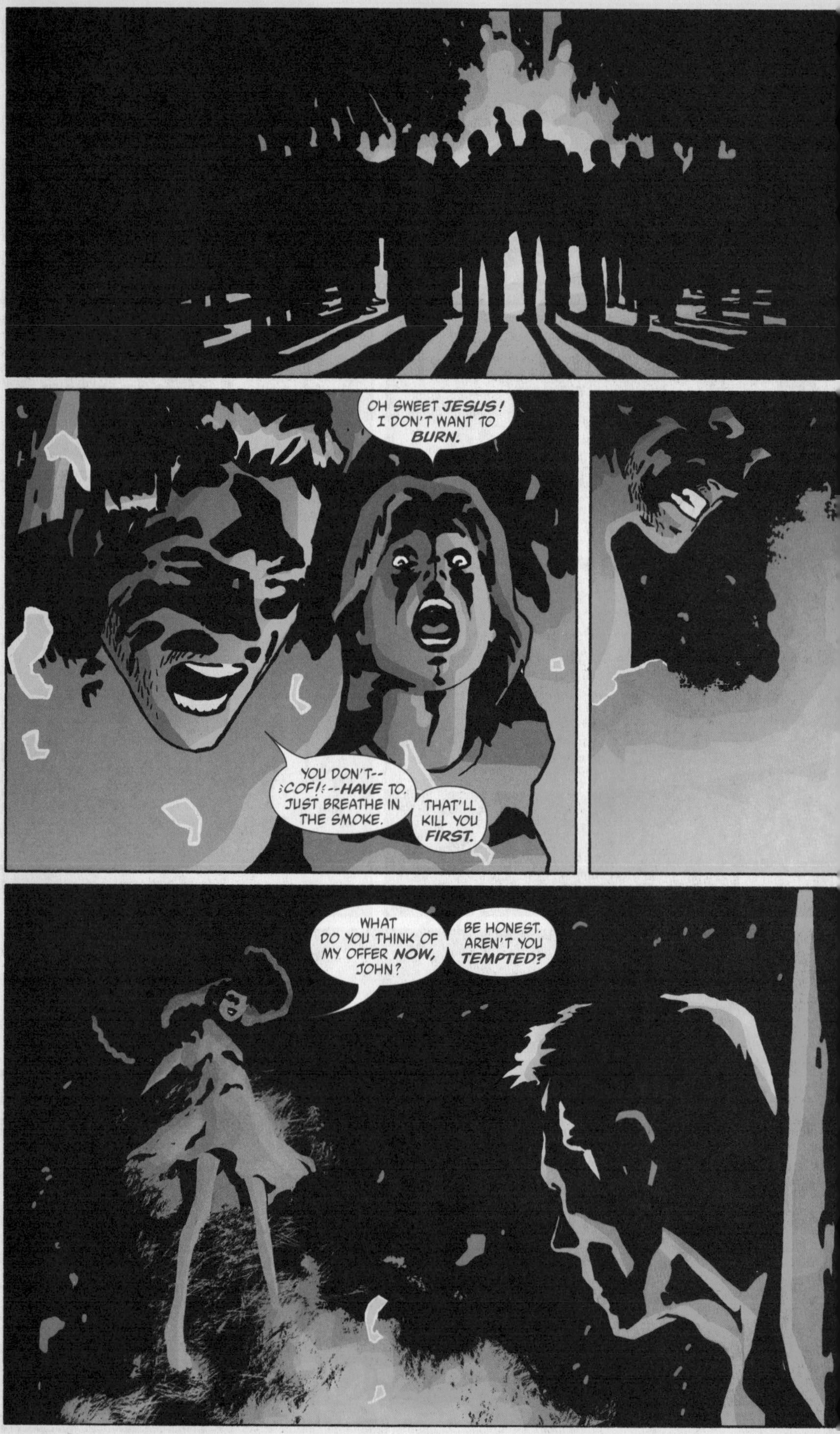
OH SWEET JESUS! I DON'T WANT TO BURN.
YOU DON'T-- COF! --HAVE TO. JUST BREATHE IN THE SMOKE.
THAT'LL KILL YOU FIRST.
WHAT DO YOU THINK OF MY OFFER NOW, JOHN?
BE HONEST. AREN'T YOU TEMPTED?

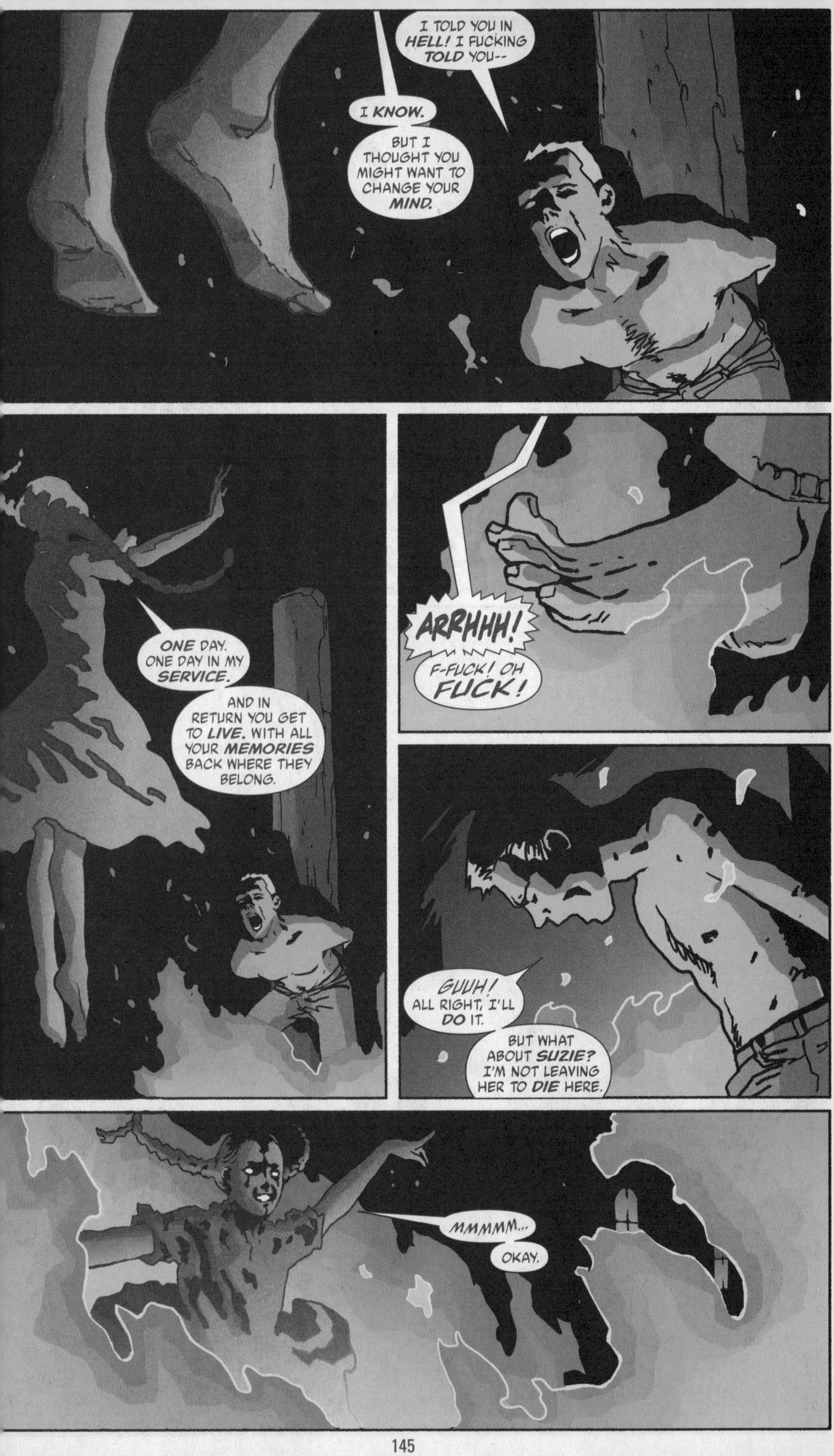
I TOLD YOU IN HELL! I FUCKING TOLD YOU--
I KNOW.
BUT I THOUGHT YOU MIGHT WANT TO CHANGE YOUR MIND.
ONE DAY. ONE DAY IN MY SERVICE.
AND IN RETURN YOU GET TO LIVE. WITH ALL YOUR MEMORIES BACK WHERE THEY BELONG.
ARRHHH!
F-FUCK! OH FUCK!
GUUH! ALL RIGHT, I'LL DO IT.
BUT WHAT ABOUT SUZIE? I'M NOT LEAVING HER TO DIE HERE.
MMMMM...
OKAY.

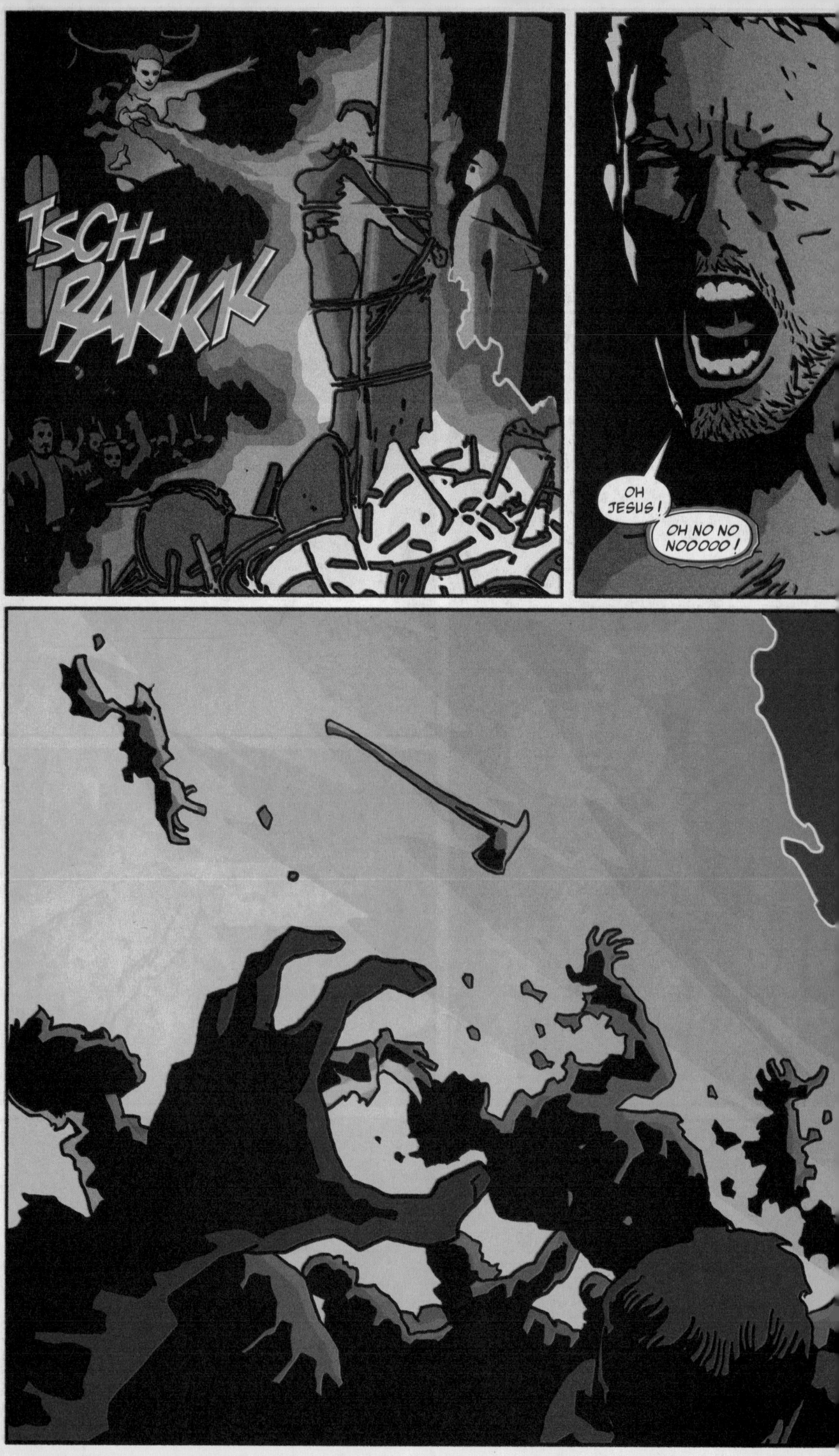
TSCH-BAKKK
OH JESUS!
OH NO NO NOOOOO!

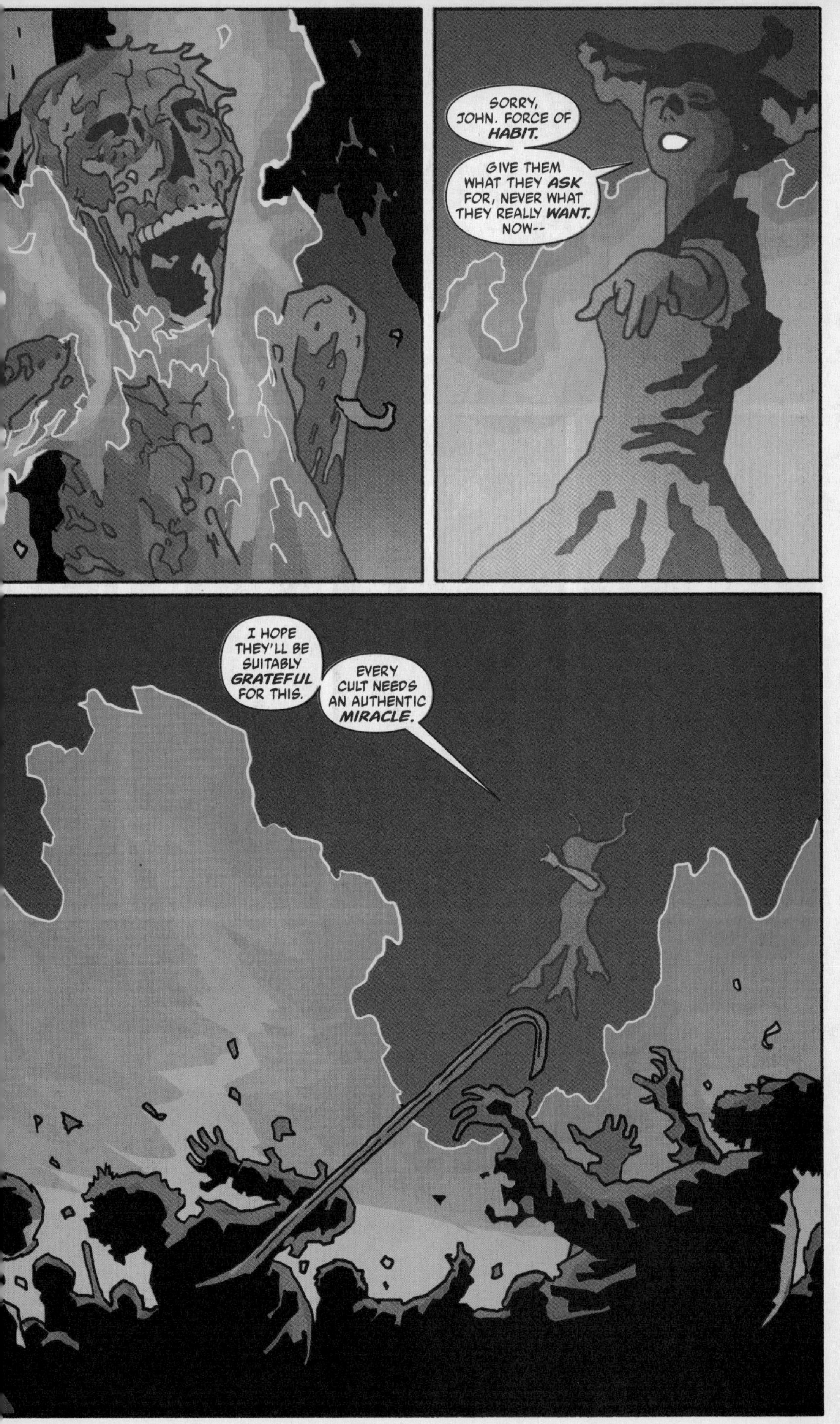

SORRY, JOHN. FORCE OF HABIT.
GIVE THEM WHAT THEY ASK FOR, NEVER WHAT THEY REALLY WANT. NOW--
I HOPE THEY'LL BE SUITABLY GRATEFUL FOR THIS.
EVERY CULT NEEDS AN AUTHENTIC MIRACLE.

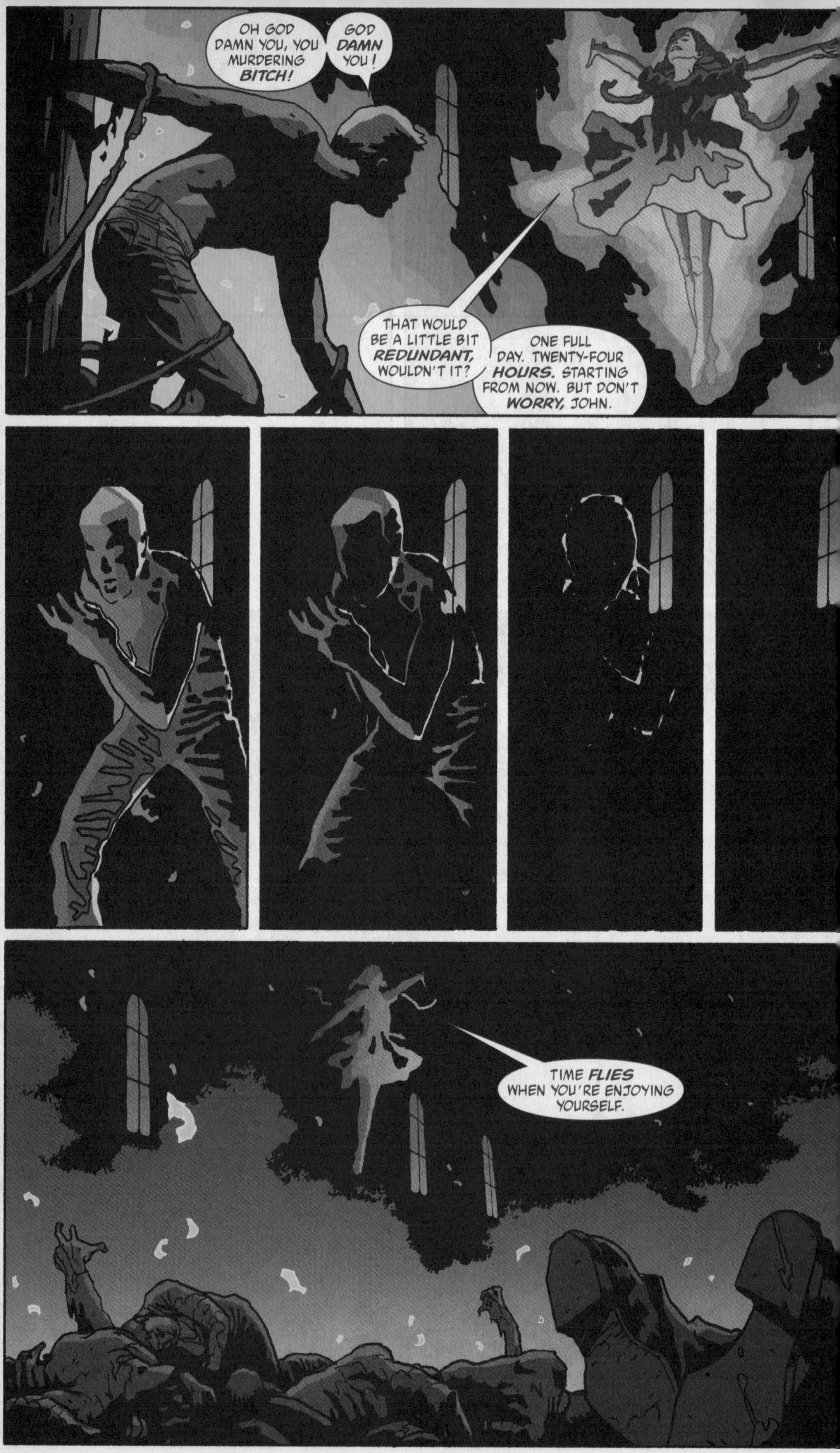
OH GOD DAMN YOU, YOU MURDERING BITCH!
GOD DAMN YOU!
THAT WOULD BE A LITTLE BIT REDUNDANT, WOULDN'T IT?
ONE FULL DAY. TWENTY-FOUR HOURS. STARTING FROM NOW. BUT DON'T WORRY, JOHN.
TIME FLIES WHEN YOU'RE ENJOYING YOURSELF.

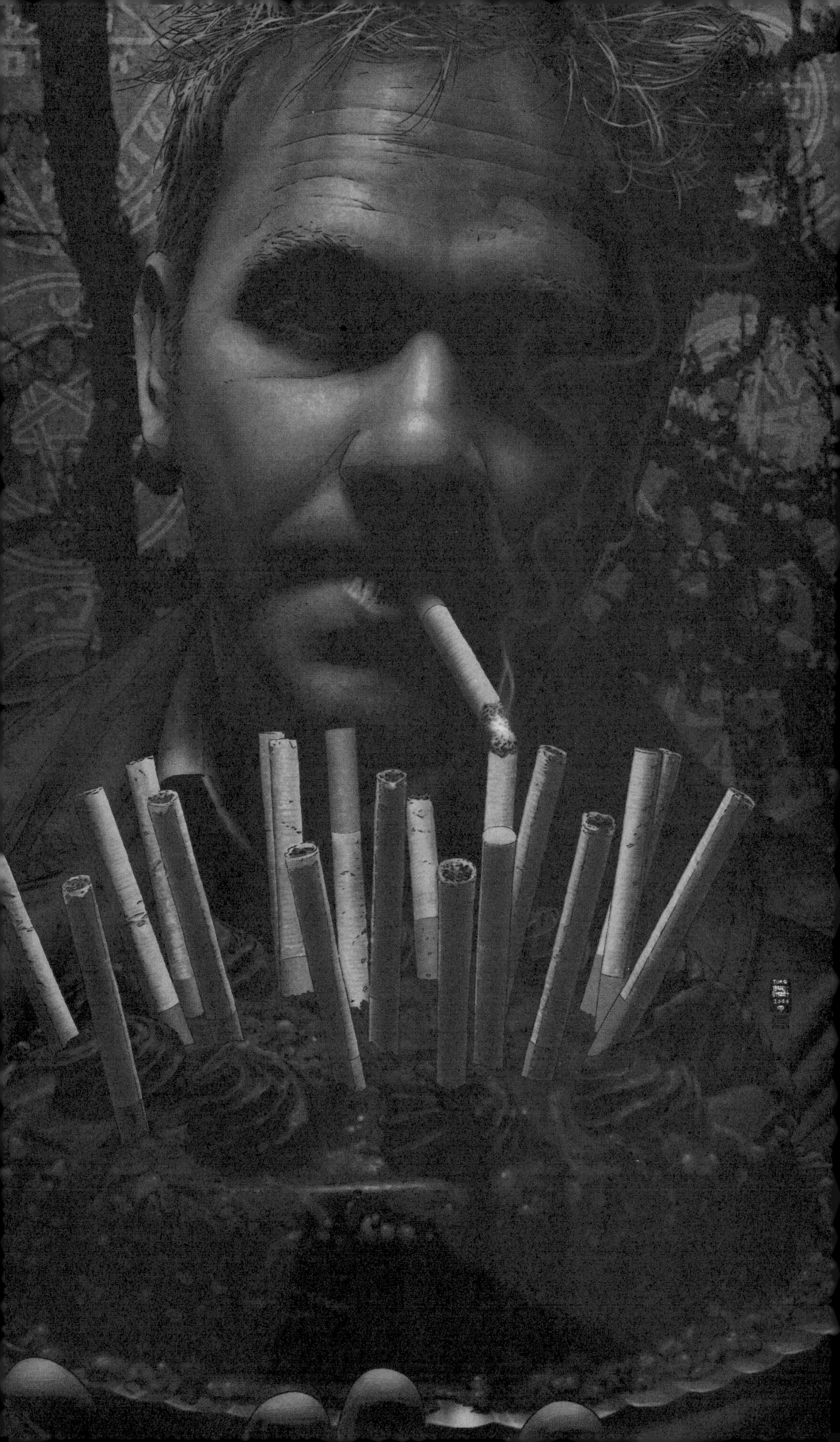

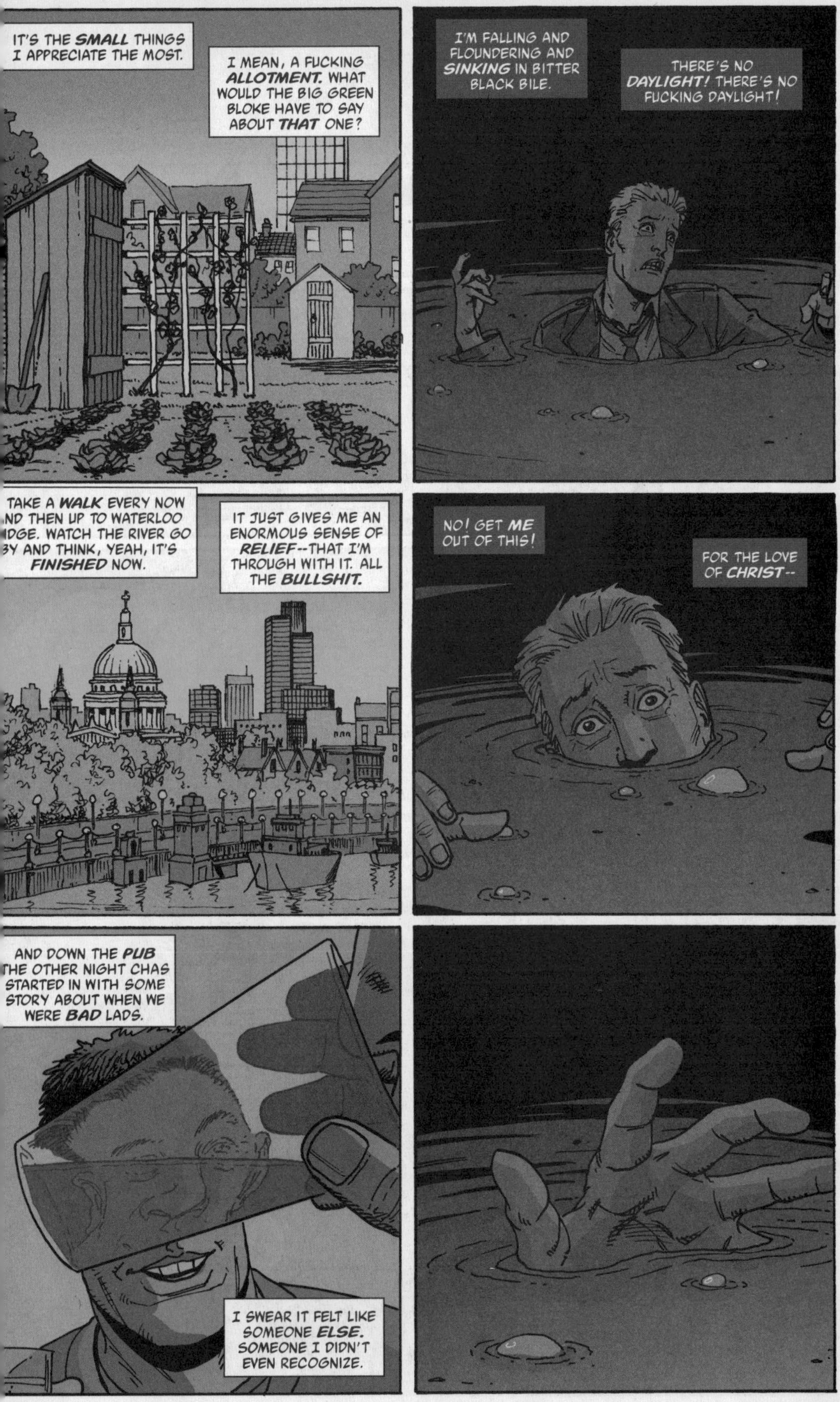

IT'S THE SMALL THINGS I APPRECIATE THE MOST.
I MEAN, A FUCKING ALLOTMENT. WHAT WOULD THE BIG GREEN BLOKE HAVE TO SAY ABOUT THAT ONE?
I'M FALLING AND FLOUNDERING AND SINKING IN BITTER BLACK BILE.
THERE'S NO DAYLIGHT! THERE'S NO FUCKING DAYLIGHT!
TAKE A WALK EVERY NOW ND THEN UP TO WATERLOO IDGE. WATCH THE RIVER GO BY AND THINK, YEAH, IT'S FINISHED NOW.
IT JUST GIVES ME AN ENORMOUS SENSE OF RELIEF--THAT I'M THROUGH WITH IT. ALL THE BULLSHIT.
NO! GET ME OUT OF THIS!
FOR THE LOVE OF CHRIST--
AND DOWN THE PUB THE OTHER NIGHT CHAS STARTED IN WITH SOME STORY ABOUT WHEN WE WERE BAD LADS.
I SWEAR IT FELT LIKE SOMEONE ELSE. SOMEONE I DIDN'T EVEN RECOGNIZE.

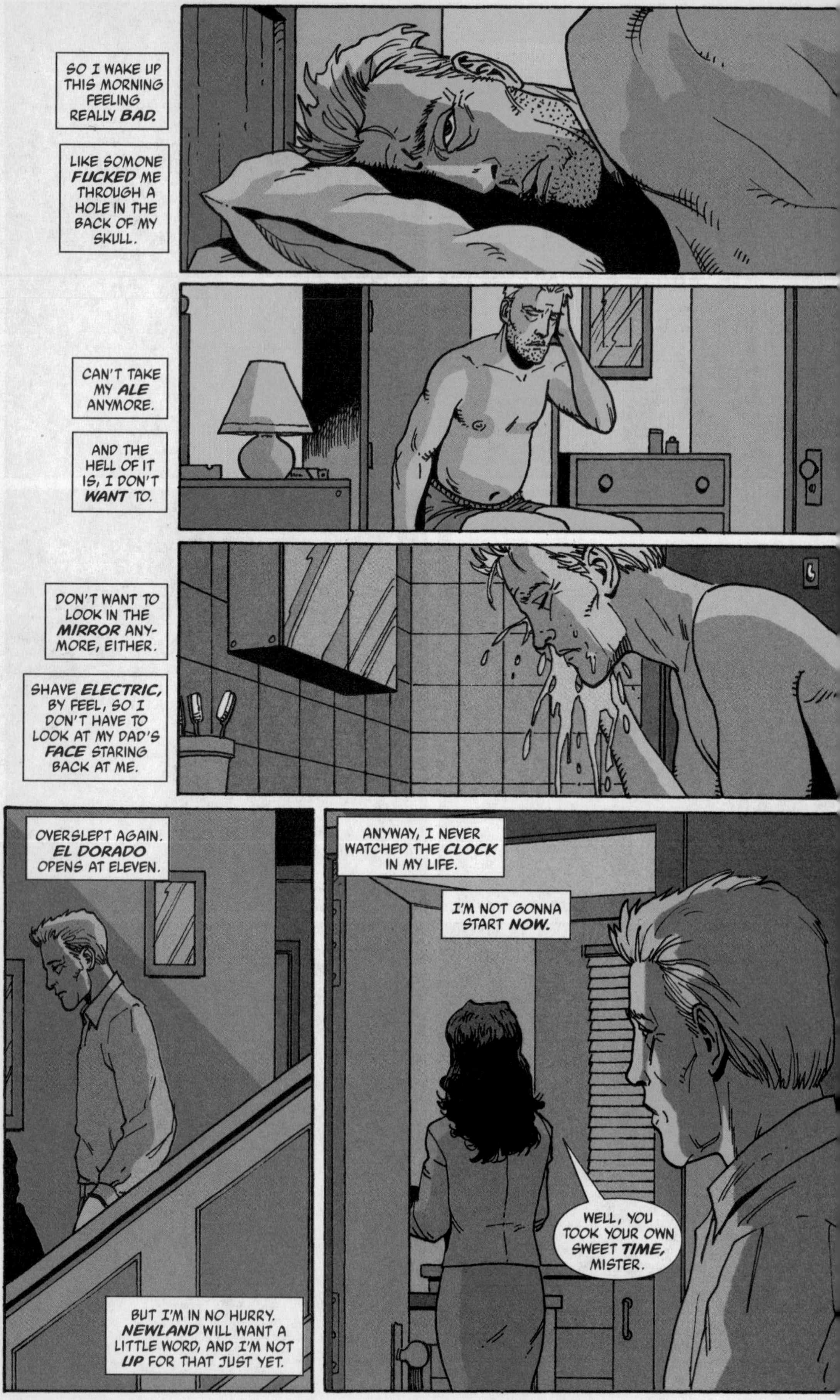
SO I WAKE UP THIS MORNING FEELING REALLY BAD.
LIKE SOMONE FUCKED ME THROUGH A HOLE IN THE BACK OF MY SKULL.
CAN'T TAKE MY ALE ANYMORE.
AND THE HELL OF IT IS, I DON'T WANT TO.
DON'T WANT TO LOOK IN THE MIRROR ANY-MORE, EITHER.
SHAVE ELECTRIC, BY FEEL, SO I DON'T HAVE TO LOOK AT MY DAD'S FACE STARING BACK AT ME.
OVERSLEPT AGAIN. EL DORADO OPENS AT ELEVEN.
BUT I'M IN NO HURRY. NEWLAND WILL WANT A LITTLE WORD, AND I'M NOT UP FOR THAT JUST YET.
ANYWAY, I NEVER WATCHED THE CLOCK IN MY LIFE.
I'M NOT GONNA START NOW.
WELL, YOU TOOK YOUR OWN SWEET TIME, MISTER.

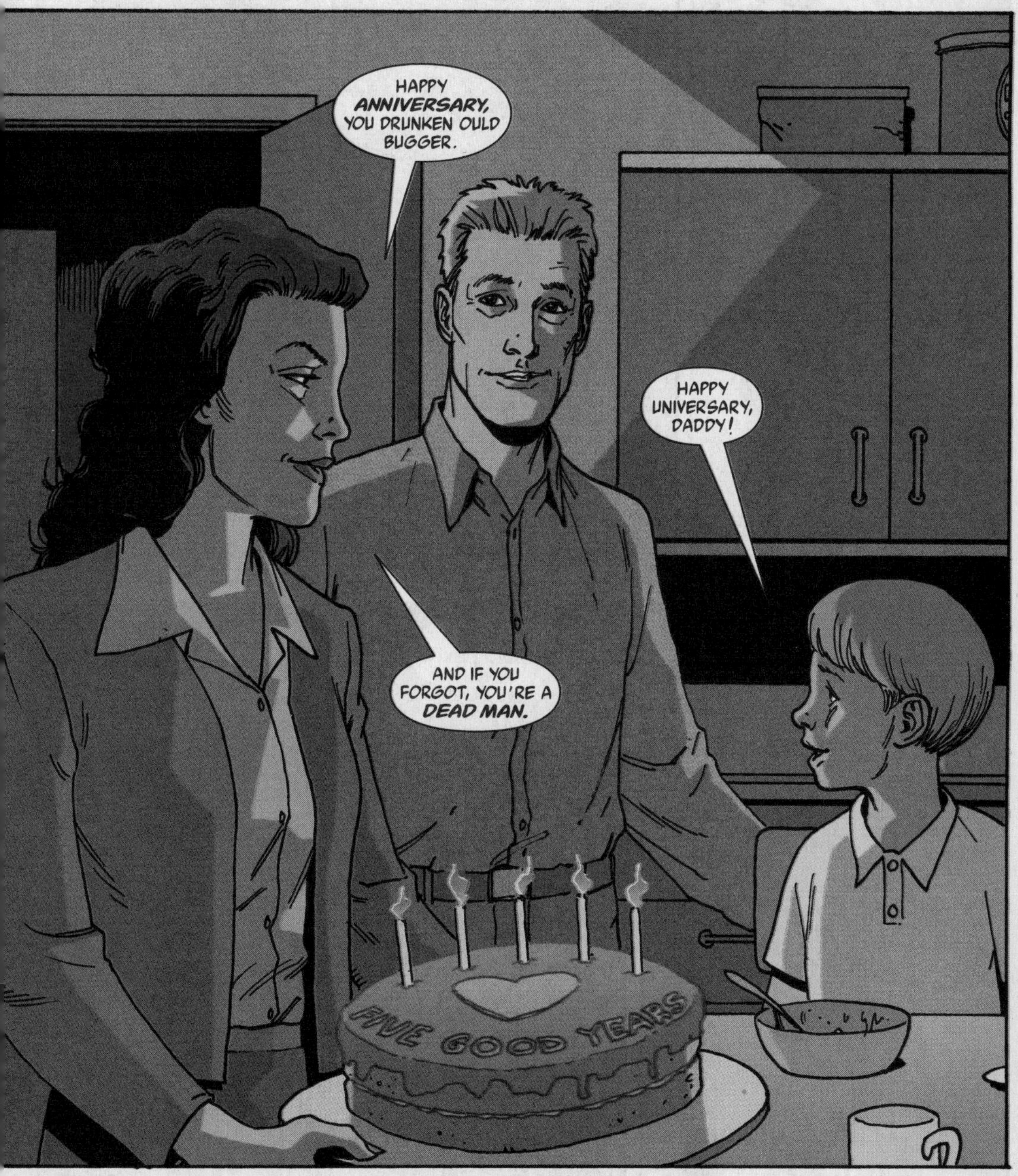
HAPPY ANNIVERSARY, YOU DRUNKEN OULD BUGGER.
HAPPY UNIVERSARY, DADDY!
AND IF YOU FORGOT, YOU'RE A DEAD MAN.
FIVE GOOD YEARS

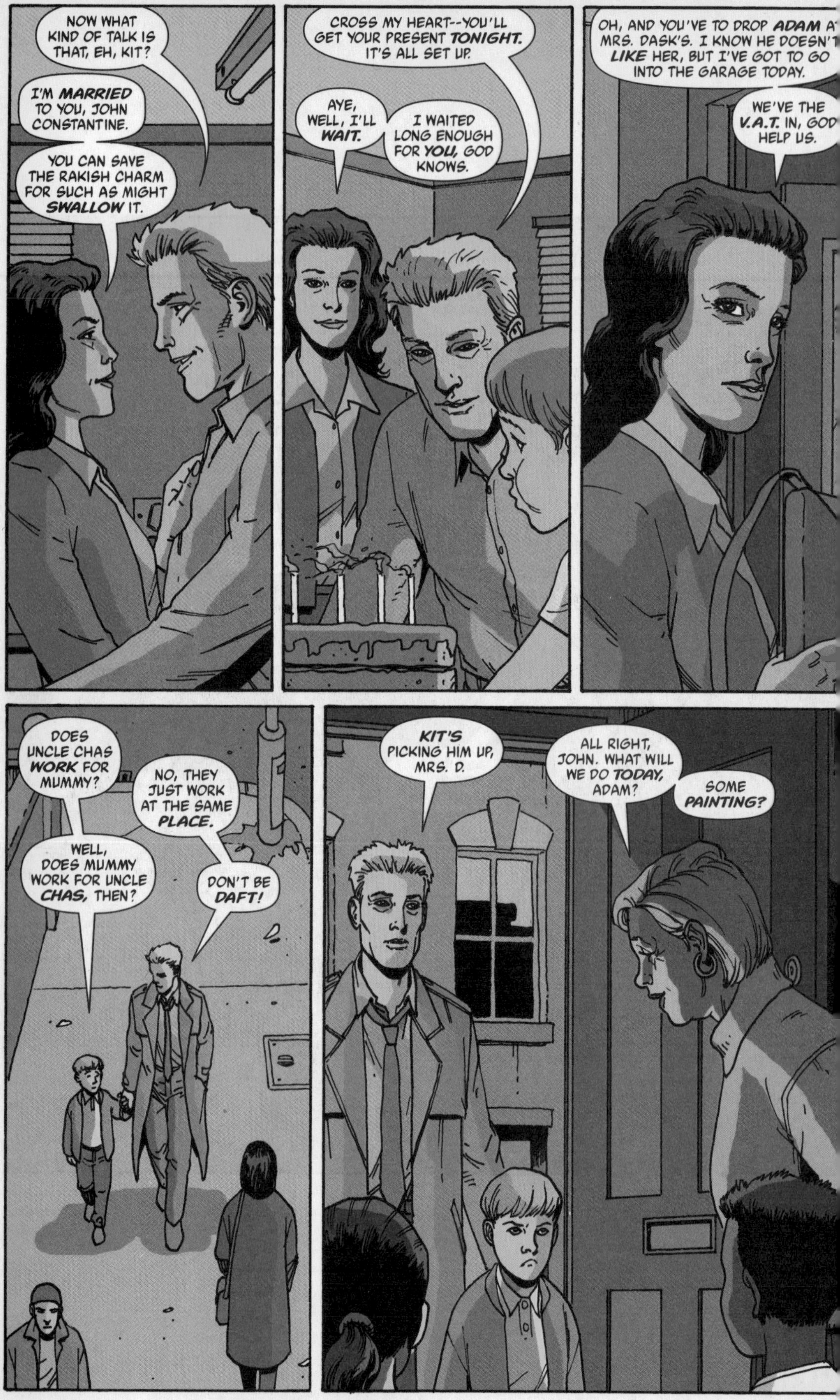
NOW WHAT KIND OF TALK IS THAT, EH, KIT?
I'M MARRIED TO YOU, JOHN CONSTANTINE.
YOU CAN SAVE THE RAKISH CHARM FOR SUCH AS MIGHT SWALLOW IT.
CROSS MY HEART--YOU'LL GET YOUR PRESENT TONIGHT. IT'S ALL SET UP.
AYE, WELL, I'LL WAIT.
I WAITED LONG ENOUGH FOR YOU, GOD KNOWS.
OH, AND YOU'VE TO DROP ADAM AT MRS. DASK'S. I KNOW HE DOESN'T LIKE HER, BUT I'VE GOT TO GO INTO THE GARAGE TODAY.
WE'VE THE V.A.T. IN, GOD HELP US.
DOES UNCLE CHAS WORK FOR MUMMY?
NO, THEY JUST WORK AT THE SAME PLACE.
WELL, DOES MUMMY WORK FOR UNCLE CHAS, THEN?
DON'T BE DAFT!
KIT'S PICKING HIM UP, MRS. D.
ALL RIGHT, JOHN. WHAT WILL WE DO TODAY, ADAM?
SOME PAINTING?

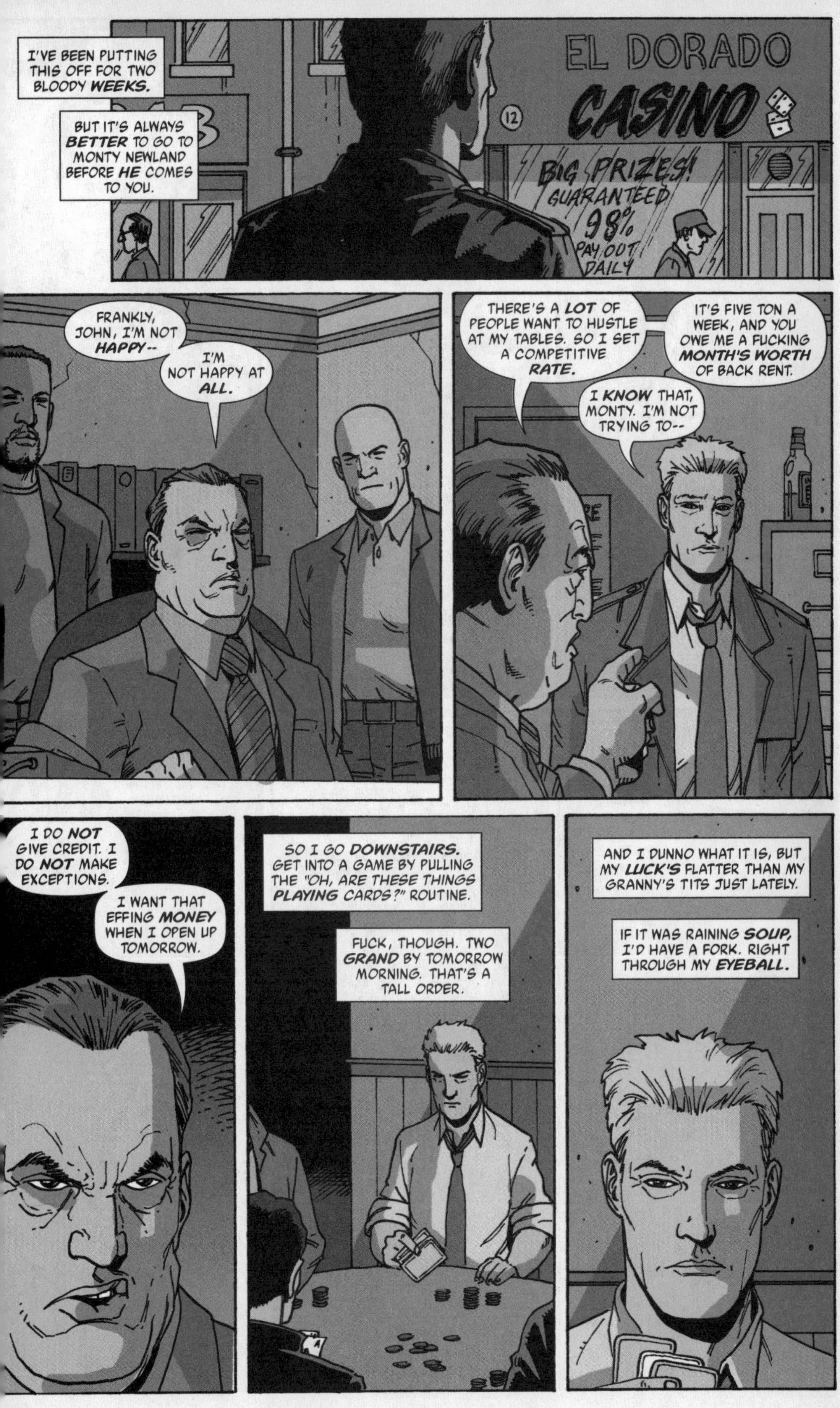
I'VE BEEN PUTTING THIS OFF FOR TWO BLOODY WEEKS.
BUT IT'S ALWAYS BETTER TO GO TO MONTY NEWLAND BEFORE HE COMES TO YOU.
EL DORADO
CASINO
BIG PRIZES!
GUARANTEED
98%
PAY OUT
DAILY
FRANKLY, JOHN, I'M NOT HAPPY--
I'M NOT HAPPY AT ALL.
THERE'S A LOT OF PEOPLE WANT TO HUSTLE AT MY TABLES. SO I SET A COMPETITIVE RATE.
IT'S FIVE TON A WEEK, AND YOU OWE ME A FUCKING MONTH'S WORTH OF BACK RENT.
I KNOW THAT, MONTY. I'M NOT TRYING TO--
I DO NOT GIVE CREDIT. I DO NOT MAKE EXCEPTIONS.
I WANT THAT EFFING MONEY WHEN I OPEN UP TOMORROW.
SO I GO DOWNSTAIRS. GET INTO A GAME BY PULLING THE "OH, ARE THESE THINGS PLAYING CARDS?" ROUTINE.
FUCK, THOUGH. TWO GRAND BY TOMORROW MORNING. THAT'S A TALL ORDER.
AND I DUNNO WHAT IT IS, BUT MY LUCK'S FLATTER THAN MY GRANNY'S TITS JUST LATELY.
IF IT WAS RAINING SOUP, I'D HAVE A FORK. RIGHT THROUGH MY EYEBALL.

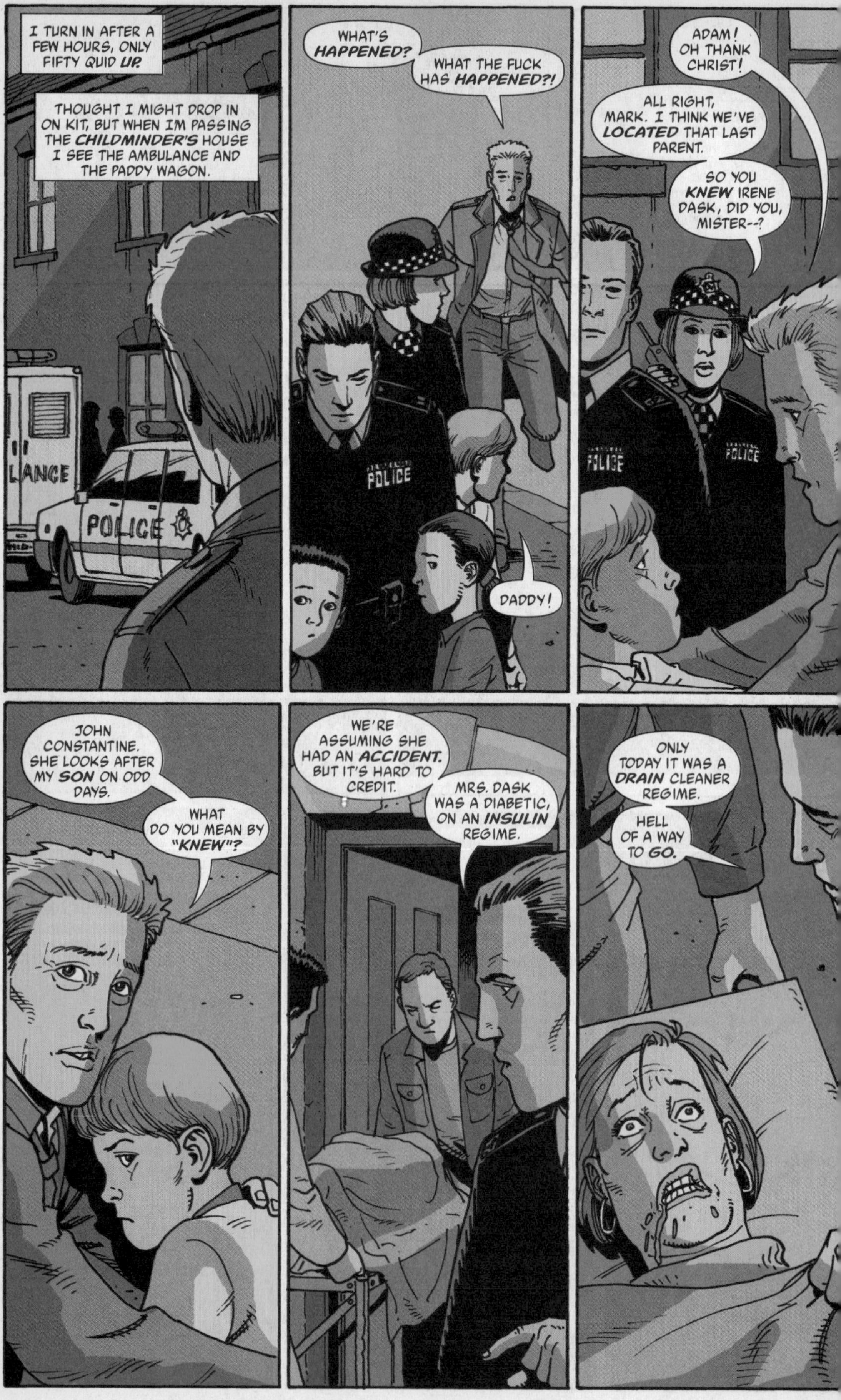

I TURN IN AFTER A FEW HOURS, ONLY FIFTY QUID UP.
THOUGHT I MIGHT DROP IN ON KIT, BUT WHEN I'M PASSING THE CHILDMINDER'S HOUSE I SEE THE AMBULANCE AND THE PADDY WAGON.
LANCE
POLICE
WHAT'S HAPPENED?
WHAT THE FUCK HAS HAPPENED?!
POLICE
DADDY!
ADAM! OH THANK CHRIST!
ALL RIGHT, MARK. I THINK WE'VE LOCATED THAT LAST PARENT.
SO YOU KNEW IRENE DASK, DID YOU, MISTER--?
POLICE
POLICE
JOHN CONSTANTINE. SHE LOOKS AFTER MY SON ON ODD DAYS.
WHAT DO YOU MEAN BY "KNEW"?
WE'RE ASSUMING SHE HAD AN ACCIDENT. BUT IT'S HARD TO CREDIT.
MRS. DASK WAS A DIABETIC, ON AN INSULIN REGIME.
ONLY TODAY IT WAS A DRAIN CLEANER REGIME.
HELL OF A WAY TO GO.

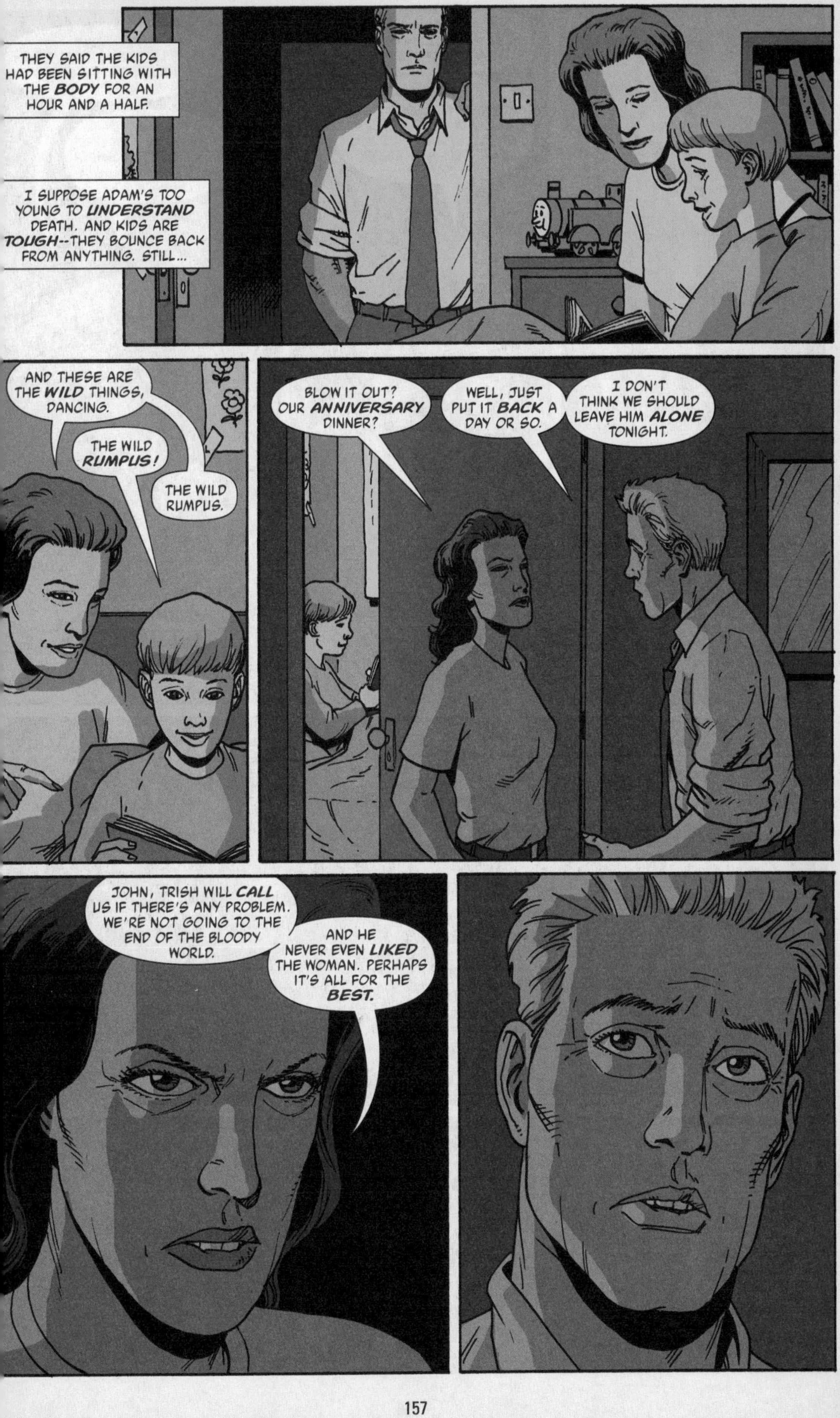

THEY SAID THE KIDS HAD BEEN SITTING WITH THE BODY FOR AN HOUR AND A HALF.
I SUPPOSE ADAM'S TOO YOUNG TO UNDERSTAND DEATH. AND KIDS ARE TOUGH--THEY BOUNCE BACK FROM ANYTHING. STILL...
AND THESE ARE THE WILD THINGS, DANCING.
THE WILD RUMPUS!
THE WILD RUMPUS.
BLOW IT OUT? OUR ANNIVERSARY DINNER?
WELL, JUST PUT IT BACK A DAY OR SO.
I DON'T THINK WE SHOULD LEAVE HIM ALONE TONIGHT.
JOHN, TRISH WILL CALL US IF THERE'S ANY PROBLEM. WE'RE NOT GOING TO THE END OF THE BLOODY WORLD.
AND HE NEVER EVEN LIKED THE WOMAN. PERHAPS IT'S ALL FOR THE BEST.

"ALL FOR THE BEST"?

YEAH.

WELL, KIT GREW UP IN BELFAST. I SUPPOSE THAT MAKES YOU A BIT HARD, LIKE.

AND SHACKING UP WITH YOU, AND ALL. NOT FOR THE FAINT-HEARTED, IS IT?

REMEMBER WHEN WE BLAGGED THAT CRUCIFIX THAT WOULDN'T STOP BLEEDING? DID YOU EVER TELL HER ABOUT THAT?

PROBABLY NOT. LISTEN, IS YOUR TRISH STILL OKAY FOR SITTING TONIGHT?

DO WHAT? YOU KNOW HOW SHE IS WITH KIDS. SHE'S NOT GONNA MISS A CHANCE TO--

CONSTANTINE!

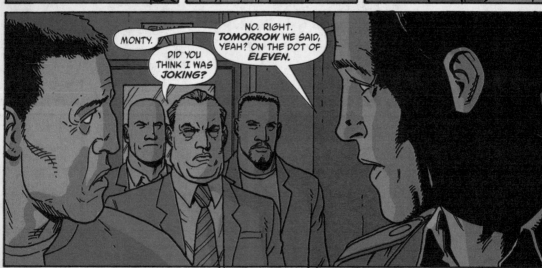

MONTY.

DID YOU THINK I WAS JOKING?

NO. RIGHT. TOMORROW WE SAID, YEAH? ON THE DOT OF ELEVEN.

YOU SHOULD NOT BE DOWN HERE ON THE PISS.

YOU SHOULD BE COUNTING UP YOUR PENNIES AND MAKING SURE YOU GET THE RIGHT FUCKING ANSWER.

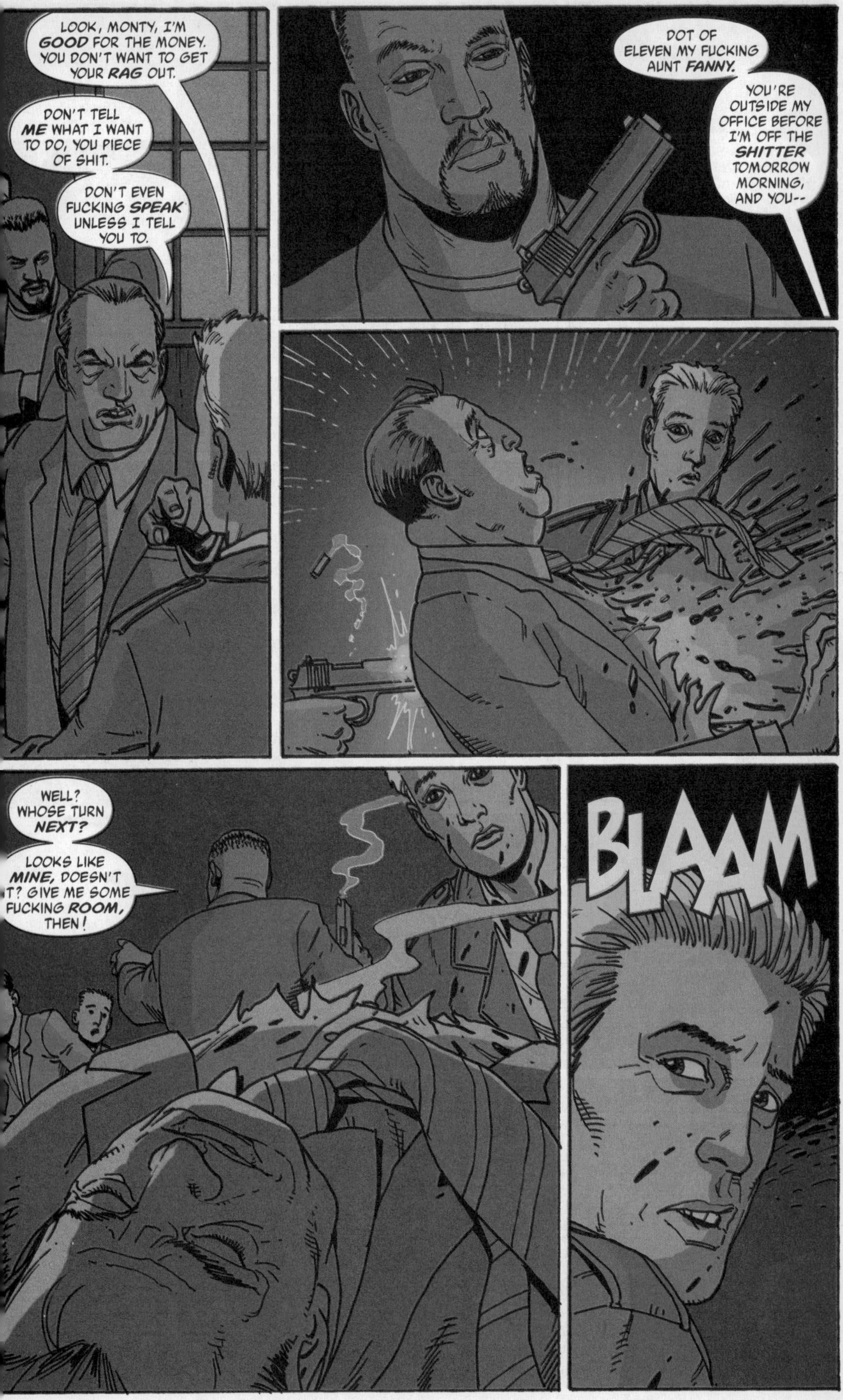
LOOK, MONTY, I'M **GOOD** FOR THE MONEY. YOU DON'T WANT TO GET YOUR **RAG** OUT.
DON'T TELL **ME** WHAT I WANT TO DO, YOU PIECE OF SHIT.
DON'T EVEN FUCKING **SPEAK** UNLESS I TELL YOU TO.
DOT OF ELEVEN MY FUCKING AUNT **FANNY.**
YOU'RE OUTSIDE MY OFFICE BEFORE I'M OFF THE **SHITTER** TOMORROW MORNING, AND YOU--
WELL? WHOSE TURN **NEXT?**
LOOKS LIKE **MINE,** DOESN'T IT? GIVE ME SOME FUCKING **ROOM,** THEN!
BLAAM

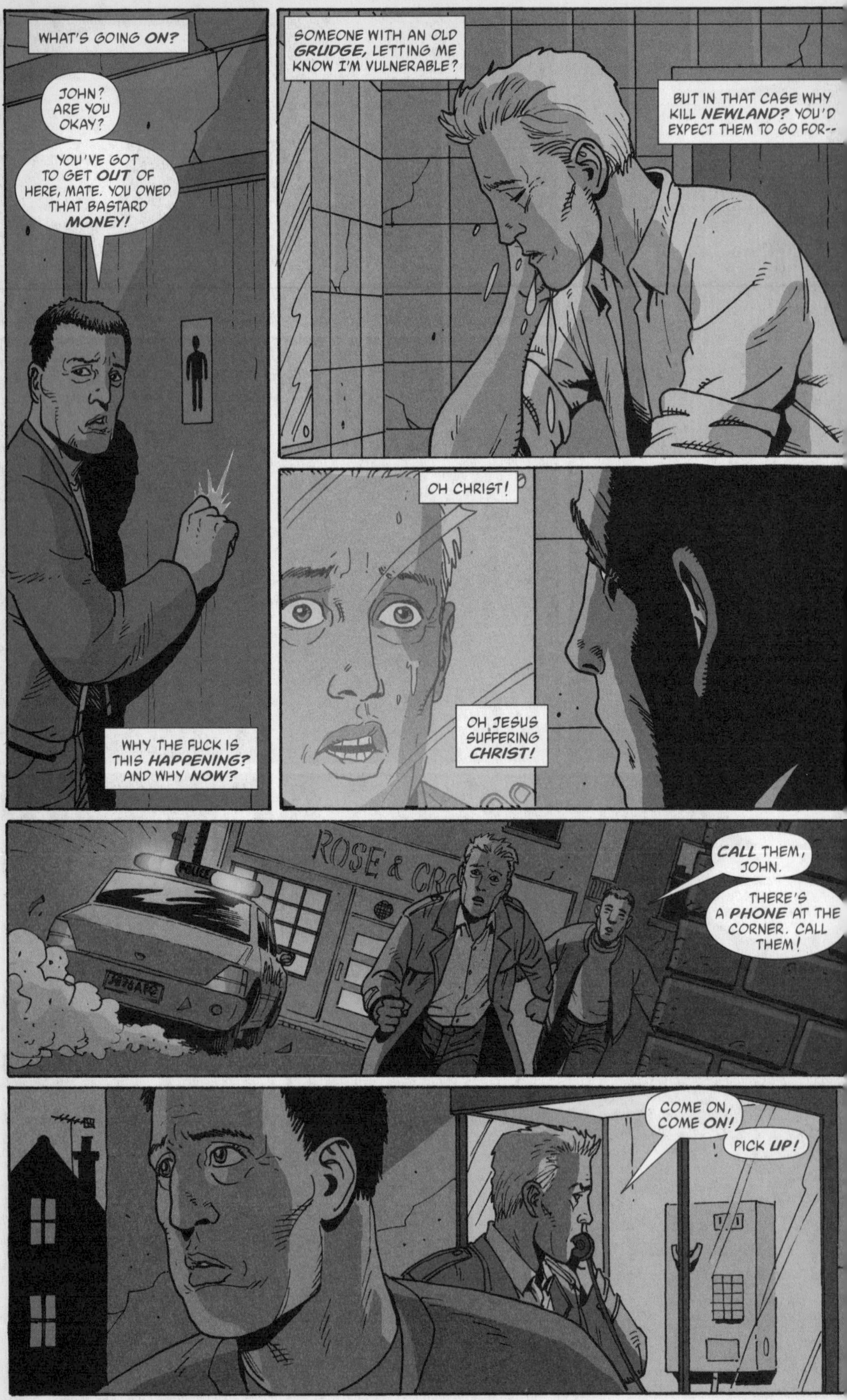
WHAT'S GOING ON?
JOHN? ARE YOU OKAY?
YOU'VE GOT TO GET OUT OF HERE, MATE. YOU OWED THAT BASTARD MONEY!
WHY THE FUCK IS THIS HAPPENING? AND WHY NOW?
SOMEONE WITH AN OLD GRUDGE, LETTING ME KNOW I'M VULNERABLE?
BUT IN THAT CASE WHY KILL NEWLAND? YOU'D EXPECT THEM TO GO FOR--
OH CHRIST!
OH JESUS SUFFERING CHRIST!
ROSE & CRO
POLICE
CALL THEM, JOHN.
THERE'S A PHONE AT THE CORNER. CALL THEM!
COME ON, COME ON!
PICK UP!

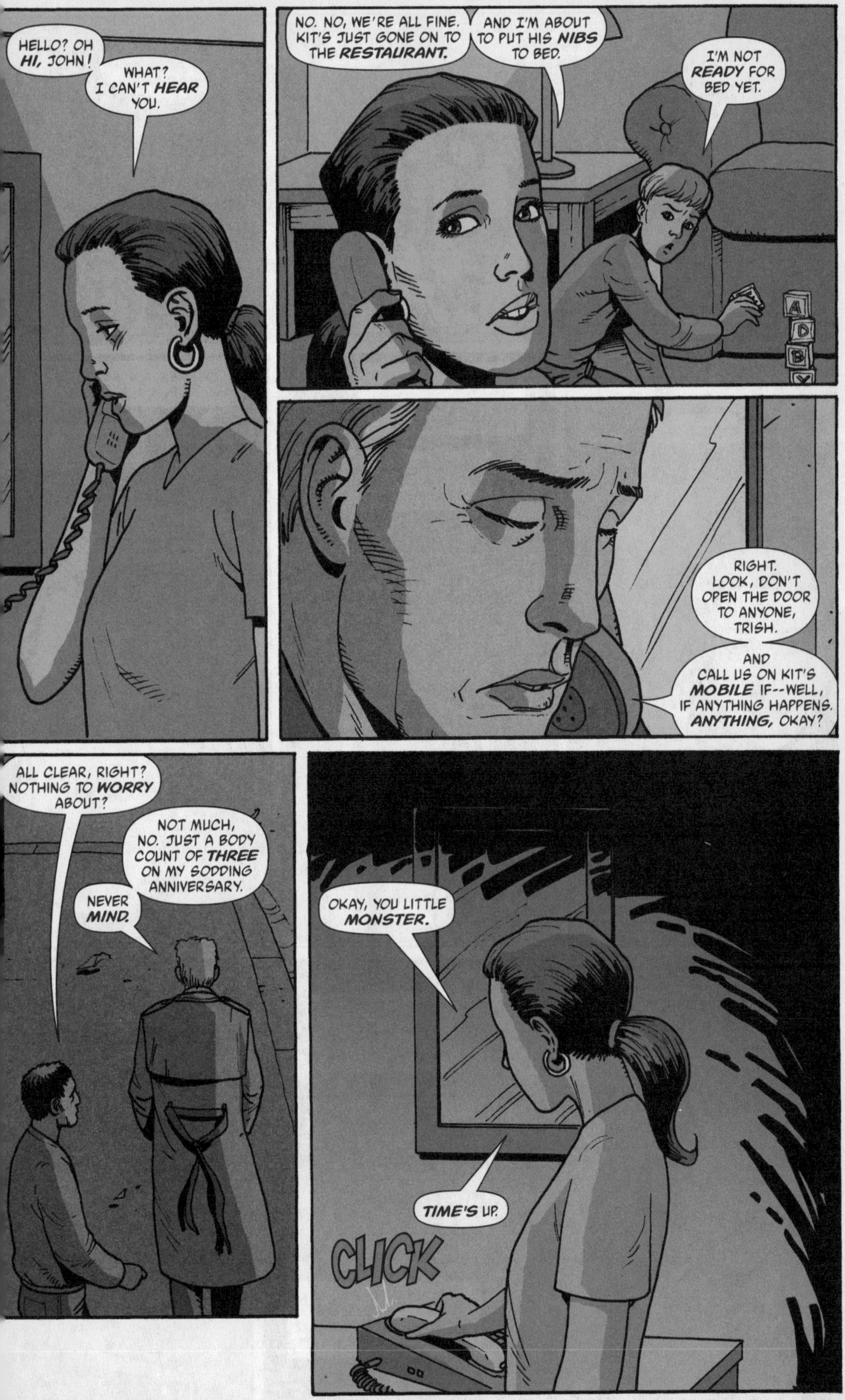

HELLO? OH HI, JOHN!
WHAT? I CAN'T HEAR YOU.
NO. NO, WE'RE ALL FINE. KIT'S JUST GONE ON TO THE RESTAURANT.
AND I'M ABOUT TO PUT HIS NIBS TO BED.
I'M NOT READY FOR BED YET.
RIGHT. LOOK, DON'T OPEN THE DOOR TO ANYONE, TRISH.
AND CALL US ON KIT'S MOBILE IF--WELL, IF ANYTHING HAPPENS. ANYTHING, OKAY?
ALL CLEAR, RIGHT? NOTHING TO WORRY ABOUT?
NOT MUCH, NO. JUST A BODY COUNT OF THREE ON MY SODDING ANNIVERSARY.
NEVER MIND.
OKAY, YOU LITTLE MONSTER.
TIME'S UP.
CLICK

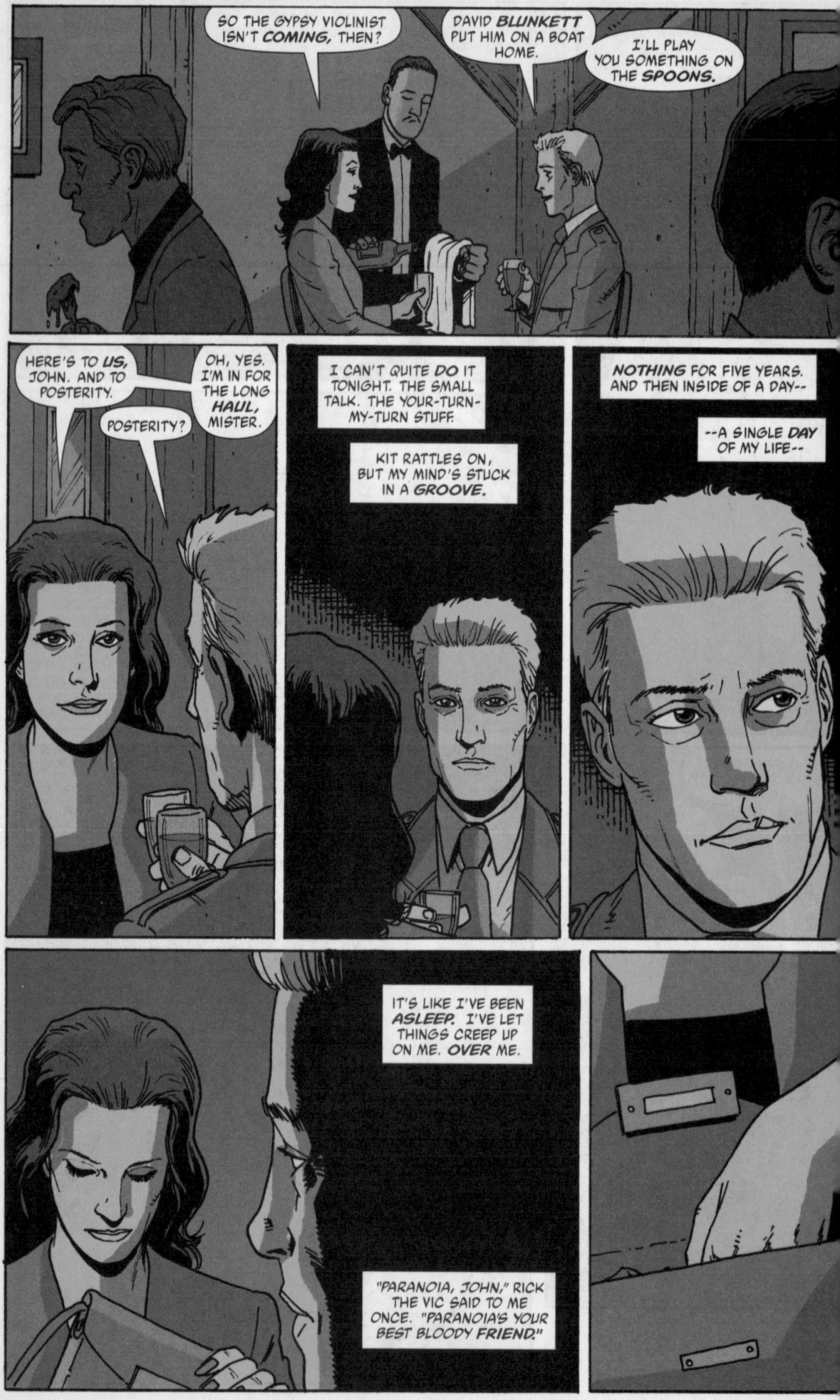

SO THE GYPSY VIOLINIST ISN'T COMING, THEN?
DAVID BLUNKETT PUT HIM ON A BOAT HOME.
I'LL PLAY YOU SOMETHING ON THE SPOONS.
HERE'S TO US, JOHN. AND TO POSTERITY.
POSTERITY?
OH, YES. I'M IN FOR THE LONG HAUL, MISTER.
I CAN'T QUITE DO IT TONIGHT. THE SMALL TALK. THE YOUR-TURN-MY-TURN STUFF.
KIT RATTLES ON, BUT MY MIND'S STUCK IN A GROOVE.
NOTHING FOR FIVE YEARS. AND THEN INSIDE OF A DAY--
--A SINGLE DAY OF MY LIFE--
IT'S LIKE I'VE BEEN ASLEEP. I'VE LET THINGS CREEP UP ON ME. OVER ME.
"PARANOIA, JOHN," RICK THE VIC SAID TO ME ONCE. "PARANOIA'S YOUR BEST BLOODY FRIEND."

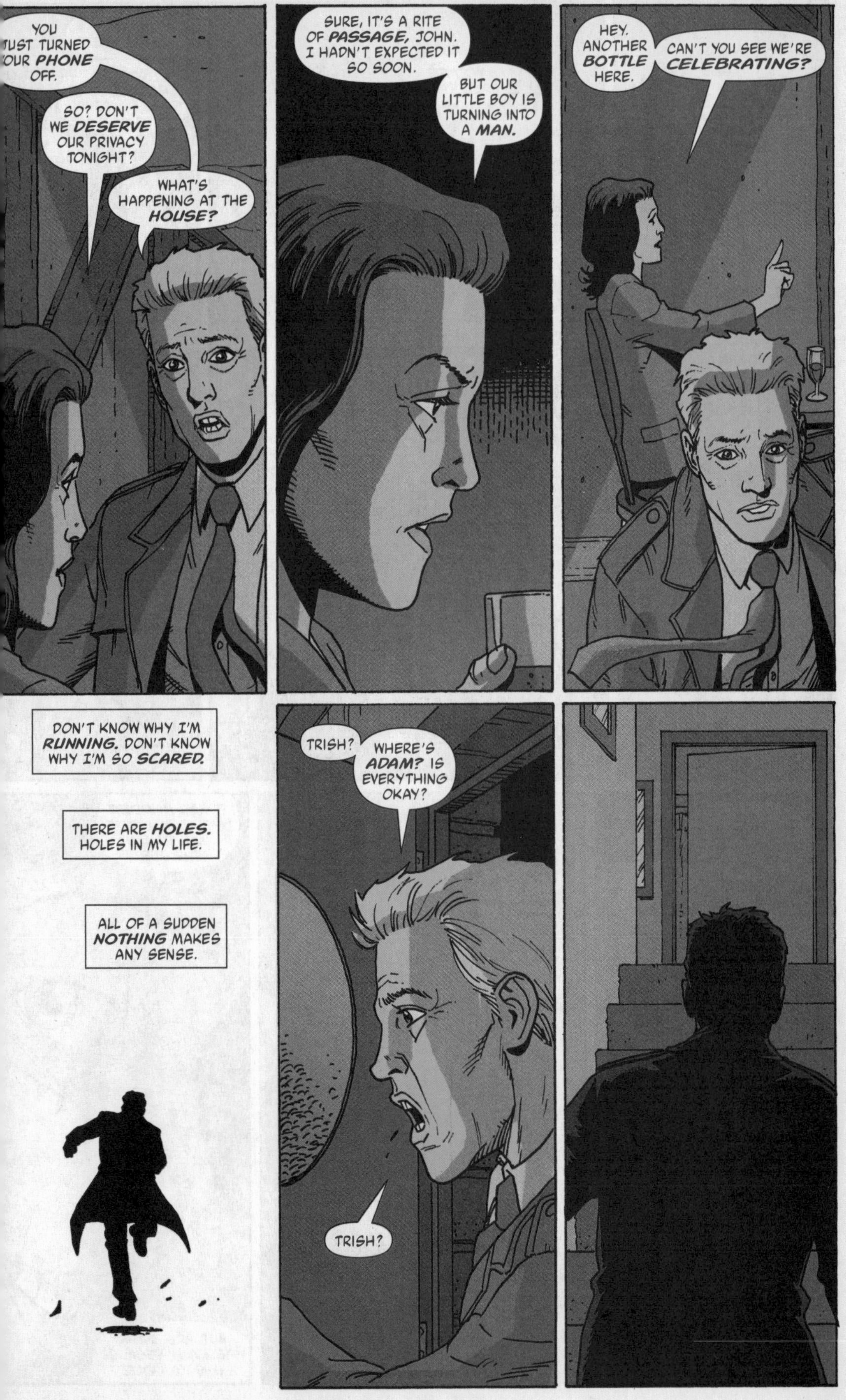

YOU JUST TURNED YOUR PHONE OFF.
SO? DON'T WE DESERVE OUR PRIVACY TONIGHT?
WHAT'S HAPPENING AT THE HOUSE?
SURE, IT'S A RITE OF PASSAGE, JOHN. I HADN'T EXPECTED IT SO SOON.
BUT OUR LITTLE BOY IS TURNING INTO A MAN.
HEY. ANOTHER BOTTLE HERE.
CAN'T YOU SEE WE'RE CELEBRATING?
DON'T KNOW WHY I'M RUNNING. DON'T KNOW WHY I'M SO SCARED.
THERE ARE HOLES. HOLES IN MY LIFE.
ALL OF A SUDDEN NOTHING MAKES ANY SENSE.
TRISH?
WHERE'S ADAM? IS EVERYTHING OKAY?
TRISH?

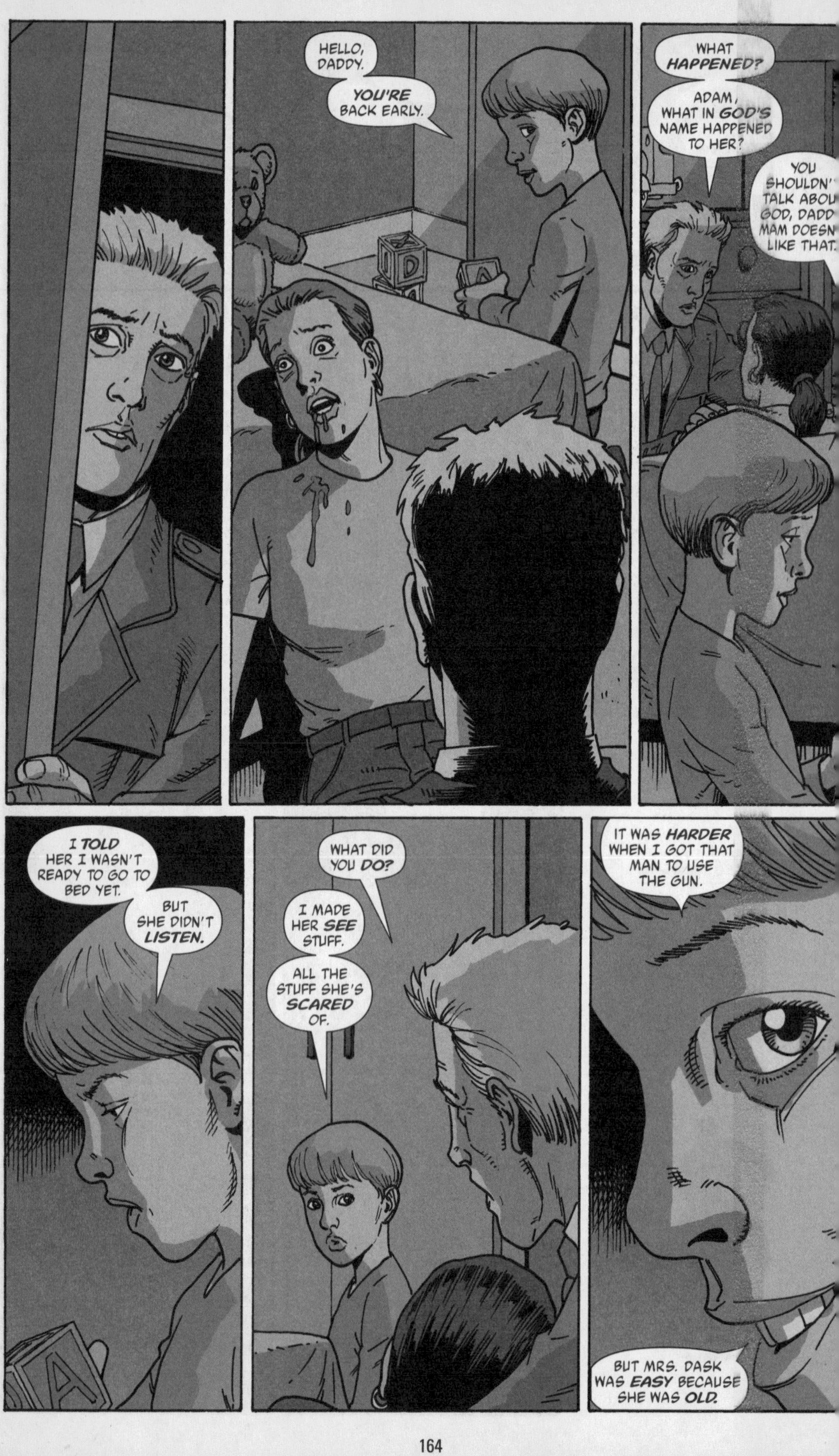
HELLO, DADDY.
YOU'RE BACK EARLY.
WHAT HAPPENED?
ADAM, WHAT IN GOD'S NAME HAPPENED TO HER?
YOU SHOULDN' TALK ABOU GOD, DADD MAM DOESN LIKE THAT.
I TOLD HER I WASN'T READY TO GO TO BED YET.
BUT SHE DIDN'T LISTEN.
WHAT DID YOU DO?
I MADE HER SEE STUFF.
ALL THE STUFF SHE'S SCARED OF.
IT WAS HARDER WHEN I GOT THAT MAN TO USE THE GUN.
BUT MRS. DASK WAS EASY BECAUSE SHE WAS OLD.

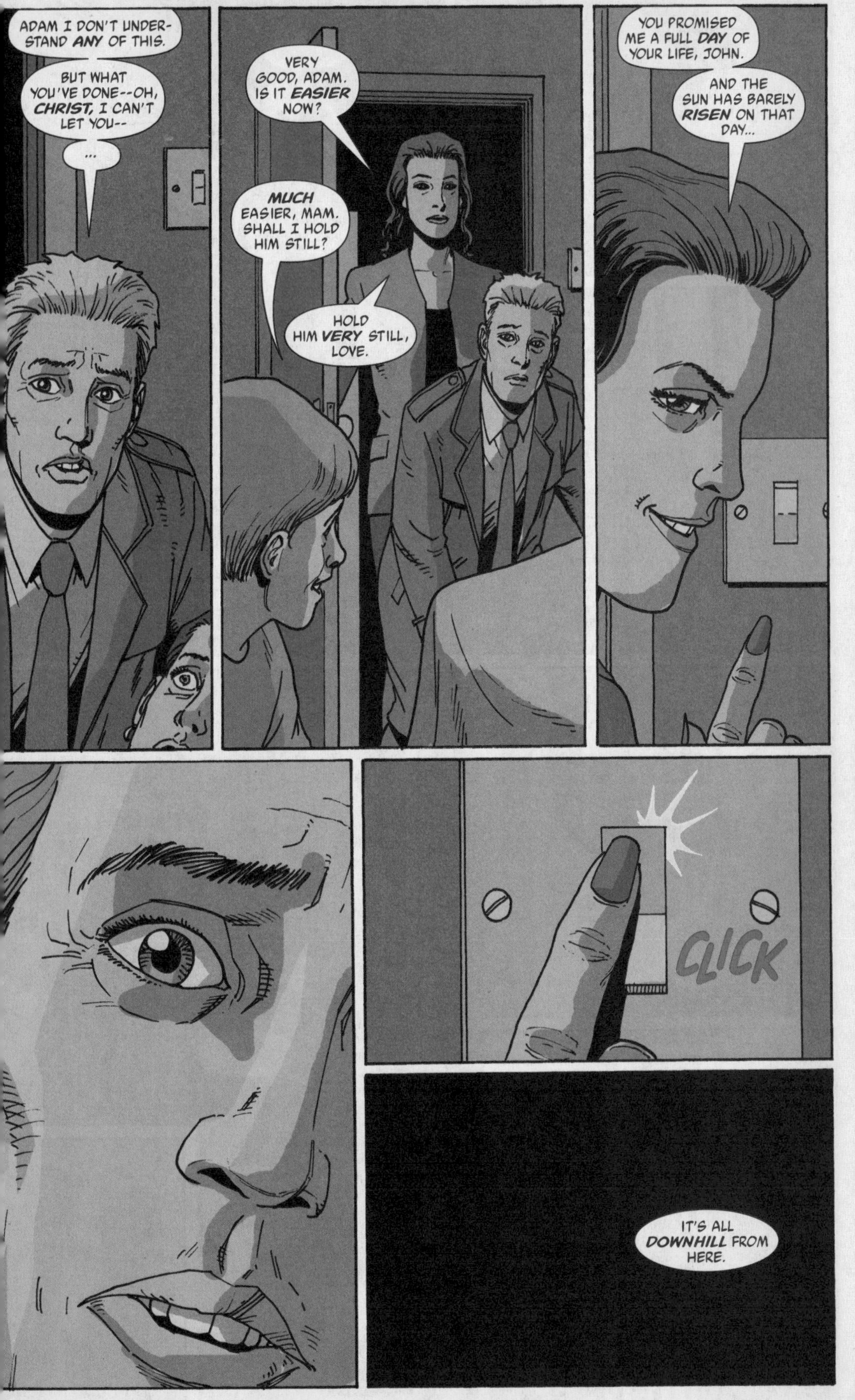

ADAM I DON'T UNDER-STAND ANY OF THIS.
BUT WHAT YOU'VE DONE--OH, CHRIST, I CAN'T LET YOU--
...
VERY GOOD, ADAM. IS IT EASIER NOW?
MUCH EASIER, MAM. SHALL I HOLD HIM STILL?
HOLD HIM VERY STILL, LOVE.
YOU PROMISED ME A FULL DAY OF YOUR LIFE, JOHN.
AND THE SUN HAS BARELY RISEN ON THAT DAY...
CLICK
IT'S ALL DOWNHILL FROM HERE.

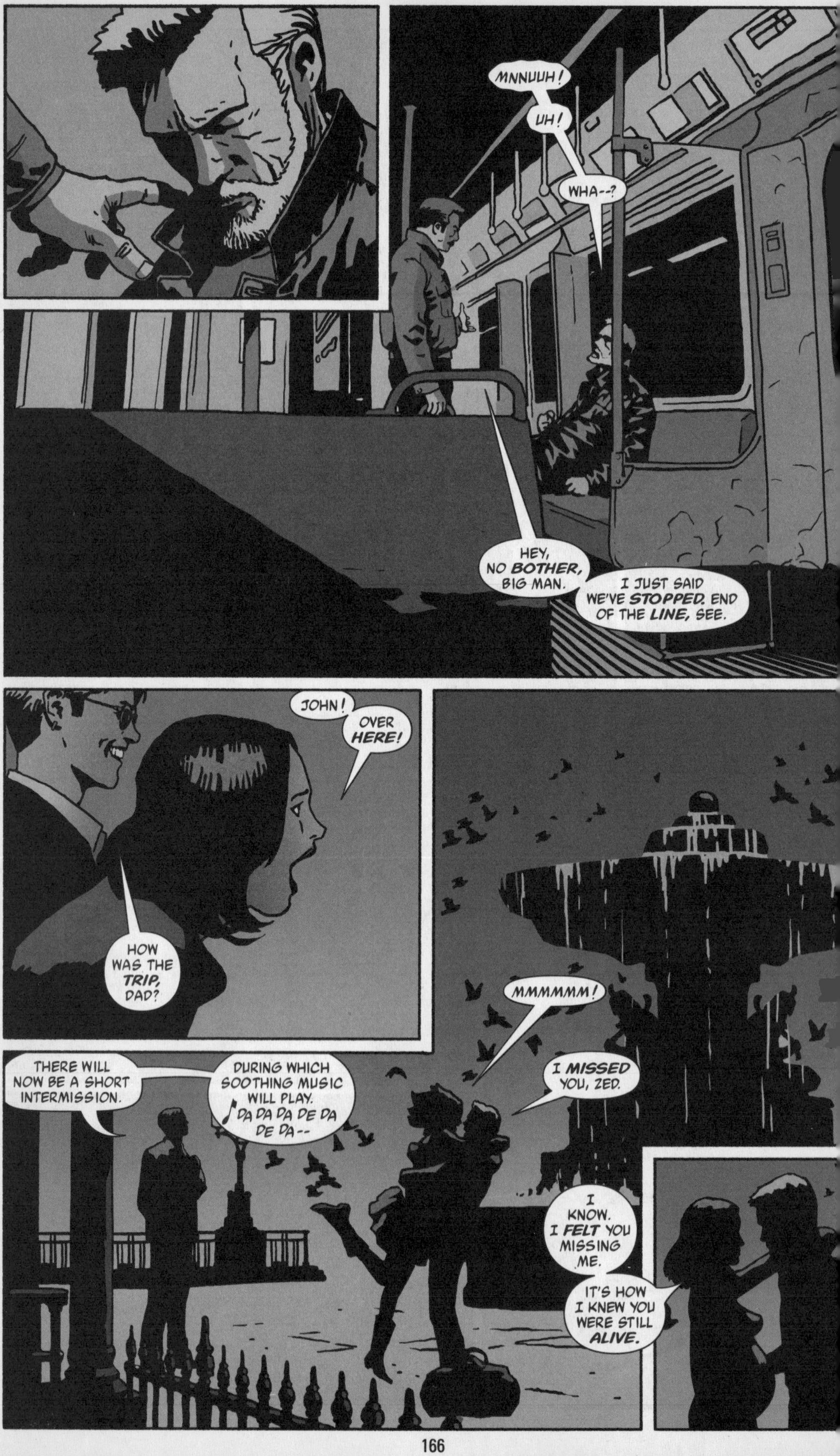
MNNUUH!
UH!
WHA--?
HEY, NO BOTHER, BIG MAN.
I JUST SAID WE'VE STOPPED. END OF THE LINE, SEE.
JOHN!
OVER HERE!
HOW WAS THE TRIP, DAD?
MMMMMM!
THERE WILL NOW BE A SHORT INTERMISSION.
DURING WHICH SOOTHING MUSIC WILL PLAY. ♪ DA DA DA DE DA DE DA--
I MISSED YOU, ZED.
I KNOW. I FELT YOU MISSING ME.
IT'S HOW I KNEW YOU WERE STILL ALIVE.

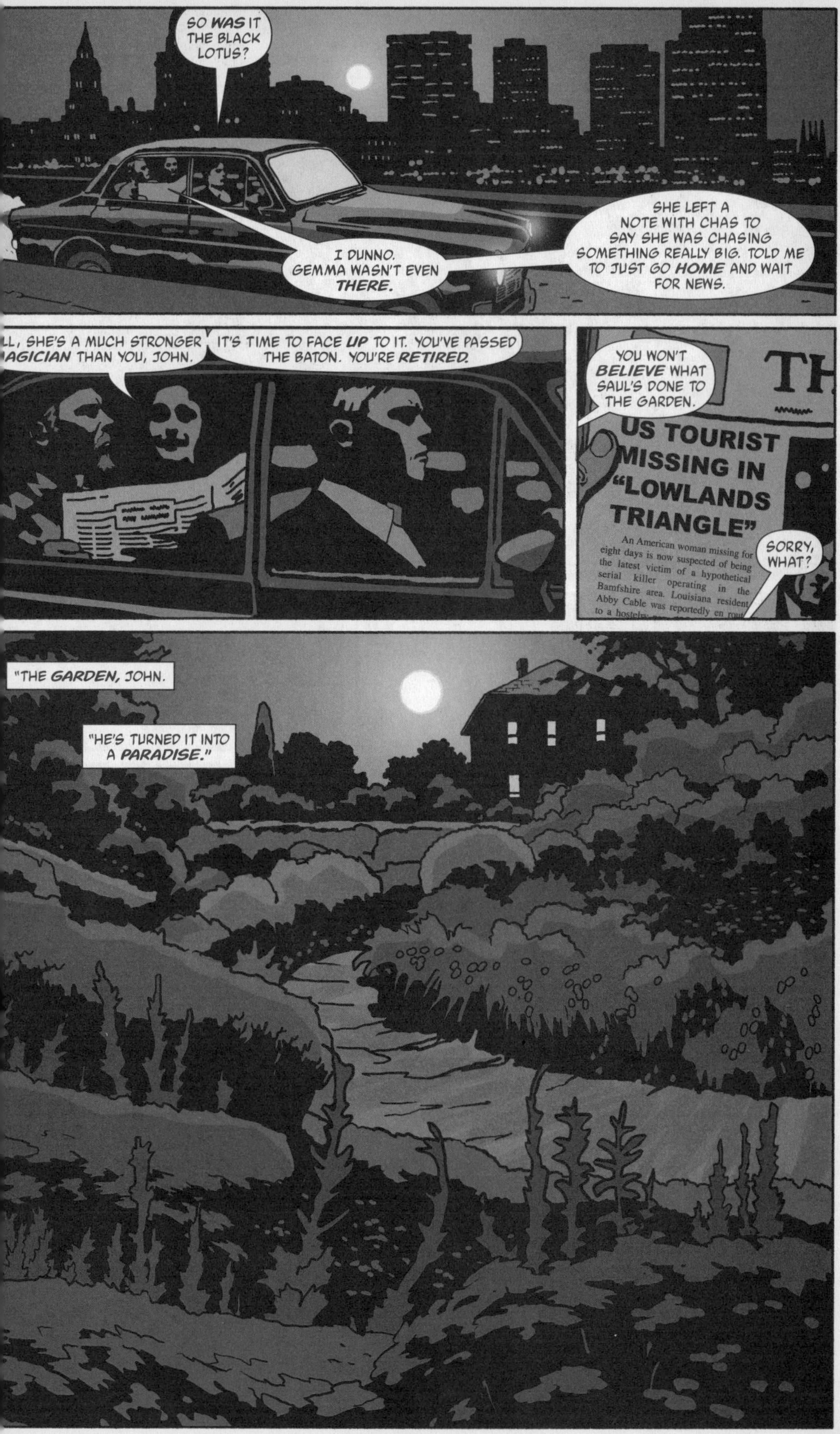
SO WAS IT THE BLACK LOTUS?
I DUNNO. GEMMA WASN'T EVEN THERE.
SHE LEFT A NOTE WITH CHAS TO SAY SHE WAS CHASING SOMETHING REALLY BIG. TOLD ME TO JUST GO HOME AND WAIT FOR NEWS.
LL, SHE'S A MUCH STRONGER AGICIAN THAN YOU, JOHN.
IT'S TIME TO FACE UP TO IT. YOU'VE PASSED THE BATON. YOU'RE RETIRED.
YOU WON'T BELIEVE WHAT SAUL'S DONE TO THE GARDEN.
TH
US TOURIST MISSING IN "LOWLANDS TRIANGLE"
An American woman missing for eight days is now suspected of being the latest victim of a hypothetical serial killer operating in the Bamfshire area. Louisiana resident Abby Cable was reportedly en
SORRY, WHAT?
"THE GARDEN, JOHN.
"HE'S TURNED IT INTO A PARADISE."

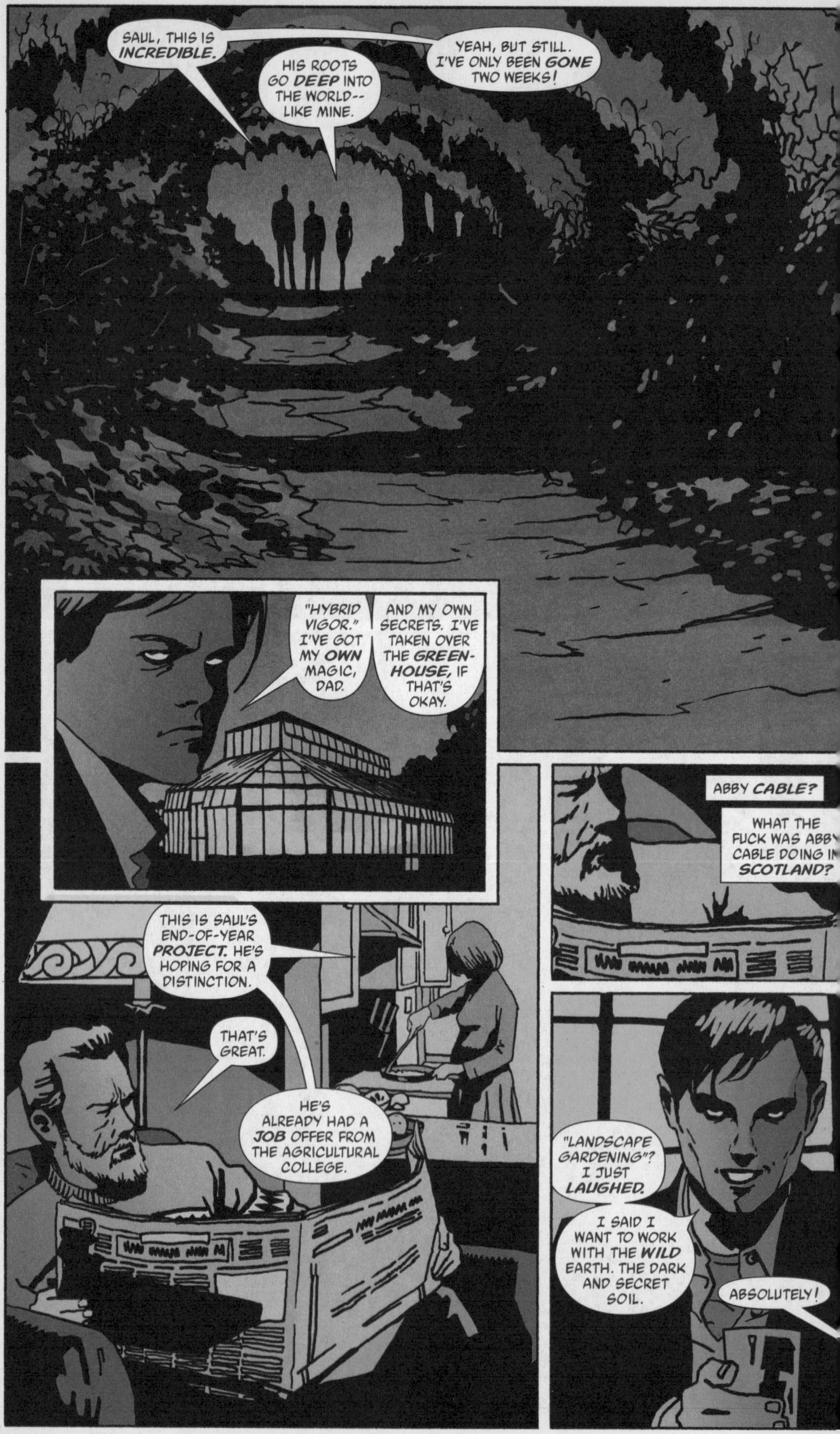
SAUL, THIS IS *INCREDIBLE.*
HIS ROOTS GO *DEEP* INTO THE WORLD-- LIKE MINE.
YEAH, BUT STILL. I'VE ONLY BEEN *GONE* TWO WEEKS!
"HYBRID VIGOR." I'VE GOT MY *OWN* MAGIC, DAD.
AND MY OWN SECRETS. I'VE TAKEN OVER THE *GREEN-HOUSE,* IF THAT'S OKAY.
ABBY *CABLE?*
WHAT THE FUCK WAS ABBY CABLE DOING IN *SCOTLAND?*
THIS IS SAUL'S END-OF-YEAR *PROJECT.* HE'S HOPING FOR A DISTINCTION.
THAT'S GREAT.
HE'S ALREADY HAD A *JOB* OFFER FROM THE AGRICULTURAL COLLEGE.
"LANDSCAPE GARDENING"? I JUST *LAUGHED.*
I SAID I WANT TO WORK WITH THE *WILD* EARTH. THE DARK AND SECRET SOIL.
ABSOLUTELY!

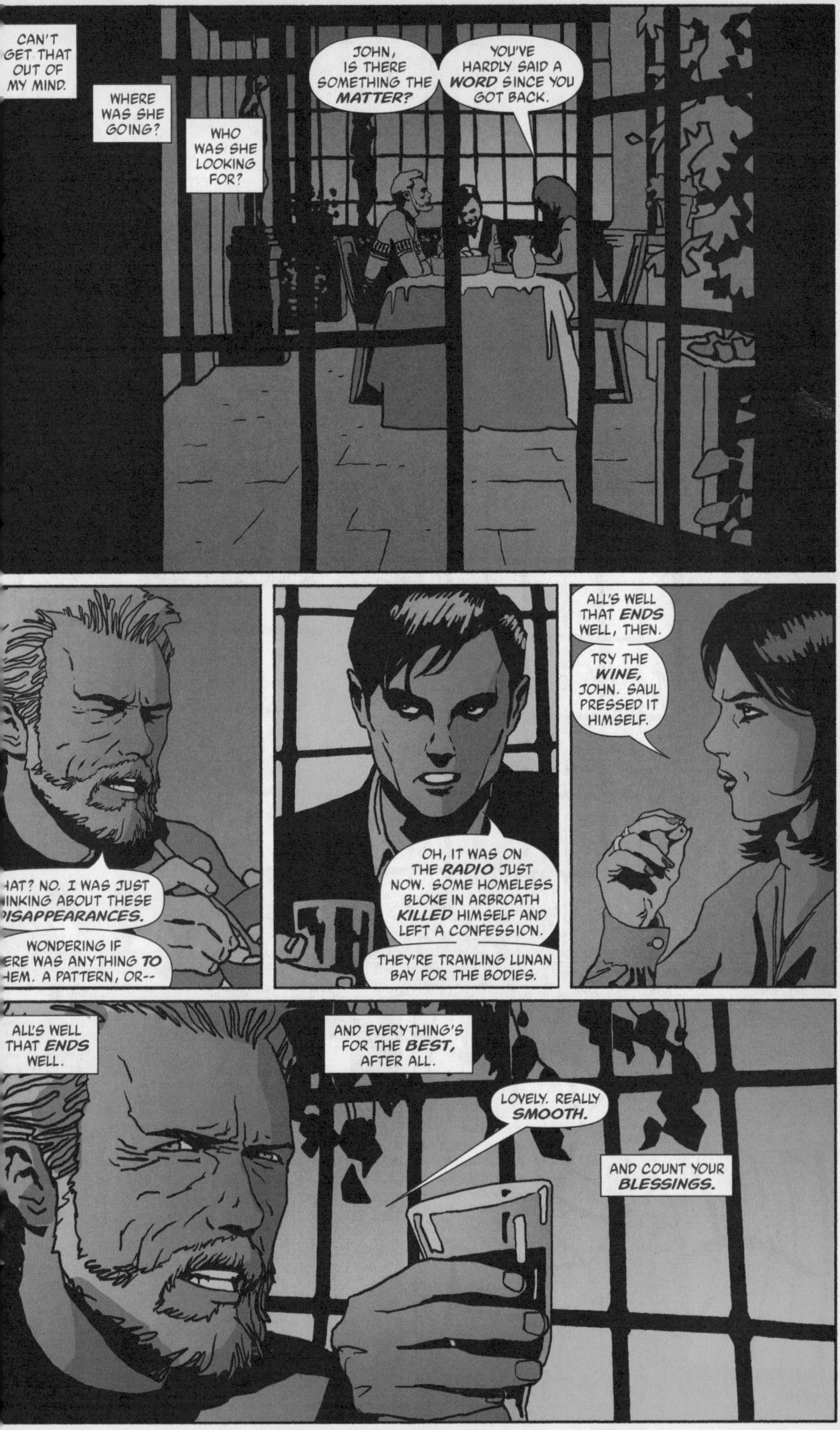
CAN'T GET THAT OUT OF MY MIND.
WHERE WAS SHE GOING?
WHO WAS SHE LOOKING FOR?
JOHN, IS THERE SOMETHING THE MATTER?
YOU'VE HARDLY SAID A WORD SINCE YOU GOT BACK.
HAT? NO. I WAS JUST INKING ABOUT THESE ISAPPEARANCES.
WONDERING IF ERE WAS ANYTHING TO HEM. A PATTERN, OR--
OH, IT WAS ON THE RADIO JUST NOW. SOME HOMELESS BLOKE IN ARBROATH KILLED HIMSELF AND LEFT A CONFESSION.
THEY'RE TRAWLING LUNAN BAY FOR THE BODIES.
ALL'S WELL THAT ENDS WELL, THEN.
TRY THE WINE, JOHN. SAUL PRESSED IT HIMSELF.
ALL'S WELL THAT ENDS WELL.
AND EVERYTHING'S FOR THE BEST, AFTER ALL.
LOVELY. REALLY SMOOTH.
AND COUNT YOUR BLESSINGS.

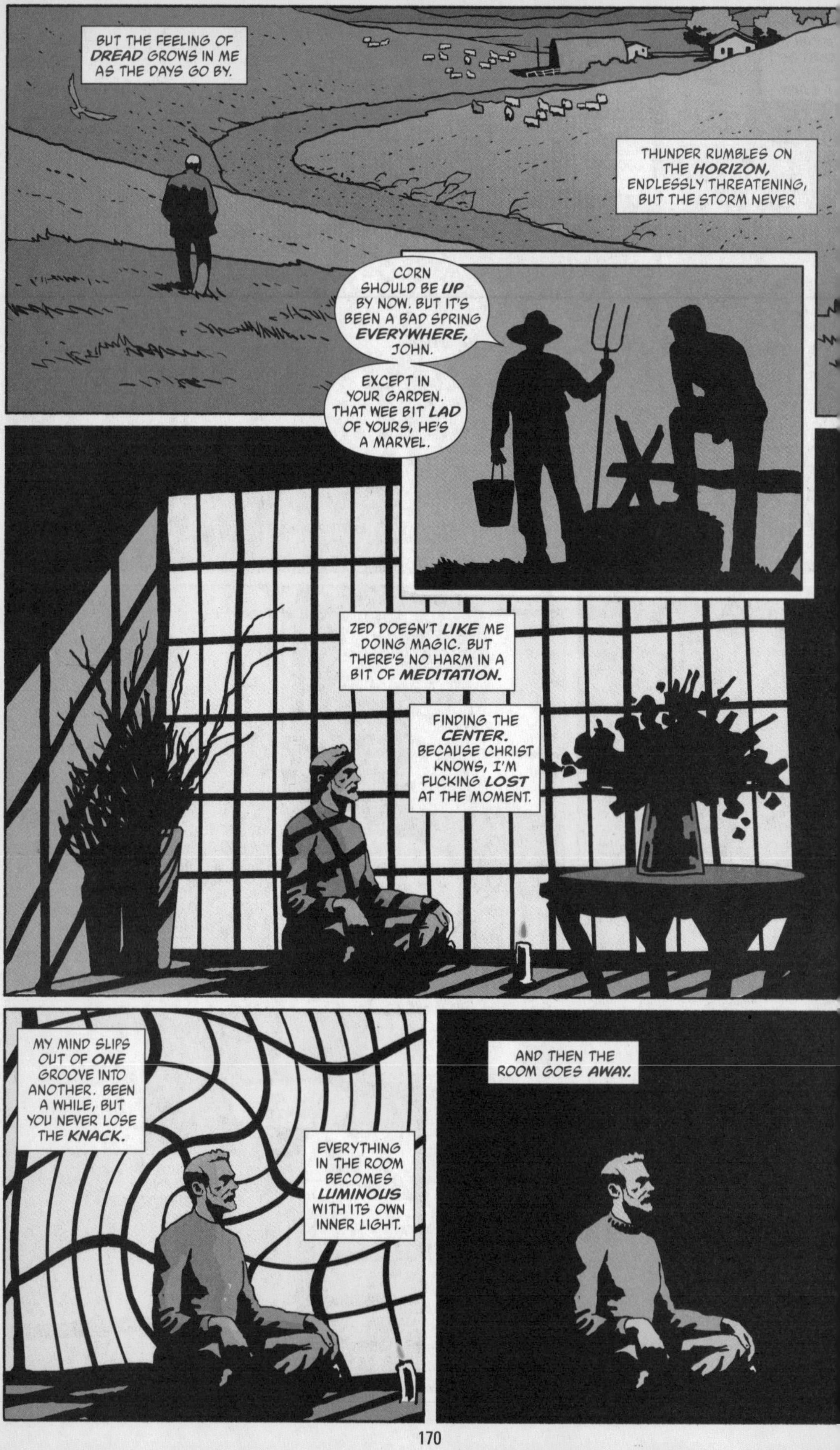

BUT THE FEELING OF DREAD GROWS IN ME AS THE DAYS GO BY.
THUNDER RUMBLES ON THE HORIZON, ENDLESSLY THREATENING, BUT THE STORM NEVER
CORN SHOULD BE UP BY NOW. BUT IT'S BEEN A BAD SPRING EVERYWHERE, JOHN.
EXCEPT IN YOUR GARDEN. THAT WEE BIT LAD OF YOURS, HE'S A MARVEL.
ZED DOESN'T LIKE ME DOING MAGIC. BUT THERE'S NO HARM IN A BIT OF MEDITATION.
FINDING THE CENTER. BECAUSE CHRIST KNOWS, I'M FUCKING LOST AT THE MOMENT.
MY MIND SLIPS OUT OF ONE GROOVE INTO ANOTHER. BEEN A WHILE, BUT YOU NEVER LOSE THE KNACK.
EVERYTHING IN THE ROOM BECOMES LUMINOUS WITH ITS OWN INNER LIGHT.
AND THEN THE ROOM GOES AWAY.

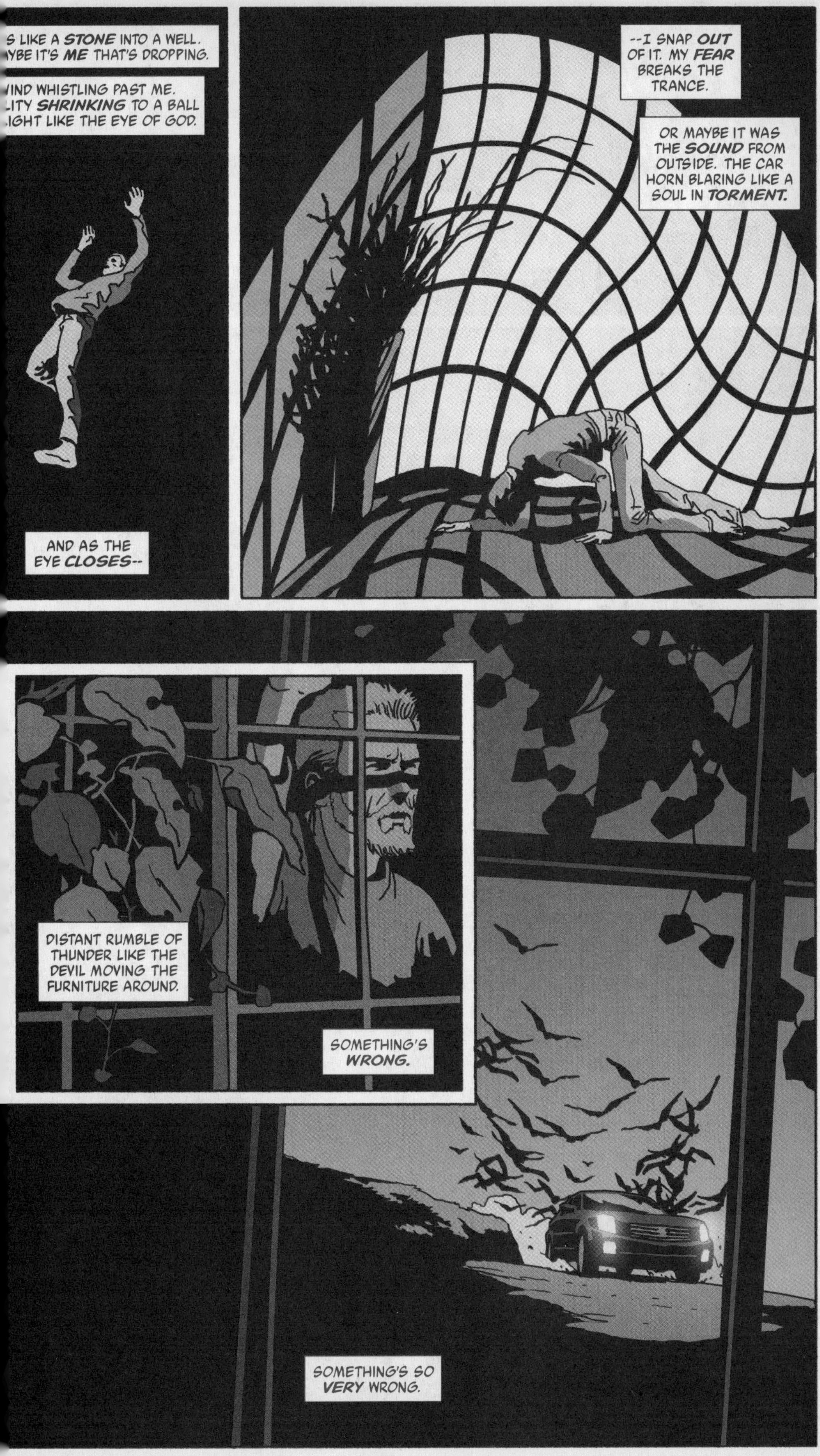
S LIKE A STONE INTO A WELL. AYBE IT'S ME THAT'S DROPPING.
VIND WHISTLING PAST ME. LITY SHRINKING TO A BALL IGHT LIKE THE EYE OF GOD.
AND AS THE EYE CLOSES--
--I SNAP OUT OF IT. MY FEAR BREAKS THE TRANCE.
OR MAYBE IT WAS THE SOUND FROM OUTSIDE. THE CAR HORN BLARING LIKE A SOUL IN TORMENT.
DISTANT RUMBLE OF THUNDER LIKE THE DEVIL MOVING THE FURNITURE AROUND.
SOMETHING'S WRONG.
SOMETHING'S SO VERY WRONG.

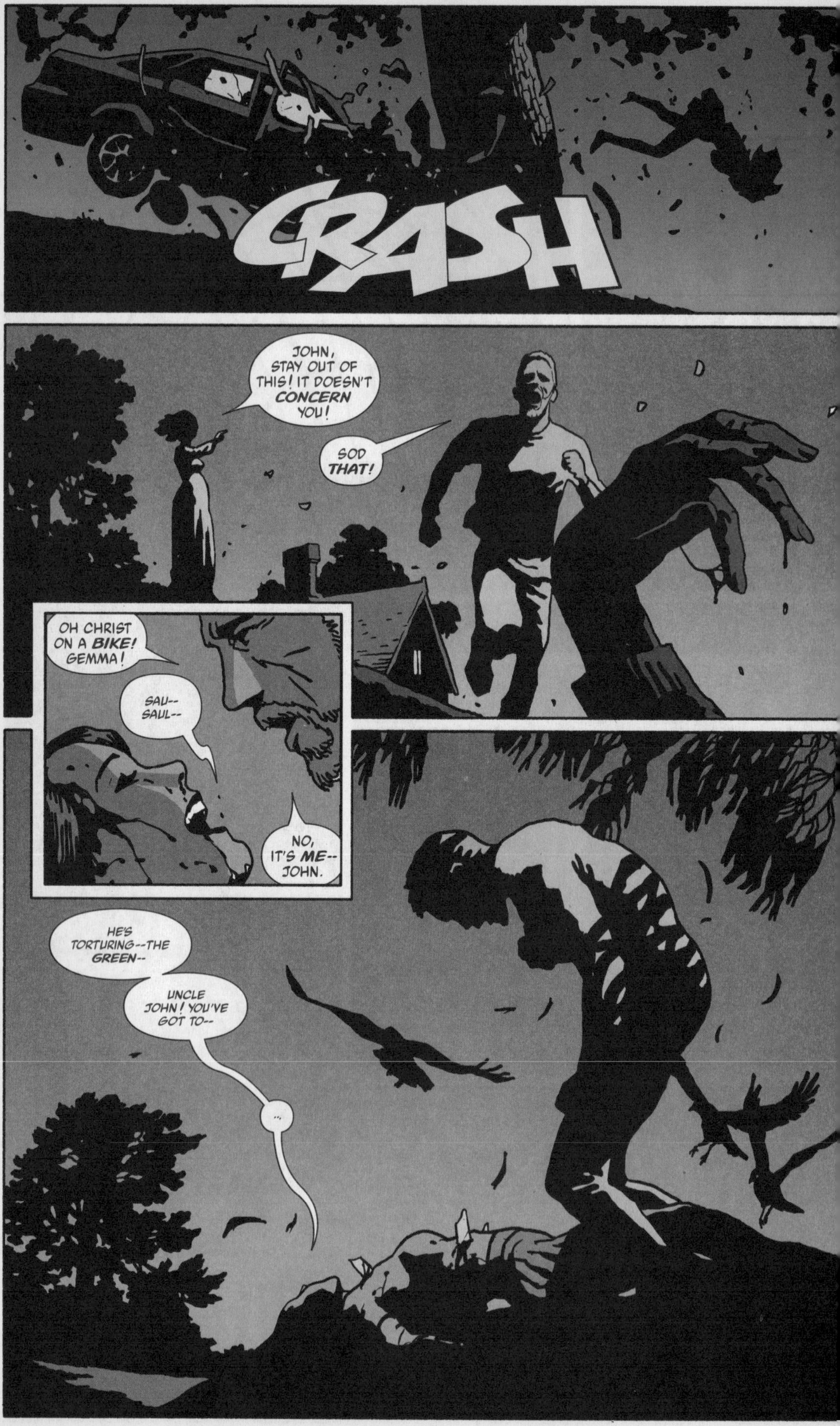
CRASH
JOHN, STAY OUT OF THIS! IT DOESN'T **CONCERN** YOU!
SOD **THAT!**
OH CHRIST ON A **BIKE!** GEMMA!
SAU-- SAUL--
NO, IT'S **ME**-- JOHN.
HE'S TORTURING--THE **GREEN**--
UNCLE JOHN! YOU'VE GOT TO--
...

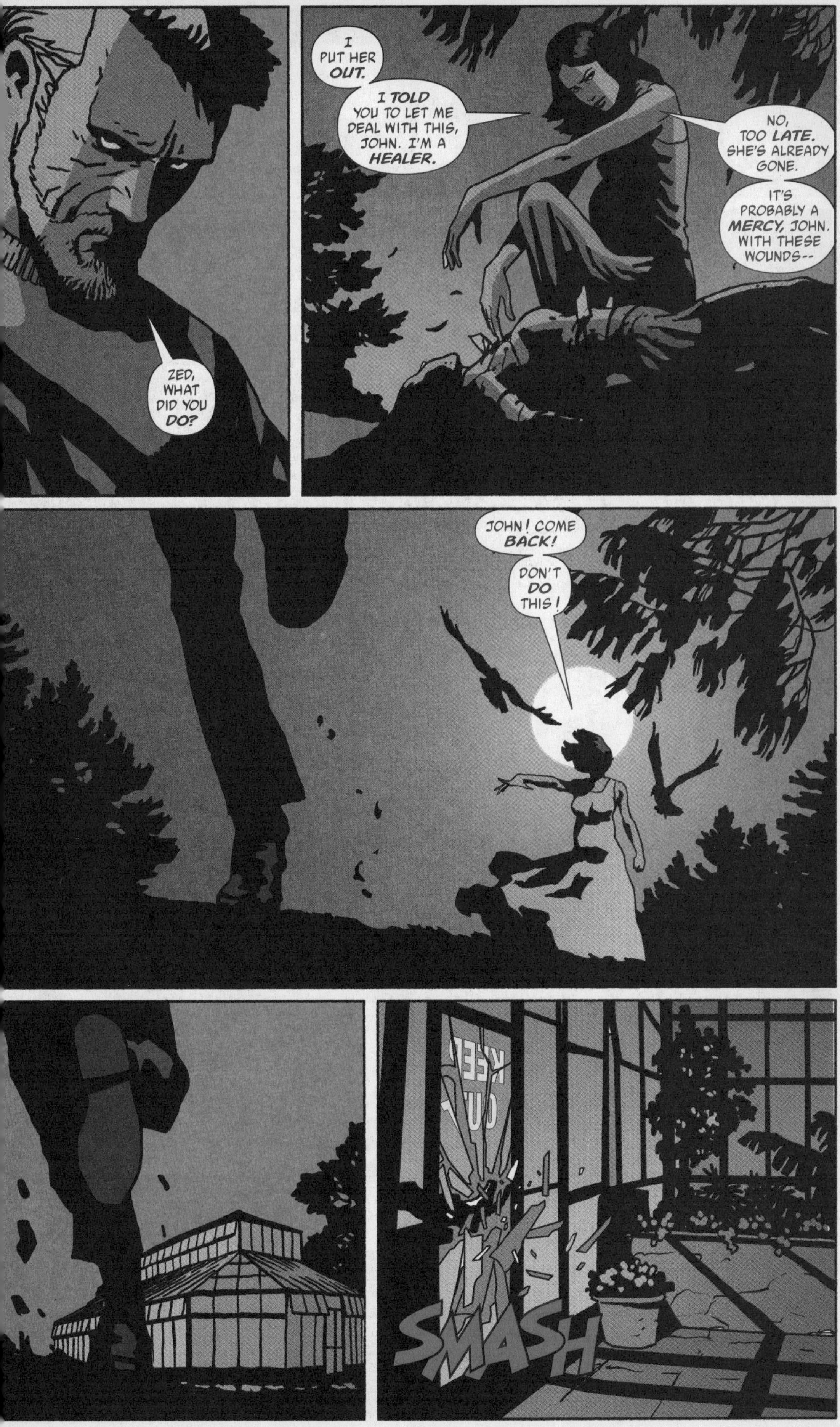
ZED, WHAT DID YOU DO?
I PUT HER OUT.
I TOLD YOU TO LET ME DEAL WITH THIS, JOHN. I'M A HEALER.
NO, TOO LATE. SHE'S ALREADY GONE.
IT'S PROBABLY A MERCY, JOHN. WITH THESE WOUNDS--
JOHN! COME BACK!
DON'T DO THIS!
SMASH

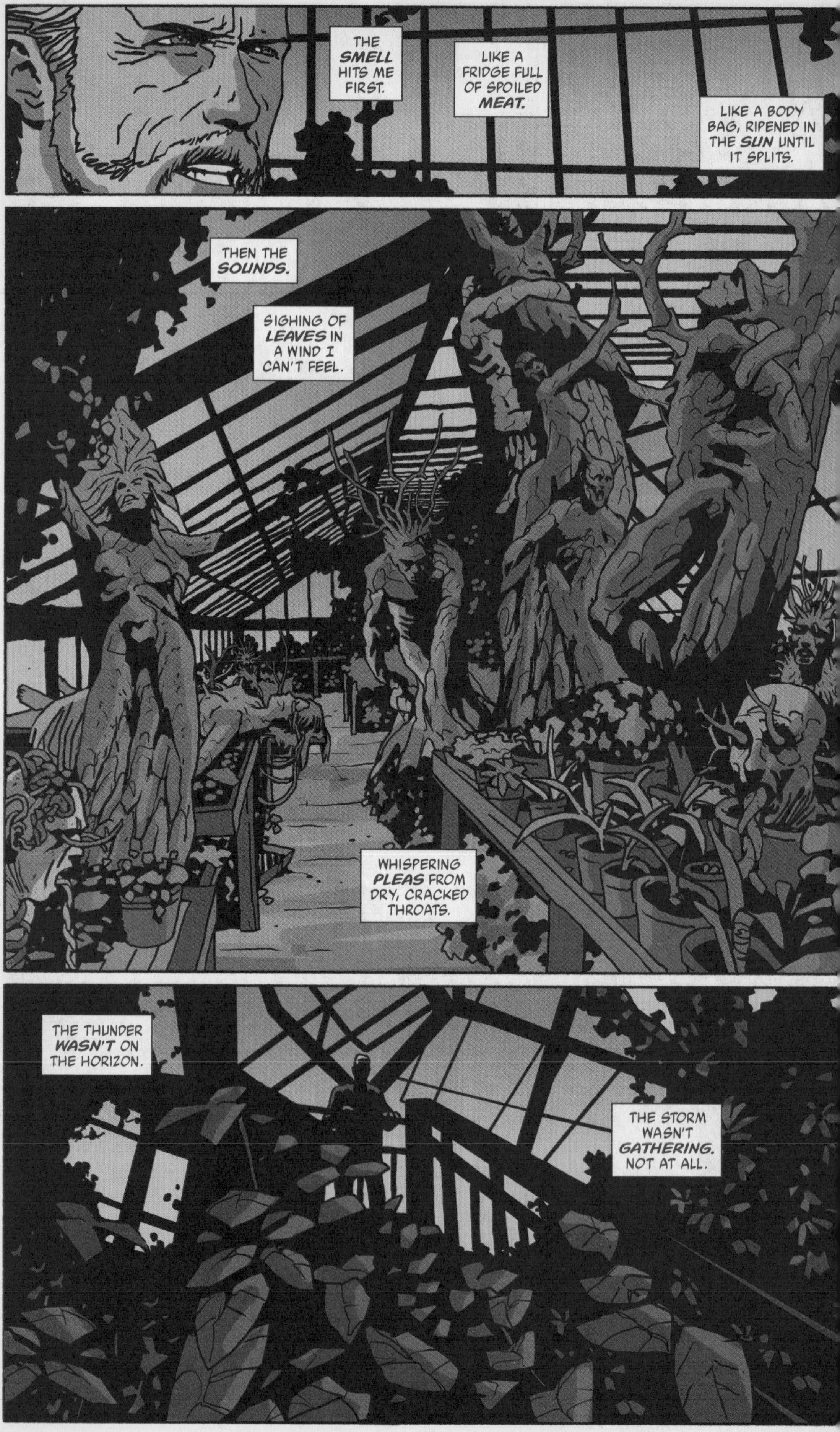
THE SMELL HITS ME FIRST.
LIKE A FRIDGE FULL OF SPOILED MEAT.
LIKE A BODY BAG, RIPENED IN THE SUN UNTIL IT SPLITS.
THEN THE SOUNDS.
SIGHING OF LEAVES IN A WIND I CAN'T FEEL.
WHISPERING PLEAS FROM DRY, CRACKED THROATS.
THE THUNDER WASN'T ON THE HORIZON.
THE STORM WASN'T GATHERING. NOT AT ALL.

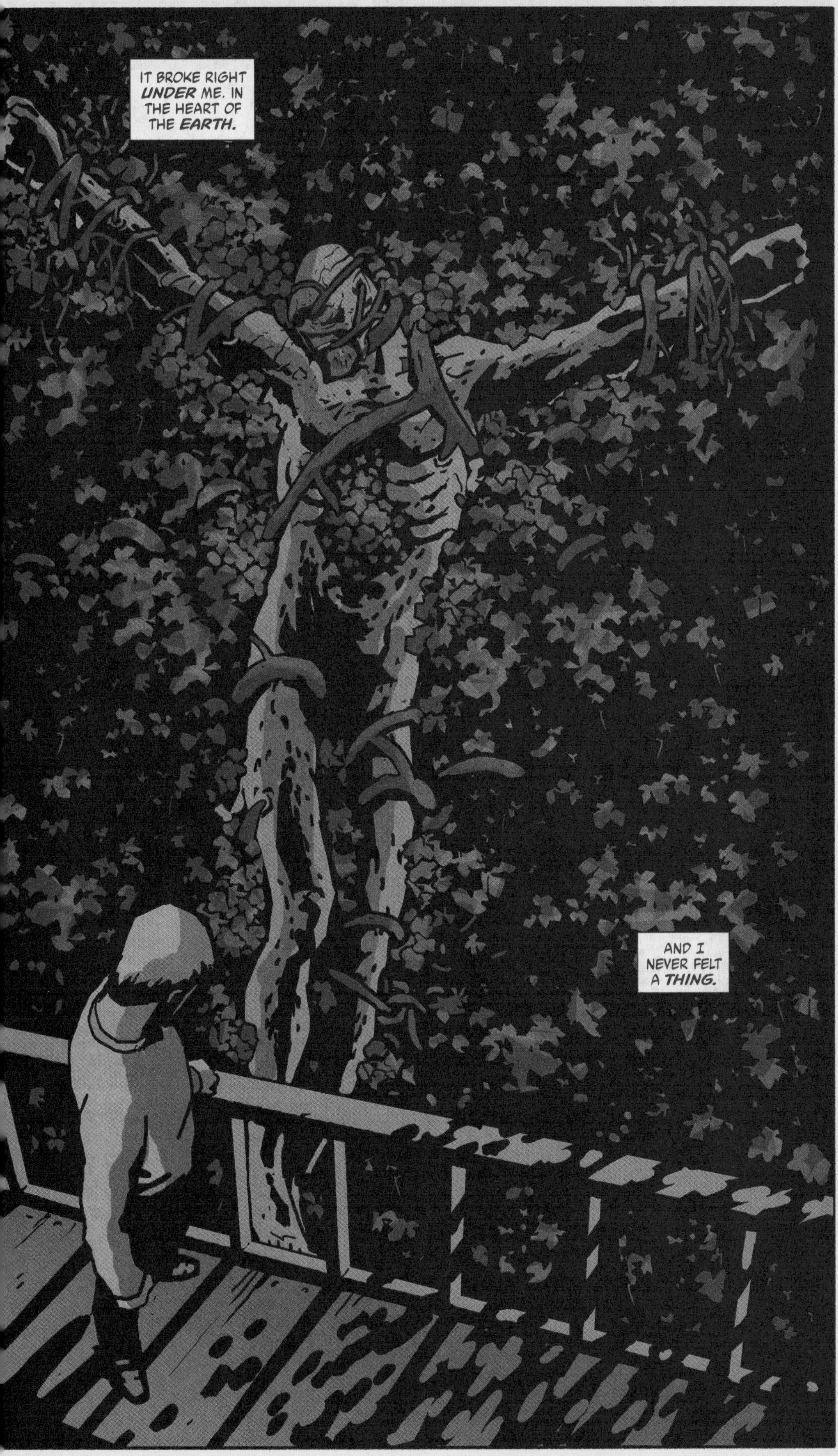
IT BROKE RIGHT UNDER ME. IN THE HEART OF THE EARTH.
AND I NEVER FELT A THING.

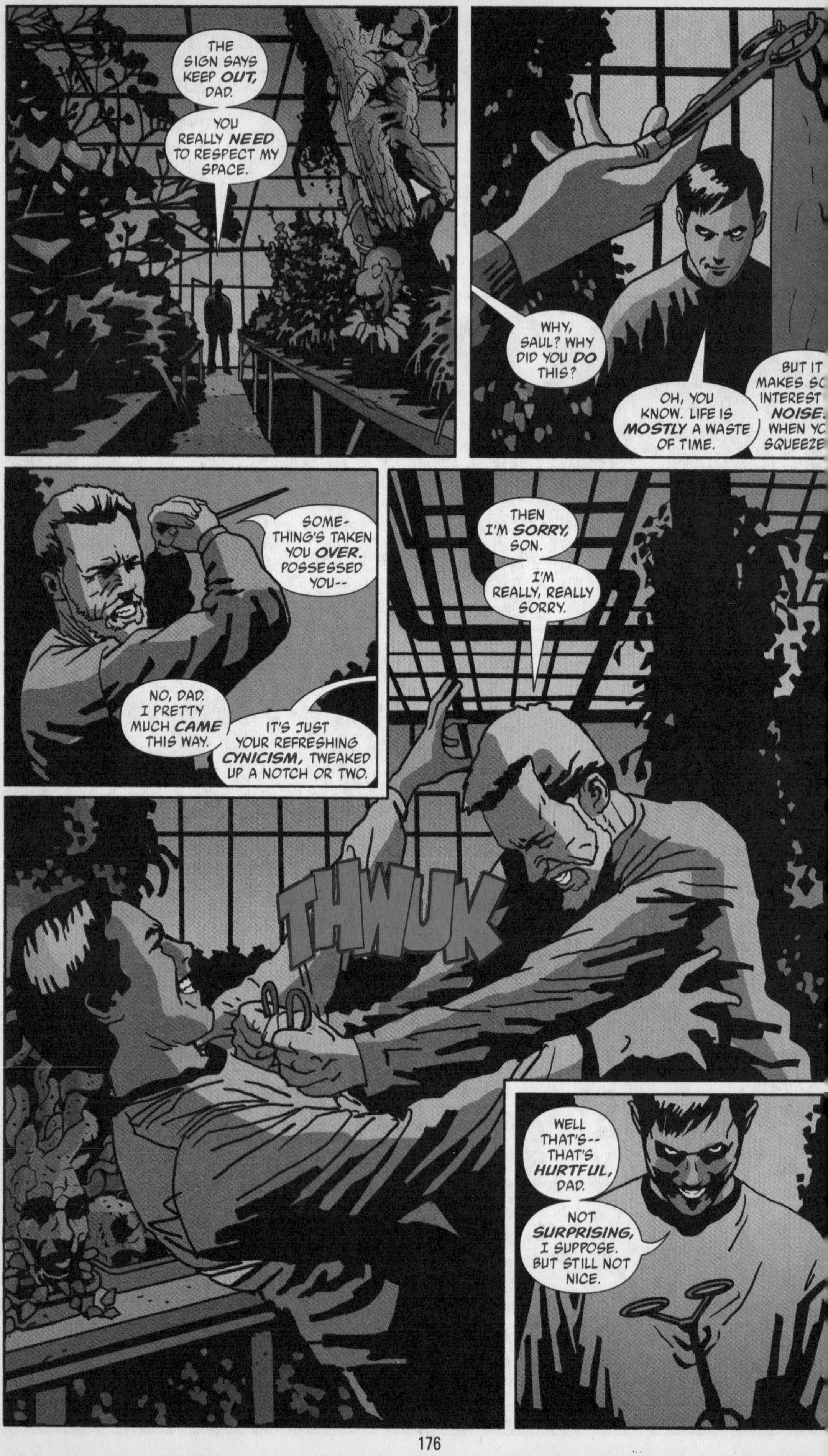
THE SIGN SAYS KEEP OUT, DAD.
YOU REALLY NEED TO RESPECT MY SPACE.
WHY, SAUL? WHY DID YOU DO THIS?
OH, YOU KNOW. LIFE IS MOSTLY A WASTE OF TIME.
SOME-THING'S TAKEN YOU OVER. POSSESSED YOU--
NO, DAD. I PRETTY MUCH CAME THIS WAY.
IT'S JUST YOUR REFRESHING CYNICISM, TWEAKED UP A NOTCH OR TWO.
THEN I'M SORRY, SON.
I'M REALLY, REALLY SORRY.
THWUK
WELL THAT'S-- THAT'S HURTFUL, DAD.
NOT SURPRISING, I SUPPOSE. BUT STILL NOT NICE.

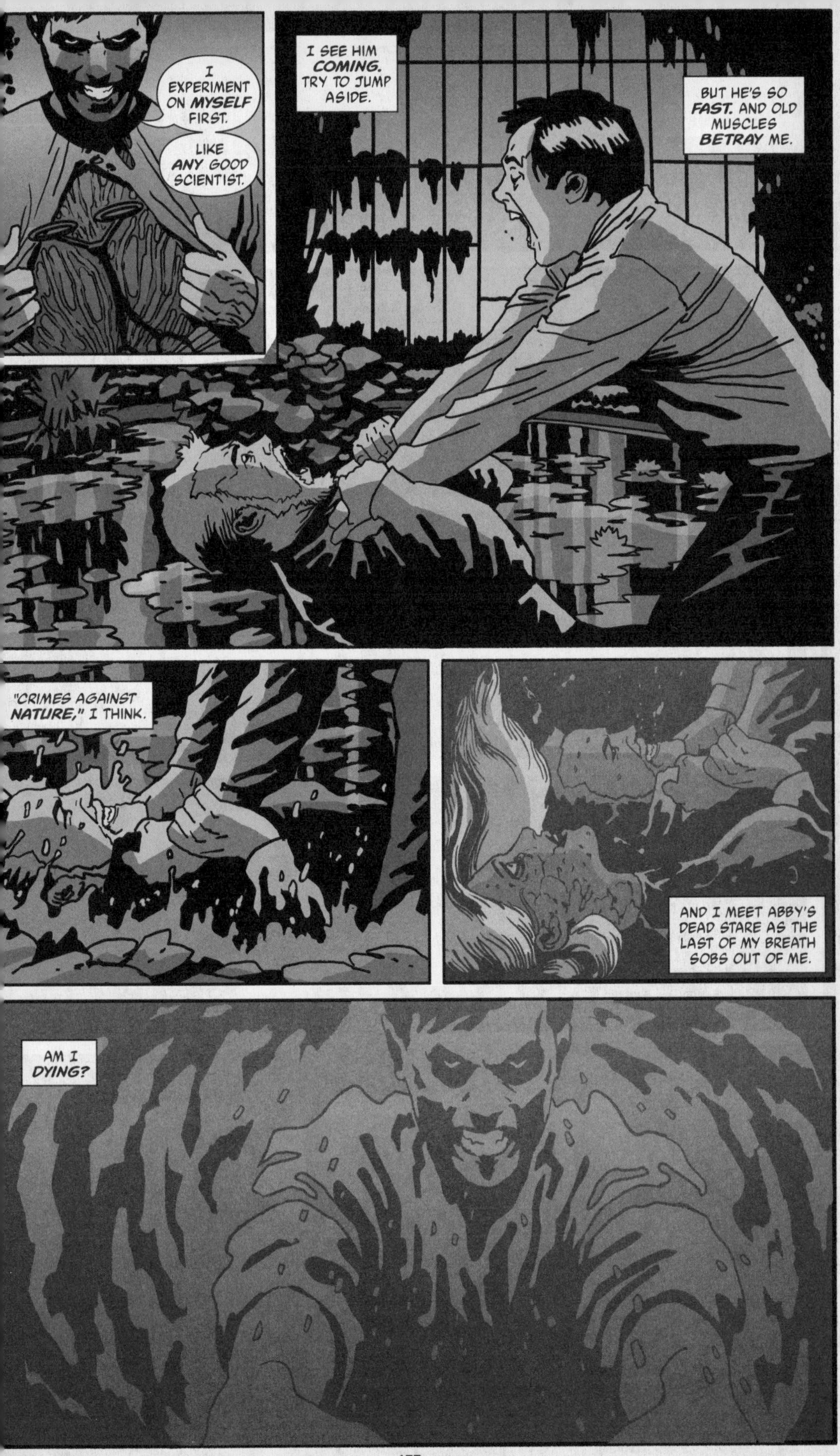
I EXPERIMENT ON MYSELF FIRST.
LIKE ANY GOOD SCIENTIST.
I SEE HIM COMING. TRY TO JUMP ASIDE.
BUT HE'S SO FAST. AND OLD MUSCLES BETRAY ME.
"CRIMES AGAINST NATURE," I THINK.
AND I MEET ABBY'S DEAD STARE AS THE LAST OF MY BREATH SOBS OUT OF ME.
AM I DYING?

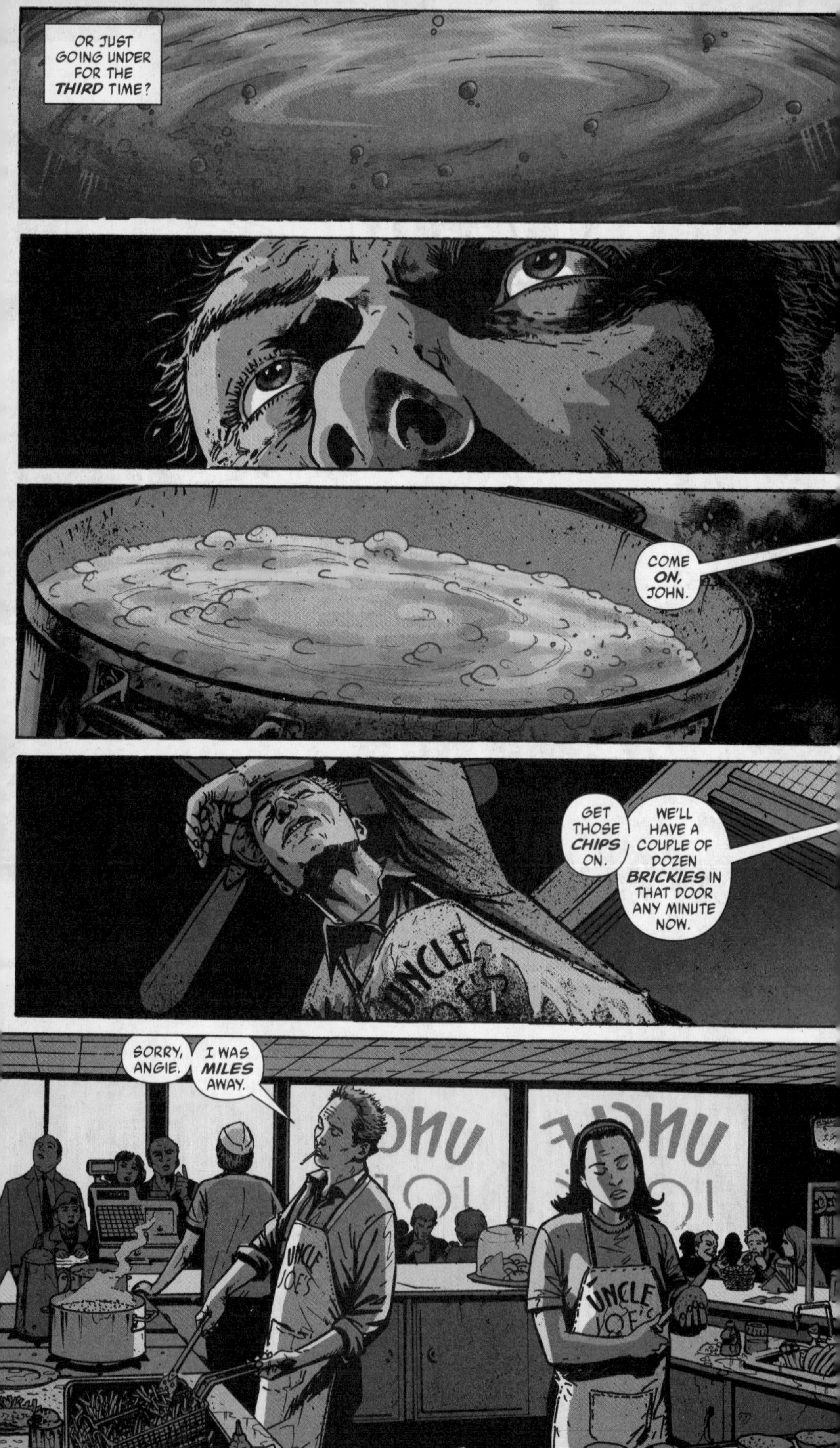
OR JUST GOING UNDER FOR THE THIRD TIME?
COME ON, JOHN.
GET THOSE CHIPS ON.
WE'LL HAVE A COUPLE OF DOZEN BRICKIES IN THAT DOOR ANY MINUTE NOW.
SORRY, ANGIE.
I WAS MILES AWAY.
UNCLE JOE'S

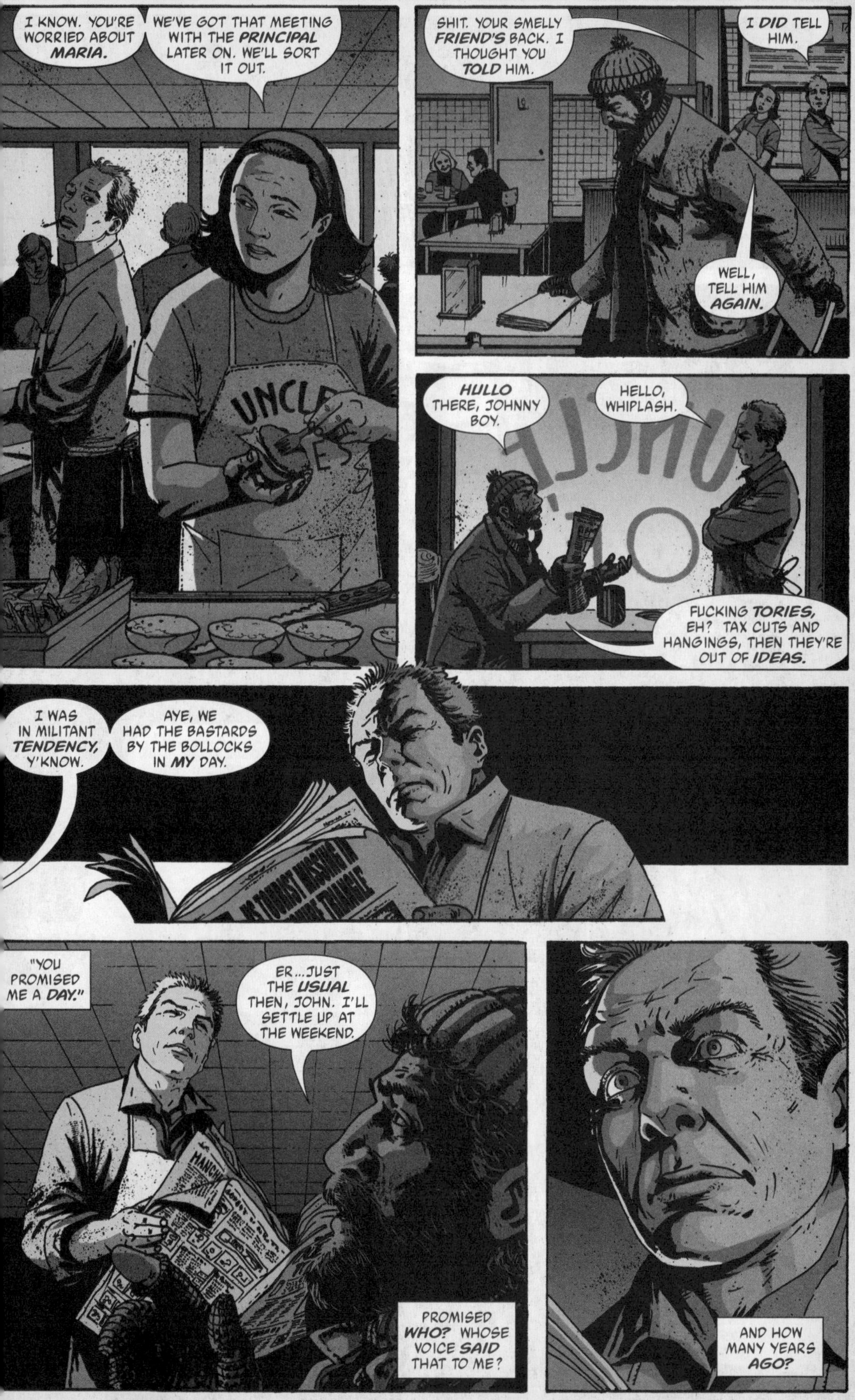
I KNOW. YOU'RE WORRIED ABOUT MARIA.
WE'VE GOT THAT MEETING WITH THE PRINCIPAL LATER ON. WE'LL SORT IT OUT.
SHIT. YOUR SMELLY FRIEND'S BACK. I THOUGHT YOU TOLD HIM.
I DID TELL HIM.
WELL, TELL HIM AGAIN.
HULLO THERE, JOHNNY BOY.
HELLO, WHIPLASH.
FUCKING TORIES, EH? TAX CUTS AND HANGINGS, THEN THEY'RE OUT OF IDEAS.
I WAS IN MILITANT TENDENCY, Y'KNOW.
AYE, WE HAD THE BASTARDS BY THE BOLLOCKS IN MY DAY.
"YOU PROMISED ME A DAY."
ER...JUST THE USUAL THEN, JOHN. I'LL SETTLE UP AT THE WEEKEND.
PROMISED WHO? WHOSE VOICE SAID THAT TO ME?
AND HOW MANY YEARS AGO?

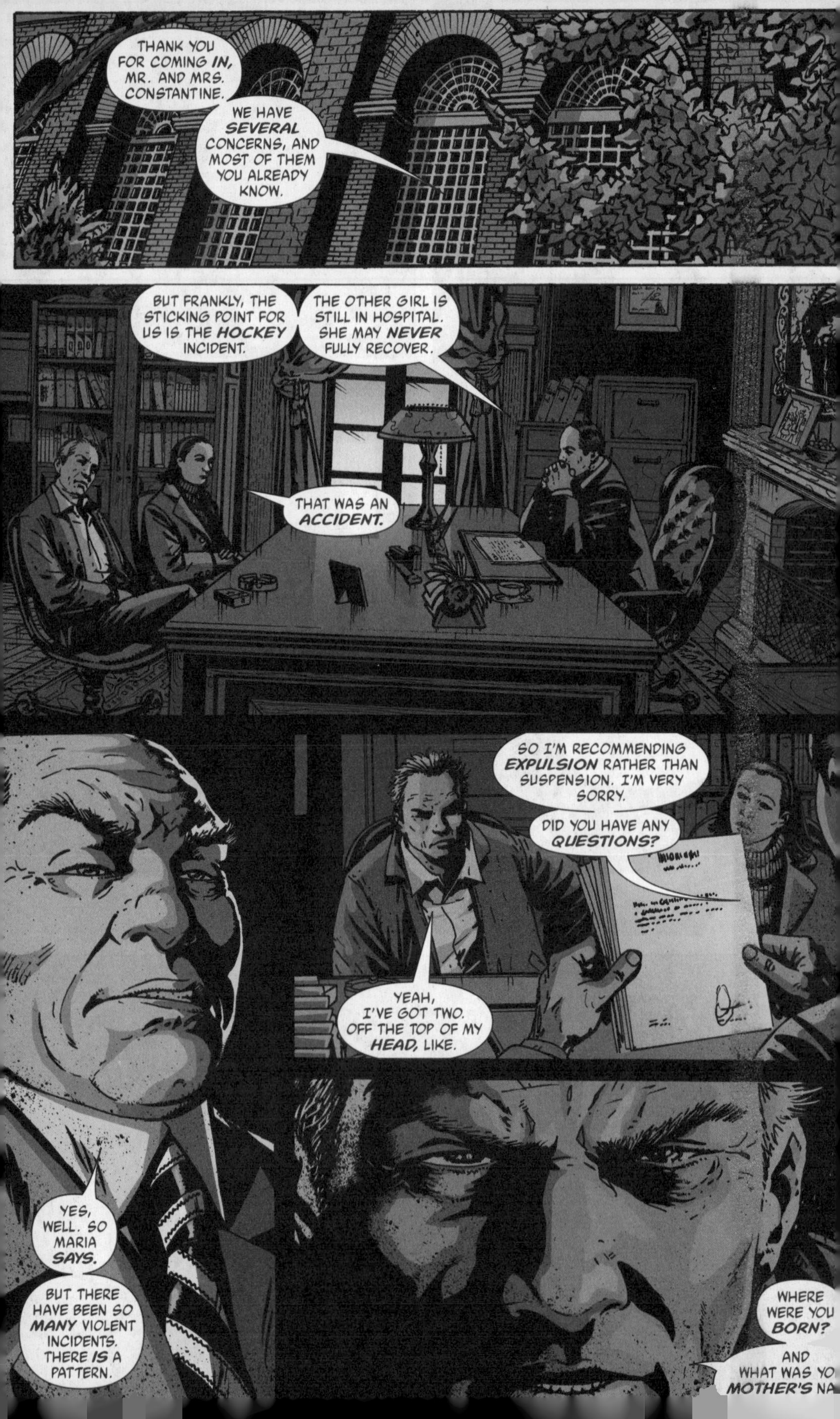
THANK YOU FOR COMING *IN,* MR. AND MRS. CONSTANTINE.
WE HAVE *SEVERAL* CONCERNS, AND MOST OF THEM YOU ALREADY KNOW.
BUT FRANKLY, THE STICKING POINT FOR US IS THE *HOCKEY* INCIDENT.
THE OTHER GIRL IS STILL IN HOSPITAL. SHE MAY *NEVER* FULLY RECOVER.
THAT WAS AN *ACCIDENT.*
YES, WELL. SO MARIA *SAYS.*
BUT THERE HAVE BEEN SO *MANY* VIOLENT INCIDENTS. THERE *IS* A PATTERN.
SO I'M RECOMMENDING *EXPULSION* RATHER THAN SUSPENSION. I'M VERY SORRY.
DID YOU HAVE ANY *QUESTIONS?*
YEAH, I'VE GOT TWO. OFF THE TOP OF MY *HEAD,* LIKE.
WHERE WERE YOU *BORN?*
AND WHAT WAS YO *MOTHER'S* NA

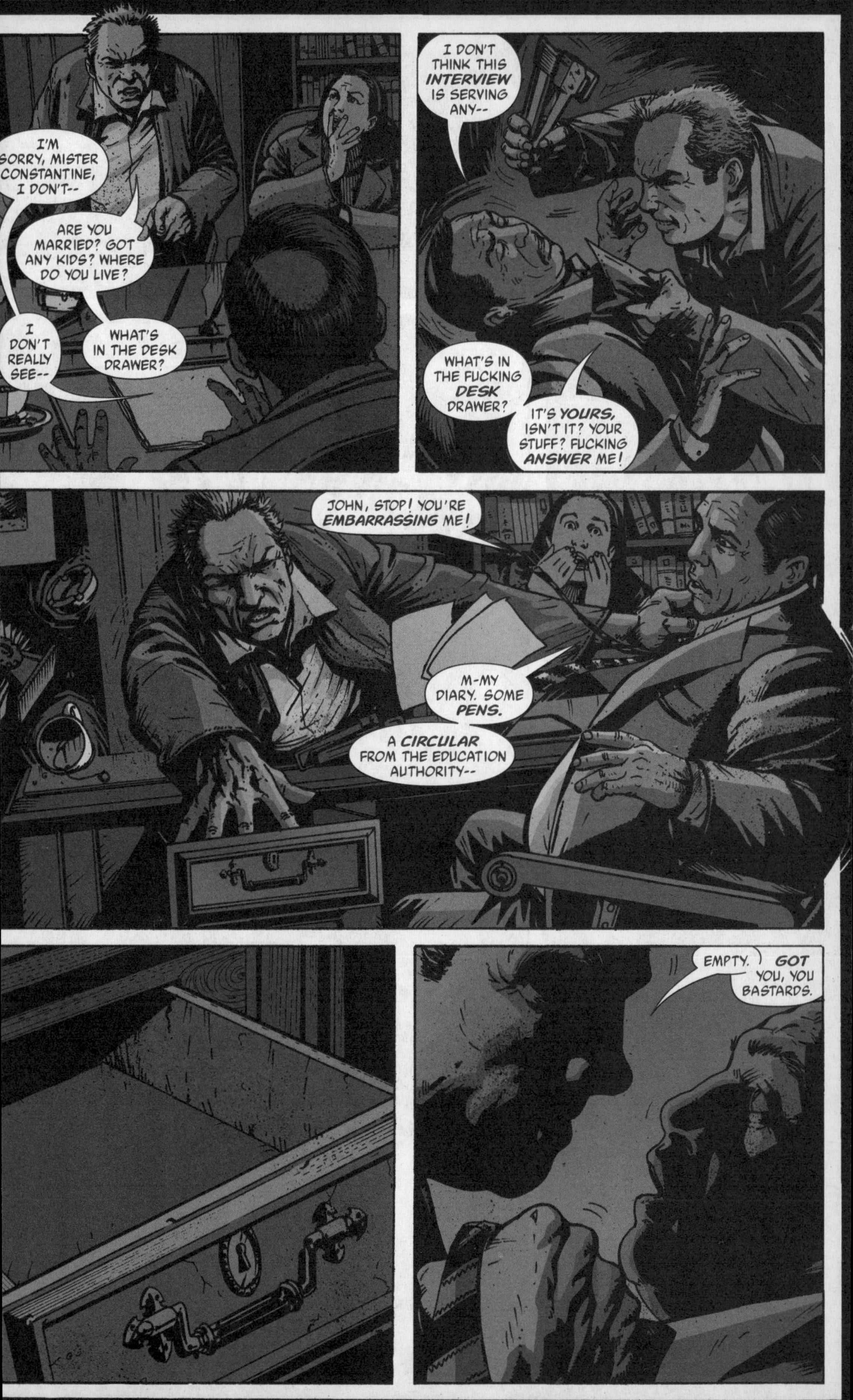
I'M SORRY, MISTER CONSTANTINE, I DON'T--
ARE YOU MARRIED? GOT ANY KIDS? WHERE DO YOU LIVE?
I DON'T REALLY SEE--
WHAT'S IN THE DESK DRAWER?
I DON'T THINK THIS INTERVIEW IS SERVING ANY--
WHAT'S IN THE FUCKING DESK DRAWER?
IT'S YOURS, ISN'T IT? YOUR STUFF? FUCKING ANSWER ME!
JOHN, STOP! YOU'RE EMBARRASSING ME!
M-MY DIARY. SOME PENS.
A CIRCULAR FROM THE EDUCATION AUTHORITY--
EMPTY.
GOT YOU, YOU BASTARDS.

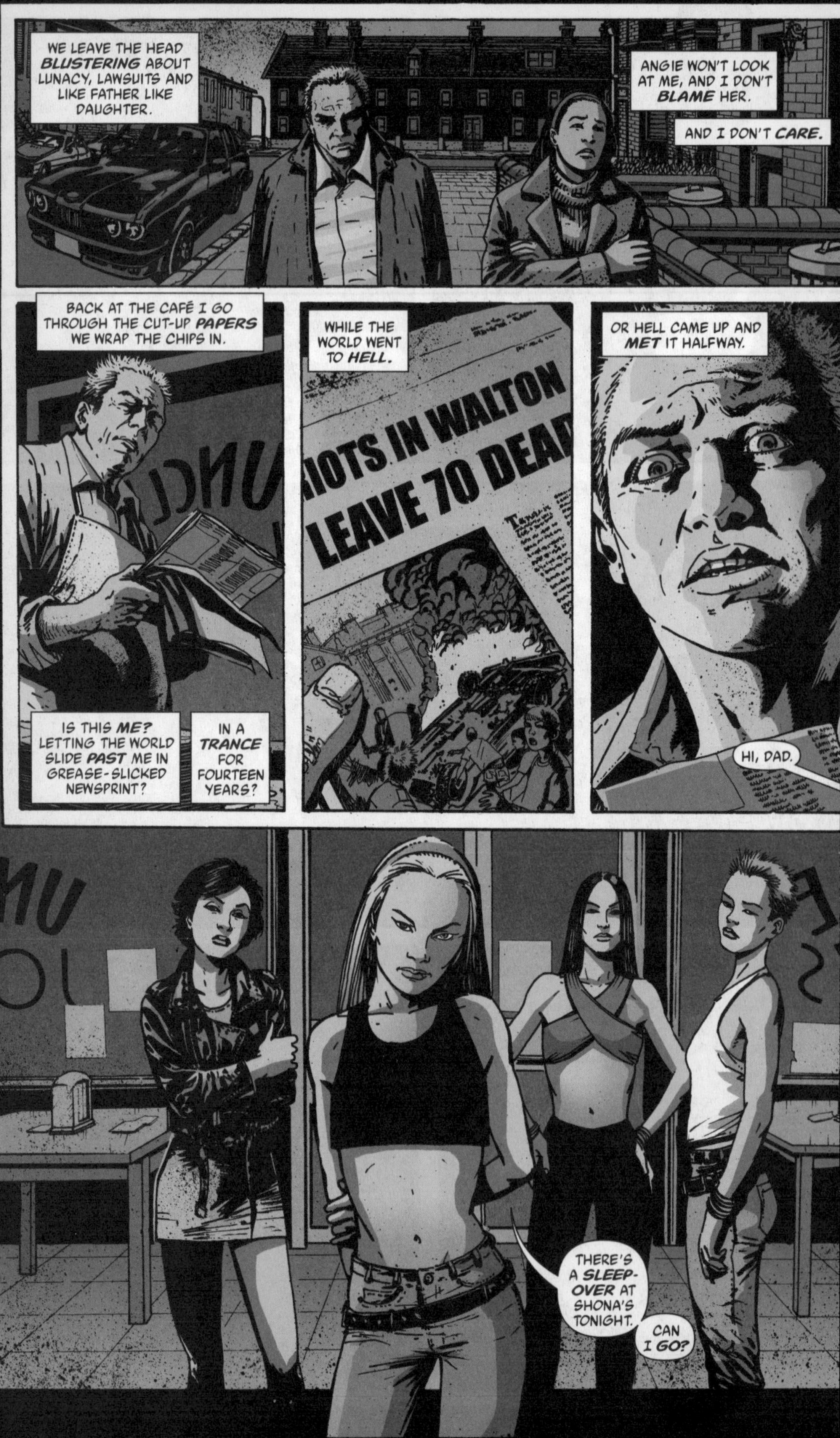
WE LEAVE THE HEAD BLUSTERING ABOUT LUNACY, LAWSUITS AND LIKE FATHER LIKE DAUGHTER.
ANGIE WON'T LOOK AT ME, AND I DON'T BLAME HER.
AND I DON'T CARE.
BACK AT THE CAFÉ I GO THROUGH THE CUT-UP PAPERS WE WRAP THE CHIPS IN.
IS THIS ME? LETTING THE WORLD SLIDE PAST ME IN GREASE-SLICKED NEWSPRINT?
IN A TRANCE FOR FOURTEEN YEARS?
WHILE THE WORLD WENT TO HELL.
RIOTS IN WALTON
LEAVE 70 DEAD
OR HELL CAME UP AND MET IT HALFWAY.
HI, DAD.
THERE'S A SLEEP-OVER AT SHONA'S TONIGHT.
CAN I GO?

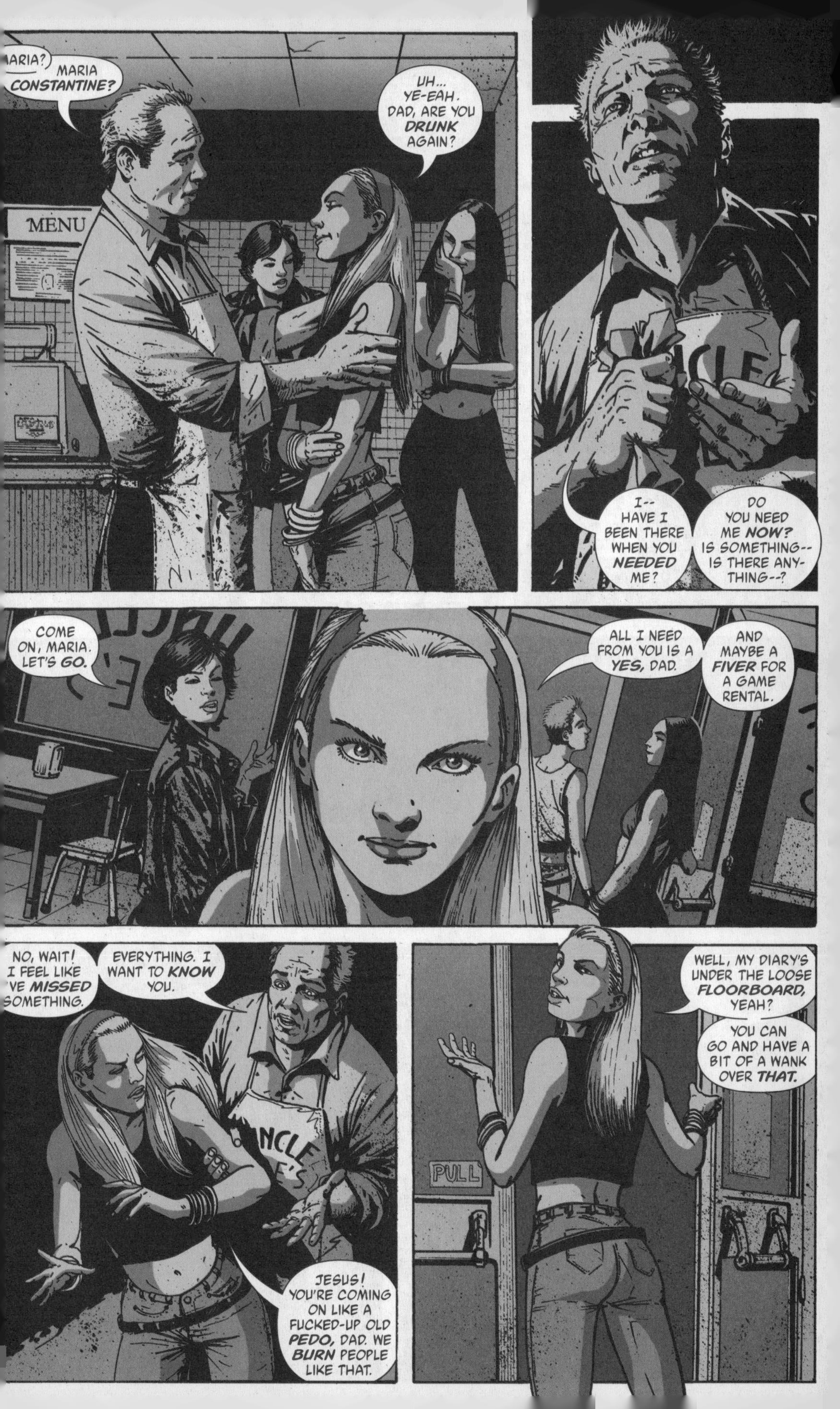

ARIA? MARIA CONSTANTINE?
UH... YE-EAH. DAD, ARE YOU DRUNK AGAIN?
MENU
I-- HAVE I BEEN THERE WHEN YOU NEEDED ME?
DO YOU NEED ME NOW? IS SOMETHING-- IS THERE ANYTHING--?
COME ON, MARIA. LET'S GO.
ALL I NEED FROM YOU IS A YES, DAD.
AND MAYBE A FIVER FOR A GAME RENTAL.
NO, WAIT! I FEEL LIKE VE MISSED SOMETHING.
EVERYTHING. I WANT TO KNOW YOU.
JESUS! YOU'RE COMING ON LIKE A FUCKED-UP OLD PEDO, DAD. WE BURN PEOPLE LIKE THAT.
WELL, MY DIARY'S UNDER THE LOOSE FLOORBOARD, YEAH?
YOU CAN GO AND HAVE A BIT OF A WANK OVER THAT.
PULL

SHE DOESN'T LOOK *BACK*.

FOURTEEN YEARS *OLD*. SHE'S GOT THINGS TO DO. PLACES TO BE.

THE STUFF OF MY NIGHTMARES, THROWN LIKE *DUST SHEETS* OVER THE WORLD.

DISGUISING *EVERYTHING*.

AND I'VE CAUGHT REALITY OUT IN A BARE-FACED *LIE*. BUT I STILL CAN'T WAKE UP.

AND I CAN' SHAKE THE FEELING THA I'M IN A *FIGHT* I'V ALREADY LOS

OH SHIT! I GOT *BLOOD* ON MY TIGHTS!

HEY, IT'S *MY* TURN. YOU ALREADY HAD A GO!

LOOK IN HIS *EYES*.

YOU CAN SEE HE'S *FEELING* IT.

EYES, *PLURAL?*

I THINK YOU LOST *COUNT*, SHONA.

WHOA! FUUUUUUC

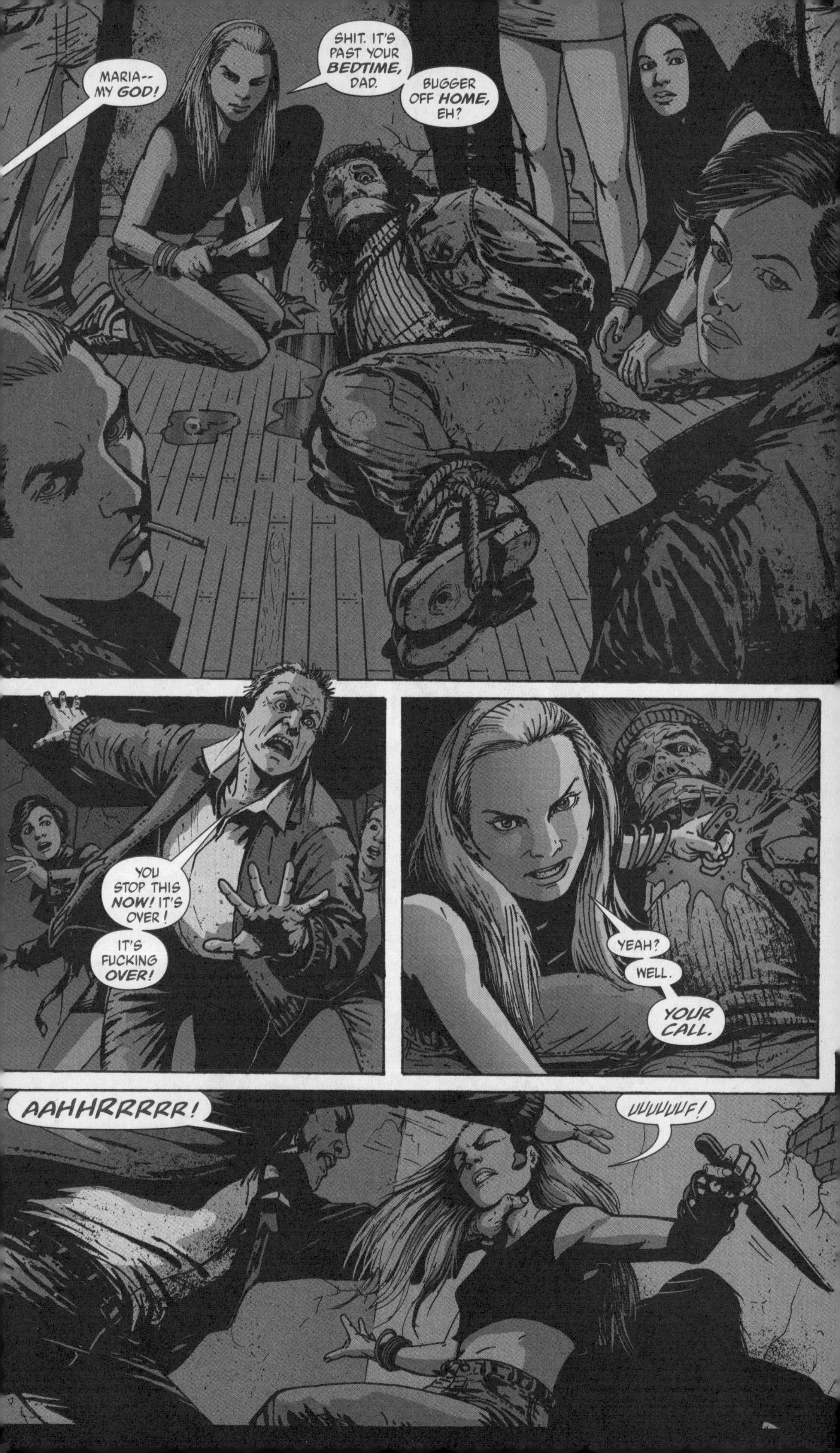
MARIA-- MY GOD!
SHIT. IT'S PAST YOUR BEDTIME, DAD.
BUGGER OFF HOME, EH?
YOU STOP THIS NOW! IT'S OVER!
IT'S FUCKING OVER!
YEAH?
WELL.
YOUR CALL.
AAHHRRRRR!
UUUUUUF!

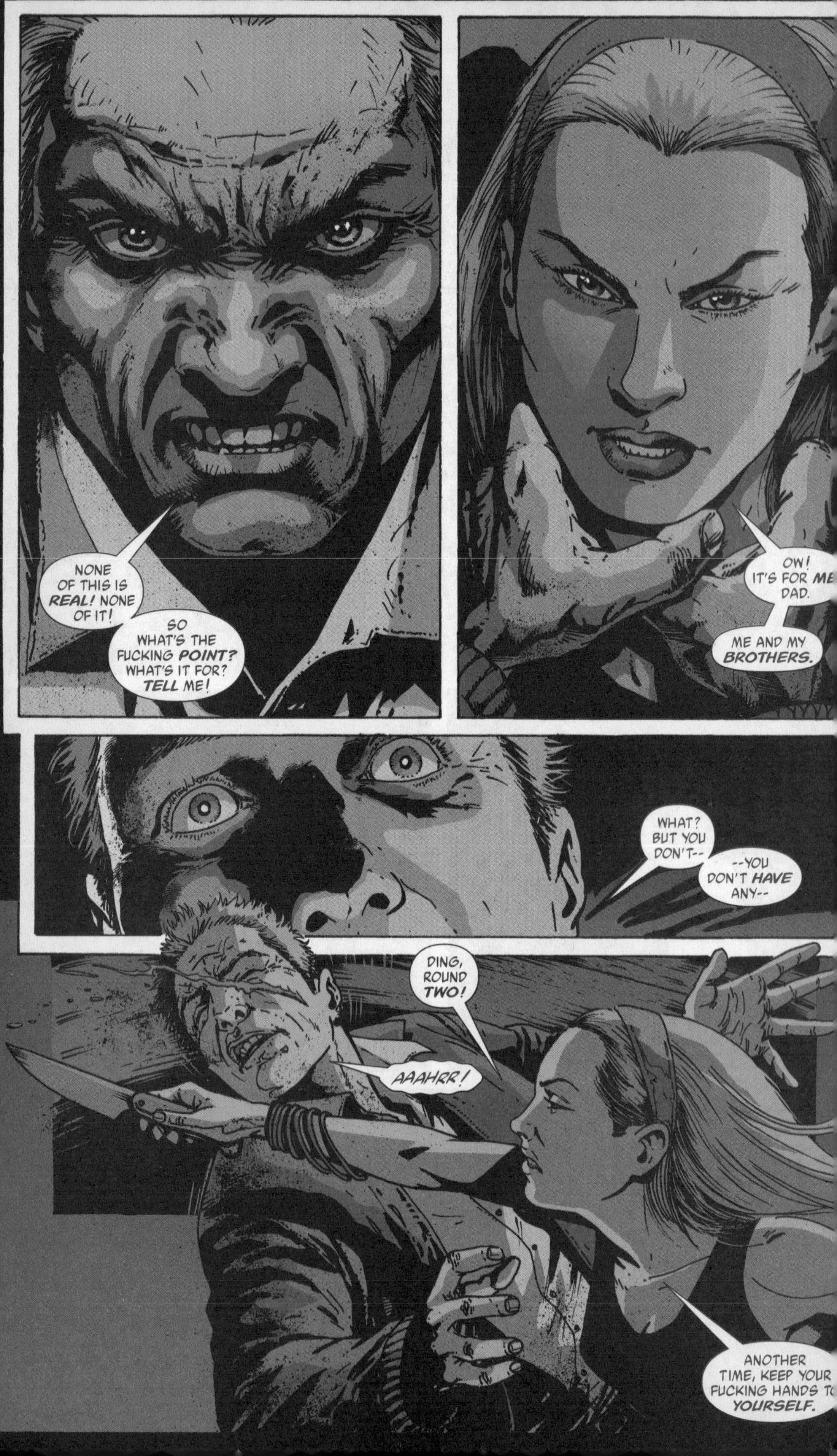
NONE OF THIS IS REAL! NONE OF IT!
SO WHAT'S THE FUCKING POINT? WHAT'S IT FOR? TELL ME!
OW! IT'S FOR ME DAD.
ME AND MY BROTHERS.
WHAT? BUT YOU DON'T--
--YOU DON'T HAVE ANY--
DING, ROUND TWO!
AAAHRR!
ANOTHER TIME, KEEP YOUR FUCKING HANDS TO YOURSELF.

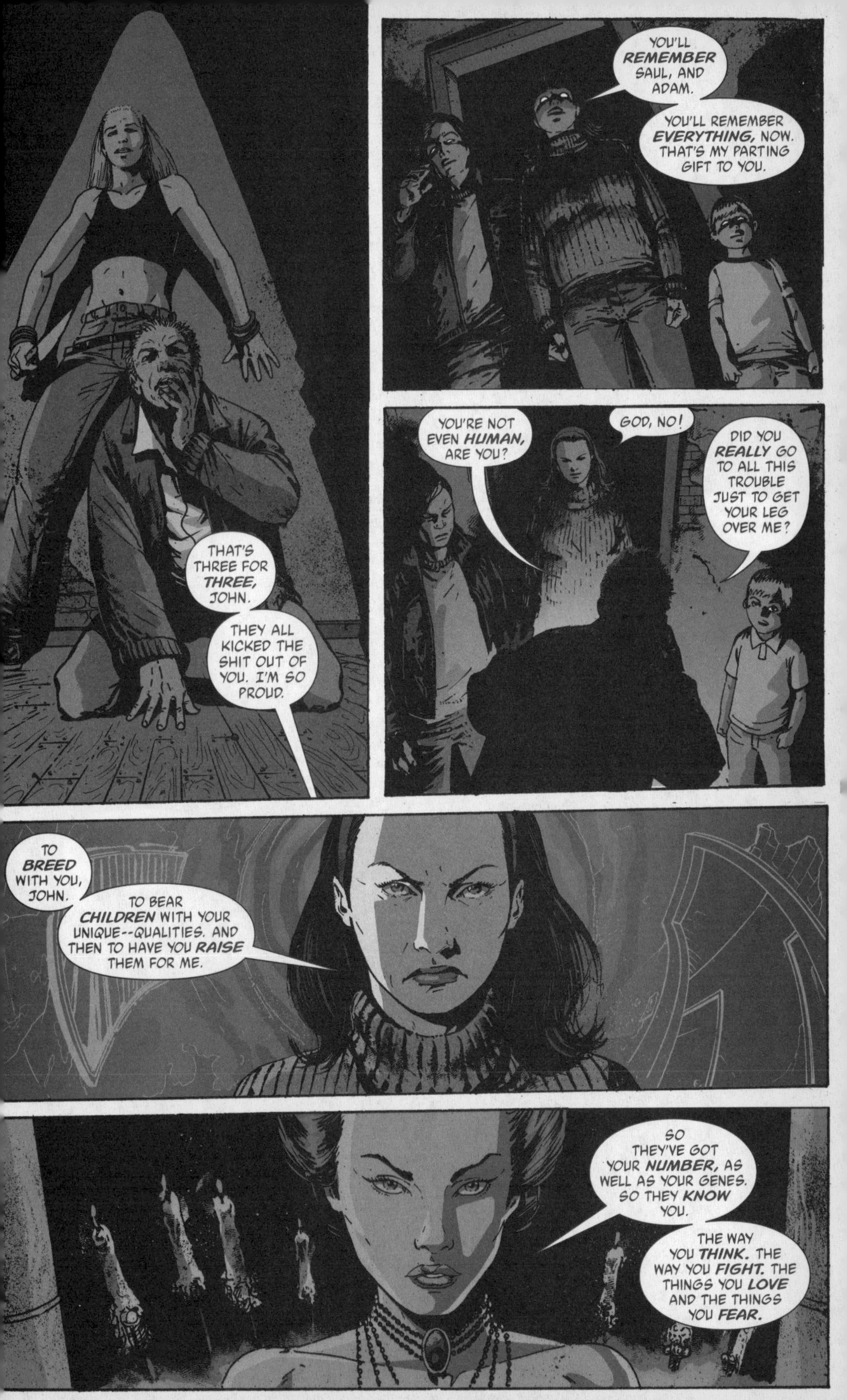
YOU'LL REMEMBER SAUL, AND ADAM.
YOU'LL REMEMBER EVERYTHING, NOW. THAT'S MY PARTING GIFT TO YOU.
THAT'S THREE FOR THREE, JOHN.
THEY ALL KICKED THE SHIT OUT OF YOU. I'M SO PROUD.
YOU'RE NOT EVEN HUMAN, ARE YOU?
GOD, NO!
DID YOU REALLY GO TO ALL THIS TROUBLE JUST TO GET YOUR LEG OVER ME?
TO BREED WITH YOU, JOHN.
TO BEAR CHILDREN WITH YOUR UNIQUE--QUALITIES. AND THEN TO HAVE YOU RAISE THEM FOR ME.
SO THEY'VE GOT YOUR NUMBER, AS WELL AS YOUR GENES. SO THEY KNOW YOU.
THE WAY YOU THINK. THE WAY YOU FIGHT. THE THINGS YOU LOVE AND THE THINGS YOU FEAR.

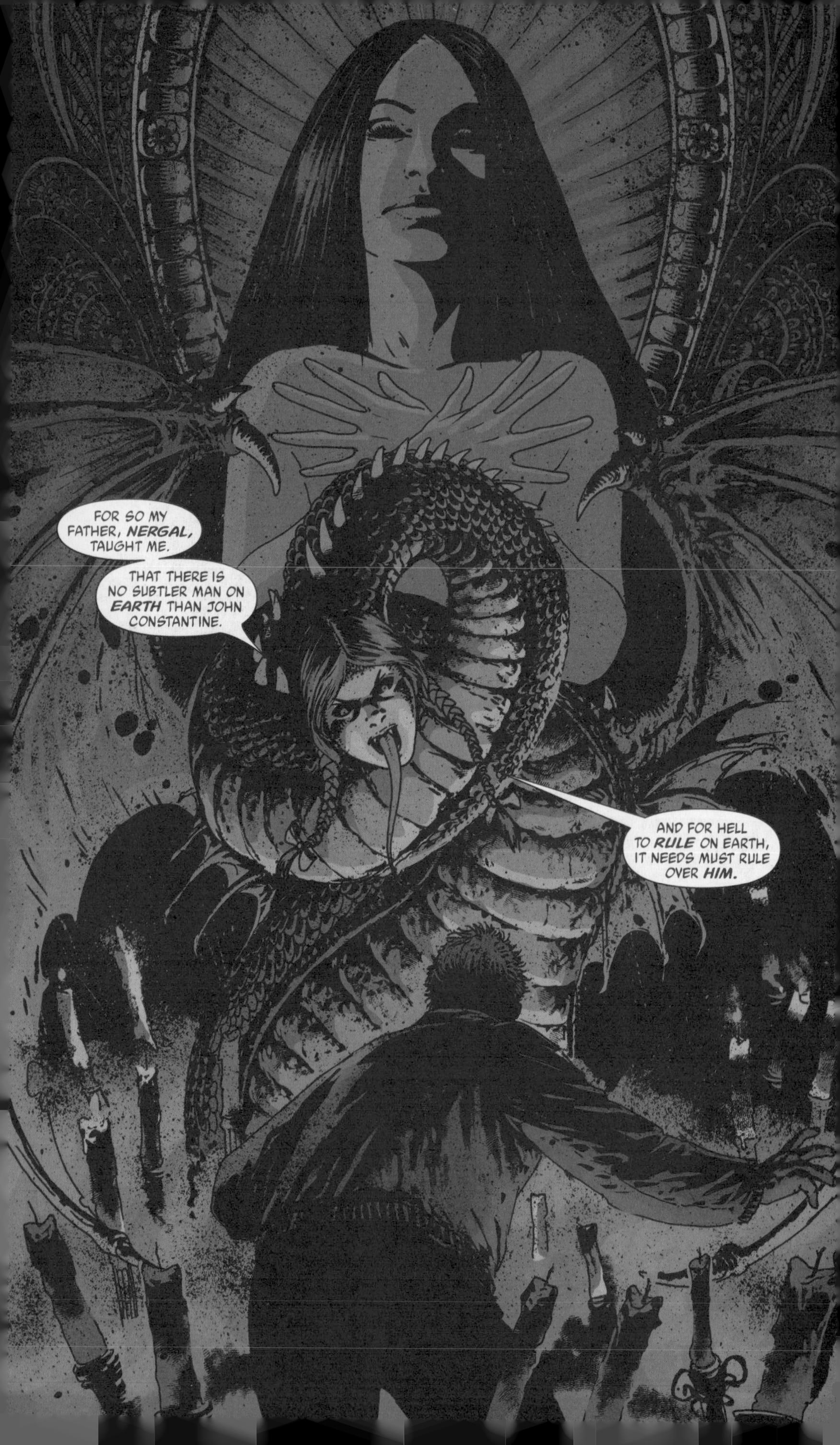
FOR SO MY FATHER, NERGAL, TAUGHT ME.
THAT THERE IS NO SUBTLER MAN ON EARTH THAN JOHN CONSTANTINE.
AND FOR HELL TO RULE ON EARTH, IT NEEDS MUST RULE OVER HIM.

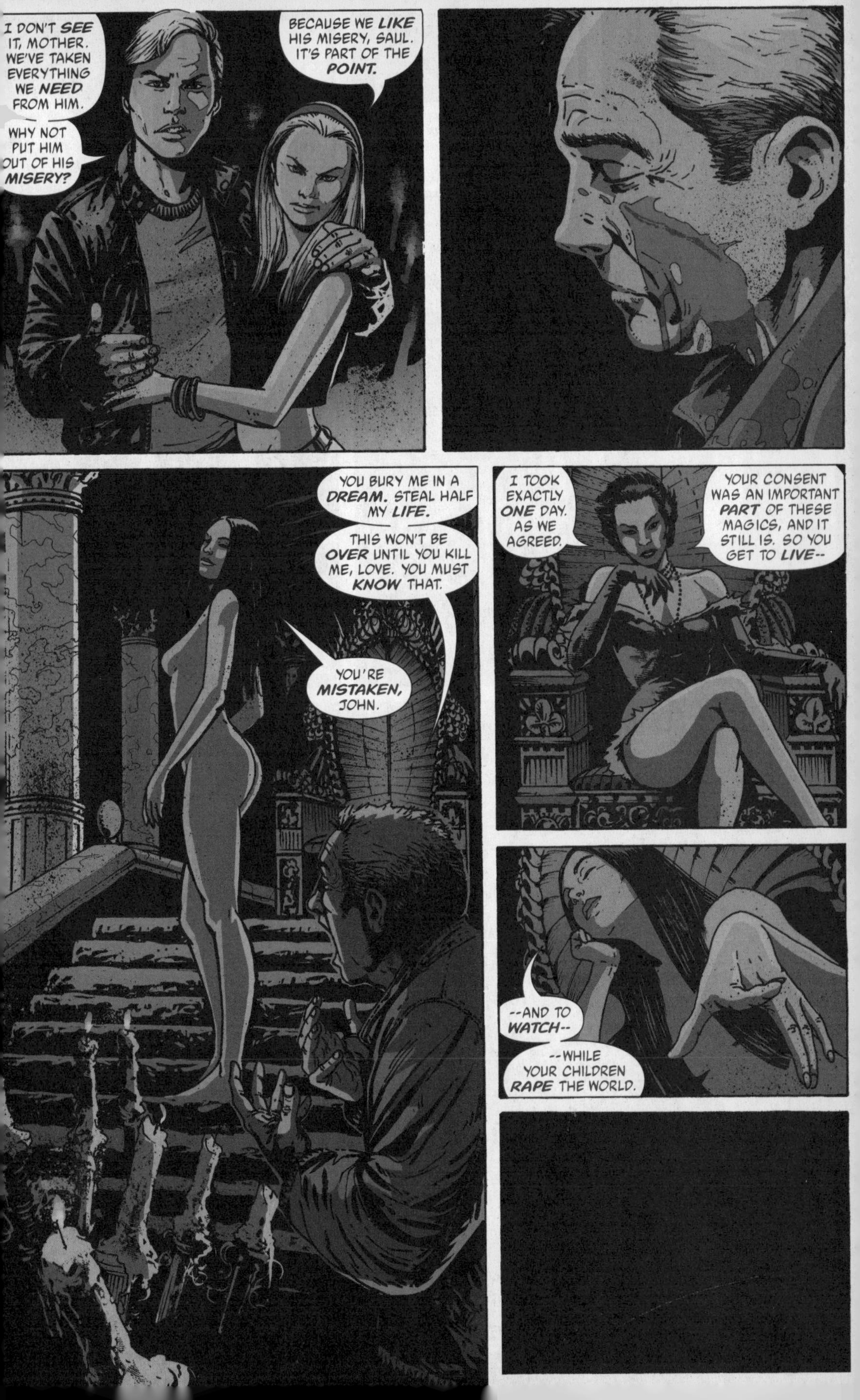
I DON'T SEE IT, MOTHER. WE'VE TAKEN EVERYTHING WE NEED FROM HIM.
WHY NOT PUT HIM OUT OF HIS MISERY?
BECAUSE WE LIKE HIS MISERY, SAUL. IT'S PART OF THE POINT.
YOU BURY ME IN A DREAM. STEAL HALF MY LIFE.
THIS WON'T BE OVER UNTIL YOU KILL ME, LOVE. YOU MUST KNOW THAT.
YOU'RE MISTAKEN, JOHN.
I TOOK EXACTLY ONE DAY. AS WE AGREED.
YOUR CONSENT WAS AN IMPORTANT PART OF THESE MAGICS, AND IT STILL IS. SO YOU GET TO LIVE--
--AND TO WATCH--
--WHILE YOUR CHILDREN RAPE THE WORLD.

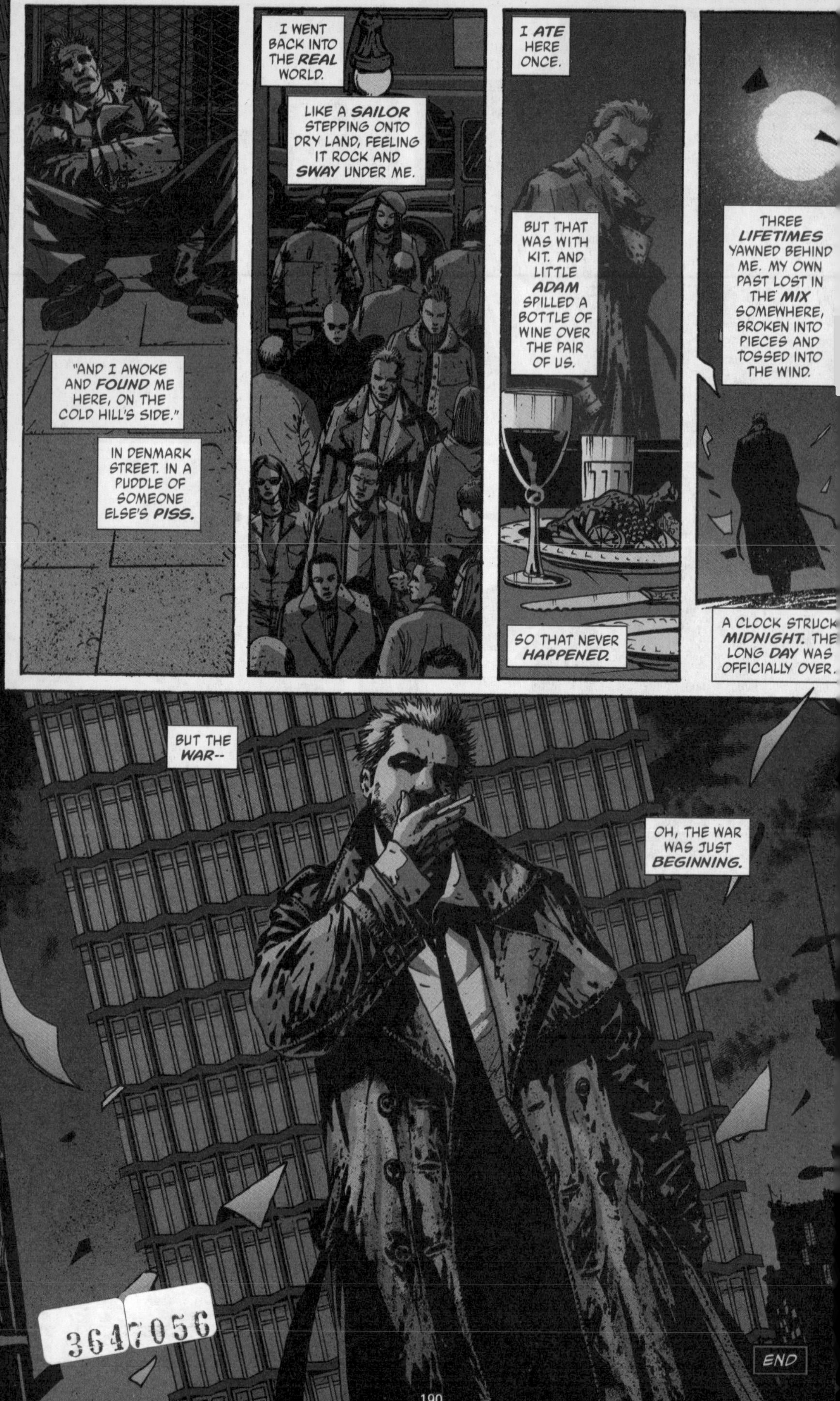
"AND I AWOKE AND FOUND ME HERE, ON THE COLD HILL'S SIDE."
IN DENMARK STREET. IN A PUDDLE OF SOMEONE ELSE'S PISS.
I WENT BACK INTO THE REAL WORLD.
LIKE A SAILOR STEPPING ONTO DRY LAND, FEELING IT ROCK AND SWAY UNDER ME.
I ATE HERE ONCE.
BUT THAT WAS WITH KIT. AND LITTLE ADAM SPILLED A BOTTLE OF WINE OVER THE PAIR OF US.
SO THAT NEVER HAPPENED.
THREE LIFETIMES YAWNED BEHIND ME. MY OWN PAST LOST IN THE MIX SOMEWHERE, BROKEN INTO PIECES AND TOSSED INTO THE WIND.
A CLOCK STRUCK MIDNIGHT. THE LONG DAY WAS OFFICIALLY OVER.
BUT THE WAR--
OH, THE WAR WAS JUST BEGINNING.
END